D1289589

The Road to Charleston

The Road to Charleston

NATHANAEL GREENE AND THE AMERICAN REVOLUTION

John Buchanan

UNIVERSITY OF VIRGINIA PRESS

Charlottesville and London

University of Virginia Press
© 2019 by the Rector and Visitors of the University of Virginia
All rights reserved
Printed in the United States of America on acid-free paper

First published 2019

1 3 5 7 9 8 6 4 2

Library of Congress Cataloging-in-Publication Data

Names: Buchanan, John, 1931– author.
Title: The road to Charleston : Nathanael Greene and the American Revolution /
John Buchanan.
Description: Charlottesville : University of Virginia Press, [2019] | Includes
bibliographical references and index.
Identifiers: LCCN 2018046409 | ISBN 9780813942247 (cloth : alk. paper) |
ISBN 9780813942254 (ebook)
Subjects: LCSH: Southern States—History—Revolution, 1775–1783—
Campaigns. | South Carolina—History—Revolution, 1775–1783—Campaigns. |
Greene, Nathanael, 1742–1786.
Classification: LCC E236 .B83 2019 | DDC 973.3/457—dc23

LC record available at https://lccn.loc.gov/2018046409

Cover art: Illustration for "Drums" (detail), Newell Convers Wyeth, American
(1882–1945), ca. 1928; oil on canvas, 26½ × 40⅛ inches. (The Nelson-Atkins Museum
of Art, Kansas City, Missouri; gift of Sarah and Landon Rowland, 2006.6;
photo courtesy Nelson-Atkins Media Services/Jamison Miller)

Frontispiece: Nathanael Greene, 1742–1786; oil painting by Charles Willson Peale.
(Courtesy of Independence National Historical Park Collection)

Maps by Nat Case, INCase, LLC.

Susi Erhardt Buchanan, 1928–2012

Some individuals may recollect all the little events of which the great result is the battle won or lost; but no individual can recollect the order in which, or the exact moment at which they occurred, which makes all the difference as to their value or importance.

—The Duke of Wellington

Did it ever occur to you, sir, what an opportunity a Battlefield affords a liar.

—Thomas "Stonewall" Jackson

Give me six eyewitnesses and I'll give you six different stories.

—Detective Sergeant Joe Volpato, NYPD

Contents

Illustrations

Figures

Maps

Acknowledgments

I am immensely grateful to the late Professor John D. W. Guice, Ben Rubin, Christine Swager, and Bob Swager for willingly accepting the daunting task of reading the entire manuscript. Their sage comments made this a better book. Mistakes, omissions, and assertions are my responsibility, not theirs.

Two peer reviewers also waded through the manuscript, and then graciously waived anonymity. Mark Lender changed my thinking on a significant subject, and also offered other suggestions that made eminent sense and were gratefully accepted. (James Kirby Martin advised me on the significant subject raised by Professor Lender and kindly sent me articles that were most helpful.) In his peer review, Lawrence Babits also added much to the improvement of the manuscript with suggestions I accepted with many thanks. These noted scholars bear no responsibility for my conclusions.

Portions of the manuscript were read by Charles Baxley, Greg Brooking, Dennis Conrad, Bert Dunkerly, Frances H. Kennedy, Steven Rauch, and Dr. Steven D. Smith. Although they bear no responsibility for what I have written, their comments and suggestions not only helped but also increased my knowledge of the Southern Campaign.

Steven Rauch also twice shared with me his deep knowledge of the British 1779 Georgia campaign. The tour he led of such sites as Augusta, Kettle Creek, and Briar Creek was invaluable in getting a feel for the terrain where actions took place.

I have always believed that military history demands field as well as archival and library research, and in this regard I would have been lost without my good friends and fellow independent historians Charles Baxley and David Reuwer, who took time out of their busy schedules to take me on grand tours: Hobkirk's Hill, Quinby Plantation, Goshen Point on the Stono River, and the field of Eutaw Springs. I find it difficult to adequately express my gratitude for their time as well as their generosity in sharing their wide knowledge. Charles Baxley also drove me through the countryside where Greene withdrew after his defeat at Hobkirk's Hill, which gave me a sense of this difficult terrain that I can only hope I transferred accurately and with feeling to the printed page.

I must also thank Charles and his lovely wife, Judy, for their hospitality, and for introducing me to Skye, their precious granddaughter.

I am also indebted to C. Leon Harris for sharing with me his findings on the British Legion's behavior during the action at the Waxhaws on 29 May 1780.

At Ninety Six, Ranger Sarah Cunningham and Gray Wood were liberal with their time and knowledge, and Sarah led me to valuable sources on that fascinating site.

What would I have done without the warm and generous hospitality of my dear friends Luther and Doraine Wannamaker and Chris and Bob Swager of South Carolina? On numerous occasions over the years they wined and dined and entertained me, and gave me a place to rest my weary head. The warm memories evoked are ingrained forever.

Librarians at several institutions made my quest for source material easier and were unfailingly cheerful and efficient: at the William L. Clements Library, University of Michigan; the Maryland Historical Society; the New-York Historical Society Library; the New York Public Library, especially Rare Books and Manuscripts; the Wisconsin Historical Society, and my home away from home, the venerable New York Society Library.

A warm thank-you to my friend Richard Berenson for making the print of Elizabeth Lichtenstein Johnston. Another warm thank-you to Allison Peller, who solved my endnote and font problems.

It would be churlish of me not to recognize and extend my gratitude for the efforts of those who came before me: historians and historical editors who traveled the same path, past and present. In this regard, I must pay special tribute to the late and much lamented Don Higginbotham, who found value in my previous works and encouraged me to write this volume.

I must also not ignore four scholar/teachers, sadly departed from this world, master historians all at St. Lawrence University so many years ago. Their willingness to share their knowledge helped immeasurably to develop and hone whatever skills I have in re-creating the past: Andreas Dorpalen, mentor and advisor for my senior honors thesis on the Nazi SS; Henry Reiff and his legendary course on historiography; William Mallam, whose dry sense of humor made his lectures such a pleasure; and Carl Chilson, whose passion for history was inspiring.

At the University of Virginia Press, Acquisitions Editor Dick Holway found the manuscript worthy of consideration and shepherded it smoothly through the process, ably assisted by his charming and efficient aide, Helen Marie Chandler. Assistant Managing Editor Mark Mones handled editorial production with confident professionalism and was always available to answer my questions. I am grateful to Publicity and Social Media Director Emily

Grandstaff for being in touch early and often, giving the book diligent attention. I also appreciated the solid work of Jason Coleman and Emma Donovan.

All writers should have a copyeditor of Marilyn Campbell's skill and sensitivity. She also saved me from bloopers. I have an intense dislike of cluttered maps, and cartographer Nat Case gave me precisely what I requested. The state maps contain only sites mentioned in the text. Steve Moore delivered a fine index.

Susi, my dear wife of sixty years, first reader and gentle advisor, did not live to see the completion of the manuscript, but to the end her encouragement did not flag, and among her last words to me were—"Keep writing."

Chronology

1778

29 December	British forces take Savannah, GA

1779

31 January	British forces occupy Augusta, GA
14 February	Battle of Kettle Creek, GA
14 February	British forces evacuate Augusta
3 March	Battle of Briar Creek, GA

1780

11 February	British forces invade South Carolina
12 May	Americans surrender Charleston and Southern Army to the British
29 May	Buford's Massacre, SC
June	Carolina Back Country rises in revolt against the British
20 June	Battle of Ramseur's Mill, NC
11 July	Battle of Huck's Defeat, SC
16 August	Battle of Camden, SC
18 August	Fishing Creek (Sumter's Surprise), SC
18 August	Battle of Musgrove's Mill, SC
7 October	Battle of Kings Mountain, SC

9 November	Battle of Fishdam Ford, SC
20 November	Battle of Blackstock's, SC
3 December	Major General Nathanael Greene assumes command of the Southern Department

1781

17 January	Battle of Cowpens, SC
10–14 February	American-British Race to the Dan, NC-VA
7–20 March	Francis Marion's Bridges Campaign, SC
15 March	Battle of Guilford Courthouse, NC
6 April	Greene marches for South Carolina
7 April	General Charles Cornwallis arrives in Wilmington, NC
14 April	Light Horse Harry Lee joins Francis Marion
23 April	Marion and Lee take Fort Watson, SC
25 April	Cornwallis marches for Virginia
25 April	Battle of Hobkirk's Hill
10 May	Lord Rawdon evacuates Camden, SC
11 May	Thomas Sumter takes Orangeburg, SC
12 May	Marion and Lee take Fort Motte, SC
15 May	Lee takes Fort Granby, SC
18 May	Lee and Andrew Pickens commence second siege of Augusta, GA
21 May	Captain John Rudulph takes Fort Galphin, SC
23 May	Lee and Pickens take Fort Grierson, GA
24 May	Greene lays siege to Ninety Six, SC
5 June	Lee and Pickens take Fort Cornwallis, GA
7 June	Lord Rawdon marches to relieve Ninety Six
19 June	Greene fails to take Ninety Six and marches away

Late June–mid-July	British evacuate Ninety Six
12–18 July	Sumter's Dog Days expedition, SC
8 September	Battle of Eutaw Springs, SC
12 September	Governor Thomas Burke of NC captured by the British
13 September	Battle of Lindley's Mill, NC
19 October	Cornwallis surrenders at Yorktown, VA
17–21 November	The Bloody Scout
18 November	British evacuate Wilmington, NC
12 December	British forswear further offensive operations in or reinforcements to America

1782

26 February	Sumter resigns his military commission
Late February	House of Commons votes to abandon the war in America
27 March	New British policy is to withdraw its army from mainland America
13–14 December	British Army evacuates Charleston
14 December	Greene and the Continental Army march into Charleston

1786

19 June	Nathanael Greene dies at Mulberry Plantation, GA

Prologue

Sir Henry "Lay under a Tree in the Rain"

On the night of 11 February 1780, the quarrelsome, neurotic General Sir Henry Clinton (1730–1795), commander in chief of British forces in America, "lay under a Tree in the rain" on a South Carolina island then called Simmons, today manicured Seabrook where the affluent live and play. In 1780, it was described by diarists in Clinton's command as a land of "stinking water," of "deep sand, marshland, and impenetrable woods where human feet had never trod." To Sir Henry's British and German troops Spanish moss hanging from the trees gave "a very melancholy appearance to a forest." "Heat," wrote an early observer, "so intense as to be almost unendurable." Jaeger Captain Johann Hinrichs entered in his diary, "What a land to wage war in." And what he and his comrades may not have known, a land where the twin terrors of yellow fever and malaria made Charleston and the Low Country into a "great charnel house."[1]

Thus the landing of a British expeditionary force of 8,500 soldiers aimed at the reconquest of South Carolina and, perhaps, a triumphant march northward.

The Prologue is a synopsis, with some new observations (e.g., on the 1779 Georgia campaign), of the first volume of my study of the Southern Campaign, *The Road to Guilford Courthouse: The American Revolution in the Carolinas* (1997), and was written for those who have not read that book and to refresh the memories of those who have. Only quotations and new material are cited.

The Revolution had come to South Carolina in 1775 when the Rice Kings of the Low Country, who recognized no authority but their own—aside from their maker?—rebelled against British rule and overcame resistance by fellow Americans loyal to the Crown. The Rice Kings believed fervently in government of, by, and for the rich and the well-born. And who better to assume that role but themselves? Proud, even arrogant, they believed that they, having created the best of all possible worlds, were more capable than any other earthly power of managing their affairs. Yet separation from the mother country was not an overnight decision, for they did not take rebellion lightly. John Rutledge, who became wartime governor of South Carolina and a bitter and unforgiving foe of American Tories, although a staunch defender of "American rights," early on yearned for reconciliation with Britain. The Rice King Henry Laurens, one of the most important Rebels and a future president of the Continental Congress, confided to his son John a little over a month following the Declaration of Independence, which he supported, "even at this Moment I feel a Tear of affection for the good Old Country & for the People in it whom in general I dearly Love."[2]

Revolutionary fervor also abounded among the tradesmen and mechanics of Charleston, whose support was critical. One Rice King maintained in public print that "nature never intended that such men should be profound politicians, or able statesmen." Yet that man, the firebrand revolutionary William Henry Drayton, would later publicly proclaim, "Upon all public and general questions, the people are ever in the right." For he needed, as he called them, the *profanus vulgus,* his previous words a minor inconsistency for a politician with a cause. It was Drayton who undertook in 1775 a dangerous mission far to the west of Charleston and the Low Country, among the *profanus vulgus* of that remote region. He and his fellow Rice Kings knew that without the support of the Back Country, where some two-thirds of the white population lived, revolution in South Carolina was a dead letter. By adroitly isolating and neutralizing Back Country Tory leaders, and at the right moment applying overwhelming force, Drayton prevailed.[3]

In contrast to the French and Russian Revolutions, the American Revolution, the first of the great modern revolutions, did not end in tyranny. But in this first American civil war that accompanied the revolt against British rule, the Rebels engaged in acts of terror against fellow Americans loyal to the king, including individual and mob acts of murder, beating, tar and feathering, and arson. There should be no surprise about this. That is what revolutionaries do, no matter the era or the place, and that is why they so often succeed. Of North Carolina Tories, Lord Cornwallis commented that "the severity of the Rebel government has so terrified and totally subdued the minds of the people, that it is very difficult to rouse them to any exertion." Rebel terror, of course, invited retaliation from Tory Americans, and as we shall see that dreary cycle continued throughout the war. And let there be no doubt that we are looking not only at a war of independence but a true revolution. The centuries-old system of government in Europe and much of the world was monarchy. The American revolutionaries overthrew a king, abolished monarchy and hereditary aristocracy in the United States, and established an independent republic. In its time, that was a radical political revolution. And as will be made clear much later in the narrative, the Revolution's radical nature and the danger it represented did not escape the attention of European monarchs and their advisors.[4]

In 1776 the Rebels defeated and drove out of Charleston Harbor a British naval and ground reconnaissance in force. The Rice Kings were elated and continued to reign supreme in South Carolina. But over the next few years, far to the north at British headquarters in New York, and 3,000 miles away in London chancelleries, plans were being made to humble these proud men. For Britain had been thinking about a major Southern Campaign since early in the war, and after the French entered the war in 1778 as the indispensable allies of the American Rebels, there were urgent reasons for following through with a southern strategy. Not least were the protection of Britain's rich sugar islands in the West Indies against French fleets and armies and the possibility of picking up some of the French islands. Lord Germain, who as secretary of state for America ran the war from London, made that clear to Sir Henry Clinton when he wrote of "the Necessity of providing for the immediate Security of Our West India Possessions." For British sugar merchants and planters, the islands were more important than the American mainland, and the merchants had clout with the government in London.[5]

Another spur to a southern offensive was the early conviction that became an obsession of George III and his ministers that the rebellion was a "conspiracy of a minority," and that the southern Back Country contained vast numbers of loyal subjects who would rise against the minority Rebels once a powerful British army arrived. Their belief was fed by exiled royal governors and Tories, both in exile and in America, the latter described by a British officer serving in the South as "people of too sanguine Expectations." The theory went that the Tories would control the countryside once the regulars moved on. Failure to quash the rebellion in the North added spice to this theory. Yet the British leaders had held the same belief of the North, that few Americans favored rebellion. British soldiers serving in America thought otherwise. A twenty-two-year-old lieutenant, writing to his father, observed that "Perhaps never was a Rebellion so universal and intense as this." The *Stamford Mercury* in Britain published a letter containing a memorable line from another officer serving in America that was reprinted throughout the country: "remember one thing, we do not contend with an army but with a country." Although the king and his ministers had been proven wrong north of the Mason-Dixon Line, it did not change their thinking about the South. For as we know from our own times, once government settles on a belief it becomes dogma.[6]

After five years of marching and countermarching, of bloody battles in New England, Canada, New York, New Jersey, and Pennsylvania, the British held only New York City, its environs, and Providence, Rhode Island, and they would soon withdraw from Providence. The British army and its German allies won most of the battles, but lost the key battles of Trenton, Princeton, and Saratoga. Nor was their army large enough to occupy wide swaths of territory. Perhaps, the ministers in London thought, it would be best to give up the North, especially New England, turn South, and concentrate on what has been described as the "soft underbelly of the rebellion." That soft underbelly, however, turned out to be a hornet's nest. We who have lived through one misreading after another by government of regions it does not understand should not be surprised by this eighteenth-century misreading by the British government.[7]

"People of Too Sanguine Expectations"

The British began their southern operations in December 1778 with an order from Sir Henry Clinton to Lieutenant Colonel Archibald Campbell (1739–1791), commanding a little over 3,000 men, "by a rapid Movement endeavour to take possession of Savannah in the Province of Georgia." Campbell was told by Clinton and British peace commissioners that if he was successful it "may possibly open the Way for the Re-establishment of Civil Government within the provinces of Georgia and South Carolina." He carried with him "provisional Appointments" as governor of both provinces. But how was he expected to reconquer Georgia and South Carolina with such a small force? "This belief arose," Campbell wrote, "from the hope of my receiving a Reinforcement of 6000 Loyalists from the back countries in Conjunction with the Indian Tribes who were attached to Government." His commanding officer, Major General Augustine Prevost (1723–1786), explained that the "object" of the expedition "was to open the back country, to bring to the test the often made professions of loyalty of its inhabitants."[8]

Campbell was described as either "courteous, humane, polished in his manners," or "vain, arrogant and cruel." Whatever his personality, Campbell, with the assistance of a black guide, outmaneuvered Rebel Major General Robert Howe and succeeded in a "rapid Movement." On 29 December the

British assault force went ashore at daybreak and with minimal casualties by sundown were masters of Savannah. In the words of a Georgia historian, Robert Howe's report of 30 December "showed his complete confusion as to what had happened."[9]

Leaving two Hessian regiments to garrison the city, on 24 January Campbell began his 110-mile march upcountry from Ebenezer, a town eighteen miles northwest of Savannah. As he stated in separate documents, he led either 1,000–1,044 or 900 British regulars, Tory regulars (known as provincials), and militia, as recorded by his secretary. He also had four field guns and a howitzer. His initial contacts with King's Friends in the Back Country were not auspicious. He described them as "irregulars . . . under the denomination of *crackers* [italics Campbell's], a race of men whose motions were too voluntary to be under restraint and whose scouting disposition in quest of pillage" interfered with Campbell's "plan of attack" on his march upcountry. This is not surprising. Campbell's remarks mirrored the later complaints of Major General Nathanael Greene about Rebel irregulars, who came from the same people as the Tories. In the short run, it was not a serious problem for Campbell, as he faced little opposition on his march and occupied Augusta, Georgia, on 31 January 1779. He described the town as "a Number of straggling Houses, arranged in a long Street lying parallel to the [Savannah] River; at the Distance of 100 Yards," the river "150 yards wide and extremely deep and rapid." His description belied Augusta's importance. As the great naturalist William Bartram observed, Augusta "commands the trade and commerce of vast fruitful regions above it, and from every side to a great distance." Augusta was the key to both the Georgia Back Country and the Creek Indian frontier. And the Creeks were British allies.[10]

Campbell's purpose was to mobilize those "6000 Loyalists" that the British believed would rally to the Crown. For the British knew as well as the Rebel Rice Kings that the key to controlling the southern states was to master the Back Country with its majority white population. A year and a half later Lord Cornwallis would write, "The keeping possession of the Back Country is of the utmost importance. Indeed, the success of the war in the Southern District depends totally upon it." Campbell was also prepared to receive with open arms Britain's Creek allies. But the Creeks never appeared and the "6000 Loyalists" turned out to be a phantom force. There actually came forward by Campbell's count in his journal only 1,100 who "joined us with their Arms; and took the Oath of Allegiance to the King" and "were formed into 20 Companies." In a letter to Clinton he put the numbers at 1,400. Whatever the count, their zeal disappointed. According to Ensign John Wilson of 71st Foot, who served as Campbell's secretary during the expedition, "they

South Carolina and Georgia

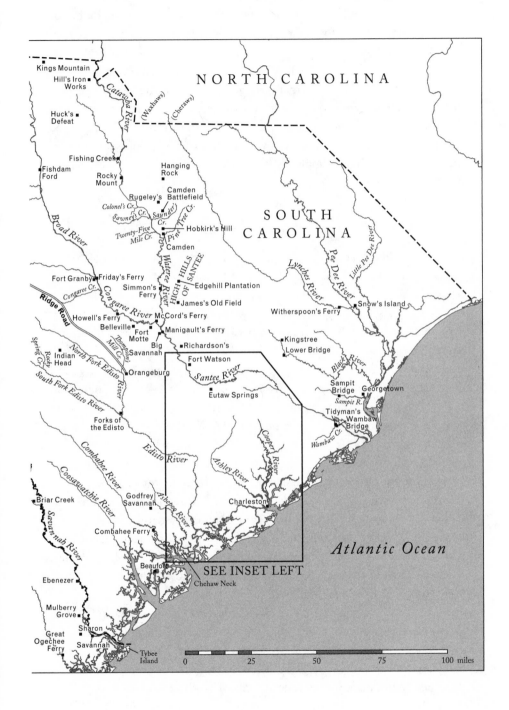

NORTH CAROLINA

SOUTH CAROLINA

Atlantic Ocean

Kings Mountain
Hill's Iron Works
Huck's Defeat
Fishing Creek
Fishdam Ford
Rocky Mount
Hanging Rock
Rugeley's
Camden Battlefield
Colonel's Cr.
Sawney's Cr.
Saunder's Cr.
Twenty-Five Mile Cr.
Pine Tree Cr.
Hobkirk's Hill
Camden
HIGH HILLS OF SANTEE
Fort Granby
Friday's Ferry
Congaree Cr.
Simmon's Ferry
Edgehill Plantation
Howell's Ferry
McCord's Ferry
James's Old Field
Belleville
Fort Motte
Manigault's Ferry
Thompson's Mill Cr.
Indian Head
Big Savannah
Richardson's
Orangeburg
Fort Watson
Santee River
Eutaw Springs
Forks of the Edisto
Edisto River
Ashley River
Cooper River
Ashepoo River
Godfrey Savannah
Charleston
Combahee River
Combahee Ferry
Coosawatchie River
Briar Creek
Savannah River
Beaufort
Ebenezer
Chehaw Neck
SEE INSET LEFT
Mulberry Grove
Sharon
Great Ogechee Ferry
Savannah
Tybee Island

Catawba River
(Waxhaws)
(Cheraws)
Broad River
Congaree River
Watree River
Ridge Road
Spring Cr.
Rocky Cr.
North Fork Edisto River
South Fork Edisto River
Witherspoon's Ferry
Lynches River
Pee Dee River
Little Pee Dee River
Snow's Island
Kingstree
Lower Bridge
Black River
Sampit Bridge
Sampit R.
Georgetown
Tidyman's
Wambaw Bridge
Wambaw Cr.

0   25   50   75   100 miles

could not be brought to any regularity; therefore no real, substantial Services from them could be depended upon, or for some time looked for but by people of too sanguine Expectations who would not consider that they were mostly Crackers, whose promises are often like their Boasts." Despite that last remark, Wilson's views on the Tory militia cannot be dismissed as mere class snobbery. For example, he further observed that when "the Militia was now ordered to strengthen the posts that were alotted them, at the different crossing places along the River it was plainly seen that they could not be depended upon; if their assistance was seriously wanted; they could not be got to turn out or assemble." Even Campbell admitted "that the Militia . . . could not be much depended upon in a general Action."[11]

"Wee Drove the Villens and Beat Them in a Fiar Fight"

Near present-day Spartanburg, South Carolina, however, a Tory colonel by the name of John or James Boyd had raised some 450 men and was joined by 250 North Carolinians under Lieutenant Colonel John Moore. In a plan hatched at British headquarters in New York City by Sir Henry Clinton, Campbell, and Boyd, Colonel Boyd's mission was to link up with Campbell in Augusta. During a successful fight with Rebels as he crossed the Savannah River into Georgia, about 100 of Boyd's men may have gotten cold feet and gone home. Boyd and his remaining 600 proceeded into Wilkes County, on Georgia's Indian frontier, and on the late morning of 14 February 1779 were camped in rugged hill country on both sides of Kettle Creek. They were seventy miles north of Augusta and a link-up with Campbell.

But Boyd was unaware that Rebel riders under Colonel Andrew Pickens (1739–1817) of South Carolina and Colonel John Dooly (1740–1780) of Georgia, 450 strong, were not only in pursuit of "Tories and horse thieves," as Colonel Dooly put it, but right behind his forces. It was 10:00 A.M., Pickens wrote many years later, when "we heard their drums a mile ahead, and they had not gone more than two miles from where they had beat their drums, when they halted at Kettle Creek to kill some cattle which they had found there and cook their breakfast."[12]

Pickens was in command and decided on a three-pronged attack: Colonel Dooly on the west, Dooly's deputy Lieutenant Colonel Elijah Clarke (1742–1799) on the east, while Pickens assaulted the center. The attack got off to a bad start. Dooly and Clarke got bogged down in the swamps, and Pickens described their lateness in coming to grips with the enemy as not as pressing "as I wished them. . . . This was not for want of courage but for want of experience & a knowledge of the necessity of obeying orders." Pickens's own advance, against orders, fired prematurely and alerted the Tories. A hot fight ensued. Dooly reported two days later "that from the first of the Ingagement to the Last it was at least 3 [h]ours Constant fireing . . . wee Drove the Villens and beat them in a fiar fight."[13]

They had indeed. Boyd was mortally wounded and died on the field. Nineteen of his men were killed, twenty-two captured. The survivors fled for their lives. Colonel Pickens recalled that "the severest conflict I ever had with the disaffected or tories was in Georgia at Kettle Creek." And Colonel Dooly's letter reminds us that in this battle and others to be described in the narrative, senior officers, Americans and British, regulars and militia alike, rode into battle on horseback. "Colonel Clark had his horse Shot Down from under him and I am sure that it must be nothing but the hand of Providence that Saved Colo Pickens and Colo Clark and my Self from begin Kild or badly wounded as we warr much Exposed on horseback During the whole Ingagement."[14]

Campbell in the meantime had decided to withdraw from Augusta. Boyd's defeat was not the reason. He made the decision one day before the Battle of Kettle Creek, marched on the day it was fought, and did not learn of Boyd's fate until the next day. The reasons were the failure of the supposed thousands of Tories to rally to the Crown and the poor quality of those that turned out; the non-appearance of Creek allies; the lack of "Provisions" as well as that vital requirement of eighteenth-century British and American armies, "Rum in this Neighbourhood to last us any Time"; and Campbell's knowledge that large Rebel forces were gathering on the South Carolina side of the Savannah River and might come across and cut communications between Augusta and Savannah. Anarchy reigned in the Georgia Back Country. Ensign Wilson wrote that "Most of the Settlements (along both the Roads) from Ebenezer to Augusta are in a ruinous, neglected State; two thirds of them deserted some of their Owners following the Kings troops others with the Rebels, and both revengefully destroying the property of each other." And as previously noted, Ebenezer was only eighteen miles from Savannah. Campbell's commanding officer, General Augustine Prevost, approved of "your movement," and added, "I always thought that our being able to keep our Post at Augusta depended on the single circumstance of the Back-Country People's joining heartily in the cause, as without that we *must be certain of finding great difficulty if not impossibility in preserving a communication to such a distance*, and I do not think it would be prudent to persevere in a measure that might bring the whole in danger" (emphasis Prevost's).[15]

Before Campbell left Augusta, an atrocity occurred that would lead to more savagery. A Rebel leader imprisoned by the British had asked Campbell for security for his wife and children. Campbell agreed and assigned Sergeant Hugh MacAlister of 71st Foot to stand guard at the man's house. Campbell reported that MacAlister was "shot and cruelly cut with Hatchets" by Rebel raiders from across the Savannah River, and that the Light Infantry "had determined to revenge MacAlister's Murder on the first favourable Occasion."[16]

"Things Here Wear a Melancholy Appearance"

Meanwhile, fifty-nine-year-old Continental General John Ashe (1720–1781), commanding 200 raw Continentals and 1,100 militiamen from North Carolina, was in search of Campbell. The Prussian Field Marshal Helmuth von Moltke once remarked, "In war with its enormous friction, even the mediocre is quite an accomplishment." For Ashe and his men, even the mediocre was out of reach. The bulk of the army was ill armed, ill trained, ill disciplined, in short, ill prepared for battle, as was Ashe, who had attended Harvard, read French, Latin, and Greek, but was not cut out for combat command. And as he admitted to General Benjamin Lincoln, "I acknowledge myself ignorant of the Geography of these parts, consequently cannot give you my opinion with the Clearness and Perspicassity I could wish." Poor Ashe. He would soon face an opponent who was a veteran of the War of Austrian Succession and the French and Indian War, and knew exactly where he was.[17]

On 20 February, while marching back to Savannah, Campbell met Lieutenant Colonel James Mark Prevost (1736–1781), younger brother of General Prevost. Young Prevost "informed me that he was in future to command the Advance Troops; and that he should be obliged to me for my Opinion and Advice as to the intentions of the Rebels, which I gave with pleasure," although one suspects that his expression of pleasure was for public consumption. According to Campbell, he explained the lay of the land to Colonel Prevost and gave him the plan of operation against General Ashe.[18]

Ashe was camped sixty-two miles south of Augusta with his rear resting at the edge of the Savannah River swamp, which was three miles wide bordering the river. Prevost discovered the American location and marched toward it with 2nd Battalion, 71st Foot, a Highland regiment wearing trews that also contained numbers of Lowland Scots and Englishmen; light infantry from the two Highland battalions; grenadiers of the 60th Foot; cavalry; and Tory units, including Major Thomas Brown's Florida Rangers. Campbell had earlier described the last as "a mere rabble of undisciplined freebooters," but they were veterans of several fights in Georgia and Florida. The 1st Battalion of 71st Foot and two field pieces were sent in another direction as a diversion.[19]

According to the pension application of a Rebel South Carolina mounted militiaman, James Fergus, he and forty other men were ordered to reconnoiter. He claimed that by posing as Tories they learned from a Tory woman of Prevost's location. After letting their horses feast on oats, they reported the next day to General Ashe "that we might expect them the next day at farthest." The following day, Fergus reported, Ashe sent Major John Ross with the rest of the militia horsemen, 160 in all, out for further reconnaissance. Ross never reported back, but Fergus said that an old man who was with Ross returned to camp and told Ashe "that the enemy was coming on us. It appeared," Fergus recalled, "that General Ashe took no notice of this, nor was there any preparation made for action till the British vanguard was fired on by our sentries."[20]

However accurate Fergus's account, filed over a half century after the battle, Ashe and his men were indeed surprised. About 3:00 P.M. on 3 March 1779, the small British army approached the still unsuspecting Americans in three columns, each six men abreast. At 150 yards from Ashe's camp they deployed into line of battle and marched on. Only then did the American pickets spot them and raise the alarm. Pandemonium must have ensued because ammunition had to be distributed before the men could form. One asks, why wait until the last minute to issue ammunition? Because the men did not have one of the most important pieces of a soldier's equipment: cartridge boxes to carry ammunition. Troops given cartridges previously had either damaged or lost them due to the lack of cartridge boxes. What a simple matter: a leather pouch slung over one's shoulder with a strap to carry ammunition and protect it from the elements and loss. Simple yet critical. Were the end not tragic our vision of American soldiers running to meet the approaching enemy would be comical. General Ashe described men "carrying their cartridges under their arms, others in the bosom of their shirts, and some tied up in the corners of their hunting shirts." As if that was not bad enough, some men were issued the wrong caliber of cartridges.[21]

The end was predictable. The Rebels were ordered not to fire until the British were within thirty-five yards. They apparently fired first but did little damage. The British returned fire, then presented their favorite weapon. At double-quick, the hard-bitten regulars charged. They reached the American lines in less than twenty seconds. Protruding from the ends of their five-foot muskets were some sixteen inches of cold steel. Earlier in the war a British general observed, "The onset of the bayonet in the hands of the valiant is irresistible." It certainly was at Briar Creek that day. The Rebels had been neither trained for bayonet fighting nor did they possess them, and the sight bearing down on them was more than they could stand. The Halifax, North

Carolina, regiment in the second line became a mob as it stampeded for the swamps. Its commander, the hapless "political socialite," Colonel Thomas Eaton, ran so fast he left his boots in his tent. An American officer on the left, probably General William Bryan, shouted that they had been outflanked and thereby precipitated a rout of the rest of the army, most on foot, James Fergus and his comrades on horseback. General Ashe was among the fleeing riders. Only eighty valiant Georgia Continentals—probably recruited in North Carolina and Virginia—under the command of General Samuel Elbert (1740–1788) stood their ground. All were either killed or captured. Elbert was among the captives.[22]

The Battle of Briar Creek, if it can be dignified as such, lasted less than fifteen minutes. But the real horror was yet to unfold. An estimated fifty to one hundred Rebels died in the swamp or river, or, as a British account stated, "many were swallowed up by one and drowned in the other." James Fergus described "several cuts or lagoons that crossed [the swamp] between the creek and the river. The banks were so steep and deep that the horses that went in could not get out again." The screams of horses and men as they slowly sank into muck and mire would have been terrible. "Here," Fergus wrote, "I left my horse and furniture, threw off my coat, and swam."[23]

All the while the light infantry and 71st Foot took their revenge for the murder of Sergeant MacAlister. They bayoneted the wounded and some of the prisoners. Campbell wrote that they "spared few that came within their reach," and a Tory described "bodies disfigured with reiterated gashes and stabs." Shrieks and pleas for mercy must have rent the air. And if that were not enough, some died when the British set fire to the brush surrounding the swamps, and "their parched and blackening bodies joined the next morning in offering a sight such perhaps as the sun never set upon among civilized nations."[24]

General Bryan was court-martialed, found guilty of personal cowardice, and resigned in disgrace. Although barely believable, Colonel Thomas Eaton, the "political socialite" who ran so fast he left his boots behind, two years later as a brigadier general commanded the Halifax District brigade at the Battle of Guilford Courthouse. With the exception of one regiment, he and his men fled that fight too. General John Ashe requested a court-martial, was cleared of cowardice but found guilty of negligence, and resigned. About a month after the battle he wrote to Governor Richard Caswell of North Carolina, "Things here wear a melancholy appearance." Ashe died of smallpox in 1781.[25]

But all was not lost. Even after this crushing defeat of the Rebels, General Prevost wrote to Lord Germain, "I cannot think it prudent to extend again immediately far upwards. . . . whilst we guard what we have already got, we hold ourselves in readiness to catch at further favorable incidents as they may occur." A British governor would sit in Savannah and Crown forces would control coastal Georgia. In the Back Country, however, the Rebels dominated for a little over a year, even formed a government of sorts, and afterward would continue the contest. Lieutenant Colonel Prevost explained why to Lord Germain: "even after so decisive a blow on that part of the Rebel arms, the frontiers, the most plentiful and populous part of the province, were still occupied by them, and their incursions and depredations on the plantations of such inhabitants who had taken protection at the time that Colonel Campbell was in Augusta made the rest apprehensive of joining us heartily and led many of them to turn zealous supporters of the rebel cause."[26]

"The Rebels Appeared Thin, Miserable, Ragged, and Very Dirty"

The following year, with continued stalemate in the North, major operations began, and at first things went very well indeed for the British.

On 12 May 1780, three months after the landings on Simmons Island, where Sir Henry Clinton "lay under a Tree in the rain," there occurred the greatest American defeat of the War of the Revolution: the British capture of Charleston, South Carolina. In one fell swoop the American Rebels lost the richest city in North America and with it the only Continental army in the South. A German officer in British service left us his amused description of the defeated army as it marched out of the citadel of the Rice Kings. "The rebels appeared thin, miserable, ragged, and very dirty. Their officers appeared to be primarily young people and poorly dressed, each in a different colored uniform, which gave the officers of their army the appearance of comedians about to commence a show, which together with their troops, without shoes, made a very comical scene." Captain John Peebles, a Scottish grenadier, had a somewhat more positive opinion. "They are a ragged dirty looking set of People as usual, but more appearance of discipline than what we have seen formerly & some of their officers decent looking men."[27]

South Carolina, in Rebel hands since 1775, was stunned by the disaster. Many erstwhile Rebels, among them imperious Low Country Rice Kings, put property before honor and flocked to their conquerors. The way seemed open for the British to pursue their strategy of marching west to pacify the rest of the state, raise Tory militia regiments, then roll northward through North Carolina and Virginia to seal their reconquest of the South. In that late spring and early summer of 1780, British and provincial regiments fanned out from Charleston and without initial resistance established strongpoints throughout the state.

George Washington, however, had another take on the British southern offensive. Some six months later he wrote that "they have not a stamina of force sufficient for such extensive conquests, and by spreading themselves out as they are now doing, they will render themselves vulnerable."[28]

And soon after the fall of Charleston the unexpected occurred, for war is a roll of the dice. The Back Country Rebels rose in revolt. The importance of the Rising was fundamental. It changed the course of the war.

"Pack of Beggars"

The Back Country then comprised most of the Carolinas. It began about fifty miles west of Charleston, roughly along the line of today's Interstate 95, and stretched to the foothills of the Appalachians. It was a newly settled land, harsh and violent, and its inhabitants matched their environment. A Root, Hawg, or Die mentality prevailed. A man who lived there as a boy and teenage Rebel militiaman recalled in his old age that religion "had been for several years neglected, as is usual in almost all new settled countries. For when people have to labor hard, live hard—and that on coarse food and wear ragged clothes—they have little to spare, and it is hardly worth while for preachers, lawyers, doctors or dancing masters to attend to their case, until they get, at least, one suit of clothing and other things in proportion."[29]

Prominent among the settlers were pugnacious Scotch-Irish Protestants, either American born or immigrants from Ulster. The Rice Kings would have agreed with the assessment of them by a New England memoirist: "a mongrel race of independent but ignorant settlers, known as the 'Scotch-Irish.'" The writer may not have realized it, but "independent" was the key word in that description. Throughout this large area men scorned as a "Pack of Beggars" by Governor John Rutledge mounted their beloved horses and began a sweeping guerilla war of movement that stymied the British pacification effort. Over a seven-and-a-half-month period, June 1780 to the Battle of Cowpens in January 1781, mounted partisan militia, largely Scotch-Irish and English, with a sprinkling of Germans and French, maintained their allegiance to the Cause despite the loss of Charleston and a Continental army, despite a major disaster to another Continental army at the Battle of Camden in August 1780. Even the defeat that same month of 800 partisans led by Brigadier General Thomas Sumter—the most important partisan commander during the first phase of the Back Country Rising—did not stop them. The Rebel partisan militia demoralized the Tory militia and held their own against British regulars and American provincial regulars in actions large and small, some lost to memory in the mists of time. The irony of the Revolution in South Carolina is that it was started by the Rice Kings of the Low Country and saved by the "Pack of Beggars" of the Back Country. Had the British occupation been accepted in the Back Country, had those "Beggars" not risen and bought the time necessary for operations by a refurbished Continental army under a brilliant general, the Southern Campaign, indeed the war itself, would have taken on an entirely different hue.[30]

Partisan, guerilla, irregular warfare—whatever one wishes to call it—has been practiced around the world since ancient times, and certainly before that in the foggy realm of prehistory. Eighteenth-century European and American regular soldiers were quite familiar with partisan war, whether by the irregulars of the Back Country or by regular army units like British light infantry, German jaegers, and Lieutenant Colonel Henry "Light Horse Harry" Lee's Legion of horse and foot. What in Europe was known as *petite guerre* (little war) had come to the specific attention of armies in Central Europe as recently as the 1740s in the War of Austrian Succession. Among Americans the men of the Carolinas and Georgia did not have a monopoly on effective partisan operations. The tactics of Massachusetts militia during the disastrous British withdrawal from Lexington in 1775; the actions of New Jersey militia in 1776 and beyond; the fighting between Cowboys and Skinners in Westchester County, New York; the destruction of a Hessian regiment by New England militia in 1777 at the Battle of Bennington; and the 1777 actions of New England militia in cutting General John Burgoyne's communication and supply lines in northern New York State during the Saratoga campaign: all attest to that. Partisan, guerilla, irregular war—it was an age-old story by the time the Carolina and Georgia militia rose against the British in 1780.[31]

That said, it can also be stated without equivocation that the Rebel partisans of the Carolinas and Georgia waged guerilla war brilliantly and profoundly affected the outcome of the War of the Revolution.

To understand this fierce struggle, indeed, the entire Southern Campaign, it is important to realize that the Back Country Rising had two distinct phases. The first phase began in June 1780, following the British capture of Charleston, by July was in full swing, and ended in the spring of 1781. The second phase opened with the return of an American regular army, the Continentals, under Major General Nathanael Greene, to South Carolina in mid-April 1781. Greene's arrival marked the beginning of sustained joint operations between regulars and partisan militia. With two exceptions, the first phase depended entirely on the efforts of the Back Country militia. The first exception was the action at Hammond's Store on 29 December 1780, in which Colonel William Washington's 3rd Continental Light Dragoons and mounted partisan militia volunteers cut to pieces some 250 Georgia Tories.

The second exception was the mix of regulars and militia who won the critical Battle of Cowpens that burst Lieutenant Colonel Banastre Tarleton's bubble. Leaving those two actions aside, there were at least forty-three engagements ranging from skirmishes to severe actions fought between Rebel partisans and British forces. Although there were a few clashes with British regulars (e.g., Fishdam Ford and Blackstock's), most were fought by Rebel militia versus Tory militia and provincial regulars, the latter American Tories trained as regulars. In other words, between Americans, in a contest that was the first American civil war as well as a struggle for empire. The Rebels won almost all of these actions, especially the critical ones, and we ask ourselves why.[32]

There were two main reasons. Of crucial importance, as in the rest of America the British never had enough troops to occupy and control the interior country. And once they left the coastal areas and the lifeline of the British Navy they were dependent upon supplies they could either carry or plunder from the countryside. Lieutenant General Charles, 2nd Earl Cornwallis (1738–1805), whom General Sir Henry Clinton left in command in the South following the fall of Charleston, had available to him about 4,870 British, German, and provincial regulars fit for duty. Cornwallis wrote that "Without good cavalry we can do nothing in this country." Yet in his little army he had only some 140 regular cavalry: about 100 provincial British Legion horse and 40 to 50 British 17th Light Dragoons. In the finest cavalry country east of the Appalachians, faced with a mounted enemy waging a classic hit-and-run guerilla campaign, his Lordship had to depend upon mounted Tory militia to supply the difference in numbers and control the countryside once most of the regular British Army passed on. That had always been part of British strategy in America. For as stated earlier but worth repeating, the government in London labored under the delusion that throughout America the Rebels were a minority in contrast to vast numbers of Loyalists only awaiting the arrival of British troops to rise up and smite their oppressors. The British experience in Georgia related earlier should have, at the least, caused ministers in London to pause and reflect. This is not to deny the presence, especially in the Southern Back Country, of thousands of Tories. (We should also note that fervor for the cause, whether Tory or Rebel, ranged from diehard to lukewarm to one Solomon Beason: "half-Whig, half-Loyalist, as occasion required.") Lord Cornwallis described Tory militia along northern South Carolina, some raised by himself, "on the very extensive line from Broad River to Cheraws ... in general weak, or not much to be relied on for their fidelity." But Colonel Robert Gray, a prominent Tory militia commander, estimated that the population of the Ninety Six District in the western Back Country was half Tory, and Cornwallis reported that Major Nisbet Balfour (1743–1823) and

Major Patrick Ferguson (1744–1780) had raised 4,000 militiamen in that district, "so regulated that they could with ease furnish about 1500 men at short notice for the defense of the frontier." Colonel Gray put Tories in the Orangeburg District, lower down in the state, as "almost unanimous." But overall Tory numbers in South Carolina were far less than London thought, estimated by Colonel Gray at "about one third of the whole" in South Carolina. A careful modern student of the Tories placed their number at "about 22 percent." And in the realm of leadership the Tory forces were lacking.[33]

With few exceptions, the Rebel partisan commanders proved superior to Tory commanders. A good example is the Georgia Tory Thomas Brown. He was an able and vigorous leader later in the war. But at a critical time in 1775, with the South Carolina Back Country hotly contested between Rebels and Tories, he and his fellow leaders failed to strike. Without British regulars, he wrote, "we are of opinion twould be an experiment rather too hazardous." Men who make such decisions may be estimable in many respects, but they neither defeat nor win revolutions. Tory leaders were hard to find even after the great British victory at Charleston and their push upcountry. "I have used my best endeavours," wrote Major Nisbet Balfour to Cornwallis in early June, "to find out proper people for militia officers in this and other districts, but I cannot find a single man of any property or consequence that has not been in rebel service." There later appeared in the South some skillful and daring Tory commanders whom we will discuss as they appear in the narrative: David Fanning of North Carolina, William Cunningham of South Carolina, and Benjamin Thompson of Massachusetts. But their exploits were of short duration and came too late to affect the outcome of the war. The astute observation of the Tory officer Colonel Robert Gray still rings true: Rebel militia commanders "established a decided superiority in the militia line," whereas "The officers of the Royal militia being possessed themselves nor were able to inspire their followers with the confidence necessary for soldiers."[34]

In defense of the Tories, by 1780 the Rebels had been in control for five years. Their militia units were organized and had spent those years violently suppressing their Tory neighbors. British Major General Augustine Prevost recognized this, writing in 1779, "It must be said for the back country people . . . that the Rebels were already in arms and in possession of all the passes so as to prevent in a great measure every chance of communicating with the King's troops, besides having considerable bodies in different parts of the country purposely watching their motions." Rebel militia had also gained operational experience in the 1776 campaign in Appalachia against the Cherokees, although some Tories joined their Rebel neighbors in what was regarded as a common cause. Following the British invasion of the South in 1780, however, Tory militia leaders had to be selected and the rank and file armed and organized, a time-consuming process. As the historian Jim Piecuch has pointed out, another reason for the weakness of the Tory militia was the flight in March–April 1778 of many of the boldest Tories, some 600 from South Carolina and about 200 from Georgia, to sanctuary in East Florida. Although they provided valuable manpower in defense of that British province, their absence in the South Carolina and Georgia Back Country in 1780 meant that a strong Tory element was unavailable in the attempt to carry out London's strategy of cementing British rule after the regular army moved on. Early victories by Rebel militia led to a loss of faith in the Tory militia by British commanders. Cornwallis considered them "dastardly and pusillanimous." Nisbet Balfour, who had helped raise some 4,000 Tories in the Ninety Six District, nevertheless by November 1780 believed that "The idea of militia being of consequence or use as a military force I own I have now totaly given up," and it "can only be of service in keeping the piece of the country against plunderers etc." A provincial regular who will play an important role in our tale, Major John Harris Cruger, wrote, "I think I shall never again look to the Militia for the least support." Even the sympathetic inspector of militia, Major Patrick Ferguson, expressed a half-hearted opinion of his charges, writing to Cornwallis, "There is very great difficulty in bringing the militia under any kind of regularity. I am exerting myself to effect it without disgusting them, and, on the whole, not without effect."[35]

But another British officer, said to be Lieutenant Colonel Francis, Lord Rawdon, who was Cornwallis's very able deputy in the field, defended the Tories. "It has been the fashion to say that the Loyalists were few in number; & that their activity in our cause was never such as ought to have a claim upon our gratitude." Rawdon, if he was the writer, considered this an "unjust opinion." He cited the thousands of Tories who were steadfast in their attachment to Britain and gave up all rather than remain in America. That was true, but it does not address the key questions of the Tory militia's leadership and their followers' effectiveness in battle, and here Rawdon himself admitted that their performance fell short. "If a succession of misfortunes diminished the numbers & broke the spirits of these people, the circumstance does not weaken the testimony of their attachment."[36]

The opinions of Cornwallis, Balfour, and Cruger cannot be dismissed. They were intelligent observers, they were on the spot, they knew far more about local conditions than the ministers in London, and theirs was not the emotion of the dispossessed: ex-royal governors and Tories in exile in England or remaining behind, bending the ears of ministers of the Crown and British officers with their tales of vast numbers of King's Friends awaiting deliverance and their chance to rise and smite their oppressors. Yet as we saw during the British invasion of Georgia, the promised 6,000 Tory militiamen turned out to be a ghost army.

To lack of faith the British officer corps added snobbery. Colonel Robert Gray reported that "almost every British officer regarded with contempt and indifference the establishment of a militia among a people differing so much in customs and manners from themselves." Nor did they hide their feelings. Cornwallis was aware of the problem and urged officers and troops to "treat with kindness all those who have Sought protection in the British Army." Yet a few weeks later, as described by his Lordship's commissary, Charles Stedman, Tory "militia were maltreated by abusive language and even beaten by some officers in the quarter-master-general's department." Ironically, British officers' views of Back Country inhabitants, Tory or Rebel, mirrored that of the Low Country Rice Kings—just a "Pack of Beggars." Or as Lord Germain would have it, "American peasants."[37]

The big three among Rebel militia commanders were Thomas Sumter (1734–1832), Francis Marion (1732–1795), and Andrew Pickens (1739–1817). No Tory leaders emerged at the right time to challenge these men. Sumter was difficult, a poor tactician and strategist, and generally uncooperative with Continental commanders. Yet he possessed during the first phase of the Rising an uncanny ability to recruit men in the face of crushing defeats to Continental armies and, on one dramatic occasion to be described shortly, to his own militia force. Genius is not a word to be used lightly, but if there was one among them it was the moody Francis Marion, wise in the ways of the guerilla and also willing to combine his militia with regulars for specific operations. From far western South Carolina emerged a dour Scotch-Irishman, the highly regarded Andrew Pickens, whose cooperation with Continental officers at the Battle of Cowpens and during the second phase of the Rising was beyond reproach. They were backed up by less well known but formidable commanders, such as Elijah Clarke, Edward Lacey and Edward Lacey Jr., William Chronicle, Benjamin Cleveland, Isaac Shelby, John Sevier, John Twiggs, and others, as well as tough rank-and-file fighters. Without the efforts of Sumter, Marion, and other militia leaders and their followers during the Rising's first phase, there would have been no solid foundation for Nathanael Greene to build upon. They bought the time necessary prior to his arrival on the scene, and in doing so they changed the course of the war.

The majority in the Back Country opted for rebellion in 1780 and rose against British forces following the fall of Charleston for multiple reasons: family and religious ties, even though some families split on the issue; preferment promised and either delivered or otherwise; men of influence and substance drawing to them people within their sphere; and generally the native born as well as foreign born who had been in America for decades and were well along the road to their personal vision of liberty, which did not translate into an orderly imperial society. Some writers, however, have vastly overstated the presence of huge numbers of slaves, especially in the Low Country, as a major, in some cases, primary factor behind the Revolution in the South. That it could be a factor, perhaps decisive with some individuals, cannot be denied. But it was not a major reason behind the revolt in the South, and it has been argued that it was not even a secondary reason. The claim that "greed for slaves could become a motive for Revolutionary service" and that "many did, particularly in the Back Country, fight the Revolution for slaves" ignores chronology and will be dealt with in chapter 3. The assertion that the South Carolina "pacification program broke down primarily because of British attempts to use slaves as weapons against their masters" has been correctly labeled by Jim Piecuch as a "considerable overstatement." Nevertheless, the slavery motivation has been disseminated in books and other media aimed at a wide reading public, including such gross misstatements as "Theirs was a revolution, first and foremost, mobilized to protect slavery." Effectively countering these claims, the late Don Higginbotham wrote with regard to the alleged racial motive, "More convincing evidence is required before we can accept the view that the slavery issue was paramount or even a somewhat lesser motive for independence." He added, "An excessive emphasis on the racial motive could lead to the erroneous notion that the southern parts of America would not have joined their northern neighbors had the southern peoples been as predominantly white as were those in the middle and New England provinces." And over 240 years ago the influential Henry Laurens, while acknowledging the dangers of British invasion, which "instigated insurrections by our Negroes . . . inroads by Neighbouring Tribes of Indians," believed that "the practices of & insidious acts of false Brethren [Tories]" were "far more to be dreaded."[38]

"Remember Buford!"

During and after the siege of Charleston, there came prominently to the attention of Americans and Britons alike a dashing and ruthless twenty-six-year-old British cavalry officer of flawed character, Lieutenant Colonel Banastre Tarleton (1754–1833). He is usually described as a stocky man with a powerful frame and coarse features. But Thomas Young, a Rebel militiaman taken prisoner by Tarleton's troops, recalled otherwise. "I rode by his side for several miles. He was a very fine looking man, with rather a proud bearing, but very gentlemanly in his manners." Tarleton commanded the British Legion, which at that time consisted of about 270 cavalry and infantry. The Legion was largely recruited in New York City from Irish, Scottish, and English immigrants, either deserters from the American army or refugees from Rebel-held areas. Attached to the Legion were forty to fifty British regulars of 17th Light Dragoons.[39]

Tarleton's troopers committed brutal acts against soldiers and civilians in actions before Charleston's surrender. After the city fell and Tarleton's command was turned loose as the British marched upcountry, Lord Cornwallis concluded his instructions to the young cavalryman with an admonition: "I must recommend it to you in the strongest manner to use your utmost endeavors to prevent the troops under your command from committing irregularities, and I am convinced that my recommend[ation] will have weight when I assure you that such conduct will [be hi]ghly aggreable to the commander in chief." It is obvious from this that Sir Henry Clinton had expressed to Cornwallis his displeasure with the Legion's conduct.[40]

Tarleton failed to take either Cornwallis's recommendation or Clinton's displeasure to heart. Over three months after Cornwallis's letter, Tarleton wrote to his Lordship that "Many of the insurgents, having taken certificates and paroles, don't deserve lenity. None shall they experience. I have promised the young men who chuse to assist me in this expedition the plunder of the leaders of the faction. If warfare allows me, I shall give these disturbers of the peace no quarter. If humanity obliges me to spare their lives, I shall convey them close prisoners to Camden. Fire and confiscation must take place on their effects etc. I must discriminate with severity." This letter strengthens belief in a reputed exchange after the war between Horace Walpole and Richard Brinsley Sheridan. "Tarleton boasts of having slaughtered more men and lain with more women than anybody else in the army," said Walpole, to which Sheridan, who had known Tarleton before the war at Middle Temple, replied, "Lain with! What a weak expression! He should have said ravished. Rapes are the relaxation of murderers!"[41]

During the British advance into the Back Country, Tarleton's command destroyed a 350-man Virginia Continental unit (3rd Virginia Detachment) at the Waxhaws. For over two centuries it has been charged that the British Legion indulged in a massacre after the American commander, Colonel Abraham Buford, tried to surrender and his troops had laid down their arms. In recent times, that version has been challenged. But the denials that the Legion committed massive atrocities fail to take into account the wounds to hands and arms suffered by Buford's soldiers. In a fine piece of research, C. Leon Harris transcribed and analyzed the pension applications of 177 veterans said to have been at the fight—an unusually large figure. Of those, 134 provided details of the battle, and a large proportion of them suffered wounds to hands and arms, which indicates that they were not armed. As Harris notes, in modern forensic investigations wounds to hands and arms "are regarded . . . as evidence that the injured party had no weapon or other device for self defense and resorted to using the hands or arms to protect more vital parts of the bodies."[42]

The testimony of two British officers, downplayed by revisionists, also supports the massacre argument. Tarleton himself, who had his horse shot from under him, wrote that "Slaughter was commenced before Lieutenant Colonel Tarleton could remount another horse." He was candid in describing what happened. "The loss of officers and men was great on the part of the Americans, owing to the dragoons effectually breaking the infantry, and to a report amongst the cavalry that they had lost their commanding officer, *which stimulated the soldiers to a vindictive asperity not easily restrained*" (italics mine). I fail to see how his testimony can be dismissed, especially as he admitted that his troopers were out of control, taking revenge on men who had thrown down their arms, and that he had difficulty bringing them to order. And I do not accept the dismissal of Charles Stedman's claim that "*The virtue of humanity was totally forgot*" (italics mine), because he "was not an admirer of Tarleton." Stedman, a Philadelphia Tory, was Cornwallis's commissary and was with his Lordship's main force. Although not present at the action, he certainly talked to British participants shortly afterward. It is true that Stedman did not like Tarleton, but few did, for he was not a likeable fellow. Are we then to dismiss any adverse comments on Tarleton by his fellow officers?[43]

It is also claimed that only a "few" soldiers of the Legion "cut Americans down without justification or bayoneted the wounded." Yet Tarleton and Buford's wagon master, Obed Britt, stated that the fight lasted only "a few minutes." Can we accept that only a "few" soldiers in "a few minutes" killed 113 men and wounded 150? I think not. The evidence is strong that the Legion indulged in atrocities until finally brought under control.[44]

On one matter there can be no argument. Colonel Buford was an incompetent combat commander whose deployment and firing orders guaranteed the destruction of his force. For readers who remain betwixt and between, there is the reasonable conclusion of the late Don Higginbotham: "The details of the slaughter—at what point did Buford offer a white flag, and did Tarleton try to restrain the Legion from senseless killings—are hopelessly confused." Higginbotham then delivered a fair verdict on the cavalryman: "Although . . . Tarleton may not have been a butcher, he nonetheless was ruthless by the standards of warfare in his day." Tarleton's dark side was never distant, and it was he who had earlier set the tone for the actions of his command.[45]

Now let us deal with what is really important. Whatever specifically happened at the Waxhaws on that tragic day of 29 May 1780 is eclipsed by the perception of Rebels far and wide that indeed a massacre of helpless men had occurred. Thus enraged passions and the cries of Rebels on many a southern battlefield of "Tarleton's Quarter" and "Remember Buford!" as they retaliated against helpless Tory militiamen and executed them, most notably at Hammond's Store and Pyle's Massacre. Cries of "Buford's Play" were also raised at Cowpens, but there atrocities were prevented by the quick actions of Brigadier General Daniel Morgan and his officers.[46]

"My Lord Hook Was Shot Off His Horse"

The first large-scale Back Country action took place between Rebel and Tory militia 20 June 1780 at Ramseur's Mill (modern Lincolnton), North Carolina, some twenty miles north of the South Carolina line. Some 1,000 Tories gathered on the high ground were attacked by about 400 North and South Carolina Rebels commanded by Ulster-born Colonel Francis Locke (1732–1796) of North Carolina. Many Tories were unarmed, perhaps most of them. Although an unknown number of Rebels failed to press home the attack, their bolder comrades advanced. In a vicious hand-to-hand fight in which some of the dead were left with gunlocks imbedded in their skulls, the Rebels drove their fellow Americans from the high ground and prepared for a counterattack that never came, as the dispirited Tories melted away and went home.[47]

Ramseur's Mill was the first fissure in London's theory of Back Country Tories controlling the countryside following victories by British regulars. In America British soldiers who had to deal with reality were not as sanguine as George III and his ministers. Brigadier General Charles O'Hara would later describe London's obsession as a "Fatal infatuation!" Cornwallis was furious over the debacle. He wrote to his deputy in the field, Lieutenant Colonel Francis, Lord Rawdon, "The affair of Tryon County has given me great concern, altho' I had my apprehensions that the flame would break out somewhere." His Lordship's "apprehensions" may well have been after the fact, but his "great concern" was on the mark. The North Carolina Rebel partisan leader, Yorkshire-born William Richardson Davie (1756–1820), wrote after the war, "in a few days that district of country lying between the [Catawba] River, the mountains and their line [South Carolina] was entirely cleared of the enemy."[48]

Matters seemed to be going very well in South Carolina, however, where strongpoints had been established and according to official reports resistance ended. Captain Christian Huck of the British Legion, commanding a detachment of Legion horse, other provincial regulars, and Tory militiamen destroyed William Hill's iron works, which the Rebels depended on for armaments. Whereupon Cornwallis, setting aside his misgivings the day before over the Ramseur's Mill debacle, wrote to Sir Henry Clinton that Huck's feat, coupled with the submission of the Back Country Rebel post of Ninety Six, had "put an end to all resistance in South Carolina." His Lordship should have heeded his own "apprehensions that the flame would break out somewhere." For beyond humbled Charleston dark passions simmered. Huck continued his raid of arson and destruction through Rebel country. But at dawn on 11 July, while Huck and his men slept, a hastily summoned force of Rebel militia crept forward unseen, unheard, and unleashed a deadly assault. A teenage militiaman, James Potter Collins, recalled that Captain Huck climbed into the saddle, drew his saber, and shouted, "disperse you damn rebels, or we will put every man of you to the sword." Collins wrote, "Our rifle balls began to whistle among them, and in a few minutes my Lord Hook was shot off his horse" and killed. His command was decimated. The memory of this important victory lived on for at least several generations. Ninety-three years later a woman recalled that "I believe it was at this same time and place that Col. Hook lost his head perhaps as good a day's work as was done during the Revolution."[49]

Huck's Defeat was crucial for its psychological effect. Militia had soundly defeated Tory regulars, including dragoons of the hated and feared British Legion. Even Cornwallis admitted that the state of affairs in South Carolina might not be as he had recently reported: "The unlucky affair that happened to the detachment under Captain Huck of the Legion has given me great uneasiness." Had he known the full story his feeling would have gone beyond uneasiness. Some in the Back Country with Rebel sympathies had been unsure whether it was wise to challenge British power after the loss of Charleston and Tarleton's coup in the Waxhaws. But they took heart after Huck's Defeat and began to flock to the standard raised by Brigadier General Thomas Sumter, a gifted leader but difficult personality, who came to be known as the Gamecock.[50]

Sumter was an excellent horseman, a trait highly valued among men who went to war on horseback. He was described by a contemporary as "rather a small, but very active man. Saw him place one hand on the saddle, and vault into the saddle without putting a foot in the stirrup." The Gamecock began his campaign with an unsuccessful assault on Rocky Mount, a British post on the west bank of the Catawba River just south of modern Great Falls, South

Carolina. It consisted of three log buildings on the crest of a high hill surrounded by open woods. De Lancey's New York Volunteers, 150 strong, held the post. Although most of the eight-hour action involved sniping, it also revealed early on Sumter's devotion to a primitive tactic. He ordered a frontal assault that failed, with Colonel Andrew Neel and six men dying needlessly. A few days later, 6 August 1780, about twenty miles east of Rocky Mount, his planned frontal assault across a creek and a ravine against provincial regulars and Tory militia at Hanging Rock turned into a flanking movement, either by error or fear on the part of local guides. Whatever the case, the Rebels rolled up the British flank and probably would have overrun their final position had not the victors found the liquor supply and gotten roaring drunk. The British had drawn up for a last stand in a "hollow square" with fixed bayonets. But the Rebels, wrote William Richardson Davie, who took part in the action, loaded with plunder and reeling from strong drink, "filed off unmolested along the front of the Enemy about 1 O'clock."[51]

The Hero of Saratoga

Meanwhile, a small regular American army, the Continentals, consisting of two Maryland brigades and the Delaware Regiment, were marching southward under the command of Major General Horatio Gates to replace the army lost at the surrender of Charleston. Any attempt to defend Gates's performance at the Battle of Camden is hopeless, for he had neither the skill nor the stomach for combat command. On 16 August 1780, a few miles north of Camden, South Carolina, Gates sent his incompetently deployed army of regulars and Virginia and North Carolina militia against a British force largely made up of first-rate regulars led by Lord Cornwallis. The Virginia militia took one look at the bayonet-wielding Redcoats advancing on them and stampeded for the rear. With the exception of one regiment, the North Carolina militia "fled different ways, as their hopes led, or their fears drove them," an American officer wrote. The Continentals stood their ground, counterattacked, at first drove the enemy, then were surrounded after the militia collapsed and cut to pieces, while their general, the Hero of Saratoga, astride the swiftest horse in the American army, sired by the famous stud Fearnaught, fled with the militia. To rally them, he claimed. The enormity of the disaster was still apparent over a year and a half later, when Captain Walter Finney of the Pennsylvania Line marched through on his way to join General Greene: "This day we past over the ground whare Gen. Gaits was Defeated, the Road for several miles was Strow'd with Broken Arms, Wagons, Harness, etc in Short it wear the Aspect of a Direful Calamety." Other diarists traveling separately made similar observations. Gates did not stop until three days later and 180 miles northward in Hillsborough, North Carolina. There he watched the survivors of the Continentals he had abandoned straggle in over the next few weeks. "General Gates used the utmost expedition in getting from the lost Field," wrote Colonel Otho Holland Williams, who had been at the battle. And Alexander Hamilton asked, "Was there ever an instance of a General running away as Gates has done from his whole Army? And was there ever so precipitous a flight. . . . It does admirable credit to the activity of a man at his time of life."[52]

Another disastrous encounter with a seemingly invincible British army. To cap it off, two days later at Fishing Creek in South Carolina, in an action that came to be known as "Sumter's Surprise," Thomas Sumter and 800 of his followers, including a Maryland regiment, were attacked and routed while they rested by Banastre Tarleton's force of 170. Many were taken prisoner, but the son of one of Sumter's officers reported that "there were thick briar patches around, which enabled some of the Americans to dodge away and escape before the cavalrymen could ride around and intercept them." Sumter himself, sleeping half-clothed under a wagon, leaped onto a horse bareback and made his escape. An important Tory provincial officer, Lieutenant Colonel Evan (or Euan) McLaurin, wrote British Lieutenant Colonel Nisbet Balfour that "Gates defeat did not entirely discourage the Disaffected—but the defeat of Sumter will effectually cool them of this." McLaurin was right about Gates, wrong about the impact of Fishing Creek on the "Disaffected." Despite the Gamecock's carelessness and humiliation, Cornwallis reported to Clinton that "the indefatigable Sumpter is again in the field, and is beating up for recruits with the greatest assiduity."[53]

"Picked Men Well Mounted"

Gates had been routed, but the partisans fought on, and more often than not frustration was the lot of the British and their Tory allies. The Back Country command of the British inspector of militia, Major Patrick Ferguson, was relentless in its pursuit of Rebels, who were just as tireless in maintaining a presence and engaging in the classic guerilla tactic of avoiding combat unless the situation and terrain suited them. Ferguson faced uncommon men who were natural leaders and firm in their devotion to the Cause. Many of them— Elijah Clarke of Georgia and Isaac Shelby and John Sevier of North Carolina in particular—had been schooled in Indian wars. They were gifted partisan leaders, and riding behind them were hard men accustomed to weapons, horses, and rough life in the field. Even Major General Nathanael Greene, soon to replace the hapless Gates as commander of the Southern Department, and whose highly critical views of militia were well known and often justified, admitted to Alexander Hamilton that "there is a great spirit of enterprise among the back people, and those that have come out as volunteers are not a little formidable to the enemy. There are also some particular corps under Sumter, Marion and Clarke that are bold and daring."[54]

Bold and daring they were, and that is nowhere better seen than in a strike deep into Tory country that ended in one of the fiercest actions of the war. It took place on the heels of the American disasters at Camden and Fishing Creek. Among the Rebels at this fight were Over Mountain Men who lived on the edge of the frontier, across the Appalachians where the waters ran west, in what is now East Tennessee. On 17 August 1780, 200 riders described by one of their leaders, Colonel Isaac Shelby (1750–1826), as "picked men well mounted," left their North Carolina camp "one hour before sundown." Besides Shelby of North Carolina, their leaders were Colonel James Williams (1740–1780) of South Carolina and Colonel Elijah Clarke of Georgia. There was no overall commander, and a keen student of the Southern Campaign has remarked that it is the only battle he knows won by a committee. According to Shelby, they rode forty miles "mostly at a canter" through the night without stopping, although another participant, Major Samuel Hammond, stated that they stopped to eat and rest for an hour. More important than the facts of the march, the force arrived undetected at Musgrove's Mill, South Carolina, "within half a mile of the enemy camp just at break of day." They had anticipated dealing with 200 Tory militia. Instead, they found themselves facing 500 Tories, 200 of whom were provincial regulars. But they had to fight. Their horses were blown, could go no farther without rest. In an action described by Colonel Shelby as "one of the hardest ever fought in the United States with small arms," they successfully defended their position against a confident, advancing foe, then, with whoops and yells, charged. In a desperate melee they broke the enemy and put him to flight, inflicting a casualty rate of 40 percent while taking few losses.[55]

At Musgrove's Mill the Rebel militia behaved with élan. According to the Tory officer Lieutenant Colonel Evan (or Euan) McLaurin, that cannot be said of the Tory militia. "The militia at that time behaved as usual. The greatest part fled and left a few honest men to be sacrificed. The Necessity of not depending on the Militia will daily become more evident."[56]

Far to the east another partisan commander of uncommon ability was also giving the British fits in their attempt to pacify South Carolina. Colonel

Francis Marion, known to posterity as the Swamp Fox, was a distinguished veteran of the 1760–1761 Cherokee war. Unfortunately, no contemporary image of him is known to exist, but we know that he was a small, dark-visaged man with thick, misshapen knees and ankles. Marion was a strict disciplinarian. When he commanded a regular regiment early in the war, 2nd South Carolina, a young lieutenant described him as "an ugly, cross, knock kneed, hook-nosed son of a bitch." Marion understood perfectly the function of a guerilla leader. He avoided defending fixed positions and stayed on the move. Superior mobility was one of the secrets of his success, and he made every effort to mount his men well. Cornwallis's talented deputy in field command in South Carolina was Lieutenant Colonel Francis, Lord Rawdon (1754–1826), who will play a prominent role in our tale. Writing not just of Marion but of the partisans as a whole, Rawdon admitted that Rebel mobility was the reason why "we have never been able to bring them to a decisive action."[57]

So Lord Cornwallis, after scoring one of the overwhelming British victories of the war at Camden, still found himself facing a popular uprising in the Back Country. His orders from Sir Henry Clinton were quite clear: he could invade North Carolina only if Charleston and South Carolina were secure, for they were "*the principal and indispensable objects of his attention*" (italics Clinton's). Cornwallis knew that South Carolina remained in revolt, but he had long believed that it could not be held without securing North Carolina and Virginia and prepared to march north in defiance of his instructions. At the end of August he looked forward to leaving South Carolina to escape the sickly season, which lasted from June until late October and brought with it some 100 miles from the coast the scourge of armies in the Deep South—malaria. He hoped "to move my first division in eight or nine days into North Carolina by Charlottetown and Salisbury," although "I dread the convalescents not being able to march, but it is very tempting to try it, as a move of forty or fifty miles would put us into a much better climate." But escaping sickness was not his reason for heading north. His conception of strategy, not climate, dictated his moves. First, however, he had to safeguard his left, or western, flank in North Carolina. He assigned that mission to a Tory militia force commanded by an officer in whom his Lordship lacked confidence yet gave awesome responsibility—Major Patrick Ferguson.[58]

On 29 August 1780 Cornwallis wrote to Sir Henry Clinton, "Ferguson is to move into Tryon County with some militia, whom he says he is sure he can depend upon for doing their duty and fight well; but I am sorry to say that his own experience, as well as that of every other officer, is totally against him." Then why did his Lordship give Ferguson this critical mission?

Because Ferguson was Sir Henry's man, and Sir Henry was Cornwallis's boss. Sir Henry had appointed Ferguson inspector of militia. Cornwallis inherited Ferguson and was stuck with him. And I suspect that Cornwallis's letter to Clinton was his way of covering his backside in case anything went wrong.[59]

"The Sword of the Lord and of Our Gideons!"

While Cornwallis bivouacked the main army at Charlotte, North Carolina, Ferguson and his command, about 1,100 strong, marched into the western parts of the state east of the mountains. Except for some seventy men of the American Volunteers, a regular provincial unit from the North, the force was made up of Back Country Tory militia whom Ferguson had trained. One of Ferguson's assignments was to intercept the Georgia partisan chief, Colonel Elijah Clarke, who was retreating after his defeat at Augusta, Georgia (a subject covered in chapter 5). With 300 to 400 men, women, and children, Clarke was attempting to seek refuge over the mountains. Ferguson's main responsibility, however, was to shield Cornwallis's main army from attacks by Back Country and Over Mountain militia. On or about 10 September, from his camp in Gilbert Town, Ferguson sent his famous message to Colonel Isaac Shelby and the Over Mountain Men. "If they did not desist their opposition to British arms, he would march over the mountains, hang their leaders, and lay their country waste with fire and sword."[60]

Ferguson had challenged hard men, and their answer was swift. About two weeks later a little over 1,000 riflemen rode eastward once again, over the mountains to where the waters ran east, with the cry, "The Sword of the Lord and of our Gideons!" They were led by Colonels Isaac Shelby and John Sevier (1745–1815) of North Carolina and William Campbell (1745–1781) of Virginia. Four days later they rendezvoused with North Carolina Back Country militia.[61]

Shortly after that Ferguson issued another famous message, this one to the men of North Carolina. After referring to the Rebel horde as "an inundation of barbarians" and "dregs of mankind," he finished with a striking sentence: "I say, if you wish to be pissed upon by a set of mongrels, say so at once, and let your women turn their backs upon you, and look out for real men to protect them."[62]

The result was much less than Ferguson hoped for, and one wonders if his dramatic language frightened more than steeled men? Ferguson slowly retreated, heading for Charlotte and Cornwallis's encampment, while the Over Mountain Men and North Carolinians joined by South Carolinians and Georgians came on, searching for their prey. At three o'clock on the afternoon of 7 October 1781 they caught up, encircled Ferguson's position on top of Kings Mountain, South Carolina, and attacked. In one of the key actions of the war, the Rebel partisans destroyed Ferguson's command, killed the man himself, stripped him naked, and, it has long been claimed, urinated on his corpse. No one has summed it up better than Sir Henry Clinton, writing over two hundred years ago: Kings Mountain "unhappily proved the first link in a chain of evils that followed each other in regular succession until they at last ended in the total loss of America."[63]

The Tories of the Back Country never recovered from the disaster. Thereafter the Rebels maintained the initiative. Lieutenant Colonel John Harris Cruger, commanding at the important British post of Ninety Six, reported to Cornwallis that "the whole district had determined to submit as soon as the Rebels should enter it." Most important of all, the great militia victory left Cornwallis's left flank in the air. He feared, incorrectly, that hordes of Rebels were descending on him, and he thereupon retreated to winter camp at Winnsboro, South Carolina. There he stayed for four months before resuming his offensive. By then, however, he faced an American general who had much to teach him about the art of war.[64]

Before Nathanael Greene's arrival, Thomas Sumter and his band inflicted two bloody defeats on British regulars in South Carolina. At Fishdam Ford elements of the British Legion horse and mounted infantry of 63rd Foot, commanded by Major James Weymss (pronounced weems), were defeated and Weymss taken prisoner. A furious Cornwallis then ordered Lieutenant Colonel Banastre Tarleton to engage in an eighteenth-century version of search and destroy. Tarleton searched, found, but failed to destroy. At Blackstock's Farm the dashing young cavalryman met Sumter in battle and suffered the first defeat of his career. In his finest hour in combat command, Sumter deployed his men skillfully in defensive positions and repulsed and dealt heavy losses to 63rd Foot with long-range rifle fire. At the tail end of the action Sumter was badly wounded and carried from the field. A weaker man in mind and physique would have died. But for all his faults, there was steel in Sumter. He lived but was laid up for several months. As it turned out, that was a boon for the Cause. Sumter's sidelining meant that the new commander of the Southern Department would not be burdened at this critical stage of the campaign by the Gamecock's difficult personality and non-cooperation with Continental generals.

"For God's Sake . . . Send Greene"

Between the summer of 1776 and late 1780 four major generals had commanded the Southern Department. One was not there long enough to judge his abilities in that theater, and of his three successors each revealed in dramatic fashion his unfitness for theater command. Alexander Hamilton had the answer for command in the South: "for God's sake . . . send Greene."[65]

By December 1780, when he assumed command in the South, thirty-eight-year-old Major General Nathanael Greene (1742–1786) of Rhode Island was a seasoned soldier, hardened by five years of war. But when he had joined the Continental Army in 1775 outside Boston, as a brigadier general commanding the Rhode Island Army of Observation, he was a rank amateur, an anchor-smith and small merchant turned soldier whose knowledge of war consisted of wide readings in military history and eight months of parade-ground drill. Quickly, however, this broadly built, five-foot, ten-inch Rhode Islander, with the powerful arms and shoulders of his craft, came to Washington's attention. He observed that Greene's troops "though raw, irregular, and undisciplined are under much better government than any around Boston." Nathanael Greene was a quick study. His readings, his intuitive grasp of military affairs, his high intelligence, and his natural ability had already put him well on the way to the mastery of military administration and leadership. And as time went on he revealed a keen analytical mind that would come to full fruition in the Carolina maelstrom. By 1780 he had distinguished himself in combat command in all but two of the major battles in the North and as quartermaster general had become a master of the vital military arts of supply and transport. He knew failure, in his case massive failure. During the 1776 New York campaign, his decision that Fort Washington, overlooking the Hudson River on the northern tip of Manhattan, could be defended against a British attack ended in disaster. A little over 2,800 troops were captured and tons of vital armaments lost. "I feel mad, vext, sick, and sorry," Greene wrote to his friend Henry Knox. Yet Washington never lost faith in him and he rebounded from the debacle. For Greene had what was crucial to the responsibilities of command: the physical and mental fortitude to undergo not only the shock of battle but the myriad problems, decisions, disappointments, failures, and tensions endemic to war. He was the man Washington had wanted to command the Southern Department instead of Congress's pet general, Horatio Gates. Following Gates's disaster there were South Carolinians who had lobbied for Greene's appointment. "You have your wish in the officer appointed to the Southern command," Washington wrote to John Mathews, who would later become governor of the state. Although Greene would take his orders from Washington, he had the political astuteness to keep successive presidents of the Continental Congress informed in detail of his operations.[66]

General Greene found his army "without Discipline and so addicted to plundering, that the utmost Exertions of the Officers cannot restrain the Soldiers." He acted quickly to restore order. A soldier who returned to camp after being absent without leave was tried, convicted, sentenced to death, and hanged in front of the entire army. The message was clear, the reaction of the troops stoic: "New lords, new laws."[67]

While Greene whipped the beaten troops into shape to fight again, he led part of the army from Charlotte east to the Pee Dee River near Cheraw, South Carolina, and sent his brilliant deputy, Brigadier General Daniel Morgan (1735–1802), with the cream of the army, 600 light troops, to take command in the area west of the Catawba River. That was Greene's first flouting of a hoary military maxim: never divide your force in the face of a superior enemy. He did so largely because food supplies had been picked clean in the Charlotte area. Greene was dead long before Napoleon became famous, but he applied the Napoleonic principle that an army divides to live, unites to fight. It was also important to keep up the morale of Rebels west of the Catawba. Greene ordered Morgan to "give protection to that part of the country and spirit up the people, to annoy the enemy in that quarter." Although Thomas Sumter was recovering from his grave wounds suffered at Blackstock's and was unable to take the field, he still considered himself in command west of the Catawba. Furious at Morgan's presence in his area and at Greene for giving Morgan command there, he refused to cooperate. That did not deter the rough-and-ready Virginia frontiersman. On 17 January 1781, with his light troops and several hundred partisan militia, the charismatic Morgan, the American army's finest combat commander, taught other Rebel generals how to use irregulars in concert with regulars in a formal, set-piece battle. On the field of Cowpens in South Carolina, Morgan met Banastre Tarleton, commanding Cornwallis's light troops. In the tactical masterpiece of the war, Morgan and his men destroyed Tarleton's command—with one exception: the British Legion horse fled the field when ordered to charge. The battle-hardened American troops, wrote Lieutenant Thomas Anderson of the Delaware Regiment, "that night . . . lay amongst the Dead & Wounded Very Well pleased With Our days Work." Morgan wrote to his friend William Snickers that they "came running at us as if they Intended to eat us up," but "I have given him a devil of a whiping."[68]

Cornwallis's reaction? "The late affair almost broke my heart." Enraged by the loss of the eyes and ears of his army, his Lordship vowed to catch Morgan and free the 500 or more prisoners taken at Cowpens. He explained his reasoning to his civilian superior, Lord George Germain, secretary of state for the American Department.

My plan for the winter's campaign was to penetrate North Carolina, leaving South Carolina in security against any probable attack in my absence. . . . I hoped to be able to destroy or drive out of South Carolina the corps of the enemy commanded by General Morgan, which threatened our valuable district of Ninety Six, and I likewise by rapid marches to get between General Greene and Virginia and by that means force him to fight without receiving any reinforcements from that province or, failing that to oblige him to quit North Carolina with precipitation and thereby encourage our friends to make good their promises of a general rising to assist me in re-establishing His Majesty's Government.

But South Carolina was not secure—and Cornwallis knew it.[69]

When he learned of Morgan's great victory, Greene mounted for a three-day, 100-odd-mile ride through bandit-and-Tory-ridden country accompanied by a guide, an aide, and three dragoons. He joined Morgan and two other senior officers at Beattie's Ford on the banks of the Catawba, where he sat on a log by the river and held one of his rare councils of war. He had written earlier that month to Alexander Hamilton, "I call no councils of war, and I communicate my intentions to very few." For Greene would have agreed with the boy colonel of the Civil War, Arthur MacArthur, father of Douglas MacArthur, who told his son, "Doug, of Councils of war breed defeatism and timidity." Greene's council lasted only twenty minutes. The decision was made to continue Morgan's retreat and join the main column, which Greene had ordered to march northward under the command of General Isaac Huger (pronounced yewgee). Greene wrote to Huger, "I am not without hopes of ruining Lord Cornwallis, if he persists in his mad scheme of pushing through the Country. . . . Here is a fine field and great glory ahead."[70]

Thus began in that rain-soaked winter of 1781, following the scenario Greene hoped for, a long pursuit across the breadth of North Carolina, across swollen rivers and streams, over wretched roads that were quagmires by day and moonscapes at night. Cornwallis burned his baggage train in order to convert his army into a light, fast-moving force. But he always found his prey one river ahead of him. At the Yadkin he stared helplessly at deep, swift-flowing waters. For lack of boats, which the Americans had taken to the opposite bank, he was forced to march several miles upstream to find a passable fording place. To Sir Henry Clinton in New York it was as if Cornwallis had disappeared into the vast hinterland of North America. Which indeed he had. General James Robertson, British civil governor of the Province of

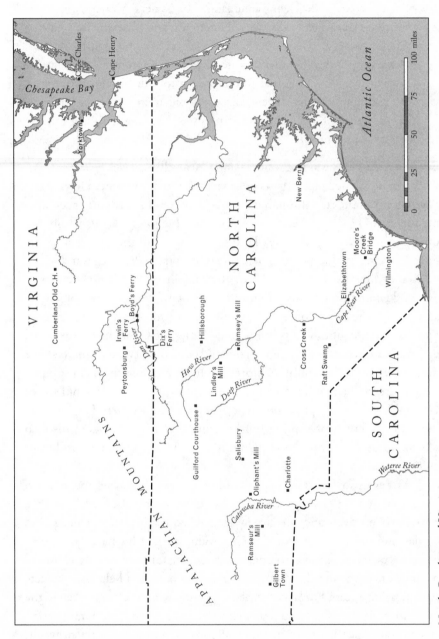

North Carolina and Virginia

New York, wrote that Sir Henry "wishes to take no step until the arrival of the English mail, and until we hear from Lord Cornwallis, of whom . . . we know nothing but by Rebel reports for six weeks."[71]

At Guilford Courthouse, North Carolina, Morgan's column and the main army met, and there Greene decided to continue the retreat, for without large numbers of militia to augment his regulars he was not strong enough to meet Cornwallis in battle. And it was there that Daniel Morgan, in such severe pain from rheumatism and probably sciatica he could not sit a horse, was forced to decline continued command of the light troops and bid adieu to the southern army. In his memoirs written long after the war, Henry "Light Horse Harry" Lee claimed that Morgan's refusal to continue might be construed by others as "a conviction that his reputation had been accidentally acquired, and could not survive the vicissitudes of war." The statement was libelous. Lee's shameful literary betrayal of his old comrade in arms was refuted by Richard Pindell, a surgeon with 1st Maryland. "Genl Morgan having been so diseased by the Rheumatism . . . he was compelled to return home in a Litter, and not from any defections as has been represented by Little Harry Lee in his Memoirs."[72]

There now ensued one of the most important and difficult operations of the war, indeed of any war: retreat and escape with the enemy in hot pursuit. It is known to posterity as the Race to the Dan. Both armies marched swiftly day and night, so close to each other the Americans could hear British bugles sounding reveille. When news came that the main American army had successfully crossed the Dan River, ten miles inside Virginia at the present site of the village of South Boston, the British advance heard the American rear guard cheer before it made its own way to the river and crossed. Once again, due to Greene's advance planning and the tireless, unsung work of Colonel Edward Carrington and his Quartermaster Corps, all the boats on the river had been gathered to carry Greene's army across the Dan, which was in full flood, and were now on the American side. Once again Cornwallis had failed to corner his quarry.[73]

That was on 14 February 1781. Subsequently, after resting and refitting Greene and his army recrossed the Dan, for he knew that he could not leave North Carolina Rebels alone to face Cornwallis and thus lose faith in the Cause. And the militia was gathering, from North Carolina and Virginia, even riflemen from the Blue Ridge. Nowhere near as many of the latter as Greene had been led to believe and hoped for, but at least some of those feared mountain marksmen had answered the call.

Almost one month to the day after the American army had crossed the Dan, Greene and Cornwallis met on 15 March 1781 at Guilford Courthouse in a battle described by Greene as "long, obstinate, and bloody." At the end the Americans withdrew, the British were left in possession of the field, and thus by eighteenth-century standards won the contest. But their ranks were thinned and battered to the point that the army needed to seek sanctuary and the lifeline of the British Navy. Cornwallis is reputed to have said, "I never saw such fighting since God made me. The Americans fought like demons." The British marched into battle 1,924 strong and came out of it with about 1,392 standing. Lieutenant General Charles, 2nd Earl Cornwallis's "mad scheme" had come to naught. He had crippled his army. And he could not remain in the hinterland. Sergeant Berthold Koch of the Hessian von Bose Regiment summed up Cornwallis's situation in a few well-chosen words: "The situation was now very bad for us. We had won, but we had no foodstuffs, no shoes on our feet, and no shirts on our bodies. . . . It was decided to begin the return march to the sea."[74]

We are now ready to begin the second and final chapter of the crucial Southern Campaign—the long and bitter road to Charleston.

1

"We March Tomorrow Directly for South Carolina"

"I Can Give You No Particular Instructions"

The year 1780 and the first half of 1781 were not auspicious times for the "glorious Cause." The British failure to subdue the northern states after several bloody battles had led to stalemate. There had not been a major action in the North since the drawn Battle of Monmouth in June 1778. It was as if the war there had been put on hold. The relative inactivity of American regulars and their legitimate grievances about short rations—and those poor to boot—and long months without pay had produced among them a sullen atmosphere to which were added the minor but cumulative irritations of military life that swelled out of proportion to their importance. All combined to create explosive situations in the camps of long-suffering Continentals. The mutinies in 1780 of the Massachusetts Line, the Connecticut Line, and 1st New York Regiment were followed in January 1781 by the far more serious mutinies of the Pennsylvania and New Jersey Lines. All were suppressed, the latter two with difficulty, but little could be done to alleviate the causes.[1]

For all practical purposes the Continental treasury was empty, public credit a joke. Nor were the states better off. Pleas for supplies for the army in the Carolinas were answered by Maryland officials that there was "Not a copper in the Treasury" and that the state was "without credit." In May 1781 Rebel finances crashed. France, the indispensable ally, was getting wobbly, faced with internal problems that nine years later would lead to its own revolution. On the surface there seemed good reason for Sir Henry Clinton to write the Duke of Northumberland that the Southern Campaign "would be the last of French assistance or American resistance"—provided, he was careful to note, that a calamity did not befall the British army.[2]

George Washington might have seconded Sir Henry had he read that letter. Gloom permeated his own correspondence. He wrote in October 1780, "I see nothing before us but accumulating distress. We have been half our time without provisions and are likely to continue so. We have no Magazines nor money to form them, and in a little time we shall have no Men, if we had money to pay them. We have lived on expedients till we can live no longer." That was written two days before the pivotal American victory at Kings Mountain in South Carolina, and a little over three months before Brigadier General Daniel Morgan and his force of regulars and Back Country partisan militia destroyed Lieutenant Colonel Banastre Tarleton's command of Cornwallis's light troops at the Battle of Cowpens.[3]

Yet the situation remained grave, for even those splendid victories did not alleviate Washington's view of "the unhappy state of our finance (which seems to be the source from whence flows all our difficulties)." That condition would last for the rest of the war. But in the Lower South, where a Back Country partisan campaign had foiled the British pacification effort, fighting had raged almost nonstop since the early summer of 1780 and showed no signs of abating. And it was to the South that George Washington sent a fighting general.[4]

The Southern Department when Greene took over included Pennsylvania, Maryland, Virginia, North Carolina, South Carolina, Georgia, and their western frontiers beyond the Appalachians, although Greene's army would operate only in the Carolinas and Georgia. As noted briefly in the Prologue, Congress had appointed four major generals in succession to command the department. The first was that bundle of eccentricities Charles Lee, a retired British officer turned Rebel, who was there only for the summer of 1776 before Congress recalled him to the North, presumably to teach Washington how to run the war. Lee left with his inflated reputation intact. The three men who followed him were not that fortunate. The serial womanizer Robert Howe of North Carolina lost Savannah and ran afoul of the political minefields of South Carolina and Georgia. Benjamin Lincoln of Massachusetts, a good man but promoted beyond his capacity, failed to retake Savannah and lost Charleston, and with it the only Continental army in the South. Of Horatio Gates, enough has been said in the Prologue. Following Gates's debacle at Camden, Congress in despair turned over the choice of the next commander of the Southern Department to George Washington. As we know, he immediately chose Major General Nathanael Greene of Rhode Island, the man he favored above all of his subordinates. Washington ordered Greene to "keep me constantly advised of the state of your Affairs and of every material occurrence." His further instructions to the new commander reveal both his faith in Greene and his own strength of character as commander in chief, for he readily admitted his ignorance of the southern situation and in effect gave Greene carte blanche.[5]

> Uninformed as I am of the enemy's force in that quarter, of our own, or of the resources which it will be in our power to command for carrying on the War, I can give you no particular instructions but must leave to you to govern yourself intirely according to your own prudence and judgment and the circumstances in which you find yourself. I am aware, that the nature of the command, will offer you embarrassments of a singular and complicated nature; but I rely upon your abilities and exertion for every thing your means will enable you to effect.

"Wedded to My Sword"

"We march tomorrow directly for South Carolina," wrote Major General Nathanael Greene. On the surface, this decision appeared foolhardy. His army of Continentals numbered about 1,840 whereas British and provincial regulars awaiting him were just shy of 10,000 strong. But the king's men were spread thin in separate garrisons in South Carolina and Georgia: Georgetown, Charleston, and Savannah on the coast; the river posts of Fort Motte, Fort Watson, and Fort Granby guarding the line of communications and supply between Charleston and the near Back Country garrisons at Camden and Orangeburg; and in the far Back Country Ninety Six and Augusta. Greene also counted on the partisan militia to cooperate and augment his strength. Cornwallis himself had admitted to the effectiveness of these irregulars a few weeks before he abandoned South Carolina to its fate: "the constant incursions of refugees, North Carolinians and Back Mountain men, and the perpetual risings in different parts of this province, the invariable successes of all these parties against our militia, keep the whole country in continual alarm and render the assistance of regular troops every where necessary."[6]

Upon Greene's orders, on Friday morning, 6 April 1781, Lieutenant Colonel Henry "Light Horse Harry" Lee swung into the saddle and led his Legion cavalry from its bivouac near Greene's camp at Ramsey's Mill on Deep River in North Carolina and rode south by southeast toward Cross Creek (modern Fayetteville). Lee's Legion infantry had left the previous day. To strengthen Lee's command, Greene detached a company of light infantry from the Maryland Continentals led by a sterling officer, Captain Edward Oldham.[7]

Henry Lee Jr., 1756–1818; oil painting by Charles Willson Peale. (Courtesy Independence National Historical Park Collection)

We should get to know Henry Lee Jr. (1756–1818), for he would become a key player in Greene's Southern Campaign. Better known as Light Horse Harry, he was of the Virginia Lees, high-born, proud, arrogant, intensely ambitious, eager for fame and glory. The historian Charles Royster summed up his character in one splendid sentence. "He expected to be obeyed by soldiers and honored by civilians because he was braver, smarter, and better than they were." That hauteur did not go unobserved. "In the eyes of some of his fellow officers during the war," Royster wrote, "Henry Lee was a spoiled brat." He was indeed—but he was also the most gifted partisan commander in the American army.[8]

"He was one of the finest looking men and best riders on horseback," recalled a North Carolina militiaman who "had the satisfaction of an intimate and familiar conversation with Colonel Lee." Thin, of medium height, he was described by contemporaries as "light and agile," of "weakly form, and not qualified, in personal strength, to make a heavy charge in battle." His were the skills and cunning of the regular partisan, relying on mobility, intelligence gathering, ambuscade, sudden raids, quick withdrawals. He was bold but also noted for careful reconnoitering and planning prior to a mission, for he was no harum-scarum fellow. After his martial talents became known, General Charles Lee (no relation), well known for the telling comment, said that "Lee . . . seems to have come out of his mother's womb a soldier." On

18 June 1776, age twenty, he was commissioned a captain in the Regiment of Virginia Horse, which was renamed 1st Continental Light Dragoons when it was mustered into the Continental Army in Morristown, New Jersey, at the end of March 1777. Early notice of his gifts, by the enemy as well as Americans, came in 1777–78, during the winter of Valley Forge. The Hessian diarist Captain Johann Ewald noted that Lee's dragoons "constantly alarmed our outposts." Lee's 5th Troop was part of the screening force protecting the Continental Army from surprise by the British Army in Philadelphia and vicinity, and also engaged in scouting, foraging expeditions, waylaying deserters, and clashing with British patrols. At eleven o'clock on the night of 19 January 1778, elements of 17th Light Dragoons and Queen's Rangers, estimated by various sources at forty to two hundred men, commanded by Major Frederick Crewe, set out to bag, wrote Sir William Howe's aide de camp, Friedrich von Muenchhausen, "a rebel dragoon captain by the name of Lee, who has alarmed us quite often by his boldness." Lee was at his headquarters in a stout stone house at Scott's farm, about five miles from Valley Forge and some sixteen miles from Philadelphia. He had eight officers and men with him. The British attacked at sunrise and tried to force their way into the house. A quartermaster sergeant fled, leaving Lee with seven men. Lee's leadership proved decisive, as the Americans drove off the attackers with well-aimed fire, including one round that knocked off the helmet of a British captain whose name would become infamous in the South: Banastre Tarleton.[9]

Lee reported the action to Washington, who in General Orders gave his "warmest thanks to Captn Lee & Officers & men of his Troop," informing "the army that Captn Lee's Vigilance baffled the enemy's Designs by judiciously posting his men in his quarters." Washington followed this up with a private letter to "My Dear Lee": "Altho I have given you my thanks in my general Orders of this day for the late instance of your gallant behaviour I cannot resist the Inclination I feel to repeat them again in this manner." Washington's closeness to Lee and the preferment he showed him would inflame jealousies that already existed simply because he was a Lee, and would later plague the young cavalryman.[10]

The following month Washington, as part of a grand forage for provisions to combat what he described as "this fatal crisis—total want and a dissolution of the Army," ordered Lee to proceed to Delaware and Maryland to gather cattle and food and gave him authority to "impress . . . any number of Waggons you . . . need." General William Smallwood was in command there, but Washington "intrusted this business to the zealous activity of Capt. Lee" and informed Smallwood that "Every aid you can possibly afford him is demanded by the exigency of the occasion." Captain Lee, not General Smallwood, was given control of foraging. Once again Lee's performance was exceptional. Hundreds of cattle, large amounts of flour, and other provisions were sent to Valley Forge.[11]

George Washington thought so highly of the young Virginian that in March 1778 he proposed that Lee, then twenty-two, join his staff as an aide-de-camp. In his reply, in the formal language of the eighteenth century, Lee assured Washington that "to deserve a continuance of your Excellency's patronage, will be a stimulus to glory, second to none, of the many, that operate on my soul," and "that I most cheerfully will act in any character your Excellency may call me to." Yet he declined the appointment, stressing his bond with his fellow officers and rank and file, and in one sentence revealed his true nature: "Permit me to premise that I am wedded to my sword, and that my secondary object in the present war, is military reputation." Washington was not at all put out. He replied that Lee's candor "cannot but strengthen my good opinion of you—as the offer on my part was purely the result of a high Sense of your merit, and as I would by no means divert you from a Career ... affording more frequent opportunities of acquiring military fame, I entreat you to pursue your own Inclinations as if nothing had passed on this subject, and to be assured of [my] good wishes."[12]

Two days later Washington wrote to Henry Laurens, president of the Continental Congress, praising Lee and his light dragoons and officers for "having uniformly distinguished themselves by a conduct of zeal, prudence and bravery," and recommending that Lee be promoted to major and given the "command of two troops of Horse ... to act as an independent partisan Corps." Washington had read his man correctly, adding, "Capt. Lees genius peculiarly adapts him to a command of this nature—and it will be most agreeable to him, of any station, in which he can be placed." Four days later, 7 April 1778, Congress enacted Washington's recommendations. By a partisan corps Washington meant a regular force able to engage in either conventional operations or in the type of warfare waged by irregulars, or guerillas as we say today.[13]

Lee's best-known exploit in the North came in August 1779 at Paulus Hook, New Jersey (now Jersey City), and it brought to full boil the simmering resentment of some of his fellow officers. The sixty-five-acre site jutted into the Hudson River. Two thousand yards across the river was New York City, headquarters of the British commander in chief, Sir Henry Clinton. Paulus Hook was almost an island. A two-mile salt marsh and creek, both flooded at high tide, lay between Paulus Hook and the mainland. On the hook the British maintained a substantial post. Outside the wall facing the mainland was a flooded ditch and a double row of abatis (logs imbedded in the ground with sharpened ends facing outward). Blockhouses and redoubts completed the defenses. Lee had played a minor role in General Anthony Wayne's successful storming of Stony Point in the Hudson Valley. Probably inspired by that morale-lifting victory, and perhaps jealous of Wayne's feat, Lee turned his eyes to Paulus Hook. Given the topographical difficulties, preparations for an attack demanded careful reconnaissance and planning—two of Lee's fortes. When he was ready he gave Washington his plan and asked that he be allowed to storm the post. Washington studied the plan, made changes, and gave him the go-ahead. He also gave Lee command of the operation. Lee's infantry assault force of 300 was drawn from Virginia and Maryland Continentals in the division commanded by General William Alexander, who preferred to be called Lord Stirling. Alexander made no objections. But the men were taken from the regiment of another Virginian, Colonel Nathaniel Gist. That Gist did not take kindly to troops from his regiment being commanded by Lee is an understatement. Transferred temporarily to Lee's command with his 300 men was Gist's subordinate Major Jonathan Clarke, who was also unhappy. Nevertheless, the operation began on the late afternoon of 18 August.[14]

It was a stunning success: despite the column's getting lost and the attack being set back two hours; despite being abandoned halfway through by many Virginia officers and men; despite, wrote Captain Levin Handy of Maryland, having "a morass to pass of upwards of two miles . . . and several canals to ford up to our breast in water." By Lee's orders, Handy's van "advanced with bayonets fixed, pans open, cocks fallen, to prevent any fire from our side," and "we gained their works and put about fifty of them to the bayonet, took one hundred and fifty-seven prisoners." Lee's command then made a successful withdrawal.[15]

Sir Henry was furious, Washington elated. He praised Lee by name and the attacking force in General Orders; extolled him to the president of the Continental Congress for a "remarkable degree of prudence address enterprise and bravery" in an attempt "critical and success brilliant"; and wrote in a private letter to his stepson, John Parke Custis, "this was a brilliant transaction . . . under the Comd. of Major Lee of the light Dragoons." Lee, it seemed, had confounded his enemies. Then it all seemed to come crashing down.[16]

Major Clarke brought court-martial charges against Lee on eight counts and had him arrested. One charge was that Major Lee had lied to Clarke about his time in grade, that Clarke was senior and should have been in command. To be gentle, Lee apparently did dissemble regarding the date of his appointment, but it was unnecessary for him to do so because Washington had given him command of the operation. That overrode seniority. Lee was infuriated, and the final charge probably induced white-hot rage: "behaving in a manner unbecoming an officer and a Gentleman." He was convinced that Colonel Nathaniel Gist was behind a "cabal" to blacken his name. And there is no doubt that Gist and other Virginia officers, including two generals, were intensely jealous of

Lee and determined to humble him. The officers of the Continental Army were a fractious lot. John Adams memorably described them two years earlier to Abigail Adams. "I am wearied to Death with the Wrangles between military officers, high and low. They Quarrell like Cats and Dogs. They worry one another like Mastiffs, Scrambling for Rank and Pay like Apes for Nuts." Nathanael Greene would suffer such wrangles later on in the South.[17]

The court-martial board sat for just over a week hearing evidence. Lee was acquitted, totally exonerated, with some charges, including "behaving in a manner unbecoming an officer and a Gentleman," declared unfounded, the rest with explanations as to why they were decisively rejected. Washington announced the decision in General Orders, and Congress in a resolution praised Lee's "remarkable prudence, address and bravery," appropriated $15,000 for Lee to divide among the noncommissioned officers and men who took part in the operation, and ordered a gold medal struck for Lee. He would be the only soldier in the army below the rank of general to be awarded a gold medal—overkill for an action certainly meritorious but even described by Washington as giving "the enemy another little stroke." The most telling tribute, and proof of the commander in chief's favoritism, was a letter to Lee saying that thereafter he could mark his communications *private,* which meant they would be read only by Washington, not by his aides.[18]

Lee had come out of it triumphant. Yet his biographer felt that "probably it was a trauma which left a permanent mark." And another historian wrote of the episode that Lee's "pride and confidence never recovered," and "thereafter his rage fed on the realization that others doubted his judgment, accomplishment, and character." These judgments are questionable. Of course it had some sort of effect on him, probably the very human desire for sweet revenge. Trauma, however, is overused in our time, and we should shrink from applying it to people dead for almost two centuries without direct evidence from the subject and his actions or people very close to him. As we shall see, the man whose exploits we will follow as our story unfolds did not lack confidence. As for pride? He had it, and retained it beyond full measure.[19]

This was the man Washington described as having "great resources of genius" and sent south to serve under Nathanael Greene.[20] It would prove to be a productive pairing—with, however, a sad ending.

"War Is an Intricate Business"

We left Light Horse Harry marching east toward Cross Creek while Greene with the main army marched southwesterly toward South Carolina. Greene trusted key subordinates enough to send them on detached missions, but he continually worried about them. (Greene was also not above micromanagement. It is fortunate that helicopters and the instant communication of our time were not available to him, for one can easily see him in his command helicopter circling the field of Cowpens, advising Daniel Morgan how to fight a battle for which Morgan needed no instructions. When it came to tactics, Morgan was the innovator, Greene the pupil.) Lee's actual mission, Greene wrote, was "to mask our real designs" and lead Cornwallis to infer from Lee's movements that his Lordship's army was Greene's real target. Lee was to march eastward as far as he thought necessary to fool Cornwallis. He was then to turn south and also march for South Carolina, with the possibility "to effect a surprise on the enemies posts on the Santee" River. But if Cornwallis decided to pursue Greene and came "pretty close," Lee should rejoin the army. "Give me constant information of your Movements, and the intelligence you may get." Greene also included words of caution in his orders to Lee as he sent him off. "You have only to remember that our force is small, and you cannot afford to waste men without a valuable object in contemplation." Revealing that he knew his man, Greene added, "Remember that you command Men, and that their powers may not keep pace with your ambitions." But he ended on an encouraging note: "I have every confidence in your prudence, and flatter myself that nothing will be left unattended which may promote the honor or interest of the American Arms."[21]

The decision to leave Cornwallis in North Carolina licking his wounds while Greene marched for South Carolina was typical of the general from Rhode Island. Since taking command of the Southern Department in December 1780, this most cerebral of American Revolutionary War generals had revealed an artful combination of daring, prudence, unorthodox field strategy, and adaptability to changing situations. His intention immediately following the Battle of Guilford Courthouse was to pursue Cornwallis and engage him in a campaign of attrition. (How ironic that after being chased across North Carolina and losing a battle the hunted had become the hunter.) On 18 March, three days after Guilford Courthouse, he wrote to Washington, "Lord Cornwallis will not give up this Country without being soundly beaten," and "I am in hopes by little and little to reduce him in time again." Agreeing with Light Horse Harry that the best tactic was "to attack the enemy upon their march," he had intended to fight as soon as he could catch up with Cornwallis and instructed Lee to hang on the British rear and keep sending up-to-date intelligence. Be ready for battle "on the shortest notice" he wrote Lee, and sent riflemen to reinforce him. Greene also had another purpose in ordering Lee's aggressive actions. Lee wrote in his memoirs that Greene ordered him to hang upon the rear of the British Army "lest the inhabitants of the region through which he passed might presume that our army had been rendered incapable of further resistance, and might flock to the royal standard." According to Banastre Tarleton, Lee succeeded. The Englishman wrote in his own memoirs that Cornwallis's army was "insulted" and "disturbed" by the American "light troops."[22]

Not seriously, however. Cornwallis's march discipline was tight. According to Sergeant Major William Seymour of the Delaware Line, "Lord Cornwallis, with his army, made such precipitate and forced marches, that it was a thing impossible to overhaul them, he leaving the sick and wounded behind with a flag, keeping his rear so close that we could not pick up not so much as one of his stragglers."

And on at least one occasion the American army was delayed in its pursuit by the necessity of applying military justice, not least as an example to would-be transgressors. On 25 April, Seymour reported, a court-martial tried, convicted, and sentenced to death Solomon Slocum of 2nd Maryland "for desertion to the enemy, joining with them, and coming in as a spy into our camp. . . . he was hanged on a tree by the roadside in full view of all who passed by." The same quick justice prevailed with the British, as Cornwallis made clear after his victory at Camden: "I have ordered in the most positive manner that every militia man who had borne arms with us and had afterward joined the enemy should be immediately hanged." And he did not leave it solely to subordinates. "I have myself ordered several militia-men to be executed who had voluntarily enrolled and borne arms with us, and afterwards revolted to the enemy." Modern readers accustomed to lengthy appeals, shocked by the swiftness with which these executions were carried out, should keep in mind that "The past is a foreign country. They do things differently there."[23]

Even if Greene had been able to catch Cornwallis, he could not have fought him. He had written earlier to Governor Abner Nash of North Carolina that the British "operating force is diminished in such a manner, that I am not without hopes of turning their victory into a defeat"—then added a caveat: "if the militia don't leave me." Militia being militia, short-timers all, they did leave him, "in great numbers" he wrote to Joseph Reed, "to return home to kiss their wives and sweet hearts." By 29 March he informed Nash that he lacked the strength to take on Cornwallis for lack of provisions and sufficient manpower. He bemoaned that "the greatest advantages are often lost by short terms of service." He also knew that Cornwallis's troops "are good . . . and fight with great obstinacy."[24]

Since January Cornwallis's army had been whittled from some 3,300 to about 1,450, while Greene's regulars were some 1,840 strong. But without considerable additional numbers Greene never meant to risk his little army in a potential winner-take-all battle. That would have been foolish and potentially disastrous. Above all, the army had to be kept intact, for as soon as it had come to a test of arms between mother country and colonies, the fate of the Revolution and the army became one. Ever flexible, Greene had changed his plans and also his orders to Lee. Since he could not fight Cornwallis, his aim was to draw his Lordship out of North Carolina in order to give that state a chance to recuperate from the fighting and passage of armies and raise its quota of soldiers. A master logistician as well as a fighting general, he was also thinking of supplies. He wrote to his faithful aide, Major Ichabod Burnet (1756–1783), who had been with his general since the Battle of Germantown in 1777, "Another reason for my moving into South Carolina is the enemy have now almost the entire command of the supplies of the state, and by going there we shall be able to share it with them at least." In his *Memoirs* Light Horse Harry Lee laid claim to the idea of marching to South Carolina. But the chronology of documentation does not bear him out. Greene, not Lee, was the master strategist of the Carolina campaign.[25]

Let us take a look at Greene's reasoning. The letter of 5 April 1781 to Burnet, partially quoted in the above paragraph, merits closer examination.

> In my last I gave you a hint that I was going to take a bold and I believe unexpected measure. We march tomorrow directly for South Carolina. This will oblige the Enemy either to follow us or give up there posts there. If the former takes place it will draw the war out of this State [North Carolina], if the latter we shall gain more than we can lose. Should [we continue?] in this State and follow the enemy down towards Wilmington, they will hold their ground in both States; for strange as it may appear the Enemy by moving northward secure their conquests southward. If we can oblige the enemy to retire into South Carolina we shall just undo all that they have been doing all winter, at such an expence of blood and treasure.[26]

This is a confusing letter. If Cornwallis follows him, the war will leave North Carolina. If he does not, "we shall gain more than we can lose," and it was the latter that turned out to be true. But if the British move "northward" they will "secure their conquests southward," which turned out not to be true. Yes, if the British left North Carolina and followed Greene to South Carolina, it would "undo all that they have been doing all winter, at such an expence of blood and treasure"—but in North Carolina. He repeated this a few weeks later in a letter to the president of the Continental Congress. "I thought it most adviseable to push my operations into South Carolina to recover the expiring hopes of the People; to divide with the Enemy the supplies of the Country . . . to break up their little posts of communication, and if possible oblige Lord Cornwallis to return to the State for their protection. *This last was the great object of the movement*" (italics mine). The key state, however, was South Carolina. If Cornwallis had followed Greene, or taken his army by sea to Charleston, that would have added 1,435 seasoned British (1,001), German (228), and provincial (206) regulars to British strength in South Carolina, which could have had a marked effect on the military situation in that state. I find Greene's reasoning strange. But now let us return to the narrative and to what actually happened.[27]

In moving south Greene once again flouted the rules of warfare. A little over three months earlier he had broken the rule that one never divides one's army in the face of a stronger enemy. That decision had worked brilliantly, leading to Tarleton's disaster at Cowpens. Now Greene broke the rule that one never leaves a dangerous enemy in one's rear. He wrote to another officer, "Don't be surprised if my movements don't correspond with your ideas of military propriety. War is an intricate business, and people are more often saved by means they least look for or expect."[28]

He also once again revealed his ability to adapt to changing conditions. The previous year he had written to Thomas Sumter, "It is not a war of posts but a contest for States dependent upon opinion. If we can introduce into the field a greater [regular] army than the enemy, all of their posts will fall of themselves; and without this they will reestablish them though we should take them twenty times." Aware, however, that a large regular army was not in the cards, he began a war of posts and had ordered Lee to attack the "enemies posts on the Santee" River.[29]

A key part of Greene's plan was the ability of his Continentals to confront the British in formal set-piece battles while the mounted Back Country irregulars continued the hit-and-run guerilla tactics that had kept Rebel resistance alive during the first phase of the Carolina campaign. Of equal importance, he also meant that the partisans would engage in joint operations with his regulars. He meant both to be part of a general plan of operations. To that end he had written to the commander of the South Carolina militia, Brigadier General Thomas Sumter, of his plans and to request cooperation. He asked Sumter to order his two main subordinates, Francis Marion and Andrew Pickens, "to collect all the Militia they can to co-operate with us." He also asked Sumter to gather all the provisions possible, "for on this our whole operations will depend," and to inform Greene "of your prospects, and the probable force I may expect to cooperate with us." Given their past performances, Marion and Pickens could be depended upon to answer Greene's call and serve the Cause selflessly. Of Thomas Sumter, we can only wait and see as we wend our way on the road to Charleston.[30]

Well aware of his numerical weakness, Greene expected a new draft of Virginia militia. As observed in the Prologue, he was not a fan of militia and had often made known in sharp language his feelings on their lack of discipline, their wasteful ways, their unmilitary habits, their here today, gone tomorrow mentality. But he needed them to augment his Continentals, and he did concede that the militia horsemen of the Back Country and the frontier were formidable. In a letter to Major General Friedrich von Steuben, whom he had left in Virginia to contain British forces there and prevent them from cutting the passage of supplies from the North to the southern army, he observed that the "militia of the back Counties would be most agreeable." From Governor Thomas Jefferson he urgently requested that 1,500 men be called up for three months to replace the militia going home after only six weeks of service. Few men were raised, and when the military situation changed and Virginia became endangered they were kept in the state. From Maryland Greene had asked for its quota of regulars, but despite assurances received, the troops were not raised until August and were then sent to join Washington's main army. Greene was on his own, his entreaties in vain. He complained bitterly to von Steuben that "One point is absolutely necessary to be settled by Congress, which is, whether the militia or State troops shall be under the Orders of the continental officers or not." For "if the views of a State are opposed to the general plan of operations, and the force in the field can only be employed at such points as they shall think proper, no Officers can be safe in his measures, nor can the War be prosecuted upon a general scale." Greene must have known that the matter would not be settled by Congress, given the lack of power of that body over the states. He would have to push on and trust that the South Carolina militia would answer his call to arms.[31]

Following his orders to keep Washington informed, Greene wrote of his plan to the Great Virginian, "I am determined to carry the war directly into South Carolina." Ever cautious with regard to logistics and security in the event of misfortune, he ordered that baggage and supplies not traveling with the army proceed under escort to Charlotte, North Carolina, at that time a crossroads village. For "by having them in the upper Country," he informed Washington, "we shall always have a safe retreat, and from those inhabitants we may expect the greatest support." His judgment was correct. From the upper country around Charlotte, on both sides of the North Carolina–South Carolina line, Rebel partisans had swarmed in the spring and summer of 1780 and created a nightmare for British forces attempting to establish control over the Carolina Back Country. Greene, however, intended to march directly toward the British post at Camden. He was well aware of the risk he was running. "I shall take every measure to avoid a misfortune, but necessity obliges me to commit myself to chance and trust my friends will do justice to my reputation if any accident attends me."[32]

"My Dear You Can Have No Idea of the Horrors of the Southern War"

For it was to a grim landscape that he was marching, "a poor barren part of the country," Sergeant Major William Seymour reported. "The inhabitants chiefly of a Scotch extraction, living in mean cottages, and are much disaffected, being great enemies of their country." Some if not most of those Highlanders had probably been among the Scots who had been overwhelmingly defeated in February 1776 by Rebel militia at the Battle of Moore's Creek Bridge. Rebel and Tory partisan bands had been raiding each other's settlements since May 1780, following the fall of Charleston to the British. Murder, arson, and pillage were common in the Carolinas and Georgia. A teenage Andrew Jackson grew up amid this horror and never forgot a Rebel driven mad by the murder and mutilation of a friend in a fury hunting down and murdering twenty Tories. Jackson later said of him, "he was never a happy man afterward." The law of the jungle prevailed as men stalked men. Greene wrote, "The whole country is in danger of being laid waste by Whigs and Torrys, who pursue each other with as much relentless fury as beasts of prey." Although they probably never met, he was describing such men as the South Carolina Back Country Rebel Tarlton Brown, who left us a vivid description of his reaction when, "Hearing that British Tories and Indians had murdered our father and sixteen more of his neighbors, burning to ashes his house and all within it, our mothers and sisters escaping to the woods, with little or nothing to support upon, no male friend to help them, my blood boiled within my veins, and my soul thirsted for vengeance." Brown's "Memoirs" do not reveal whether he ever caught up with his father's killers, but there were other scores to settle. Tarlton Brown was one of the hard men on both sides who did not hesitate to take vengeance swiftly whenever and wherever the opportunity arose. In April 1780, riding with eighty South Carolina and Georgia partisans, Brown described such an incident. "Crossing the Edisto [River] at Givham's Ferry, we fell in with a man who assisted [Thomas] Brown in hanging the five brave fellows at Wiggins' Hill. We gave him his due, and left his body at the disposal of the birds and beasts."[33]

Nor were acts of revenge restricted to the crackers of the Back Country. William Martin Johnston of Savannah was a gentleman, a Tory of the

American gentry class, and a captain of provincial regulars. He married Elizabeth Lichtenstein, a beautiful young Savannah woman of the same class. His favorite brother, John, known in the family as Jack, was taken by Rebels and hanged. Many years after the war, living in Nova Scotia, Elizabeth Lichtenstein Johnston told the following tale to one of her grandsons. After Jack was hanged, her husband was absent for some days, and upon returning said to her, " 'I expect some friends here tonight, and would like supper for them at 11 o'clock; tell the negroes to have food also for their horses. I expect about twenty men.' " The men arrived at about the appointed hour. "Some of them were gentlemen I knew, friends of your grandfather, but others ... were bad looking men, not gentlemen." After supper, as the men were leaving, she asked her husband when he would be back. " 'Bet, if I return at all I will be back in twenty-four hours.' I slept little that night, and spent the next day in anxious prayer for his safe return." Captain Johnston returned at two o'clock that afternoon. He embraced Elizabeth, then "threw his sword and pistol on the table, both of which I could see had been used. I said to him, 'William, where have you been?' He replied, 'Bet, never ask me where I have been or what I have done, but we don't owe the rebels anything for Jack.' "[34]

Elizabeth Lichtenstein Johnston, c. 1764–1848, in early life; reproduced from Elizabeth Lichtenstein Johnston, *Recollections of a Georgia Loyalist,* rev. and ed. Arthur Wentworth Eaton (New York: Bankside Press, M. F. Mansfield & Company, 1901).

Greene's wife, Catharine, the fascinating Caty, was pressing him to allow her to join him. Despite Greene's deep and lasting love and his intense desire to have her by his side, in a letter written three days after the Battle of Guilford Courthouse he argued against it. "Nothing but blood and slaughter prevails here and the operations are in a Country little short of a wilderness, where a delicate woman is scarcely known or seen. While the war rages in the manner it does you will have little opportunity of seeing me." But Caty persisted, and three months later he penned another lurid description of conditions in the Carolinas. "My dear you can have no idea of the horrors of the Southern war. Murders are as frequent here as petty disputes are to the northward.... The Gentlemen in this quarter think themselves extreme happy if they can get their wives and families into some place of safety."[35]

"Without Supplies Neither a General nor a Soldier Is Good for Anything"

Much of the land had been picked clean by raiders, and Greene the concerned husband, the keen strategist, the fighting general, dared not neglect the key to armies in the field: supply and transport, or logistics as we say today. Training, experience, and esprit can carry an army beyond what normally might be expected of it, but eventually the lack of wherewithal will cause the best of armies to grind to a halt. The armies of the Revolution were small in contrast to those of the Napoleonic era and onward, when hundreds of thousands to millions of troops were mustered. Yet the amount of supplies that even the small armies of the Revolution required is staggering. Greene's papers contain a list of "Items Provided by Quartermaster Department" for the Southern Department alone that is seven-and-one-quarter pages long, two columns per page. And the list, the editors note, "is not exhaustive."[36]

Greene had experienced at first hand the vital role of getting supplies and forage to the army in the years 1778–1780. He found the Quartermaster Department, Washington wrote, "in a most confused—distracted and destitute state," but "by his conduct and industry has undergone a very happy change . . . such as enabled us, with great facility, to make a sudden move with the whole Army & baggage from Valley Forge in pursuit of the Enemy." Washington also included a sentence that reveals Greene's overall conduct of operations, whether as a staff officer or in field command. "In a word he has given the most general satisfaction and his affairs carry much the face of method and System." Greene hated the job, for it took him away from combat command. "I am taken out of the Line of Splendor," he complained bitterly at the time to Joseph Reed, and he might have added, where glory is to be had. For eighteenth-century officers, unlike those of our time, were not shy in speaking publicly of glory in war. To Washington, who in the army's extremity had prevailed upon the man he trusted most to accept the position, Greene wrote, "No body ever heard of a quarter Master in history." Yet he would certainly have agreed with the World War II German commander Field Marshal Erwin Rommel: "Before the fighting proper, the battle is fought and decided by the Quartermasters." Generals from ancient times to our own have testified to this truth. "Without supplies neither a general nor a soldier is good for anything," wrote the fifth-century B.C. Spartan mercenary commander Clearchus. George Washington echoed Clearchus in stark language when he informed a South Carolina delegate to Congress of Greene's appointment. "I think I have given you a General; but what can a General do, without men, without arms, without cloathing, without stores, without provisions?"[37]

Thus Nathanael Greene's experience as quartermaster general of the Continental Army was a critical part of his on-the-job training as a soldier, and in the South he had been on top of that aspect of his command from the beginning. When he had first come south to relieve Horatio Gates as commander of the Southern Department, he spent his first night in camp in Charlotte studying the resources of the countryside with Colonel Thomas Polk, Gates's chief of commissary. Polk later told the New England Rebel Elkanah Watson that "by the following morning he better understood them than Gates had done in the whole period of his command."[38]

Yet if Greene was a proven master of supply and transport, one might ask why his southern army was continually plagued by dire shortages of clothing, food, ammunition, and the entire gamut of supplies required to maintain an army in the field? The differences in the two great American regions tell the tale. The North had a much larger population, mostly rural and agricultural but with well-established manufactures and artisans. There Greene had been close to his sources of supply. What was needed was good organization and an iron determination not to be thwarted, and on both counts Greene was masterful: "forage the Country naked," he ordered a subordinate, and when Pennsylvania farmers cried out and "beset me from all quarters . . . like Pharoh I harden my heart."[39]

The South, however, with its thin population spread over a vast area, its few manufactures and skilled artisans, was incapable of meeting the demand for the full range of supplies needed by the army. Most of the Southern Army's supplies had to come by land from the North, and thus we must keep in mind during any discussion of logistics in the Southern Campaign the resources available for supply and transport. We are on eighteenth-century means and time. The common means were wagons drawn by horses at a walk, oared river craft, or sailing ships. Yet unlike northern rivers, southern rivers ran west to east, and for most of the war the British Navy controlled the coastal waters and the British Army all the ports south of Virginia. An example drives this situation home. On 4 April 1781 Greene wrote to the Board of War that Colonel William Washington's dragoons were in dire need of clothing. They had been wearing the same clothes for nine months under conditions of "severe service" and the clothing was close to a state of "decay." He sent Lieutenant Ambrose Gordon with the letter to Philadelphia to present to the board and return with the goods. On 31 August Captain John Hamilton, Greene's deputy clothier general, found eight wagonloads of clothing that had arrived in Charlotte, some five months after Greene's request. But the wagons had been contracted only as far as Charlotte, and no other wagons were available. By at least 10 September the clothing had not reached Colonel Washington's dragoons.[40]

Greene's correspondence before and after the Battle of Guilford Courthouse reveals a commander ever aware that food, clothing, ammunition, forage for horses, and other supplies were the fuel that stoked the army's engine. In the North, rerouting and commandeering of supplies en route was not unknown. Conditions in the South, however, were such that the job of supplying the army was made even more difficult by administrative structures at the state and local levels that were primitive in contrast to the North. Disorganization was the rule, not the exception. In January 1781 Greene had to write a detailed letter to Colonel Nicholas Long, deputy quartermaster general for North Carolina since 1776, explaining the difference between the departments under his command. In March Long admitted that "a Number of Officers being appointed by several different powers," such as the governor, the board of war, the council extraordinary, did not communicate with him and were beyond his "Directions." Greene complained repeatedly that supplies meant for the Continental Army in the South were being intercepted, confiscated, and issued elsewhere by militia officers. Colonel Thomas Wade, a South Carolina state contractor who had been collecting and forwarding supplies for the army, wrote "for God Sake lets have no more Low Land Militia Guards to guard Public Property." Despite Greene's best efforts he was not able to stop this practice. Of these "embezzlements." he wrote,

> the distance is so great and the waggoners so unfaithful that great abuses prevail on the road, and besides it has been so much the custom for Stores to be stopped on the way by order of the different Governors and officers either commanding or residing in the different States

through which the Stores pass that the packages are often broken and issues made without being accounted for. These last two evils I have been endeavoring to prevent ever since I have been in this department. But customs however improper which have received a sanction from long indulgence are difficult to prevent.[41]

No discussion of the wherewithal that maintained eighteenth-century armies can ignore the contributions of camp followers, or, as I prefer to call them, support troops. Sutlers (civilian contractors) were necessary for eighteenth-century armies to operate. Cornwallis, for example, wrote to another British general, "The cattle drivers are absolutely necessary; we cannot do without them." Nor could armies do without women followers. Sarah Osborn, wife of Sergeant Aaron Osborn of Greene's commissary department, "busied herself washing, mending, and cooking for the soldiers," as she stated in her pension application. Nursing the wounded was also one of the duties of women following the army. Often denigrated as whores, most of these women were the wives, sweethearts, and widows of soldiers who for one reason or another—poverty often—followed their men to war. George Washington, accustomed to the refined ladies of his own class, did not welcome the presence of women from the great unwashed. But he knew that he had either to accept them or, he wrote, "lose by Desertion, perhaps to the enemy, some of the oldest and best Soldiers in the Service." In the words of the historian of the camp followers, the women who shared the hardships of the men "helped maintain the health and welfare of the army." Without them the army could not function.[42]

The gathering of the necessities of war also encountered Americans' already highly developed sense of the sanctity of private property. In the midst of a war, with the issue hanging in the balance, Americans bristled at the thought that what belonged to them could in emergencies be taken for the greater good. As Thomas Jefferson reminded Greene, a "free People think they have a right to an Explanation of the Circumstances which give rise to the Necessity under which they suffer." An example, which also had its amusing moments, was the problem of acquiring horses for Greene's cavalry. It began before the Battle of Guilford Courthouse and continued thereafter.[43]

Virginia was the home of fine stock, and in February 1781 Greene turned for help to Governor Thomas Jefferson. Cavalry was "so essential," wrote Greene, that Jefferson should take steps necessary to obtain horses for the 1st and 3rd Continental Dragoons. Jefferson immediately sent Greene blank impressment documents. Aware of his countrymen's sensitivities with regard to private property, Greene warned senior cavalry commanders that officers using the impressment power should proceed with "great delicacy" and "treat the Inhabitants with tenderness." They should not impress valuable stud horses, and they were to keep complete records and give proper certificates to the owners. "Otherwise the people will think they are plundered."

His warnings were either too late, not circulated properly, or ignored by junior cavalry officers. Colonel William Washington's officers took many stud horses in their prime, "valued at 800 to 1000 hard dollars." Jefferson wrote on 24 March that dragoon officers had "transgressed extremely." One of the offending officers was a lieutenant of 3rd Continental Light Dragoons with the marvelous name of Epaphroditus Rudder. His behavior was downright scandalous. He impressed a horse named Romulous, appraised at 750 pounds specie, from one David Deardins and then "swoped it with Colonel George Gibson for a gelding and ... Two Hogsheads of tobacco to boot."[44] These offenses whetted the legislative appetite for meddling. The Virginia legislature passed three resolutions that Greene described as so restrictive that the army could "not purchase by voluntary sale a horse that I would trust a dragoon on," for it would be placing them in jeopardy "to mount them on such cattle."

Greene apologized for the dragoons' transgressions but claimed that only two or three horses of superior quality had been brought to his camp, whereas "most of the horses that have been impressed are rather inferior." He stressed that cavalry superior in quality as well as numbers was necessary if the army and militia were "to prevent the enemy from attempting surprise at a distance from which so many disagreeable consequences happened last campaign." He added, "The use and value of them had been but little attended to in the Southern Department," a reference to Horatio Gates's neglect of cavalry, even though the partisans had already proven the worth of a mounted force. "Without cavalry," Greene continued, "we can never reconnoiter the enemy, attempt a surprise, or indeed keep ourselves from being surprised."

Greene obviously stewed over this vexing matter, and the longer he thought about it the more frustrated he became. That is not surprising given his generally low opinion of legislators. Three years earlier he had written of the Continental Congress, "The Congress have so many of those talking Gentlemen among them that they tire themselves and every body with the long, laboured speeching that is calculated more to display their own talents than promote the publick interest." On 28 April he wrote a brutally candid letter. Although addressed to Jefferson, it was directed at the Virginia legislature. Greene wrote hundreds of good letters, but this is one of his best and casts light on the important subject of civil-military relations.[45] "It is to be lamented that Officers and men will not exercise more discretion and prudence when entrusted with the execution of any order which seems to invade the rights of a Citizen not perfectly comfortable with the Laws and constitution of the land. And it is to be equally lamented that a Legislature should from resentment for the misconduct of a few individuals, bring upon an army employed for their service inevitable ruin and upon the community disgrace and distress."

A bit hyperbolic toward the end, but the point was well made. Greene explained that he had given an order "to guard against the evils complained of" and enclosed a copy. He also pointed out that "Particular situations and particular circumstances often make measures necessary that have the specious show of oppression, because they carry with them consequences pointed and distressing to individuals. It is to be lamented that this is the case, but pressing emergencies make it political and somewhat unavoidable." Following a review of the circumstances leading to the controversy and his efforts to redress grievances, Greene entered a realm that throughout history has vexed citizens, politicians, and soldiers of free societies, and should especially interest we in the twenty-first century: what do officials responsible for coping with a crisis or a serious threat do when the needs—ever debatable—of the emergency conflict with the rights of individuals? Greene made his position quite clear. "The rights of the individual are as dear to me as any Man. But the safety of the community I have ever considered as an object more valuable." He castigated the Virginia legislature. "Already we have experienced in many instances, the ill Consequences of neglecting the Army when surrounded with difficulties and threatened with ruin. Great expence of blood and treasure have attended this policy and to redress the grievances of a few individuals when it will entail calamity upon the Community will be neither political or just."

Greene ended his letter on a sarcastic note and again did not spare hyperbole. "If horses are dearer to the Inhabitants than the lives of Subjects or the liberties of the People there will be no doubt of the Assembly persevering in their late resolution, otherwise I hope they will reconsider the matter and not oblige me to take a measure which cannot fail to bring ruin upon the Army, and fresh misfortunes upon the Country."

The lawmakers of Virginia stood fast. Prior to the Battle of Hobkirk's Hill in April 1781, Greene's cavalry mustered eighty-seven men, of whom thirty-one had no mounts. Yet the heavens did not fall in. A combination of thoughtless cavalry officers and meddling legislators had made the army's job more difficult, but it did not have a major bearing on the campaign. Nevertheless, the affair is of interest to us on two levels: as an example of the specific frustrations faced by Greene, and in general of the constraints under which a free society wages war, and of the contrasting opinions of soldiers and civilians.

Ironically, after Cornwallis left Wilmington and invaded Virginia, some of the finest horses in Virginia were transferred to British forces, and there was nothing Governor Jefferson or the legislature could do about it. As Cornwallis marched north to Virginia, slaves flocked to his army, and many brought with them fine stock from their masters' stables. Captain Johann Ewald of the Jaeger Corps provided us with a description of the result. "Every officer had four to six horses and three or four Negroes, as well as one or two Negroes to cook and maid. Every soldier's woman was mounted and also had a Negro and Negress on horseback for her servants. Each squad had one or two horses and Negroes, and every non-commissioned officer had two horses and one Negro. Yes, indeed, I can testify that every soldier had his Negro who carried his provisions and bundles. The multitude always hunted at a gallop."[46]

"Our Wants Are without Number, and Our Difficultey without End"

Manpower problems also bedeviled Greene. In late October 1780 two companies of artificers, men skilled in the crafts—wheelwrights, harness makers, gunsmiths, carpenters, and others—marched from New Jersey to join Greene. But by early May of the next year he complained that most of "their time of service expir'd are gone home." He hoped for reinforcements and in February 1781 Congress assigned the Pennsylvania Continentals to Greene's Southern Department. But the Pennsylvanians' mutiny in January and the difficulty outfitting the troops delayed their departure. The first division under Brigadier General Anthony Wayne did not march from York, Pennsylvania, until 26 May, the second division marched even later, and by then events in Virginia made it imperative that Wayne join the Marquis de Lafayette's small army to resist the ravaging of that state by British forces under Cornwallis. Lafayette himself with 1,200 light infantry had been ordered by Washington on 6 April to join Greene, but the same events in Virginia made it impossible for Lafayette to leave that state undefended. In fact, Greene, aware that Virginia could not be left to the mercy of the enemy, on 1 May ordered Lafayette to "take . . . command in that State and conduct Military operations as circumstances shall dictate to be proper." Fearing that the young Frenchman might let his desire for glory overcome due caution, he warned Lafayette, as he had Light Horse Harry Lee, to use his force carefully. "I have only one word of advice to give you, (having entire confidence in your ability, zeal and good conduct), that is not to let the love of fame get the better of your prudence and plunge you into a misfortune, in too eager a pursuit of glory. This is the voice of a friend, and not the caution of a general." Lafayette would follow that advice to good effect.[47]

Throughout the campaign for the Carolinas Greene's correspondence contains a litany of desperate problems with regard to the mechanics of war that would have crushed lesser men. To continually dwell upon them, how-ever, would bore the reader to distraction. Our point is that amid the panoply of war, the strategy and operations and tactics, the smoke and din of battle, courage and cowardice, cheers and tears, a myriad of administrative prob-lems, many without solution, test the mettle of the commander. "Our wants are without number, and our difficultey without end," Greene wrote. Yet he persevered in managing his army. As with all successful commanders before and after, Greene knew that to ignore the administrative aspect of war was to set the stage for failure. We are not referring to simple pen-pushing, or, as the Duke of Wellington put it, "mere quill driving." The Iron Duke himself said, "My rule was to do the business of the day in that day," and his final adversary, Napoleon, wrote to his brother, "The good conduct of my armies comes from the fact that I devote an hour or two every day to them."[48]

But one man, no matter how competent, how dedicated, could not attend to all the nitty-gritty necessary to supply the army. To drive home the enormity of the task, consider the statistics offered for a later war in which horsepower still predominated. The American Civil War general William Tecumseh Sherman wrote in his memoirs, "To be strong, healthy, and capable of the largest measure of physical effort, the soldier needs about three gross pounds of food per day, and the horse or mule about twenty pounds." Those amounts were virtually impossible to obtain in the sparsely populated and much fought over Carolina and Georgia Back Country, and we can be certain that men and horses rarely if ever came close to receiving Sherman's standard. Man and beast would often go hungry. Yet every effort had to be made.[49]

To accommodate this and other logistical missions, to study rivers and streams and topography, and to further establish rear area supply and trans-port, Greene required a subordinate of intelligence, ability, diligence, and unwearied patience. Upon arriving in the southern theater of war in late 1780 he found that man in Colonel Edward Carrington (1748–1810) of Virginia. A former artillery officer, Carrington was resourceful and tireless. Greene immediately appointed him deputy quartermaster general for the Southern Department and never regretted his choice. When Carrington ran afoul of the Continental Army's quartermaster general, that self-righteous and ven-omous hack Timothy Pickering, Greene sprang to Carrington's defense. "The War here is upon a very different Scale to what it is to the northward," he wrote to Pickering, and "A man of great resource is essential to the opera-tions." Colonel William Richardson Davie, who had become, reluctantly, Greene's commissary general, wrote of Carrington's appointment, "a more fortunate choice could not have been made." Carrington, one of the Revolu-tion's unsung heroes, would more than live up to his billing.[50]

Davie's appointment as commissary general, in charge of feeding the army, was another brilliant choice. A gifted small-unit combat commander, Davie in December 1780 was preparing to raise a cavalry regiment for service under Brigadier General Daniel Morgan. In his own words Davie was "fired with the prospect of serving under this celebrated commander" when Greene did to Davie what Washington had done to him. He asked Davie to leave combat command and accept the post of commissary general. Poor Davie. He wriggled, squirmed, pleaded, but Greene was adamant and persuasive. In desperation, Davie finally observed that "although he knew something about the management of troops, he knew nothing about *money or accounts,* that he must therefore be unfit for such an appointment." Greene easily countered. "The General replied that as to *Money* and *accounts* the colonel would be troubled with neither, that there was not a single dollar in the military chest nor any prospect of obtaining any, that he must accept the appointment." Davie bowed to Greene's demand, "under an express promise that it should be for as short a time as possible"—which turned out to be the duration.[51]

"I Am Quite Tired of Marching about the Country in Quest of Adventures"

Meanwhile, what of Cornwallis? What was he about? His plan to secure South Carolina by pacifying North Carolina had gone awry. Now his Lordship found himself facing the reality of King's Friends who either failed or were prevented to rally to the colors and king's enemies who forced him to change his plans.

On 20 February 1781, a little less than a month before the Battle of Guilford Courthouse, Cornwallis had issued a proclamation declaring that he had "driven the rebel army out of" North Carolina and calling "upon all loyal subjects to stand forth and take an active part in restoring good order and government." The Tory leader Colonel John Pyle, commanding 400 militia, attempted to join Cornwallis but on 25 February encountered Light Horse Harry Lee's Legion and the militia of Andrew Pickens. The result was the slaughter of about ninety of Pyle's men in what came to be known as Pyle's Massacre. The terrorized survivors fled. If that were not enough to devastate Tory morale, on the early morning of 4 March a band of King's Friends intent on joining Cornwallis approached Banastre Tarleton's lines. Tarleton had been assigned by Cornwallis to escort Tory units to safety. But Tarleton's dragoons mistook the Tories for Rebels, charged, "and those who did not disperse Expeditiously were cut to pieces." When Tarleton realized the error riders were sent to round up the terror-stricken men, but they would hear neither apologies nor assurances of protection. The following evening an American dragoon patrol found Tories driving cattle to Cornwallis's camp. They killed twenty-three drovers. Word of these incidents spread far and wide, and if after Pyle's Massacre there had been any glimmer of hope among the King's Friends that their day of deliverance might arrive, it died amid the shrieks of men being hacked to death by hard-charging dragoons of both sides.[52]

After the Battle of Guilford Courthouse, Cornwallis issued another proclamation. (British officers were enamored of proclamations.) "WHEREAS by the blessing of almighty God His Majesty's arms have been crowned with signal success by a compleat victory . . . I have thought proper . . . to call upon all loyal subjects to stand forth and take an active part in restoring good order and government." His Lordship described in a letter to Sir Henry Clinton the reaction of those who came and observed an army that did not give the appearance of having won a "compleat victory." "Many of the inhabitants rode into camp, shook me by the hand, said they were glad to see us, and to hear that we had beat Greene, and then rode home again; for I could not get one hundred men in all the Regulators' country to stay with us even as militia." The Tories behaved that way not out of supineness but from their experience of British armies, which more often than not arrived, departed, and left their American allies at the mercy of the Rebels. As a local Quaker told one of Cornwallis's officers, "they had been so often deceived in promises of support and the British had so often relinquished posts, that the people were now afraid to join the British army, lest they should leave the province, in which case the resentment of the revolutioners would be exercised with more cruelty, that although the men might escape, or go with the army, yet such was the diabolical conduct of these people, that they would inflict the severest punishment upon their families."[53]

The previous autumn in Norfolk, Virginia, a Tory woman wrote, "In the same extraordinary manner as our public affairs were ever conducted . . . just as the poor people came forward to show their loyalty, in the hope that the British troops would remain permanently, suddenly in the month of November" she was told that the "troops would embark the next morning. This took us unprepared in every way," and "Our poor landlady, a Mrs. Elliot, sat with her head back and her mouth extended, scarce in her senses from the shock, till at last she found speech to articulate; 'Well, this is the third time we have been so served by the British. We have shown our loyalty, and they have left us to the rage and persecution of the Americans for doing them service.'"[54]

This was a pattern that repeated itself throughout the country. Captain Frederick Mackenzie, a British officer who served in the Northern Campaign, confided to his diary, "Our taking post at different places, inviting the

Loyalists to join us, and then Evacuating those posts, and abandoning the people to the fury of their bitterest Enemies, has deterred them from declaring themselves until affairs take a decisive turn in our favour." But once the British left those posts, they did not return.[55]

With the exception of Burgoyne's disaster in the Saratoga campaign in northern New York State, the British army could march where it wished, winning battles, creating turmoil and distress, but once they were gone the Rebels either reestablished their control through the use of terror or waged bitter guerilla war with Tory partisans—or both. The British admiral Samuel Graves described the movement of Britain's armies succinctly: the army marched like "the passage of a ship through the sea whose track is soon lost." Cornwallis repeated the pattern. "With a third of my army sick and wounded, which I was obliged to carry in waggons or on horseback, the remainder without shoes and worn down with fatigue ... [I] thought it best to look for some place of rest and refitment."[56]

But the king's enemies were in the field and busy. Cornwallis had not intended to march to Wilmington on the coast. His goal was Cross Creek (modern Fayetteville), at the head of navigation of the Cape Fear River. From there he expected supplies to be sent to him upriver from Wilmington. In January 1781, following Cornwallis's orders, Lieutenant Colonel Nisbet Balfour, commanding at Charleston, had ordered Major James Henry Craig to sail from Charleston on three warships—*Blonde, Otter,* and *Delight*—with six companies of 82nd Foot, numbering 210 rank and file, Cornwallis's convalescents, and a small detachment of artillery with two brass 3-pounders and two iron 6-pounders, about 300 men in all, and establish a base at or around Wilmington. Other watercraft were three galleys, an artillery transport, three boats to carry provisions, an oat ship for victuals, and several smaller boats. Craig's "principal" assignment was "to gain the navigation" of the Cape Fear River. This would enable him to carry out his principal mission of "supplying Cornwallis's army at Cross Creek with provisions etc." Craig took Wilmington on 29 January and immediately skirmished with Rebel militia. By 10 February, because "of our small force," Craig found it impractical to hold "the town itself. We are therefore fortifying with redoubts a situation just below the town." He was never in any danger, but he soon discovered that he could not carry out his critical assignment of supplying Cornwallis. Readers, however, should remember Craig's presence in Wilmington, for it would eventually lead to bitter fighting between North Carolina Rebels and Tories and, several months later, to one of the most dramatic actions of the Revolution.[57]

Cornwallis had been informed that provisions were ample at Cross Creek and Scottish Highland settlers would join him "to a Man." Yet his Lordship found them "not equal to my expectations." He had written to Craig on 21 February, before the Battle of Guilford Courthouse, to prepare to supply his army and investigate the possibility of securing "the navigation of the Cape Fear River." Craig received a duplicate of this letter precisely one month later, after the battle. He replied that it would be "impracticable . . . to send anything up [the Cape Fear River] until the country is more settled." In other words, Rebel militia prevented it. He also had little in the way of supplies. Cornwallis was shocked when he arrived at Cross Creek and found "to my great mortification and contrary to all former accounts, that it was impossible to procure any considerable amount of provisions, and there was not four days forage within twenty miles." He claimed that he had been led to believe that food, forage, and assistance could be brought up the river by the British garrison at Wilmington without "the least obstructions from the people of the country." Yet he found that "the navigation of Cape Fear, with the hopes of which I had been flattered, was totally impracticable, the distance from Wilmington by water being one hundred and fifty miles, the breadth of the river seldom exceeding one hundred yards, the banks generally high, and the inhabitants on each side most universally hostile." For Rebel militia in an area thought to be controlled by King's Friends occupied the high banks and peppered supply boats with such hot fire they all turned back. His misinformation may have come from local Tories, because Major Craig had not misled him. Whoever was responsible, under these circumstances, Cornwallis continued, "I am determined to move immediately to Wilmington."[58]

It was a sad march. Five officers died of their wounds on this leg of the journey to the sea. One was irreplaceable. In Elizabethtown, North Carolina, the army buried the intrepid field commander of 33rd Foot, Cornwallis's own regiment. His Lordship mourned deeply Lieutenant Colonel James Webster. "I have lost my scabbard," he said. On 7 April, the day after Greene wheeled his army and marched for South Carolina, the exhausted survivors of what Nathanael Greene had called Cornwallis's "mad scheme" to pursue him through North Carolina arrived at Wilmington.[59]

Cornwallis now faced decision time. Should he follow Greene, reinforce the small army he had left behind, and thus meet his primary responsibility—the security of South Carolina? Or should he follow the siren song of Virginia, the destination that was his obsession? He found excuses for not immediately recognizing his duty. He wrote to Clinton on 10 April 1781 "expressing my wishes that the Chesapeake may become the seat of war—even, if necessary, at the expence of abandoning New York." It must noted that the Royal Navy wanted to establish a port in the Chesapeake to refit its ships, because its main port, New York, had treacherous sand bars outside the harbor, and

Halifax was too far away and difficult in winter. But I believe Cornwallis had convinced himself long before that "Until Virginia is in a manner subdued, our hold of the Carolinas must be difficult if not precarious." Even before receiving Cornwallis's letter, Clinton wrote to the earl giving him permission to go to Chesapeake Bay "in a frigate as soon as you have finished your arrangements for the security of the Carolinas and you judge that affairs there are in such a train as no longer require your presence, directing at the same time such troops to follow you thither as Your Lordship is of opinion can best be spared." Can there be any doubt of Clinton's intention? Can there be any doubt as to where Cornwallis's duty lay? Although the earl did not receive the letter until June, when he was already in Virginia, Clinton's instructions with regard to the security of the Carolinas, especially South Carolina, was a repeat of the order he had given Cornwallis over a year before. This letter, written on 13 April and received by Cornwallis in June, is more testimony to how long it took in an age of foot, horse, and sail for orders and intelligence to be transmitted.[60]

It is true that Cornwallis made arrangements to return to South Carolina if necessary. In early April he had written from near Wilmington to Lieutenant Colonel Balfour, "should the enemy threaten South Carolina, I must not stay here. I think it improbable, but this war has taught me to think nothing impossible." On 24 April, he wrote again to Balfour, instructing him to send troop transports to Wilmington in case he decided to take his army back to South Carolina. He was then aware that Lieutenant Colonel Francis, Lord Rawdon, commanding in the South Carolina Back Country, was in peril. Writing on the same day to Major General William Phillips, commanding British forces in Virginia, he admitted his "fear that Lord Rawdon's posts will be so distant from each other and his troops so scattered as to put him into the greatest danger of being beat in detail." Yet he found excuses for not marching in pursuit of Greene. "By a direct move towards Camden I cannot get time enough to relieve Lord Rawdon, and should he have fallen, my army would be exposed to the utmost danger from the great rivers I would have to pass, the exhausted state of the country, the numerous militia . . . and the strength of Greene's army, whose Continentals alone are at least as numerous as I am." However dubious his claim that he could not reach Rawdon in time, then why not wait in Wilmington for the transports he had ordered and sail to Charleston? Because "I could be of no use on my arrival at Charlestown, there being nothing at present to apprehend at that post." But what was to prevent him from then marching upcountry to either reinforce Rawdon if he had not "fallen" or take up the fight in the interior himself? The record is silent. We can be sure, however, that the Noble Earl, as Sir Henry Clinton liked to call him, would have thought of another excuse. Yet he knew, as he wrote to Phillips and other correspondents, of "the almost universal spirit of revolt which prevails in South Carolina."[61]

No, Cornwallis had long ago settled on his destination, his arrangements to the contrary mere window dressing for the record. On 10 April, Cornwallis wrote General Phillips a letter that helps to reveal the state of mind of a harried and deeply disappointed commander. "I assure you that I am quite tired of marching about the country in quest of adventures." As he had once thought the key to holding South Carolina was the suppression of rebellion in North Carolina, he now decided that the key to the entire rebellion was to abandon North Carolina, abandon New York, and "bring our whole force into Virginia; we then have a stake to fight for, and a successful battle may give us America." He repeated this in a straightforward way on 23 April to his civilian superior in London, Lord Germain. "I have . . . resolved to take advantage of General Greene's having left the back part of Virginia open, and march immediately into that province to attempt a junction with General Phillips." But in that letter to Phillips he also admitted, "whether after we have joined we shall have a sufficient force for a war of conquest I should think very doubtful." He also wrote to Phillips that he hoped by marching north to draw Greene out of South Carolina in pursuit. Yet he wrote to Clinton "that the return of General Greene to North Carolina, either with or without success, would put a junction with General Phillips out of my power."[62]

Before we comment on these strange, contradictory thoughts, let us be fair to Cornwallis. Although not a strategist of note, he was a sound eighteenth-century tactician, a bold field commander, and a lion in battle, always where he needed to be at the dying time, tall in the saddle, riding into the thick of it, facing death to rally his troops at moments of crisis. But . . .

Had his Lordship come unhinged? His biographers treat his decision gently, maintaining that had he received news of a disaster in South Carolina he would have returned. But Sir Henry Clinton's biographer, William Willcox, in one of the best books written on the war, was harsh in his analysis of the earl's actions. "Cornwallis's decision to join him [Phillips] cannot be fully explained. It seems to have been the act of a man driven beyond the limits of clear thinking." Willcox's judgment is compelling. Consider what Cornwallis had been through between October 1780 and March 1781. Poised with his victorious army at Charlotte to begin the reconquest of North Carolina, he had suddenly lost his left wing under Ferguson at Kings Mountain, forcing him to retreat to winter quarters. Subsequently, he sent his favorite subordinate, Banastre Tarleton, in pursuit of Daniel Morgan only to lose almost all of his light troops in Tarleton's disaster at Cowpens. There followed the frustrating chase of first Morgan, then Greene, across North Carolina, which further debilitated his army. His victory in name only at Guilford Courthouse left his army desperately in need of, in his own words, "rest and refitment." The retreat of his crippled force to the coast again revealed the weakness of the King's Friends and the strength of the king's enemies. Then, fully aware that the situation of British forces in South Carolina was perilous, he made the fatal decision to chase his delusion and head north to Virginia. Can we doubt that his Lordship's mental state was, at the very least, confused?[63]

On 25 April 1781, Lieutenant General Charles, 2nd Earl Cornwallis, relinquishing his responsibility to secure the Carolinas, pursuing his dream of a grand, climactic battle that "may give us America," turned his worn and decimated little army northward, where he found more adventures and fulfilled his American destiny.

That, however, was six months away, while to the southward there awaited Major General Nathanael Greene and his battered but unbowed little army more battles "long, obstinate, and bloody."

2

"We Must Endeavor to Keep Up a Partizan War"

"Untill a More Permanent Army Can Be Collected"

"I have not the Honor of your Acquaintance but am no Stranger to your Character and merit." The writer was Nathanael Greene, the recipient Francis Marion, who led a mounted brigade of South Carolina militia. Despite those felicitous words, more often than not Greene was a biting critic of militia. Early in the war, following the American debacles on Long Island and at Kip's Bay on Manhattan, with reference to formal, open-field engagements, he wrote to his brother Jacob: "The policy of Congress has been the most absurd and ridiculous imaginable, pouring in militia men who come and go every month. A military force established upon such principles defeats itself. People coming from home with all the tender feelings of domestic life are not sufficiently fortified with natural courage to stand the shocking scenes of war. To march over dead men, to hear without concern the groans of the wounded, I say few men can stand such scenes unless steeled by habit or fortified by military pride." Five years later, writing from North Carolina, where he had found some 1,700 militia muskets in "miserable" storage conditions, he exploded: "These are some of the happy effects of defending the country with Militia; from which the good lord deliver us."[1]

On the brink of his reentry into South Carolina, Greene continued his barrage of criticism of militia efforts in a letter to Samuel Huntington, president of the Continental Congress. "The Militia in our interest can do little more than keep Tories in subjugation, and in many places not that." But keeping the Tories in check was one of the important missions of Rebel militia.

He continued: "These states were in a better condition to make exertions last Campaign than this." There was a good measure of truth to that statement. He then wrote, "The well effected last year spent their time and substance in fruitless exertions." Yet that was not true, and Greene must have known it. As was made clear briefly in the Prologue and at length in *The Road to Guilford Courthouse*, in the last half of 1780, during the first phase of the Rising, the Rebel partisan militia saved the Revolution in the Carolinas and changed the course of the war.[2]

The following year Greene wrote a letter on the subject of the militia to Governor Thomas Nelson Jr., of Virginia. Expressed in measured, unemotional language, it briefly but precisely explained his thoughts on a regular army and defined regular troops as professionals, at the time a rare use of that word.

> Your own experience no doubt teaches you the great impolicy of depending too much on Militia. Regulars alone can insure your safety. Men will not yield to the hardships of Camp, nor submit to the severity of discipline without a certain line of duty prescribed as something professional, and by the force of discipline are made to encounter dangers and hardships as the most honorable attendants of a Soldiers life. I would by all means recommend drafting for three or four Years at least; short enlistments are dangerous, and can give you no permanent security. Before you can finish a Character for the duties of the Field, twelve months experience and severe service are absolutely necessary. Eighteenth Months Men are but little better than raw undisciplined militia. Before you can reap any material advantage from them their times of enlistment will expire, and leave you perhaps at a moment when everything is at stake . . . and the too frequent calls on the Militia, serve to weaken the powers of industry, destroy the means of agriculture, and break up the resources of the Country.[3]

Greene's opinion of militia was widely known and not well taken by many, North and South. In a letter to Greene from his good friend Joseph Reed, president of the Pennsylvania Council, Reed touched upon the historic roots of conflicts between regulars and militia and offered sage advice. Writing from Philadelphia on 16 June 1781, Reed stated that people there

> insist that you hold the Militia in Contempt & are too much inclined to attribute Failures to them. . . . My sentiments of Militia have been ever pretty much the same but I see plainly that . . . the great Body of the People of America will never allow them to support a permanent Force equal to the Defence of the Country & that of course we must

give up the contest or cherish the Militia. The successes which they have obtained to the Northward, at Kings Mountain & elsewhere seem also to give them some meritorious Claims. The Jealousy which has taken place, especially in this State between Continental Troops & them [militia] very much resembling the Behaviour of the Regulars [British troops] & our Provincials last War [French and Indian War] keeps up an Attention to this Point & tho it may be forgiven in inferior Officers, depend upon it, the Bulk of the Country resent any Indignity attempted towards them. In short at this Time of Day we must say of them as Prior of a Wife, "Be to their Faults a little blind And to their Virtues very kind."[4]

Greene answered on 6 August. "I am far from despising the Militia, I have ever considered them the great palladium of American liberty." Although we might take that statement with at least a modicum of salt, Greene the pragmatist was well aware of the absolute necessity of militia in the fight for freedom. A little later that year he wrote to Thomas McKean, who had succeeded Samuel Huntington as president of the Continental Congress, "I conceive the support of the militia is the very ground work of our Independence for the regular force can never maintain our cause independent of them." But, he added in his letter to Joseph Reed, "It was my duty to state the force of the Militia of this Country in its proper light." And that he did in the letter to Huntington. For after the criticisms quoted earlier, he observed that "The conflict may continue for some time longer, and Generals Sumter and Marion deserve great credit for their exertions and perseverance, but their endeavours rather serve to keep the contest alive than lay a foundation for the recovery of the States." The final words of that letter explain what Greene was driving at. What he meant by laying a "foundation for the recovery of the States" was a general plan of operation in which the partisan militia and Greene's regular army fought in concert with each other in order to drive the British from the South. Greene was right that hit-and-run guerilla raids and ambushes, even overwhelming victories such as Kings Mountain, vital as they were, could not win the campaign and free the Carolinas and Georgia.[5]

In 1780 there had been only a small window of opportunity for combined operations when Horatio Gates and his Continentals and militia entered South Carolina only to be quickly and thoroughly thrashed at the Battle of Camden. The partisans, therefore, had no regular army to work with even had they been willing. Although Gates brought his army back to Charlotte after Cornwallis withdrew to winter quarters, he had not a clue how to use partisans, either in formal battle or combined operations. The partisans, however, in their generally uncoordinated way, in 1780 had blocked the British pacification effort, kept the Cause alive, and bought the time necessary for an effective Continental general to combine the respective talents of regulars and partisans.

When Nathanael Greene praised Marion's "Character and merit" he was obviously buttering up a key militia commander. But there was more to his words than that. Greene might disdain militia, but he was also a realist. The apparent contradiction between praising a militia officer and heatedly criticizing the policy of depending upon militia for the war effort is readily explained in another sentence in the same letter to Marion. "Untill a more permanent Army can be collected than is in the Field at present, we must endeavor to keep up a Partizan War and preserve the tide of sentiment among the People as much as possible in our Favour."[6]

"Untill a more permanent Army can be collected": that is the key phrase. But that "permanent Army" was never collected. Throughout the war, North and South, the Continental Army was never large enough to win the war by itself. (How ironic that the American and British armies had this in common and were dependent on their respective militias, and in the case of the British also provincial regulars.) At times the Continentals required militia units to join in formal, open-field battles, as had occurred in the South: disastrously at Camden, gloriously at Cowpens, and with some success at Guilford Courthouse. But the everyday missions of militia were to control the countryside, keep the Tories in check, protect lines of communication and supply, deny the enemy provisions and forage, gain intelligence of enemy intentions and movements, and, in George Washington's words, "harass their troops to death." That is precisely what the Back Country partisans had been doing and continued to do.[7]

"He Was Obliged . . . to Enter into a Long Vindication of His Conduct"

Resistance by South Carolina and Georgia partisans did not cease while Greene and Cornwallis were maneuvering and fighting in North Carolina. Between the Battle of Cowpens on 17 January 1781 and the reentry of Greene's Continentals into South Carolina in April of that year, about thirty-three partisan actions took place. Space prevents description of all of them and a listing would be a bore. Some, however, merit our attention.[8]

Even though "I am extremely short of ammunition," on 9 February 1781 Brigadier General Thomas Sumter summoned his partisan brigade to action in order to carry out his plan to roll up the British posts guarding the supply and communication lines between Charleston and Camden and other Back Country posts. The previous year, prior to the terrible wound he had suffered

Thomas Sumter, 1734–1832; oil painting by Rembrandt Peale. (Courtesy Independence National Historical Park Collection)

during his victory over Banastre Tarleton at Blackstock's, Sumter was able to raise several hundred riders. But his glory days had passed, although he did not know it. When he left the Catawba River on 16 February only 280 men rode behind him. He was headed for the newly constructed British post of Fort Granby on the Congaree River, at the site of present-day Columbia, South Carolina. Its garrison of 300 provincial regulars and militia was commanded by a Maryland Tory, Major Andrew Maxwell. Sumter began his siege on 19 February. Fearful that Lord Rawdon at Camden would send a relief column to the fort's aid, Sumter asked Francis Marion "to move in such a direction as to attract his attention, and thereby prevent his designs."[9]

Marion was unhappy about all of this, for he had good intelligence of British strength and strongly doubted that Sumter could succeed. Sumter, as commanding general of the South Carolina militia, was Marion's nominal superior—with the emphasis on nominal. Marion, however, was a far wiser guerilla leader, exhibiting a fine combination of boldness and prudence that served him and his men well. He also cooperated with Continental officers. Sumter on the other hand was addicted to bloody frontal assaults, even though his major victories during the first phase of the Rising came from an inadvertent flank attack at Hanging Rock and at Blackstock's well-deployed riflemen in a strong defensive position. Those lessons, however, were apparently lost on him. He also exhibited all the characteristics of a prima donna who deeply resented reporting to, taking orders from, or cooperating with higher authority, especially Continental officers, and specifically Nathanael Greene. It has been argued that Greene had no authority over Sumter because he was a militia officer, without Continental rank, and therefore only Governor John Rutledge could give him orders. Francis Marion on the other hand was obliged to obey Greene's orders because he held a Continental rank as well as a militia commission. Both statements are true. But Andrew Pickens, who held only a militia commission, never questioned Greene's orders and never failed to cooperate. The different reactions of Sumter and Pickens to cooperating with Greene came down to a matter of character.[10]

Greene had written to Marion on 11 February that he had asked Sumter to "call out all the Militia of South Carolina & Employ them in destroying the Enemies Stores & perplexing their Affairs," and that Marion should "Communicate & Concert" with Sumter. "Communicate & Concert" with the Gamecock was the last thing Marion wanted to do, and the intelligence he had received argued against Sumter's ability to accomplish his purpose. Marion's biographer Hugh Rankin speculated that rather than serve under Sumter the Swamp Fox "sulked" and dismissed most of his brigade.[11]

Sumter's siege of Fort Granby lasted from 19 to 21 February. Lord Rawdon marched out of Camden commanding a relief force of 600 infantry, 100 cavalry, and two field pieces. If Marion had any thoughts about diverting this force, it would have been a mission impossible given their comparative strengths. Rawdon assumed Sumter would retreat northward and detached Major Robert McCleroth with 270 infantry and a field piece to block him while Rawdon tried to circle and attack Sumter from the other side. But Sumter learned of Rawdon's approach, withdrew from Fort Granby on the night of the 21st, and marched thirty-five miles south down the Congaree and Santee Rivers. He took with him boats that had been tied up on the river. Rawdon learned of this and sent word to Lieutenant Colonel John Watson Tadwell Watson to be on the lookout for them.[12]

Sumter's next attempt was on the British post at Belleville commanded by Lieutenant John Stuart of 71st Foot (Fraser's Highlanders). He assaulted it on 22 February under heavy fire, tried to burn the buildings, failed, and withdrew. According to the British commandant at Charleston, Lieutenant Colonel Nisbet Balfour, Sumter lost "18 killed, a few taken, and many horses." That affair took no more than half an hour. Leaving men behind to maintain a siege, Sumter withdrew to Manigault's Ferry on the Santee River and camped. One of Sumter's officers, Wade Hampton, on patrol near this place met a British force. A skirmish ensued and several of Hampton's men were captured.

On 23 February Sumter finally had some luck. At a place called Big Savannah he ambushed a British supply column and took many prisoners. Even more important were the twenty wagons full of arms, ammunition, and clothing. This was a treasure trove for the chronically ill-supplied partisans, who rarely had supply depots and for the most part had to live off the land. This incident is probably the one referred to by British Lieutenant Colonel Watson, who wrote, "A few days ago, after Genl. Sumter had taken some waggons on the other side of the Santee, and the escort of them had laid down their arms, a party of his horse who said they had not discharged their pieces came up, fired upon the prisoners and killed seven of them. A few days after we took six of his people. Enquire how they were treated."[13]

The plunder was loaded onto the boats taken from Fort Granby. Sumter placed Captain Hugh McClure in charge of the boats and instructed him to join the land force farther down the Santee at Wright's Bluff near Nelson's Ferry. The river was high and McClure took along a local ferryman, Robert Livingston, to guide the boats. Sumter and the main force did not set out immediately. Exhaustion had set in and the partisans were resting at Manigault's Ferry on 24 February when Major McCleroth's pursuing force appeared near Sumter's camp in mid-afternoon. Rawdon reported that McCleroth, commanding 64th Foot, "upon a rumor that Marion had crossed the Santee and joined Sumter . . . unfortunately discontinued the pursuit." Using either two or three small canoes found on the riverbank, Sumter's men paddled across the swollen waters to the left bank of the Santee, holding the bridles of their swimming horses. It took them two days. Safe for the time being, they marched for Wright's Bluff to join up with Captain McClure and their plunder.

McClure, however, had run into trouble. In fact, disaster. He had lost everything: arms, ammunition, supplies. At Wright's Bluff the British had built Fort Watson. There, "in a concealed but commanding Spot," Colonel Watson had left a guard that waylaid the little river flotilla. McClure and his men escaped but the British recovered all they had lost. The magnitude of the disaster must have struck Sumter like a thunderbolt. Almost two weeks of marching and fighting and nothing to show for it. He decided to attack the fort and retake the plunder.[14]

Fort Watson was a strong post, a stockade built on top of an Indian mound surrounded by abatis at its base. The garrison had been reinforced by 400 provincial light infantry commanded by Colonel Watson. But Sumter, whose command had shrunk to 200 men, did not know that. In his slipshod manner he had neglected to reconnoiter the fort. When a wagon of a British foraging party broke down about a mile and a half from the fort, Ensign Cooper of the Provincial Light Infantry was left with twenty men to guard the wagon while it was repaired "& bring it on." Its cargo was valuable: "a mill to grind the corn." The repairs made, Cooper and his men had resumed their march when Sumter surrounded the party and called for its surrender. Watson reported that Ensign Cooper "replied Light Infantry never Surrender and began firing as hard as they could." The firing alerted the garrison, which sprang to arms and rode to the rescue. On spotting the relief column's approach, Sumter formed "to receive us." The clash was brief. Sumter and his command fled, leaving behind dead, wounded, prisoners, and "30 Horses."[15]

The survivors were unwilling to go on. Sumter then led them toward the High Hills of Santee, stopping on the way to pick up his invalid wife and their young son Tom. A mattress had to be strapped to her horse for Mrs. Sumter to ride on, and though a slave woman doubled up behind to hold her she apparently fell off the horse several times. On 6 March near Ratcliffe's Bridge on Lynches River the column ran into Tory infantry commanded by Major Thomas Fraser, which was one of many British and Tory units searching for Sumter. A sharp skirmish broke out. The Rebels had to run for it. Being mounted, they outdistanced the Tory infantry, reached the bridge, set it afire, and escaped. But they left behind ten dead comrades. Forty Rebels were wounded.

Upon reaching safety in the High Hills, Sumter left wife Mary and son Tom with friends to care for them. He rode on to his camp in the Waxhaws and released his men to go home to their families for spring planting. It was just as well. For the atmosphere in Sumter's camp, consider the words not of an enemy or a critic but his biographer and champion. "He found it cold, his men quiet and sullen. After three weeks of fruitless campaigning, they were angry, declaring that they had been led on a wild-goose chase. They felt ill-used in rescuing Sumter's family. They were bitter over leaving one-fourth of their number on unnamed battlefields." One of Sumter's foes, the Tory Colonel Robert Gray, wrote that they raised such a cry against him "for deceiving them with regard to Lord Rawdon's strength that he was obliged at a muster to enter into a long vindication of his conduct."[16]

Yet Sumter's raid down the Congaree and Santee Rivers did have one positive aspect from the Rebel point of view. It created turmoil and wild disparities in estimates of his strength. Balfour reported to Clinton that 800 men rode behind Sumter. Rawdon wrote Cornwallis that when Sumter crossed the Congaree River some thought he had 1,000 men behind him, although Rawdon judged that his force "scarcely exceeded four hundred." Even that was off the mark, for as we know Sumter was able to gather only 280 men. The reputation Sumter had gained during the first phase of the Rising meant that his mere presence caused disturbance and great uneasiness among the King's Friends and forced Lord Rawdon to sound the alarm and march with hundreds of troops to deal with the Gamecock. It is also true that partisan raids, even if successful, could not drive the British from the Lower South. The only chance for that awaited the arrival of a general to the north of them, now wending his way southward. The energies of these formidable militia fighters had to be harnessed and directed in a general plan of operation. Whether that could be done awaited events.[17]

"Almost Fatally Courageous"

While Sumter was blundering along the Congaree and Santee Rivers, another Rebel partisan leader, one of the fiercest fighters of all, was operating in the western Back Country of Georgia and South Carolina. Unknown today to a wide public, Colonel Elijah Clarke of Georgia was an illiterate backwoodsman, one of those men labeled contemptuously by their British foes and well-born Americans as crackers. He has been described as "almost fatally courageous." We met him briefly in the Prologue at the American victory at Kettle Creek, where his horse was shot from under him. During a critical moment in the bloody encounter between Americans at Musgrove's Mill, another colonel watched in awe as Clarke led his men in a wild, screaming charge. "It was in the severest part of the action," a friend of Isaac Shelby later recalled, "that Colonel Shelby's attention was arrested by the heroic conduct of Colonel Clarke. He often mentioned the circumstances of ceasing in the midst of battle to look with astonishment and admiration at Clarke fighting."[18]

On 23 March 1781, at Beattie's Mill on Little River in the Long Canes district of southwestern South Carolina, Clarke led about 180 Georgia and South Carolina partisans, some of whom were unarmed, in an action that was costly for the Tories and eventually ended in an atrocity. What details we have of the action come from Andrew Pickens, who had been sent by Greene back to South Carolina prior to the Battle of Guilford Courthouse. Greene was ever mindful of civilian morale and opinion, and shortly after Pickens arrived on the Catawba River on 20 March, he received orders from Greene to "harass the foraging parties at Ninety Six and Augusta and as much as possible encourage the desponding inhabitants." It would have been a day or so after that when Pickens and his command, riding south, met Clarke on the Broad River with the prisoners Clarke had taken at Beattie's Mill. Clarke told Pickens the following tale.[19]

A Tory party of seventy-six horse and foot led by Major James Dunlap, who commanded the cavalry at the British post of Ninety Six, was on a foraging expedition when the two forces met. Clarke sent Captain James McCall to circle and block any Tory retreat on a bridge across the river. Clarke then

Elijah Clarke, 1733–1799; c. early 1800s oil painting attributed to Rembrandt Peale. (Augusta Museum of History)

formed his men into two divisions and immediately attacked, wrote Pickens, "with vigour and resolution." Dunlap's cavalry began fleeing, "their Horse being chiefly killed in the flight." The scene must have been horrendous, horses crashing to the earth, screaming in pain as only horses can, sending their riders flying. Dunlap's infantry took shelter in the mill and outbuildings. Clarke's men poured fire into the buildings. His losses mounting, Dunlap finally surrendered. The entire Tory force was accounted for: thirty-four killed, forty-two wounded, Major Dunlap a prisoner. He was well known to the Rebels, especially Andrew Pickens, who had laid down his arms and accepted parole in 1780 following the fall of Charleston. Pickens had honored his parole. Yet late in 1780 Dunlap raided Pickens's plantation on Long Cane Creek and burned his buildings and crops. Whereupon Pickens broke his parole and went back to war, an act that meant death by hanging if he were caught. There were many among the Rebels who would have killed Dunlap on the spot. But Andrew Pickens was a man of honor. He reported to Greene that the prisoners were being sent to Virginia "by way of the mountains." But in Gilbert Town, North Carolina, an "inhuman action" occurred. While a prisoner Dunlap was murdered by "a set of Men chiefly unknown" who "forced the Guard and shot him." Pickens was outraged. He offered a reward of $10,000 for the capture of the one killer whose identity was apparently known. But the Back Country version of *omertà* settled like a thick haze over the affair. Nobody came forward to claim the reward. The murderers were never brought to justice. And it would not be the end of such atrocities.[20]

"He Had Never Seen Such Shooting in His Life"

Well to the east of the scene of operations of Andrew Pickens and Elijah Clarke, a running series of fights between Francis Marion and Lieutenant Colonel John Watson Tadwell Watson began in the first week of March and lasted until the 28th. Lord Rawdon dispatched Watson up the Santee River "for the purpose of dispersing the plunderers that infested the eastern frontier." At the same time he sent Colonel Wellbore Ellis Doyle down the Santee from Camden. The object was to catch Marion between the two British columns. Although the operation was not well coordinated, the discovery and destruction of Marion's base at Snow Island by Doyle, plus other factors, eventually wore down the Swamp Fox. Nevertheless, the series of fights between Marion and Watson reveal Marion at top form as a militia commander. He may have been down to about twenty rounds per man, but he did not hesitate to engage Watson.

Marion and Watson first met on 6 March 1781. Marion's force was about 500 strong, Watson's about 480. Watson's men included provincial regulars, Tory militia, and gunners of the Royal Regiment of Artillery with two field pieces. Marion set up an ambush at Widboo Swamp. He placed Lieutenant Colonel Peter Horry and his command on a causeway while Marion remained behind with the reserve. Part of the reserve, under Captain Daniel Conyers, was concealed in anticipation of a British cavalry charge, in which case Conyers would engage the enemy's flank. Watson, a veteran of fighting partisans, smelled trouble and sent a militia unit ahead to reconnoiter. Horry's advance was spotted. Watson deployed his artillery. Grapeshot scattered Horry's men. Watson ordered a charge. His cavalry thundered down the causeway. Captain Conyers's concealed horsemen charged in turn and took the British cavalry in the flank. Conyers killed an officer who was charging with the Tory militia. The rest of Marion's reserve charged and a melee ensued. Watson's cavalry was driven back. But he had with him five companies of provincial light infantry and he ordered them forward—bayonets fixed. Marion and his men then disappeared into the swamp. It was time to vanish, survive, and fight another day. He lost six killed and twelve wounded, Watson three killed.[21]

A few days later about fifteen miles away the two foes met at Mount Hope Swamp, where Marion had destroyed the bridge across the Santee River. Lieutenant Colonel Hugh Horry's rear guard and some thirty riflemen commanded by Captain William Robert McCottry were stationed there to prevent a crossing. But Watson brought up his two field pieces and forced the partisans to retreat under a hail of grapeshot fired across the river. At their next meeting, however, McCottry's riflemen would come into their own.

Watson left the Santee and headed for the village of Kingstree. Marion sent Major John James, commanding seventy men, including McCottry's riflemen, to Lower Bridge on the Black River. They threw the planks off the bridge, set the stringers on fire, deployed, and waited. Marion came up with the rest of the brigade and formed as a reserve. When Watson appeared he once again brought his artillery forward. But at Lower Bridge topography worked against him. The gun barrels could not be depressed far enough to bear on the Rebels across the river. The gunners tried to take their pieces to a bluff where they could depress the barrels and sweep the Rebel positions. McCottry's riflemen picked off the gunners. Watson then tried to storm the fording place. A captain waving a sword led the assault. Once again the long rifles cracked and he was shot dead. The men behind him fled. Four men tried to retrieve the body of their dead captain. They too were shot dead.

Colonel Watson would witness more of the same on 20 March at Sampit Bridge. After the action at Lower Bridge, Watson had bivouacked and rested his men for about ten days. During that time he was continually harassed by Captain Conyers's horse and Captain McCottry's riflemen. Tradition has it that he had so many dead he weighted them and sank their bodies in the deep waters of an abandoned quarry. All around him, like the terrible mosquitos of the Low Country, were Marion's men.

Watson broke camp and headed for Georgetown. Marion followed and harried him. He sent Colonel Horry's horse ahead of Watson to destroy the bridge across the Sampit River, ten miles from Georgetown. On the 20th Marion came upon the British at their most vulnerable—fording the river. McCottry's riflemen zeroed in and took a terrible toll. The rear guard was badly shot up and Watson's horse was shot from under him. He mounted another horse and directed his artillery to sweep the Rebels with grapeshot. That ended the pursuit. Marion had one man killed. Watson lost twenty killed and thirty-eight wounded. He is reputed to have said that "he had never seen such shooting in his life."

Marion had bloodied Watson but at a cost. As noted earlier, while Marion was engaged in his running fight with Watson, the other British column under Colonel Wellbore Doyle had taken and destroyed Marion's Snow's Island base. Ammunition, provisions, supplies—all gone. By then Marion had only seventy men with him and their ammunition was almost exhausted. Yet he sent McCottry and his riflemen in pursuit of Doyle. McCottry caught up with him on or near Witherspoon's Ferry on Lynches Creek. After an exchange of fire across the creek, Doyle withdrew. Marion then took up the pursuit. Following a difficult fording of Lynches Creek, Marion engaged Doyle on 30 March. Nightfall broke off the skirmish, and the next day the two forces went their separate ways.

It had been a month-long first-rate performance by Marion and his partisan brigade. Yet all was not well in Marion's camp. As one of his officers recalled, the raid on Snow's Island by Wellbore Doyle was "a most serious loss," for it left Marion desperately short of ammunition. His ranks had also shrunk. The partisan fighters were farmers. It was time for spring planting, and many men of the some 500 that rode with him to Widboo Swamp in early March had peeled off to go home. Throughout the country planting and harvest times were critical for militia. Early in the New York campaign in 1776, during harvest season, George Washington alerted the Orange County, New York, Committee of Safety that at this "extreem busy season I cannot recommend your keeping the Regiment embodied," but "it would be well to notify them all to be ready at a moments warning to Assemble at any place they may be called too." Adding to Marion's problems, the Tory leader in northeastern South Carolina, Micajah Ganey, had once again taken the field with his Tory partisans.[22]

Marion was also stewing over letters he had received from Thomas Sumter. In early March John Rutledge, the governor of South Carolina in exile, wrote Marion of his "hope that you will cultivate a good understanding with Gen'ls Sumter and Pickens and do everything in your power to forward the former's views." Forwarding Sumter's views was the last thing Marion wanted to do. He generally ignored Sumter's letters requesting cooperation and a junction of their forces and kept his distance: wisely, as we have seen.[23]

All of these problems weighed on a man known to be moody. Marion was afflicted with the Black Dog. He brooded. He called his officers to him and proposed that they leave the Low Country, head for North Carolina, or even to the mountains, raid now and then, or perhaps head north and join up with the regular army under Greene. Although the officers agreed to go along with whatever Marion decided, they were unhappy, and as the word got out other men in camp expressed negative opinions. Uncertainty reigned.[24]

Suddenly a scout, Ensign Baker Johnson, galloped into camp with electrifying news. He had spotted a "great number of Continental troops, horse and foot," on the march toward them. On that same day Light Horse Harry Lee's van of light infantry, drums beating, marched into Marion's camp. On 14 April Lee rode in with his cavalry. The Black Dog trotted off. Marion cast aside all thoughts of heading for the hills. What had led Light Horse Harry to the Swamp Fox?[25]

A vital mission for partisans that was mentioned earlier in this chapter came to full fruition in the South: military operations in conjunction with regular units. The reader will recall from chapter 1 that after Lee's initial mission of harassing Cornwallis's rear and masking Greene's turn southward, he was to wheel south, enter South Carolina, and attack the British posts on the Santee River. At the same time Greene was in touch with Thomas Sumter. Their relations had gotten off to a rocky start upon Greene's arrival in the South in 1780, due to Sumter's prima donna temperament compounded by Greene's lack of tact in a letter to the Gamecock. All seemed well, however, in their exchange of correspondence in late March and early April 1781. On 30 March Greene wrote, "I am [in] hopes by sending forward our Horse and some detachments of light Infantry to join your Militia, you will be able to possess yourself of all their little out posts before the Army arrives." He also asked for the numbers of "the probable force I may expect to cooperate with us." In none of his letters did Greene present his wishes as orders. He asked for Sumter's cooperation. Sumter replied that he expected to have 600 or 700 men gathered by 20 April—a dubious proposition given his inability to gather more than 280 men for his unsuccessful February operation related above. Upon receiving this information, Greene wrote to Lee, who had already turned southward, that Sumter was gathering men and "if you go over Santee you will fall in with him." Yet following an eight-day forced march, Lee joined Marion on 14 April.[26]

Was this by design or chance? In his *Memoirs* Lee stated that he was "instructed to join Marion." And in a letter of 22 April to Samuel Huntington, Greene stated that "I detached Lieut Colo Lee with his Legion, and part of the 2nd Maryland Regiment to join General Marian to invest the Enemy's posts on the Santee." But this was written after Greene knew that Lee and Marion had joined up and begun combined operations. In Greene's order to Lee he did not directly order Lee to join Sumter but gave him Sumter's approximate location and observed that if Lee crossed the Santee "you will fall in with him." Many years after the war Lieutenant Colonel John Eager Howard, a key regimental commander in Greene's Southern Campaign, wrote that "Lee objected to be put under Sumter's command, and Greene well knew that the service would not be promoted by it, for Sumter and Lee were both very tenacious of command and would not have acted cordially together." Had Greene in discussion with Lee left it up to him, depending on which partisan commander he met first? We know that Greene had shared his thoughts on operations with Lee, who wrote to Greene, "As you have been pleased to honor me with your confidence, I take the liberty to communicate to you my Sentiments respecting your plan of operations." We can also be sure that Greene and Lee had discussed Thomas Sumter and the difficulty of dealing with him.[27]

Whatever led Lee to Marion, it could not have been a better pairing at a better time. They had campaigned well together in 1780, prior to Cornwallis's pursuit of Greene across North Carolina and Lee's being recalled to the main army. At that time Nisbet Balfour in Charleston had referred to them as "Two very enterprising Officers, Lee & Marrian." There was an initial disagreement at this second meeting. Marion wanted to engage the British troops under Colonel Watson at Georgetown, but Lee argued to keep their combined force close to Greene's main army and carry out the general's instructions to attack the river posts. Lee was right, although according to one of Marion's officers the Swamp Fox later regretted that "his orders did not permit him to pursue Col. Watson." He must have known, however, given his extreme shortage of ammunition, that his brigade could have been of little help against Watson. In any event, Marion quickly agreed to follow Greene's orders. The next day, 15 April, Marion and Lee marched to Fort Watson and laid siege.[28]

"Cowardly and Mutinous Behavior"

Fort Watson, where Sumter had failed, was on the Santee River about seventy-five miles—plus the crossing at Nelson's Ferry—northwest of Charleston. It was the first of three British forts guarding the communication and supply lines between Charleston and the Back Country. Lieutenant James McKay of 64th Foot commanded a garrison of only 114 British and provincial regulars to hold out against Rebel besiegers numbering 420. But Fort Watson was a stout stockade resting on an Indian mound. Marion judged the mound to be forty feet high but Lee thought about thirty feet and was probably closer to the mark. (As of this writing, the mound is twenty-three feet high.) The fort walls were about six or seven feet high. The base of the mound was ringed with "three rows of Abattis," Marion wrote, and there were "no trees near enough to [provide] cover [for] our men." Lee mentioned a fosse (ditch) surrounding the fort outside the abatis.[29]

At first, Marion and Lee were unsure what to do. Their plan to cut off the fort's water supply was frustrated when McKay, according to Lee, "immediately cut a trench secured by abatis, from his fosse to the river, which passed close to the Indian mount." In his report Marion mentioned a "well near the stockade which we could not prevent them from as we had no Intrenching tools to make our Approaches." Here Marion was referring to a lack of shovels and picks to dig zigzag trenches toward the fort to get close enough to interrupt the water supply. Unable to do that, they had to get close enough to tear a hole in the abatis in order to storm the walls. The Rebels must have procured the necessary tools in the neighborhood, for according to Lieutenant McKay on the night of the 17th they "broke ground within one hundred Yards of our Works." They also captured baggage stored outside the fort. The siege was still slow and laborious, however, and Lee decided they needed artillery. On the 18th he wrote to Greene requesting a field piece, promising it would "finish the business" in "five minutes." To further emphasize the need, a few hours later he sent Dr. Matthew Irvine to plead his case in person. Greene replied the following day that it was too risky, as he couldn't afford to release enough men to guard the cannon on its journey. He also noted that his discussion with Dr. Irvine had led him to believe that a "field piece will not answer your expectations, and the only certain way of reducing the Garrison is to cut them off from Water." But he compromised by suggesting that Lee send a guard to escort the piece. Greene also mentioned that he had not heard from Sumter since 9 April.[30]

Lee persisted, as was his wont, and asked for even more. He wrote to Greene on the 23rd that he and Marion agreed that a "field piece, the addition of one hund[re]d chosen riflemen & fifty infantry we could in six days perform the most essential service." He was "miserable to find by your letter of yesterday that no field piece is on the way." What could Lee have been thinking? One hundred riflemen and fifty infantry? There were no riflemen in Greene's army. And he was camped in front of Camden, where he believed Lord Rawdon's garrison was stronger than he expected, and he still did not know what Cornwallis was up to. Lee also took liberties in his correspondence with his general. Greene had expressed some alarm in a letter of the 22nd to Lee regarding the whereabouts of Lieutenant Colonel John Watson Tadwell Watson, whom he had been told was on the march to Camden. Lee replied, "No man was ever more deceived than you are concerning Watson. He did [not] even dare to cross the Pedee but went forty miles out of his way across Wakemau & the bay."[31]

Meanwhile, one of Marion's officers, Major Hezekiah Maham (1739–1789), came up with what today's military calls a field expedient. He proposed to build a wooden tower overlooking the fort from which riflemen could pepper the garrison inside. Although Maham deserves full credit for recommending the technique, the use of siege towers was centuries old. Dionysius I of Syracuse, Sicily, erected six-story wheeled towers for his siege of Moyta in 397 B.C., and towers may have been used earlier by the Persians. But Maham's tower did not require that level of sophistication. The only tools needed were axes. Dragoons were sent to neighboring farms to fetch them. Light Horse Harry recalled that "relays of working parties were allotted for the labor, some to cut, some to convey, some to erect." Major Maham contributed the design and presided over the work. The tower was oblong in shape with a floor of logs at the top and "protected on the side opposite the fort with a breastwork of light timber." The "Arduous work," wrote Marion, was completed on the morning of 23 April. Riflemen immediately climbed to their positions on top and began their deadly fire. Under cover of that fire a detachment armed with muskets supported by Lee's infantry with bayonets fixed entered the ditch surrounding the fort and "pulled a way the abbattis" confronting them. Lieutenant McKay claimed that Marion and Lee then called upon him to surrender, but they claimed McKay raised a white flag before the summons. A minor controversy of little interest. On 23 April 1781 the fort surrendered and was torn down.[32]

McKay was furious, or at least he said so. He recorded in his journal that he was "reduced to the disagreeable necessity of Capitulating, by the Cowardly & Mutinous behavior of A majority of the men—having grounded their Arms & refused to defend the Post any longer." If that is true, we should observe that given Maham's tower looming over the garrison, placing it at the mercy of Marion's sharpshooters, one can argue that McKay's men showed good sense. The prisoners included five officers, seventy-three British regulars, and thirty-six Tory militia. As was common then, the officers were paroled and allowed to keep their side-arms and "private Baggage." The British regulars were allowed to march to Charleston to remain "out of service till exchanged." The Tories were left behind as prisoners. All captured supplies were taken over by Lee's quartermaster—except for ammunition. As we know, Marion's Brigade had been perilously low on ammunition. The capture of Fort Watson put that to right. Marion wrote to Greene that the captured munitions "will be a Sufficient Supply at present."[33]

Lee wrote a second letter to Greene on the 23rd apologizing for his first letter in which he had expressed in biting terms his disappointment in not getting a field piece, attributing his letter to the "determination I took in consequence of the disappointment which was neither more nor less than to sacrifice myself & my Infantry so as to gain a victory." Here he was saying that without an artillery piece he would have had to rely on an infantry frontal assault and implied that heavy casualties would have ensued. That was just more of Lee's dramatic prose style, for he was not given to such tactics. Now, however, our dashing cavalryman was delighted at the outcome and informed Greene that on the following day he and Marion would head for the High Hills of Santee. Such was his mood, he also wrote that "Indeed," he would be pleased to serve under Marion—"to some degree." He admired Marion and wrote that such an arrangement would "please" the Swamp Fox. Note, however, the caveat: "to some degree." Despite his claim in an earlier letter that he had chosen to serve under Marion, Light Horse Harry was not really comfortable serving under anybody but Greene. And even then was he unwilling to totally surrender his freedom of movement and action.[34]

During the siege of Fort Watson, Lee had also written to Greene requesting that he write a long "let[ter]" to Marion, who felt "[ne]glected." On 24 April, the day after Fort Watson fell but before Greene knew it, the commander of the Southern Department responded to Lee's request in felicitous fashion.

> When I consider how much you have done and suffered and under what disadvantages you have maintained your ground I am at a loss which to admire most your courage & fortitude or your address and management. Certain it is no man has a better claim to the public thanks or is more generally admir'd than you are. History affords no instance wherein an officer has kept possession of a Country under so many disadvantages as you have, surrounded on every side with a superior force, hunted from every quarter with veteran troops, you have found means to elude all their attempts, and to keep alive the expiring hopes of an oppressed militia, when all succor seemed to be cut off. To fight the enemy with a prospect of victory is nothing; but to fight with intrepidity under the constant impression of defeat, and to inspire irregular troops to do it is a talent peculiar to your self. Nothing will give me greater pleasure than to do justice to your merit, and I shall miss no opportunity of disclosing to Congress[,] the commander in Chief of the American Army and to the world in general the great sense I have of your merit & services.[35]

What a splendid paragraph, and well deserved by the recipient, who had been a key player in striking some of the first blows to the British line of supply and communications. And to cement his words of praise Greene informed Marion in the same letter that he was sending a field piece with powder and lead.

There was, however, much to be done, and the issue remained in the balance. We now return to Nathanael Greene and the circumstances surrounding a major and controversial battle in the campaign to free South Carolina and Georgia.

3

"We Fight Get Beat Rise and Fight Again"

"You May Rely upon My Unremitted Endeavours"

As Greene had marched southward and neared the South Carolina line, his thoughts were not only on what confronted him but also on what lay behind, for lack of information about Cornwallis's intentions was of deep concern to him. He requested news of his Lordship's movements from various sources, including Sumter and Marion. He wrote to the latter as late as 24 April of intelligence received that Cornwallis had crossed the Cape Fear River and was marching for South Carolina. "I beg you to take measures to discover his route and approach and have me constantly advised of both." It was false intelligence. Cornwallis had not left Wilmington. When he did leave, that very day and the next, he turned his army northward and headed for Virginia. On 30 April Greene thought that Cornwallis's cavalry commander, Banastre Tarleton, was on the march for South Carolina, and Marion promised to try to "intercept [his] cavalry if they come via Georgetown." On 1 May Greene warned Marion to "Keep a good look out for Tarleton," who could be heading for Georgetown or the "uper route." That intelligence was also false. Tarleton was with Cornwallis marching for Virginia. Thus the ever-present fog of war that has bedeviled commanders from ancient times to our own.[1]

Despite his uncertainty about his enemy's movements, Greene maintained the offensive and his determination to mold his Continentals and the partisans into a general plan of operation against British forces in South Carolina. As mentioned in chapter 2, Greene wrote to Thomas Sumter on 30 March, before he set out for South Carolina, suggesting that if he sent "forward our

Horse and some small detachments of light Infantry to join your Militia, you will be able to possess yourself of all their little out posts before the Army arrives." Greene was referring to the river forts that Sumter had failed to take during his February raid down the Congaree and Santee Rivers. He had also asked Sumter to "Take measures to collect all the provisions you can: for on this our whole operations will depend." Sumter replied on 7 April in fulsome style: "you may Rely upon my unremitted endeavours to Promote and facilitate your Designs."[2]

And he did not mean a word of it.

Sumter did face a serious manpower problem. We know that he had been able to gather only 280 men for his February foray against the British river posts, and that had ended badly, with Sumter forced to defend himself before the sullen survivors of that ill-fated operation. It is doubtful that Sumter, at the time Greene wrote his letter of 30 March, could have raised enough men to gather either copious provisions or join Greene's army in numbers large enough to have made a difference in a major action. Like farmers from ancient times, the militiamen/farmers were chained to the seasons. Spring planting time was nigh. Depending upon the last frost, planting would begin about mid-April. But preparation of the land had to begin in March. Let us be generous and give the Gamecock the benefit of the doubt. It is possible that he was not in a position to give Greene the help requested.

In the same letter Sumter broached to Greene a plan he had come up with to raise men. It became known unofficially as "Sumter's Law" and remains controversial to this day. Sumter aimed at raising five regiments of state troops for a period of ten months, to be paid as follows: "Each Colonel to receive three grown negroes and one small negro; Major to receive three grown negroes; Captain, two grown negroes; Lieutenants, one large and one small negro; The staff, one large and one small negro; The Sergeants, one and a quarter negro [under 10 years and over 40 was half a negro]; each Private, one negro." They were also to receive clothing, "a blanket . . . (and one half bushel salt for those who have families;) with two thirds of all articles captured from the enemy except negroes and military stores; and salvage allowed them for all the articles belonging to our friends which we may capture from the enemy, and to be equipped with a sword, pistols, horse, saddle and bridle, etc."[3]

One of Sumter's biographers believed he was making the best of a bad situation: widespread plundering by militiamen. "In the last analysis," Anne King Gregorie wrote, "his plan merely substituted systematic public plunder for indiscriminate private plunder." The late Don Higginbotham argued that Sumter's Law "made robbery from Loyalists official policy and tempted numerous militiamen to rob from whigs as well." The policy probably did lead to across-the-board plundering. Plunder and worse, or course, have always been common in war, with little attention paid by hardened front-line fighters, either regulars or irregulars, to the loyalties of the victims. British and German troops were quite expert looters and rapists. In New Jersey in 1776, for example, British officers agreed with the conclusion of their own deputy adjutant general, Stephen Kemble, that British and German soldiers committed "every species of Rapine and plunder." And on Staten Island that year Lord Rawdon thought it amusing when British troops tumbled local girls in the bushes. "The fair nymphs of this isle are in wonderful tribulation, as the fresh meat our men have got here has made them as riotous as satyrs. A girl cannot step into the bushes to pluck a rose without running the imminent risk of being ravished, and they are so little accustomed to these vigorous measures that they don't bear them with the proper resignation, and of consequence we have most entertaining courts-martial every day." Plunder and rape: an age-old story of armies regular or irregular. So there should be no surprise about what was going on in South Carolina. The real motive behind Sumter's Law was his inability to raise large numbers of men.[4]

Greene reluctantly approved Sumter's Law. "Altho' I am a great enemy of plundering," his strong desire for superior cavalry led him to inform Sumter that horses "belonging to Inhabitants within the Enemy's lines should be taken," but "any horses, or any other kind of property whether taken from Whig or Tory, certificates ought to be given, that justice may be done to the inhabitants hereafter." Andrew Pickens went along but Francis Marion refused to have anything to do with Sumter's plan. And when Governor John Rutledge returned to the state in August 1781 he issued a proclamation on the 5th "forbidding plundering for any reason and ordering the return of stolen property." Given the impossibility in war-torn South Carolina of enforcing orders and proclamations, it is unlikely that any certificates for seized property were handed out or stolen property returned. But in the words of Rutledge's biographer, both the governor and Greene "insisted that Tories be punished by the law, not by personal retaliation." Rutledge meant to be harsh toward Tories. But lawful seizure of Tory property had to await conditions allowing the seating of a legislature and the passing of laws of retaliation and confiscation. That time had not arrived, and the great issue of the war still hung in the balance.[5]

The controversy surrounding Sumter's Law remains alive. One historian has claimed that "greed for slaves could become a motive for Revolutionary service," and that "many did, particularly in the Back Country, fight the Revolution for slaves." There can be no doubt that the desire to own slaves could be a motive for service, and some men probably joined for that reason. But many? And how many is many? What a tempting but imprecise word. The claim also ignores chronology. As a historian has observed in another context, "In history, chronology matters." To repeat what was observed in the Prologue, the Rising had two distinct phases. The first phase began shortly after the fall of Charleston in May 1780. During this first phase Sumter had no trouble raising men. Even after the disastrous defeat of General Gates's Continental Army at Camden and Sumter's self-inflicted defeat at Fishing Creek, the Gamecock and his followers soon took the field again. Yet there was no Sumter's Law to tempt men to serve. The second phase began in mid-April 1781 with the return of Nathanael Greene and his army of Continentals to South Carolina. That phase was dominated by Greene, and it was at the beginning of the second phase that Sumter's Law went into effect. It was not a success. Even Sumter's ardent champion, the South Carolina historian Edward McCrady, admitted that Sumter's Law "was a failure." Among a Back Country white population alleged to have been obsessed by "greed for slaves," he was able to raise only three understrength regiments, not the five full-strength units he aimed at. Of those enlisted, Governor Rutledge was informed that they were "the most discontented sett of men I ever saw. . . . They are dubious from whence the authority derived by which they were raised, and whether they will ever receive what was promised them." In other words, there was no stampede to serve in order to obtain slaves.[6]

"Gunby Was the Sole Cause of the Defeat"

While Sumter struggled to raise men, Greene was closing in on the British strongpoint of Camden. Although his failure in 1776 at Fort Washington on Manhattan Island was a huge mistake, it was not controversial in the sense that everybody knew precisely what had happened and Greene never made excuses or blamed others for his mistake. The Battle of Hobkirk's Hill, however, was quite different. Was it, according to Greene, a golden opportunity lost because of the blunder of a subordinate? Or was it an example of Greene's own shortcomings as a tactician? Or was he just unlucky in battle?[7]

Greene wrote to Sumter on 14 April, "happy to understand that our plan of operation agrees with your sentiments." He then ordered Sumter to "collect your force with all possible speed, and endeavor to take a position . . . where you may be enabled to cut off, or interrupt the communication between Camden and the other posts of the Enemy, keeping it in your power to cooperate with, or *join* this Army, should the movements of Lord Cornwallis render such measures necessary."[8]

At 4:00 P.M., 19 April 1781, Greene arrived within "three miles of Camden." Sergeant Major William Seymour of the Delaware Line recorded that the regiment had marched 2,456 miles since leaving Morristown, New Jersey, on 16 April 1780. Greene reported that "The Country is extremely difficult to operate in, being much cut to pieces by Deep Creeks, and impassable Morasses; and many parts are covered with such heavy timber and thick underbrush as exposes an Army, and particularly detachments to frequent surprises." In 1781 there were about twenty-one houses within the stockade surrounding the town of Camden. The town's outer defenses consisted of eight redoubts (enclosed earthworks). One of those redoubts protected the ferry crossing on the Wateree River two miles from town.[9]

Twenty-six-year-old Lieutenant Colonel Francis, Lord Rawdon, commanded at Camden. Rawdon belonged to the centuries-old Anglo-Irish aristocracy, well known for contributing soldiers to the Crown. Arthur Wellesley, who became the iconic Duke of Wellington, was of that ilk. Rawdon's youth belied his experience. As a twenty-year-old lieutenant of grenadiers he had first seen combat when he led his men into the maelstrom at Bunker Hill, and he had served with distinction since in a variety of field and staff assignments. Rawdon and Lieutenant Colonel Nisbet Balfour, commandant at Charleston, were then the senior British officers in South Carolina, but on the list of lieutenant colonels Balfour was senior to Rawdon. In Cornwallis's absence and by the ancient rules of seniority, Balfour ought to have been in overall command in the state. But Cornwallis paid no heed to this when he restricted Balfour to command at Charleston and "the country within the Santee, Congaree, and Saluda Rivers" and gave Rawdon command on what the British referred to as the "Frontier," that is, the dangerous Back Country. In the summer of 1781, at Cornwallis's behest, Sir Henry Clinton promoted Rawdon to brigadier general, but the commission had not arrived by the time Rawdon and Greene met in battle. Many years after the war Rawdon wrote to Light Horse Harry Lee insisting that Balfour "commanded me." But whatever the finer points of the British command structure at the time, in Cornwallis's absence Rawdon was the de facto British field commander in South Carolina. He was a hard-liner with regard to prosecution of the war, writing in 1776, "I think we should (whenever we get further into the country) give free liberty to the soldiers to ravage it at will, that these infatuated wretches may feel what a calamity war is."[10]

Greene hoped to surprise Rawdon, but the young Anglo-Irishman had received intelligence of Greene's approach about two weeks before the American army arrived in the vicinity of Camden. About half a mile in front of Camden was a group of buildings called Logtown. On the night of 19 April Greene ordered Captain Robert Kirkwood (1746–1791) "if possible to take possession of Logtown, which was in full view of Camden & if [Kirkwood] could take it, to mentain it until further orders." The intrepid Kirkwood, one of the

Francis, Lord Rawdon
(1754–1826); engraving by
J. Jones after a painting by
Sir Joshua Reynolds, 1792.
(South Caroliniana Library)

finest officers in the army, moved out with his Delaware light infantry about
eight o'clock that night, "arrived before the town between 9 & 10 and about
12 OClock got full possession of the place." Scattered firing kept both forces
awake that night, "And at sun rise the next morning had a smart schirmage, Beat
in the Enemy. About two hours afterwards had the Very Agreeable Sight of the
advance of the Army." Greene's army camped at Logtown and began reconnoitering. Some skirmishing took place as his light infantry probed the defenses.
But Greene found Rawdon's garrison "too large and the works too strong" to
storm and considered his force too small to lay siege to the town. He thereupon
withdrew a "little distance" from the town and bivouacked on Hobkirk's Hill,
a sandy, pine-covered ridge running three-quarters of a mile from east to west
about a mile and a half north of Camden. To the left, or east of the ridge, Pine
Tree Creek flowed downhill past Kershaw's Mill and millpond and around the
palisaded town. Hobkirk's Hill was neither very high nor did it provide a clear

view from the ridge of the approaches to Camden. Rawdon, meanwhile, had sent for Colonel John Watson Tadwell Watson to reinforce him, and when Greene learned that Watson was on the move he shifted to the east to block any attempt by Watson to enter the town. But Watson had not begun his march. When Lee informed him that Watson was still in Georgetown, Greene moved back to his original bivouac on Hobkirk's Hill. After the battle he reported that he had hoped to lure Lord Rawdon into sallying forth.[11]

Immediately prior to the movement eastward, because he would be marching through swamps described as "deep and muddy," Greene had ordered a North Carolina militia battalion, Lieutenant Colonel Guilford Dudley commanding, to escort the artillery to the rear, twenty-seven miles from Camden. There the field pieces remained until the early afternoon of 24 April, when Greene sent a message to bring back the guns "with all haste." Colonel Dudley recalled in his pension application of 1832, "In half an hour all was in motion again, and marching all that day and until three or four o'clock the next morning without halting, sat down about five or six hundred yards in the rear of General Greene's Continental troops . . . posted in one line upon the lofty summit of . . . Hobkirk's Hill."[12]

A few days before this maneuvering there occurred in the American camp an incident that Colonel Dudley recalled as "most unpleasant and disgusting." It concerned a matter that plagued commanders throughout the war and thereafter well into the nineteenth century. A 250-man North Carolina militia battalion commanded by a Lieutenant Colonel Webb "insisted on their discharge, alleging that their term of service had expired." Militia field officers denied that this was true and refused the demand, whereupon the militiamen "evinced a spirit of mutiny, encouraged and heightened by Captain R. of that battalion, who was their chief spokesman." The men were reminded that the enemy was nigh and in a few days their services would be greatly needed, but that had no effect on their determination to go home. Greene was advised of this development. Accompanied by Colonel Otho Holland Williams, he appeared before the mutinous battalion "and used all his persuasion and eloquence to detain them but a few days longer." Williams "in the most persuasive manner reasoned with them . . . but all to no purpose. Captain R. and the others became more clamorous and General Greene, mortified and disgusted, directed Colonel Williams to write their discharge, which done, they were instantly off." Greene certainly could not have been surprised by this incident. He would have looked upon it as just another example of the militia's here today, gone tomorrow mentality.[13]

Lord Rawdon had his own worries. His force numbered only 500. Greene had some 1,500, and until the eve of the battle Rawdon thought he had far

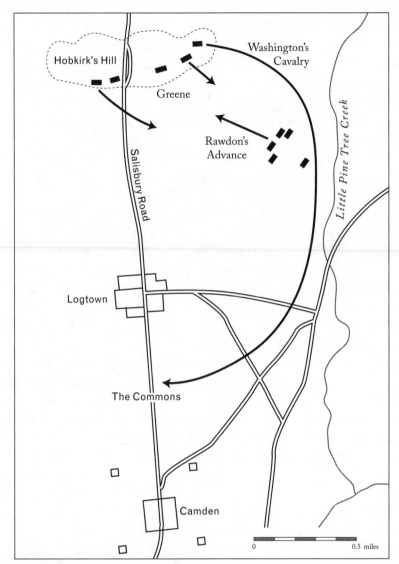

Battle of Hobkirk's Hill, 25 April 1781

more. On the 22nd 130 men of the South Carolina Royalist Regiment arrived in Camden. Rawdon still hoped for Watson to join him with about 500 men. Then he received orders from Cornwallis via Colonel Balfour to abandon Camden. "The necessity of the measure was obvious," Rawdon wrote, "but it was no longer in my power" given Greene's close proximity and Marion and Lee somewhere to his rear, thus the danger of being attacked while on the march. It was too late to do anything but hoist the white flag or fight, and young Rawdon was not a quitter.[14]

On the early morning of 25 April 1781, Greene's army was camped on Hobkirk's Hill, which "was covered with Timber," he wrote, and described the land between Hobkirk's Hill and Camden as "covered by heavy Wood and under Brush." The troops were hungry. One year later John Eager Howard recalled that "we had been two days without provision & a supply had just come into camp." The quartermaster general of the Southern Campaign, Colonel Edward Carrington, had arrived with wagons of provisions. The soldiers were allowed to stack their arms and avail themselves of the newly arrived food. That the rum had not yet arrived would have been disappointing, but there can be no doubt that the troops, who often went hungry, were delighted at Carrington's arrival. The army relaxed, unaware that Lord Rawdon had decided to attack.[15]

Rawdon had made his decision the night before when an American deserter, a drummer boy, sneaked into Camden and revealed Greene's numbers and position. Rawdon now knew that Greene's army was not as large as he thought. Another piece of intelligence revealed by the drummer boy probably sealed Rawdon's determination to attack: Greene did not have his artillery with him, the boy said; he had sent it to the rear along with his baggage train. The drummer boy did not know that the field pieces were on their way back. That night, Rawdon reported, "By arming our musicians, our drummers, and in short everything that could carry a firelock, I mustered above nine hundred men for the field." This number included sixty cavalry. From the hospital his officers gathered fifty sick or walking wounded fit to fight into a company called the "Convalescents." Of the 900, about 675 were provincial regulars: Volunteers of Ireland, New York Volunteers, King's American Regiment, and the South Carolina Royalist Regiment. The British regulars were 63rd Foot, Royal Artillery, and the "Convalescents." As quietly as 900 men can when marching together, Rawdon's battle-hardened, well-led little army slipped out of Camden about ten o'clock on the morning of the 25th. Hobkirk's Hill and Greene's army lay to the north, but Rawdon first headed south into Big Pine Tree Creek Swamp, turned east until he came to Little Pine Tree Creek, then headed north, following the creek and one of its tributaries toward the far left of the American picket line—unseen, unheard.[16]

The Americans were camped in order of battle. North of Camden and beyond, a wagon road ninety feet wide intersected Hobkirk's Hill. It was the same road that Banastre Tarleton had taken the year before on his way to the Waxhaws and the destruction of Colonel Abraham Buford's Virginia Continentals. Lieutenant Colonel Benjamin Ford's 2nd Maryland was on the far left (east). Next to it, by the wagon road, was the regiment that had fought so valiantly at Cowpens and Guilford Courthouse: 1st Maryland, Colonel John Gunby commanding. His deputy that day was the cool, unflappable

Lieutenant Colonel John Eager Howard, who had commanded the regiment brilliantly at Cowpens and had taken over in like fashion at Guilford Courthouse when Gunby was pinned under his dead horse. In overall command of the Marylanders was Colonel Otho Holland Williams. He had performed well leading the light troops during the Race to the Dan. Immediately on the other side (west) of the road was 2nd Virginia Continentals, Lieutenant Colonel Samuel Hawes commanding, and to their right Lieutenant Colonel Richard Campbell's 1st Virginia Regiment. The Virginia units were commanded by Brigadier General Isaac Huger. In reserve were a company of Maryland Continentals and Colonel Guilford Dudley's North Carolina militia battalion. The militiamen would play no part in the battle. Also in reserve was Lieutenant Colonel William Washington with his 3rd Continental Dragoons. The dragoons numbered eighty-four, but due to the shortage of horses only an estimated thirty-one to fifty-four were mounted.[17]

John Eager Howard wrote that the picket line was "about three hundred yards in front" of the American camp, though he hedged: "probably not so much, but I can not say positively as I had not seen where they were posted." The pickets were commanded by Captain Perry Benson of Maryland and Captain Simon Morgan of Virginia. They were supported by Kirkwood and his elite Delaware light infantry, who were stationed about two hundred yards behind them.[18]

The British advanced in column. "By filing close to the swamps," Rawdon wrote, "we got into the wood unperceived and, taking an extensive circuit, came down upon the enemy's left flank. We were so fortunate in our march that we were not discovered till the flank companies of the Voluntiers of Ireland, which led our column, fell in with the enemy's picquets."[19] About an hour had elapsed since Rawdon had left Camden. From this point on the evidence of what happened is contradictory.

Two nineteenth-century writers, George Washington Greene (Nathanael Greene's grandson) and Judge William Johnson (Greene's first biographer) claimed that the pickets and Kirkwood's light infantry fought stubbornly and delayed Rawdon long enough for the main army to form and even rest while they awaited battle. Sergeant Major Seymour, who was there, stated that Benson and Morgan's pickets "engaged them very vigorously for some time," then "retreated about two hundred yards across the main road, where the main picquet [Kirkwood's light infantry] of our army was formed." Seymour, who was with Kirkwood, claimed that the combined units "renewed the fire with such alacrity and undaunted bravery, that they put the enemy to a stand for some time." But Rawdon wrote, "The picquets, tho' supported, were instantly driven in and followed to their camp." Which brings us to a question: were Greene and his army surprised?[20]

In his official report Greene did not mention surprise and stated that "The line was formed in an instant." In his *Memoirs* Light Horse Harry Lee, who was not there, claimed that "Disposed for battle by the order of encampment, the American army, notwithstanding its short notice, was quickly ranged for action." William Richardson Davie, who also was not there but in Charlotte, wrote years after the war that "the line was perfectly 'settled'" and furthermore claimed that "There is not one single circumstance attending this affair that marks it as a surprise." Yet John Eager Howard, who *was* on the line with 1st Maryland, wrote about one year later, "It is impossible to ascertain the time that elapsed from the first alarm until we were attacked furiously, but it appeared to me to be not more than six, eight, or ten minutes, it might have been fifteen—however the line was not well formed, and many of the men who were washing never joined us." Greene's second in command that day, General Isaac Huger, told William Moultrie that "So little did the Americans expect the British out of their lines, that . . . a number of officers with himself were washing their feet, and that a number of soldiers were washing their kettles in a small rivulet that run by their camp when their picket was engaged by the enemy. They ran to camp as fast as they could." Some men were cooking breakfast while "our men were, for the chief part," Sergeant Major Seymour reported, "washing their clothes in a nearby spring."[21]

Can there be any doubt that the Rebel army was surprised? We can leave Greene's statement aside, for what general is going to publicly admit being surprised? Both Davie and Howard were good reporters of events, but in this case Davie was not there while Howard was on the line at Hobkirk's Hill. Furthermore, while those who were not there wrote with certainty, Howard's candor in admitting that he was hazy on elapsed time lends confidence to his testimony. The weight of the evidence points to Greene and his army being surprised.

About to take place was a classic eighteenth-century set-piece battle in which lines of infantry faced each other without attempting to take cover and traded volleys at close range until one line gave way. To the modern reader this method of fighting seems insane. But the state-of-the-art infantry weapon of the time dictated tactics. The smoothbore musket fired big lead balls that did frightful damage, knocking men to the ground, ricocheting off bones inside bodies, tearing up flesh and muscle. But it was also inaccurate. Major George Hanger, a British firearms expert and veteran of the American war, wrote that "A soldier's musket, if not exceedingly ill-bored (as many of them are)," could hit a man at eighty yards, and if one were lucky perhaps "even at 100; but a soldier must be very unfortunate indeed who shall be wounded by a common musket at 150 yards, provided his antagonist aims at him; and as firing at a man at 200 yards, with a common musket, you may just as well fire at the moon." Thus the tactic of getting within accurate range and then finding out who could best stand up to the pounding. Aggressive officers attempted to get even closer than eighty yards before firing by volleys. This required rigid discipline of the other ranks, iron-willed sergeants, and officers who were with their men at the dying time. This was the manner of combat awaiting the infantry of the two armies in the forbidding Back Country of South Carolina on the morning of 25 April 1781.[22]

There is general agreement that Greene noticed the British advancing on a narrow front as they emerged from the left, still partially in column as they began deploying into line. Greene ordered 2nd Maryland to outflank the British on the American left (east) and 1st Virginia to do the same on the right (west) and for his entire line to attack with the bayonet. Historian Mark Boatner described this maneuver as the "amateurs' delight": a double envelopment in which the enemy is outflanked on both flanks, whereupon the attacking flanking units turn and come together behind the enemy in a pincer movement. Labeling Greene's tactical plan "incompetent," he and another modern historian, John Pancake, believed Greene should have remained on the defensive, and Pancake stated that Greene "had never displayed a great deal of tactical brilliance." Light Horse Harry Lee believed that Greene's decision to attack came from "unlimited confidence. It is the only instance in Greene's command, where this general implicitly yielded to its delusive counsel."[23]

Lord Rawdon, a fine combat commander, immediately noticed Greene's attempt to outflank him and quickly ordered up his reserves to widen his line and soon outflanked the Americans. About then Rawdon got a rude surprise. Contrary to what the American deserter had told him, Greene's artillery was on the Waxhaws road and opened up, wrote Rawdon, with "heavy showers of grapeshot." Green reported that "The Enemy were staggered in all quarters" and claimed the British "upon the left [east] were retiring while our Troops continued to advance." Sergeant Major Seymour recorded that Captain Anthony Singleton, the veteran artillery commander, "levelling his pieces so well and playing with such impetuosity . . . put the enemy in great confusion, having killed and dangerously wounded great numbers of them as they crossed the main road." Nevertheless, despite the sudden hail of grapeshot, Rawdon and his officers and sergeants kept the bulk of the troops under control, their formations intact.[24]

Greene also made another controversial decision. In his official report of the battle, Greene wrote that "Lieutt Colo Washington had orders to turn the Enemies right flank [east] and charge them in the rear." He gave this order at the same time that he ordered the infantry to advance and engage the British with their bayonets. Lee would have spoken to officers who were there, and he thought that the cavalry should have been held in reserve to strike at a critical moment in the battle. Greene's friend and confidante, William Richardson Davie, agreed, and he too spoke to participants shortly after the battle. "The critique of General Lee on the disposition of the cavalry," wrote Davie, "I admit is just, had they still been held in reserve . . . the forward movement of the enemy might have been checked by a timely and spirited charge." A little later we will relate what happened when Washington reached Rawdon's rear.[25]

The critical moment was about to occur. Volleys were traded at close range. On the American side this was contrary to Greene's intention. He had ordered the regiments to eschew firing and advance with the bayonet. The Americans were advancing, however, and all seemed to be going well. Then a popular and veteran officer of 1st Maryland, Captain William Beatty, was shot dead. Other men in the company were shot down. Disorder prevailed in Beatty's company and it spread to the company next to it. This was astonishing. The 1st Maryland was the cream of the army. It had stood tall at Cowpens, driving bayonets home against British and provincial regulars and overpowering them. At Guilford Courthouse it had gone bayonet to bayonet with 2nd Battalion of Guards and forced them back. At Hobkirk's Hill, the other four companies of 1st Maryland, under John Eager Howard, were unaffected and continued to advance. The situation called for a first-rate combat commander who could think on his feet, steady his men, and march on. Colonel John Gunby was not that man. Instead of rallying his troops on the spot, Gunby blundered. He halted both companies and ordered them to withdraw "about sixty yards" and reform. He also sent an order to Howard to do the same, and when Howard and the companies he was leading complied they found Colonel Gunby, Howard later wrote, "exerting himself in forming the regiment." It was a fatal error in judgment on Gunby's part. Momentum, so important in war and sport, had been lost.[26]

It has been said that Gunby's movement was no different than Howard's at Cowpens. On the contrary, they were quite different. At Cowpens a misunderstood order led to a temporary rearward movement by the American main line of resistance that was carried out in good order. The troops never faltered as they did at Hobkirk's Hill. With the grace under pressure for which he was noted, Howard allowed the withdrawal to proceed until he gave the order to halt, face about, and engage an enemy coming on in disarray.[27]

At Hobkirk's Hill, on the far left 2nd Maryland kept advancing, as did 2nd Virginia on the right next to the road and 1st Virginia on the far right (west).

Greene rode into the fight, first with 2nd Virginia and later 1st Virginia. Guilford Dudley described "the general himself, with his cool intrepidity risking his invaluable person in the thickest of the battle." William Richardson Davie, drawing on what he had been told by men who were there, wrote years later that "General Greene exposed himself greatly in this action, especially with Campbell's regiment; so much so, that one of the officers observed to me, that his conduct during the action resembled more that of a captain of grenadiers, than that of a major-general." But despite Greene's efforts, because of Gunby's rearward movement a considerable gap existed in the American line. Rawdon took full advantage of it. Flanking fire poured in on the Americans. Colonel Benjamin Ford of 2nd Maryland was badly wounded and unhorsed and his regiment withdrew—to put it gently. On the far right 1st Virginia had got "into some disorder and fallen back a little." Davie claimed that "although they could be rallied and formed again, even with precision, they could not be made to stand the enemy's fire." Lieutenant Colonel Samuel Hawes's 2nd Virginia was doing well, driving back the British left, but the retreat of its sister regiment exposed it to flanking fire, and Greene was "obliged . . . to order Lieut Col Hawes to retire." The British thereupon advanced to the top of Hobkirk's Hill. It was then, Rawdon reported, that "The rout of the enemy was immediately decided."[28]

And what of Lieutenant Colonel William Washington and his dragoons? Where were they? What were they doing?

Colonel Washington's defenders claim that his mission was to cut off a British retreat. That is not what Greene wrote in his official report of 27 April as quoted above: "turn the Enemies right flank and charge them in the rear." Much has been made of Greene's letter to Baron von Steuben of the same date in which he wrote "gain their rear" instead of "charge them in the rear." But if we accept the latter as Greene's intention, as I do, that was the order he gave to Washington on the field that day. Why, then, did Washington fail to make the charge?[29]

In his ride around the British right flank, Washington was forced to make a wide circuit because of physical obstacles. That left him far in Rawdon's rear. As previously noted, in Greene's official report he described, "The country between that [Hobkirk's Hill] and the town is covered by heavy Wood and under Brush." John Eager Howard, one of our most reliable sources, wrote, "it is evident from the nature of the ground between Hobkirk's and Logtown, it being covered with thick underwood, the cavalry could not act in it with effect. Washington was therefore obliged to move round to the commons." The commons was the open ground in the half-mile between Logtown and Camden. Referring to a later battle but applying the experience there to

Hobkirk's Hill, Howard added, "The absurdity of cavalry charging infantry in a thick underwood, was shown at Eutau [Eutaw Springs]." This raises a question: if thick underbrush prevented cavalry from "acting in it with effect," why did Greene, who knew the lay of the land, order Washington to charge Rawdon's rear through that terrain? The answer to that question eludes us.[30]

So what did Washington do when he arrived on the commons? Howard, who certainly spoke to Washington on the day of the battle or shortly afterward, wrote in 1819 that Rawdon's force had been "partially broken," that Washington found "some wounded, and others without wounds, making their escape." Rawdon mentions only "wounded on the ground from which we had first driven" the American pickets. They were being treated by surgeons. William Richardson Davie, on the strength of information received from participants he spoke to after the battle and related years later, wrote that when Washington reached the commons he found it "filled with doctors, surgeons, wagon masters, waiters and all the loose trumpery of an army, who had pushed out to see the battle." Despite the different accounts, all are in agreement that Washington found a commons busy with people. Washington "charged this mixed multitude," wrote Davie, secured and paroled "a great number of these people," thus wasting "precious moments." Davie claimed that British officers believed that Washington should have cut through the people on the commons "without stopping, and charged the rear of the British line. They were in fact so encumbered by prisoners they could do nothing." The British officers would have been among the some "200 Prisoners and ten or fifteen officers" described by Greene as captured by Washington, who brought back with him "more than fifty" riding double with his dragoons. The day after the battle Rawdon wrote to Greene requesting that he release three British surgeons who had been treating British and American wounded but were "carried off" by Washington during the "action yesterday." Why Washington "carried off" surgeons remains unexplained. Greene agreed to return them.[31]

Although praised by Greene and other participants for his actions that day, Washington has been severely criticized by some well-regarded modern historians for not carrying out Greene's orders to "charge the Enemies rear." But I would set aside the opinions of Davie and the British officers and accept John Eager Howard's statement that the ground being covered with "thick underwood ... the cavalry could not act in it with effect." I would therefore absolve Washington of blame for not carrying out Greene's order. There remains the question of whether he should have become involved in taking prisoners and granting parole, but the evidence is too thin to speculate one way or another, and attempts at either boil down to special pleading. When he received word

William Washington,
1752–1810; oil painting
by Charles Willson Peale.
(Courtesy Independence
National Historical Park
Collection)

that Greene was retreating Washington mounted fifty prisoners behind his dragoons and headed back. Upon reaching the main army, he shed his prisoners and performed well in covering Greene's retreat, and also on the following day.

One more question must be asked of Washington's actions that day. He also knew the lay of the land, knew of that "thick underwood" between Logtown and Hobkirk's Hill. Did he therefore question Greene's order? Probably not, given his performance in a later battle in which Howard's statement, "The absurdity of cavalry charging infantry in a thick underwood, was shown at Eutau," will take center stage with regard to Washington's actions on that day.[32]

Meanwhile, the American infantry was in full retreat, although in good order. That Greene did not lose his artillery was apparently due to quick action by the gunners and luck. According to Rawdon, "The Enemy's cannon escaped by mere accident. It was run down a steep hill among some thick brush wood, where we passed without observing it, & it was carried off whilst we pursued the infantry in a contrary direction." The British pursued the Americans for "about three miles," Rawdon reported, but in an orderly manner. By that time Washington had returned, discarded the prisoners he probably should not have taken, and tended to the business at hand. "The Enemy's Cavalry," Rawdon wrote, "greatly surpassing ours as to number, horses, & appointments, our Dragoons could not risqué much, nor could I suffer those infantry to break their order in hopes of overtaking the fugitives."[33]

Rawdon broke off his pursuit and with the bulk of his little army returned to Camden, leaving Major John Coffin with his cavalry on Hobkirk's Hill. Later in the day Greene ordered Washington and Kirkwood's Delaware unit back to the scene of the fighting to find American wounded and stragglers. By a ruse they lured Coffin into an ambush and drove him back to Camden.[34]

Greene suffered 270 casualties, of whom 136 were missing: 18 percent of his force. Rawdon's loss was 258: a little over 28 percent.[35]

Greene was beside himself with frustration. "I was almost frantick with vexation at the disappointment," he wrote to his friend Joseph Reed. He was certain he'd had victory in his grasp: "had we succeeded from the disposition made," he reported to the president of the Continental Congress, "we must have had the whole Prisoners as well as full possession of Camden." In his frustration and fury he lashed out at the man he held responsible. In his official report to Samuel Huntington he was restrained. "The Enemy were staggered in all quarters, and upon the left were retiring while our Troops continued to advance, when unfortunately two companies of the right of the first Maryland Regiment got a little disordered, and unhappily Col Gunby gave an order for the rest of the Regiment then advancing to take a new position in the rear, where the two companies were rallying. This impressed the whole Regiment with an Idea of a retreat, and communicated itself to the 2nd Regiment which immediately followed the first on their retiring. Both were rallied but it was too late."[36]

To Reed, however, Greene unloaded on Gunby: "The troops were not to blame in the Camden affair. Gunby was the sole cause of the defeat and I found him much more blameable afterwards than I represented him in my public letter." We can only imagine the face-to-face exchange between the two men after the battle. Gunby demanded a court-martial to clear his name. Greene obliged him. Three days after his defeat Greene appointed General Isaac Huger, Colonel William Harrison, and Lieutenant Colonel William Washington to a court "to enquire into the Conduct of Colonel Gunby" at the Battle of Hobkirk's Hill.[37]

The "Sole Cause" for Greene's Defeat?

On 2 May the court issued its report. Most of it was positive. After Gunby's withdrawal, John Eager Howard found him "actively exerting himself in rallying the two Companies that broke from the Right, which he effected and the Regiment was again formed and gave a fire or two at the Enemy, which appeared on the Hill in front. It also appears, from other Testimony, that Colonel Gunby at several other times was active in rallying and forming his Troops." At Gunby's request, Howard in essence repeated his testimony about a year later in a letter to Gunby: "Your Regiment had orders to advance & charge the Enemy, and the left which was immediately under my notice, went on some distance very well, when I observed the right had given way, upon which I had your order to bring the left off, and they retreated." The statement was straightforward but carefully worded. Howard did not offer an opinion on whether Gunby's decision to withdraw was right or wrong. The court-martial report, however, was unequivocal on that matter. It allowed "that Colo Gunby's Spirit and activity, were unexceptionable." Then came the crusher. "But his orders for the Regt to retire, which broke the line, was extremely improper and unmilitary; and in all probability the only cause why we did not obtain a Complete Victory."[38]

Gunby was mortified. Greene was obsessed. The court-martial was right when it labeled Gunby's withdrawal "improper," and Greene was right when he described Gunby's action as "an error in judgement." But the "sole cause" for Greene's defeat? Gunby certainly had much to answer for, but Greene's obsession with laying the entire blame on Gunby was unfair. And he broadcast his belief. Not counting his official report to Samuel Huntington, he wrote at least seven letters to six individuals (two to Joseph Reed) laying the blame on Gunby. The final letter, to Horatio Gates of all people, was written a little over five months after the battle.[39]

That Gunby blundered is irrefutable. But can we be as sure as Greene that had Gunby not ordered 1st Maryland to withdraw Greene would have emerged the victor? There is the temptation to believe that if the gifted battle captain John Eager Howard had commanded instead of Gunby the two companies would have been quickly restored to order and the advance continued to the point of pushing bayonets. We must, however, set that temptation aside, for there is another very important element to consider. There were two armies on the field that day.

Lord Rawdon was a first-rate combat commander, an attribute we cannot claim for Greene despite his personal courage in battle. The talents that Rawdon displayed in his American career were harbingers of future success, for he went on to an illustrious career, which was capped with success as governor general and commander in chief in India. So it was no ordinary soldier that Greene faced at Hobkirk's Hill. Rawdon's attack was bold and caught Greene by surprise. His regiments, especially 63rd Foot and Volunteers of Ireland, were tough, veteran units, and Rawdon and his officers and sergeants handled them well. Even in the face of heavy and unexpected artillery fire the British formations recovered and advanced. Shouldn't we give young Rawdon and his outnumbered army generous credit for their skilled and gallant performance, instead of joining Greene in obsessing over who was to blame for the defeat on the American side? Shouldn't we admit that the better combat commander and better army won that day?

Greene also blamed his defeat on Sumter's failure to cooperate. Four days after the battle he wrote to Light Horse Harry Lee that he had sent Major Edmund Hyrne to Sumter, "if possible to get him to join us, but this I know he will avoid if he can with decency, for the same reason that you wish to act separately from the Army." Here Greene was all but saying that both Sumter and Lee wished to act separately from the main army in order to gain personal glory. Lee resented this and replied, "I do not conceive how you can assimilate any part of my conduct to this gentlemans, especially when you recollect that by my own request I am under General Marion," who would receive any praise due. This was another instance when Greene should have left well enough alone. Fortunately, the Greene-Lee relationship was not disrupted by this exchange. Greene also kept his correspondence with Sumter on a friendly basis and even released him from the order "to cross the Wateree and join me." But Greene's commissary general, Colonel William Richardson Davie, who saw Greene often during this period, wrote several years after the war that "General Greene was deeply disgusted with the conduct of General Sumter," considered Sumter a "mere . . . freebooter, whose sole object was plunder, and would therefore neither act under [Greene] nor in concert with him." Davie thought Greene "would certainly have arrested him but for considerations arising from the State of the Country at the time, and the hope that these rambling expeditions of Sumter might arrest the attention of the enemy, and be considered by them as connected with some plan of general operations, and thereby attract more attention than they really deserved." By "considerations arising from the State of the Country," Davie meant that Sumter was politically untouchable.[40]

Once again Nathanael Greene had taken his little army into battle. Once again he had been defeated. Yet once again he had done considerable damage to the enemy and kept his army intact and ready for further operations. He expressed it best in a famous line in a letter to the French minister to the United States.

"We fight get beat rise and fight again."[41]

4

"The Revolt Was Universal"

A Tactical Victor in Strategic Peril

At the end of the Battle of Hobkirk's Hill the Maryland Brigade on the left fell back some three and one-half to four miles to Sanders Creek. The right wing, recalled Guilford Dudley, separated from the left and continued on "through the woods, over bog and morass," to a point "nearly seven miles from Camden, where we most fortunately met General Greene.... With the general at our head, the right wing of our army then fell down and reunited with the left at Saunder's [Sanders] Creek about three or four o'clock in the afternoon."[1]

Two days after the battle, seeking food, especially cattle, Greene withdrew northward to the plantation of Colonel Henry Rugeley, which lay about thirteen miles from Camden. There, on 1 May, a grim scene took place. Dudley recalled years later that "twenty or twenty-five" prisoners taken during the battle were deserters from the American army, "some of them ... more notorious offenders than the rest." Greene ordered a court-martial, which convicted five men and sentenced them to hang for "Desertion joining the enemy and bearing arms against the United States." In his journal kept at the time, Captain Robert Kirkwood corroborated Dudley's recollection. Greene approved the sentence, for "Desertion is a Crime so Dangerous to an army that policy has dictated the mode of correction." He continued, "The indispensable necessity of giving some serious example, and the recent misfortunes the troops have suffered by the perfidy of their unworthy companions forbid the exercise of Lenity, and compel the general to admit the force of Martial Law. The Criminals are to be Executed, according to the Sentences annexed against them, at 4 oClock tomorrow afternoon." Dudley wrote that "The rest were pardoned and returned to their duty in their respective companies in the Maryland line." The five were hanged on 1 May.[2]

That unpleasant but necessary business dealt with, two days later Greene moved the army in a southwesterly direction and crossed the Wateree River and went on to 25 Mile Creek, "because, we found the enemy drew greater supplies from this quarter than any other, and we could procure supplies for our troops with less difficulty than we could on the East side." All the while Greene worried about Cornwallis's intentions. His Lordship had left Wilmington for Virginia on 25 April, the very day of the Battle of Hobkirk's Hill. But Greene wrote to Sumter on 4 May, "Last night intelligence arrived that Lord Cornwallis was moving up towards Cross Creek, and it is thought on his way for Camden, but this is altogether uncertain as our baggage and stores upon the upper route may be his object." By the latter Greene meant his supply depots at Charlotte and Salisbury in North Carolina. Greene had received that intelligence in a letter from Colonel James Emmet, a North Carolina militia officer. It was once again false intelligence, but it led Greene to order Lee to rejoin the main army immediately and to bring with him the "field pieces and all the force detached from this Army." Lee, however, on his own initiative did not immediately act upon Greene's orders and wrote on 6 May that he would wait for a day or two unless Greene ordered otherwise. Greene later surmised that Cornwallis was heading for Virginia and countermanded his order, but that does not excuse Lee's disobedience of a direct order.[3]

Greene was not totally inactive. On 4 May Captain Kirkwood and his Delaware light infantry, during a round trip of sixteen miles, "March'd to the ferry [on the Wateree] and took the Redoubt, and burned the Block House on the South side of the Wateree, then Return'd to the Army at the 25 mile Creek."[4]

Meanwhile, young Rawdon was not finished with Greene and welcomed reinforcements. On 7 May Colonel John Watson Tadwell Watson, having eluded Marion and Lee, rode into Camden with about 500 men and two field pieces. Cornwallis did not think much of Watson, writing to Rawdon, "I know that I do not make you a great present in the person of Colonel Watson." Yet Watson's arduous march is more evidence that renders false the common belief that British troops could not operate effectively in American woods and swamps. With hyperbole that can be forgiven, Watson paid tribute to "This Noble Corps, the 64th, ... almost all Gray-headed men, but such Men, that if they had no legs, they would have crawled upon their hands and knees to join Lord Rawdon." For "in a march of 50 Miles, not a Man was left behind," and "each according to their respective strength carried rails for miles, as to reach this place, we had crossed two swamps presumed impassable; one of which (Catfish Swamp), tradition reported, had never been trod by human foot, with these rails we made platforms as we went that bore our Guns and Men. . . . We proceeded up the hither side of the Santee, to a point near the confluence of the two rivers [Congaree and Wateree], & which being supposed impracticable was left unguarded. Here we crossed, and after wading 6 Creeks, which though deep, were fordable, we built a Bridge of 60 feet over the Seventh that was not so; then cutting away for about a mile and a half through the canes that grow in those swamps, we, the next morning joined his Lordship without molestation."[5]

Rawdon gave his reinforcements no time to rest. Watson wrote, "The afternoon of the day we joined Lord Rawdon, he moved out to meet Greene," for young Rawdon intended to bring Greene to battle once more: "On the night of the 7th I crossed the Wateree at Camden Ferry, proposing to turn the flank and attack the rear of Greene's army."[6]

Guilford Dudley recalled that Greene had received intelligence of Watson's arrival and was on the "lookout for a visit from Lord Rawdon with his increased force, which we were not exactly in a situation to resist with our mortified troops, whose spirits were yet rather depressed by their late repulse before Camden." Greene broke camp, Dudley wrote, and "falling back by a rapid march, gained the heights of Sawney's Creek, the strongest position I ever saw anywhere in South Carolina or perhaps anywhere else, and sat down on its summit, a stupendous hill faced with rock, having a difficult pass of steep ascent to climb up." Rawdon reported to Cornwallis that when he arrived he drove in Greene's pickets but found the American position "so strong that I could not hope to force it without suffering such loss as must have crippled my force for any future enterprise, and the retreat lay so open for him that I could not hope that victory would give us any advantage sufficiently decisive to counterbalance the loss." Nor did he dare divide his force, leaving part to pin Greene in place while the rest "attempted to get round him," for Greene's "numbers still exceeded mine" and "he would have evaded me with ease." A flanking movement and attack from the rear, however, was what Greene feared, especially as he learned of another ford some two miles away. Greene then decided to withdraw through even more rugged country, which would entail a long uphill march. Dudley reported that Greene fell back "three or four miles to a large creek of still, deep water" called Colonel's Creek.[7]

At the same time Rawdon had given up his aim of bringing Greene to battle and was retiring toward Camden. Time was of the essence, for he felt that his position on the "Frontier" was in jeopardy. As he reported to Cornwallis, Colonel Watson had brought word that the "whole interior country had revolted and that Marion and Lee," after capturing Fort Watson, had moved on to besiege Fort Motte, a key British post in the supply line between Charleston and the Back Country. Rawdon's outlook was bleak. He had scored a clear tactical victory but had not destroyed Greene's army. He was deep in the Back Country. In front of him was a beaten but unbroken foe in a strong defensive position, behind him hostile country swarming with enemies. Rawdon wrote to Cornwallis, "The situation of affairs in this province has made me judge it necessary for a time to withdraw my force from the back country and to assemble what troops I can collect at this point." In other words, a tactical victor in strategic peril.[8]

Yet even with Rawdon withdrawing to Camden, William Richardson Davie recalled that Greene was in a gloomy state of mind. On the evening of 9 May Greene and Davie conferred over a map of the Carolinas. Davie wrote that Greene felt Rawdon had the superior force and could push Greene's army back to the mountains. He believed he also had insufficient militia for "convoy and detachment service," and once again charged that "Sumter refuses to obey my orders, and carried off with him *all the active force* [italics Davie's] of this unhappy State on rambling predatory expeditions unconnected with the operations of the army." Greene intended to "dispute every inch of ground in the best manner we can—but Rawdon will push me back to the mountains; Lord Cornwallis will establish a chain of posts along the James River[,] and the Southern States, thus cut off, will die like the Tail of a snake." Davie recalled, "These are his very words, they made a deep and melancholly impression, and I shall never forget them." There is no reason not to believe Davie. Greene probably was in a pessimistic mood following a defeat he had not expected and shocked him. But though he would confide his true feelings privately to Davie, he was not about to announce them to the world. There is nothing to indicate gloom in Greene's letters of the same date to Lee, Marion, and Andrew Pickens. His tone in all of them is upbeat, and his letter to Pickens alerted the partisan commander to "Collect all the force you can and hold them in perfect readiness for the close investiture of Ninety Six which will soon be undertaken."[9]

About first light the next morning Davie was summoned to Greene's headquarters tent. Upon entering "I soon perceived some important change had taken place; 'I have sent for you,' said he, 'to inform you that Lord Rawdon has evacuated Camden—that place was the key to the Enemy's line of posts—they will now all fall or soon be evacuated—All will now go well . . . I shall march immediately to the Congaree, arrange your convoys to follow us, and let me know what expresses and detachments you will want.'" Of this, Davie wrote, "as a consequence" of Lord Rawdon's decision to evacuate Camden, Greene "instantly changed his plan of operations and assumed the offensive."

Greene's flexibility as a commander shines on this occasion. As he had done after being defeated at Guilford Courthouse, he came off another battlefield defeat and revealed his aggressive nature. To be sure, prudence was also part of his makeup. He had shown that at Guilford Courthouse when he withdrew from the field rather than risk the possible destruction of his army. In the aftermath of Hobkirk's Hill he refused to be drawn into another contest with Lord Rawdon. Yet despite those sagacious maneuvers, Nathanael Greene was a fighting general and meant to take the offensive.[10]

Meanwhile, Rawdon had indeed done what he had long thought necessary. He issued his orders to the troops on 9 May, and

> During the ensuing night I sent off all our baggage etc under a strong escort, and destroyed the works, remaining at Camden with the rest of the troops till ten o'clock the next day in order to cover the march. . . . We brought off all the sick and wounded excepting about thirty who were too ill to be moved, and for them I left an equal number of Continental prisoners in exchange. We brought off all the stores of any kind of value, destroying the rest, and we brought off not only the militia who had been with us in Camden but also all the well affected neighbors on our route, together with the wives, children, Negroes and baggage of almost all of them.

In our time we have become all too familiar with the plight of civilian refugees fleeing war zones. Those eighteenth-century American refugees were no different. They had good reason to fear what Rebel militia bands would do to them if they stayed in their homes. In Europe at the end of World War II refugees were congregated in DP (displaced persons) camps. The Tories who joined Lord Rawdon's column would end up just outside Charleston in the eighteenth-century version of a DP camp. The Rebel William Moultrie described their fate. "After their arrival in Charleston, they built themselves huts without the lines, which was called Rawdontown: many of these unfortunate women and children, who lived comfortable at their own homes near Camden, died for want, in those miserable huts."[11]

"She Was Gratified with the Opportunity of Contributing to the Good of Her Country"

While Greene and Rawdon maneuvered following the Battle of Hobkirk's Hill, Marion and Lee, after taking Fort Watson, moved on to besiege Fort Motte. Situated on high ground, it offered—as the site still does—a splendid view of the valley of the Congaree River and on to a distant horizon. One of several plantations owned by the Rice King Miles Brewton, it was called Mount Joseph Plantation, and at least one contemporary source refers to it as Buckhead. When Brewton with his family perished at sea in 1775, the plantation was inherited by his sister, Rebecca Brewton Motte, who was widowed in 1780.[12]

The plantation house, which was probably three stories, was converted into a fort by the British in early 1781. Marion described it as "Obstinate, and strong." A log palisade about nine feet high surrounded the house and protected the first two floors. Blockhouses at opposite corners of the palisade were provided with firing slits. An earthen rampart ten to eleven feet wide abutted the palisade. In front of the rampart was a ditch nine to ten feet wide and six feet deep. Abatis twenty to thirty feet away completed the outer defenses. Fort Motte was the principal depot for convoys from Charleston to Camden and also supplied Fort Granby on the Congaree River, close to where it begins at the confluence of the Broad and Saluda Rivers, and Orangeburg. Supplies were sent even farther west to the important post of Ninety Six.[13]

The fort was commanded by Lieutenant Donald McPherson and garrisoned by British, Hessian, and provincial regulars. In a letter to Cornwallis, Lieutenant Colonel Nisbet Balfour stated that the garrison numbered 120, but prisoner returns put the number at 184. Other primary sources give numbers in between. A small detachment of dragoons carrying dispatches to Camden arrived at Fort Motte a few hours before Marion and Lee laid siege on 8 May and was forced to remain there.[14]

Upon the British arrival and fortification of her plantation house, the widow Motte moved to a nearby farmhouse on a hill north of the mansion. The big house was the second home she had seen taken over by the British. After the fall of Charleston in May 1780, Sir Henry Clinton made Miles Brewton's grand home in Charleston his headquarters, banishing Mrs. Motte and her children to the top-floor servants' quarters. Rebecca Motte welcomed Lee and Marion with warmth and enthusiasm. As Lee's Legion bivouacked on the site where the farmhouse was located, Mrs. Motte insisted that Lee make "her house his quarters," and during the siege lavishly entertained Light Horse Harry and his officers, her "richly-spread table," wrote Lee, presenting "all the luxuries of her opulent country, and her sideboard" offering "without reserve the best wines of Europe—antiquated relics of happier days." Marion and his Brigade "occupied the eastern declivity of the ridge on which the fort stood."[15]

There was also hard work to be done. A vale between Fort Motte and the hill to the north where Mrs. Motte was living allowed the Rebels to get within four hundred yards of the fort. There they broke ground for a sap (trench). Light Horse Harry Lee described the process. "Relays of working parties being provided for every four hours, and some of the negroes from the neighboring plantations being brought, by the influence of Marion, to our assistance, the works advanced with rapidity." The sap was dug in a straight line through the vale and upward until it reached the elevation of Fort Motte. There it headed for the fort in zigzag fashion to prevent enfilading fire from the garrison raking the sappers. On the 10th, Lieutenant McPherson was called upon to surrender. He refused. The work went on. Meanwhile, upon his withdrawal from Camden Lord Rawdon headed in the direction of Fort Motte. Concerned that Rawdon would force them to lift the siege, the Rebels dug through the night. According to Lee, on the next night, 11 May, "the illumination of his [Rawdon's] fires" could be seen from Fort Motte, thus giving heart to the "despairing garrison." Whether this is true or another example of Lee years later dreaming up drama for his memoirs is a controversial question. Without citing a source, one of Marion's biographers went so far as to claim that upon sighting the campfires "McPherson's beleaguered troops gave a shout of triumph." Close students of the siege who know the ground well differ on whether Rawdon's fires could even be seen from the site, or, depending on where Rawdon was camped, seen only by Lee's troops. And we can only speculate on the location of Rawdon's campsite. The question narrows to those who tend to believe that the Legion could see the fires to skeptics who consider Lee's tale poppycock.[16]

What we do know from archaeological excavations is that twenty meters from the fort and ten to fifteen meters from the abatis the sap changed from zigzag to parallel. That was on the 12th, according to a letter from Marion to Greene of that date. Marion and Lee ordered the immediate preparation of bows and arrows and combustibles. (In 2015, archaeologists found an arrowhead at the head of the sap.) Lee went to the widow Motte and apologized for what they were about to do. But she declared, Lee wrote, that "she was gratified with the opportunity of contributing to the good of her country, and that she would view the approaching scene with delight." Once again on Lee's recollection, upon accidentally seeing the preparation of the bows and arrows, Rebecca Motte provided better means. She called Lee to her presence and handed "him a bow and its apparatus imported from India" and "requested his substitution of these, as probably better adapted than those we had provided."[17]

One of Marion's officers, William Dobein James, who was there, told a different story, claiming that Private Nathan Savage "made up a ball of rosin and brimstone, to which he set fire, [then] slung it on the roof of the house." But a careful study cast doubt on this, as physically it "would been a great feat." It would have been much easier to use arrows. Besides, not long afterward Lord Rawdon wrote to Cornwallis that fire arrows were used, and he certainly got his information from Lieutenant McPherson.[18]

Another flag was sent forward and Lieutenant McPherson called upon to surrender. Once again he refused. Marion and Lee acted immediately. About noon on 12 May a "scorching sun had prepared the shingle roof for the projected conflagration," Lee wrote. Rebecca Motte's bow delivered three arrows, each to a different quarter of the roof. The shingles caught fire quickly. Lieutenant McPherson sent troops to the roof to throw the burning shingles to the ground. The Rebels' 6-pounder field piece opened up, "raking the loft from end to end" with canister shot and "soon drove the soldiers down . . . McPherson then hung out the white flag."[19]

In eighteenth-century fashion there followed a convivial dinner of officers both victors and vanquished. Let Light Horse Harry fill us in on the particulars in his ornate style. "McPherson and his officers accompanied their captors to Mrs. Motte's, and partook with them of a sumptuous dinner; soothing in the sweets of social intercourse the ire which the preceding conflict had engendered." As for their hostess, "The deportment and demeanor of Mrs. Motte gave a zest to the pleasures of the table. She did it honors with that unaffected politeness which ever excites the esteem mingled with admiration. Conversing with ease, vivacity, and good sense, she obliterated our recollection of the injury she had received; and though warmly attached to the defenders of her country, the engaging amiability of her manners, left it doubtful which set of officers constituted these defenders."[20]

"I Have Sometime Determin to Relinquish My Command in the Malitia"

In the Rebel camp, however, an underlying tension existed. Once more Marion and Lee had acted effectively in tandem, but the question of overall command was ever present, as were the continuing differences between regulars and militia. Lieutenant McPherson, an officer of 71st Foot, his subordinate officers, and British and Hessian regulars surrendered to Lee. The Tories in McPherson's garrison surrendered to Marion. The question of command burst into the open after the surrender when Marion came upon Rebels—whether Lee's regulars or Marion's militia is not clear—hanging Tories. We have two versions of the incident. Lee downplayed it. He wrote that many of Marion's militia demanded that a Tory named Levi Smith who was charged with burning the houses of Rebel neighbors be punished, "but the humanity of Marion could not be overcome. Smith was secured from his surrounding enemies . . . and taken under the general's protection."[21]

Levi Smith's version is different and dramatic. Tories were being hanged and Smith was seconds from the noose. "I had nearly taken farewel of this world," he later wrote, "when . . . I perceived Gen. Marion on horseback with his sword drawn. He asked in a passion what they were doing there. The soldiers answered, 'We are hanging them people, Sir.' He then asked them who ordered them to hang any person. They replied, 'Col. Lee.'" Whereupon the little Swamp Fox took over. "I will let you know, damn you, that I command here and not Col. Lee. Do you know if you hang this man Lord Rawdon will hang a good man in his place, that he will hang Sam Cooper who is to be exchanged for him." Marion ordered Levi Smith returned to the quarter guard, and he lived to tell his tale. I see no reason to disbelieve it.[22]

Given this, it would not be unreasonable to speculate that Marion and Lee were rubbing each other the wrong way. We have Marion's outburst described above, and we also have a revealing letter from Lee to Greene written on the very day that he and Marion began the siege of Fort Motte. Lee felt "deceived in [Marion]. He is inadequate & very discontented—this discontent arises from his nature." We know that Marion was discontented at the time over the issue of horses and that he was naturally moody. But inadequate? If Lee really believed that, he was guilty of a serious error in judgment. In the same letter Lee laid the groundwork for a dispute between Major Hezekiah Maham and a long-time Marion subordinate, Colonel Peter Horry, that would plague both Marion and Greene. After writing even worse of Thomas Sumter, Lee claimed that Maham, who had been responsible for Maham's tower at the siege of Fort Watson, was urgently needed. Lee felt that Maham could raise a regiment equal to his own in one month and give Greene "one corps in the state which will be capable to serve you." Major Edmund Hyrne, who was Greene's representative with Marion and Lee, also reported Lee's recommendation to his superior and heartily supported it. "If any individual in this Country is capable of mounting a Corps, it is Major Maham, he has assiduity, capacity, and a perfect knowledge of the country—added to this he is some degree acquainted with the horse service." On 21 June Greene authorized Maham to raise a corps of 160 men.[23]

Soon after the surrender there arrived with a cavalry escort none other than Nathanael Greene himself. His arrival, Lee claimed, was due to his anxiety for the Marion-Lee force and to receive a situation report and learn Lord Rawdon's location. I doubt that those reasons were foremost on Greene's mind. He was there to stroke his moody militia commander, who once more had fallen prey to the Black Dog and was nursing a grievance against Greene over an impolitic letter the general had written.[24]

The reader will recall from chapter 1 Nathanael Greene's keen awareness of the value of cavalry in the South and the controversy that ensued in Virginia when he attempted to procure horses for Lieutenant Colonel

William Washington's 3rd Continental Dragoons. Under campaign conditions, horses were prey to the same misfortunes that befell their riders: hunger, injury, exhaustion, sickness, death. Thus the constant search for horses by both armies and the militia. (Modern readers far removed from the once vital importance of horsepower to human activities should compare Greene's urgent pleas for horses to the plight of an army today critically short of fuel, oil, and spare parts for their machines.) As early as January 1781, Greene sent Marion an order to send horses soon. Marion replied that he had only enough horses for his own men, but he would send Greene "A few more [that] may be got." Whereupon Greene came back hoping that Marion had "paid particular attention to the order sent you by Governor Rutledge for collecting horses ... what number you have and what addition you can expect." In April, following the fall of Fort Watson to Marion and Lee, Greene wrote congratulating Marion and his men, but the next day pursued the subject of horses. "Get all the good dragoon horses you can to mount our cavalry. . . . This is a great object and I beg you pay particular attention to it."[25]

On 2 May Thomas Sumter poured fuel on the embers of this fractious issue when he informed Greene that although it "will be with Great difficulty if Not impossible" for him to procure horses, "I urged Genl Pickens to have Some Got for you. Genl Marian is also in the Way of Getting Good horses, but how far I May Succeed by applying to him I Know Not." If that were not enough to irritate Greene, on the same day Light Horse Harry Lee, without Marion's knowledge, waded in. He wrote to Greene that Marion can supply "if he will" 150 dragoon horses "from his Militia, most of them impressed horses," and can "spare 60 horses which would be a happy supply." Greene's reaction in a letter to Marion two days later almost led to a rupture in their relationship. He reminded Marion that he had written several times about his desperate need of horses, begged for an early answer, then wrote these highly offending words. "I am also told the Militia claim all they take from the Tories; And many of the best horses are collected from the inhabitants On this principle. I cannot think the practice warranted either in justice or policy. If the object of the people is to plunder altogether, Government can receive little benefit from them. The horses would be of the highest importance to the public in the regular service."[26]

Once more Greene, a fine letter writer, wrote one better left unwritten. One might ask, if regulars could impress horses from Tories or any citizen, why could not militia do the same? They were fighting and dying, too, and needed horses as much as Greene's regular cavalry. Indeed, horses were vital to their success, testified to by British soldiers frustrated by their inability to corner them. Horses gave them priceless mobility. The affair is further evidence of Greene's basic distaste for militia, despite knowing that he needed them.[27]

On 6 May Marion sat down and wrote his famous reply to Greene, claiming that it had never "been in my power to furn[is]h horses. . . . The few . . . taken from [Torreys?] has been kept for service and never for private property, but if you think it best for the service to Dismount the Malitia now with me I will Direct Col Lee & Captain Conyers to do so, but am sertain we shall never git their service in the future." As for Marion himself, he had been "Determin to relinquish my command in the malatia as soon as you arrived." At the time he wrote, the siege of Fort Motte was about to begin. Marion committed to see that out, but then wished to wait "on you when [I] hope to get permission to go to Philadelphia."[28]

Greene hastened to repair the damage, first by letter. "It is not my wish to take horses from the Militia if it will injure the public service, the effects and consequences you can better judge of than I can." As far as Marion resigning and going to Philadelphia, "I will . . . add nothing more to this subject until I see you." It was obvious that a face-to-face was necessary, and when Greene rode to Fort Motte he and Marion met for the first time. A cliché best describes our reaction: Ah, to be a fly on the wall. For all we know is that they met, they talked, and the air was cleared. There would be a few bumps along the way. We already know that Marion had refused Greene's request that he take part in Sumter's Law, the Gamecock's recruitment scheme, and with one exception he would ignore in the future as he had in the past Greene's request that he take orders from and cooperate with Sumter. But the fracture in their relationship had been healed.[29]

"His Services Cannot Be Wanted at That Place"

Keeping Francis Marion content and in the field was not the only thing on Greene's mind. He was, after all, theater commander, which carried with it many responsibilities, problems, and the necessity of looking ahead and providing for a smooth transition from war to peace. Greene had many balls to juggle, and over time none were more important than his determination to prevent anarchy and set South Carolina on the path to order and justice. Two days after Fort Motte surrendered Greene wrote to Governor John Rutledge, who was still in exile in Philadelphia, and apprised him of the military situation. But most of the letter was taken up with his deep concern about the spirit of revenge in this first American civil war and the pressing importance of establishing civil government. "From the state in which I find things and the confusion and pers[e]cution which I foresee, I could wish that Civil Government might be set up immediately, as it is of importance to have the minds of the people formed to the habits of Civil rather than Military authority. This is upon the presumption we are able to hold our ground which is altogether uncertain. . . . I have not time to go into a detail of matters, but you may depend upon it that many unruly spirits will require bridling in this Country to make the people feel a happiness in the success of our arms." It is clear from this statement that Greene was as one with his commander, George Washington, in the primacy of "Civil rather than Military authority." There would also soon be another reason for pressing ahead with the establishment of a working executive and legislature and extending civil control over the state. That development will take its proper place in the course of the narrative.[30]

A more immediate matter, however, came to Greene's attention: another crisis with another militia commander, the imperious General Thomas Sumter. And once again it was at least partly of Greene's making as well as partly by some troops in Lee's command engaging in free enterprise.

The day after Fort Motte fell Greene ordered Lee to proceed "immediately with the van of the Army" for Fort Granby, located high up on the Congaree River. He was to "demand an immediate surrender of that post," and to make sure that Lee understood his meaning, Greene added, "I depend upon your pushing matters vigorously." Lee recalled that Greene wanted Fort Granby taken without delay because he expected Lord Rawdon would march to its relief, which Rawdon intended until he received faulty intelligence that Greene was advancing in the direction of Charleston. The commandant of Charleston, Lieutenant Colonel Nisbet Balfour, had joined Rawdon and told him that "the revolt was universal," that the townspeople of Charleston were disaffected, and that "his garrison was inadequate to oppose any force of consequence." Nor did Rawdon have a "deposit of provisions left on the frontier," and thus he judged it wiser to concentrate his force down country to "cover those districts from which Charlestown draws it principal supplies."[31]

On 2 May Sumter had already arrived at Fort Granby and laid siege. He felt that he could not take it without artillery and therefore left a holding force there under Colonel Thomas Taylor while he marched on the British post at Orangeburg. Sumter arrived at Orangeburg at 7:00 P.M. on 10 May. The rest of his force and a field piece sent to him by Greene arrived the following morning. Sumter acted with dispatch. A teenage militiaman, Thomas Young, described the brief artillery barrage. "The field piece was brought to bear upon the house . . . a breach was made through the gable end—then another lower down—then the centre, and they surrendered." The British commander put out the white flag at 7:00 A.M. on 11 May. Sumter reported the capture of eight officers, eighty-two privates, some "Military Stores," and "Provisions plenty." He thought the post "extremely Strong" and difficult of capture had it been "obstinately Defended." Sumter also reported that before returning to Fort Granby "I think to Move toward Santee, and endeavour to alarm Lord Rawdon." He had intelligence that many Tories were leaving for Charleston and he feared that "the Country will be Striped of every thing that is Valuable. I Wish to Deprive them of as Many horses as possible & prevent the Inhabitants from Moving and Carrying off great Quantities of Stock Which are now Collecting."[32]

Meanwhile, in accordance with Greene's orders Lee reported that he had made a "rapid march from the post at Motte's" and arrived at Fort Granby on the evening of 14 May. He described the fort as being on a "plain, which extended to the southern banks of the Congaree, near Friday's Ferry." Protected by the river on that side, it was easily "accessible" on the other three sides. But as Lee pointed out in his *Memoirs,* the fort was "completely finished, with parapet encircled by fosse [ditch] and abatis, and being well garrisoned, it could not have been carried without considerable loss, except by regular approaches." In Lee's opinion this would have required Greene's entire army "for a week at least." After reconnoitering and deciding upon approaches, Lee issued his orders. Under cover of night and an early morning fog "a battery was thrown up in point blank shot of the fort." One group of men working that night was Sumter's militia under Colonel Thomas Taylor. "Early on the morning of the 15th Cap: [Ebenezer] Finley commenced a cannonade at the same time the Legion infantry & Capt. Oldhams detachment took a position of support" thus "severing the enemy's pickets in this quarter from the fort."[33]

The British commander, Major Andrew Maxwell, was a Tory from the Eastern Shore of Maryland. His garrison, sheltering behind the stoutly built fort, numbered some 340–360 men. The evidence, however, strongly suggests that Major Maxwell was not made of stern stuff. In his *Memoirs* Lee painted a devastating portrait of the major as "neither experienced in his profession, nor fitted by cast of character to meet the impending crisis. He was the exact counterpart of McPherson [the British commander at Fort Motte]; disposed to avoid, rather than to court, the daring scenes of war. Zealous to fill his purse, rather than to gather military laurels, he had, during his command, pursued his favorite object with considerable success, and held with him in the fort his gathered spoil."

Lee sent forward with a white flag and a summons to surrender one of his senior officers, Captain Joseph Eggleston, to open negotiations. The ensuing cease-fire by Lee's force "induced the pickets and patrols, cut off by our disposition, to attempt to gain the fort." Their effort was "partially checked by the rapid movement" of Lee's cavalry. Lee was indignant at the breach of protocol and sent forward to Captain Eggleston orders to "remonstrate with Major Maxwell upon the impropriety of the conduct of his pickets and patrols." The major (concerned with the fate of his plunder?) immediately sent his adjutant with orders for the offending parties to resume their former positions. Negotiations then resumed.

Maxwell's conditions for surrender were passed to Captain Eggleston and on to Lee: (1) the "private property of every sort, without investigation of title," to be retained by its "possessors"; (2) the garrison to be returned to Charleston as "prisoners of war, until exchanged"; (3) militia should be treated the same as regulars; (4) "an escort, charged with the protection of persons and property should attend the prisoners to the British Army." There was a separate condition for Major Maxwell: "two covered wagons for the conveyance of his own baggage, free from search." Can we doubt that Maxwell had done very well for himself? Two covered wagons for one man's private baggage?

Lee considered the first condition, and without doubt Maxwell's separate condition, "repugnant," as it would prevent him from returning property plundered from Rebels. Yet Greene had ordered him to carry out the operation "without delay," Lee wrote. And nobody knew what Lord Rawdon was up to. Lee, therefore, accepted the conditions, "with the single exception" that "all horses fit for public service" would be taken by the Rebels. That was fine with Maxwell, but the Hessian officers in the garrison went "in a body" to Captain Eggleston protesting that they would not be a part of the proceeding, Major Maxwell's orders notwithstanding, "unless they were permitted to retain their horses." Just then a courier arrived from another of Lee's officers, Captain James Armstrong, who commanded a detachment of cavalry shadowing Lord Rawdon. Armstrong reported that Rawdon had crossed the Santee and was advancing on Fort Motte. This prompted Lee to consider "all horses belonging to individuals in the Fort as private property, and claiming only such, if any, belonging to the public." The surrender was then signed, and "before noon" Major Maxwell, secure in his booty, and his garrison took the road for Charleston under protective escort.

The terms of surrender were not popular. The contemporary historian William Gordon wrote that some of the militiamen left at Fort Granby by Sumter "indicated an inclination for breaking the capitulation, and killing the prisoners." According to Gordon, Greene immediately put a stop to such threatened actions with a declaration "that he would put to death any one that should be guilty of so doing." There are no documents to support any of this. But much of Gordon's knowledge of the Southern Campaign came from Greene's trusted adjutant general, Colonel Otho Holland Williams, who had written a well-respected "Narrative" of Horatio Gates's disastrous Southern Campaign. Gordon may have gotten his information from Williams.[34]

Sumter's men at Fort Granby were also angered by the actions of some American regulars. Greene wrote to Lee that "Some of your Legion behaved greatly amiss at Frydays Ferry [i.e., Fort Granby]. They sold the Arms and a large quantity of cloth. This is only meant as a hint to have them watched narrowly." A note on the bottom of the letter in Lee's handwriting reads, "Not my Legion but a detachmt from the army." Here Lee was referring to Captain Edward Oldham's company of Maryland infantry that Greene had detached to serve with Lee.[35]

Whatever his men's reaction to the surrender terms, Sumter himself was upset even before he knew of them when he learned that Lee was at Granby and had taken command. Fort Granby was Sumter's, he had gotten there first, he had left men to cut off the fort's supplies and await his return. When informed of Lee's presence he wrote to Greene the day before Maxwell's surrender, "I hope it may not be disagreeable to recall Colonel Lee, as his services cannot be wanted at that place. . . . I have the greatest respect for Colonel Lee, yet I wish he had not gone to that place. . . . I have been at great pains to reduce that place, I have it in my power to do it, and I think it for the good of the country to do it without regulars."[36]

It was too late to recall Lee and we can state with certainty that in any case Greene would have ignored Sumter's plea. When Sumter was subsequently informed that Lee had taken Fort Granby he was furious. On 16 May he tendered his resignation to Greene. He blamed it on the militia, finding "the discontent & disorder among the Militia So Great as to leave no Hope of their Subsiding Soon" and given "My Indisposition & Want of Capacity, to be of service to this Country Induces me as a friend to it to beg leave to Resign my Command, and have taken the Liberty to enclose my Commission." Greene answered the next day and returned Sumter's commission, for "I cannot think of accepting it, & beg you to continue your command." He flattered Sumter with "how important your services are to the interest & happiness of this Country; and the confidence I have in your abilities and Zeal for the good of the service." In a follow-up letter the same day Greene gave Sumter a share of the arms and public stores captured at Fort Granby. Assuaged, South Carolina's prima donna returned to service, offering more opportunities for him to plague the commander of the Southern Department and send many a man to unnecessary death.[37]

But as we leave Thomas Sumter for the time being, we cannot fail to give him credit for the capture of Orangeburg, and also for following through on his venture to the Santee to discomfit Lord Rawdon and prevent Tories flee-ing to Charleston from stripping the country of valuables, especially horses and other stock. Lord Rawdon testified to Sumter's efforts on the Santee in a letter to Cornwallis written from his camp at Monck's Corner, thirty-four miles from Charleston. Referring to either the absence or reluctance of Tories during his march to the Low Country, he wrote, "I had been five days on the Santee before a single man of the country came near me." With no supply depots left, Rawdon marched "in a wasted country," and had he attempted to remain in the Back Country, "surrounded as I should have been by a swarm of light troops and mounted militia, I conceived that my whole force must have been so employed in procuring its daily subsistence that little else could have been effected with it." Rawdon also reported "using every effort to augment our cavalry . . . but the plundering parties of the enemy have . . . stripped the country of horses."[38]

After a year and a half of campaigning to bend South Carolina to its will, the British field army had withdrawn to within thirty-four miles of Charles-ton, where on 2 June 1781 Lord Rawdon and Lieutenant Colonel Balfour were reduced to issuing a proclamation to the Tories of the Back Country.

> Although attention to the general security of the province has obliged his Majesty's troops, for the present to relinquish some of the upper parts of it, we trust, that it is unnecessary for us exhort the loyal inhab-itants of those districts to stand firm in their duty and principles; or to caution them against the insidious artifices of an enemy, who must shortly abandon to their fate, those unfortunate individuals whom they have deluded into revolt.
>
> But being well informed, that many persons, sincerely attached to his Majesty's cause, have, notwithstanding, been forced to join the enemy, as the only means of preserving themselves and their families from the savage cruelty of the rebel militia, until escape should be practicable; we desire all such to be confident, that they run no risk of suffering from us, through indiscriminate vengeance; reminding them, that the British government never extends its hand to blood, without the most convincing proofs of intentional guilt.

Those followers who had fled their homes were invited to come in to the army, and all were promised that "with the army, daily expecting powerful reinforcement, their exertions will very shortly reinstate them in the full and peaceable possession of their property . . . to receive again with confirmed security."[39]

If that were to happen, the British needed immediate reinforcements, for all of their river posts had been lost, and Nathanael Greene and his lieutenants were already besieging the last British posts in the Back Country.

"He Is a Worthy Good Man and Merits Great Respect and Attention"

It must have been with immense relief that Greene was able to turn temporarily from stroking the ruffled feathers of the Gamecock to one of the finer characters of the Revolution: the lean, dour, long-faced Scotch-Irishman, General Andrew Pickens. He had served with cool courage at Cowpens and was of immeasurable help to Greene with the militia on the long retreat through North Carolina. Upon his return to South Carolina, Pickens had taken command of the militia in the western part of the state. Greene valued him highly, writing later to Light Horse Harry Lee, "I am happy to hear that you and General Pickens are upon a perfect good footing; and I beg you will cultivate it by every means in your power. He is a worthy good Man and merits great respect and attention; and no Man in the Country has half the influence that he has."[40]

Pickens wrote to Greene on 3 May that Georgia militia "were closely besieging" Augusta, Georgia, "which is said to be very Scarce of Provision,

Andrew Pickens, 1739–1817; engraving by James Barton Longacre after a painting by Thomas Sully. (National Portrait Gallery, Smithsonian Institution)

and it was thought could not hold out long." Pickens reported that he had sent Major Samuel Hammond and a body of militia "to cooperate with the Georgia Troops on this Side of the [Savannah] River" and expressed the hope that Augusta "will soon fall." Pickens was obviously unaware that the Tory commander at Augusta, Colonel Thomas Brown, reported that he had plenty of corn and ammunition and believed his position to be secure. Pickens wrote five days later that the people in his area of operations, "except those who are at Ninety Six," are "determined unanimously" to join the Rebels. Augusta, he had learned, was "blockaded" by "the Georgians" and the men he had sent under Major Hammond. Pickens then decided to leave some of his men near Ninety Six while he marched for Augusta to join the besiegers. In a letter of 12 May he again reported the people "almost unanimous in our favour but the greatest Want of Arms to make them useful." Demonstrating an attitude toward Continentals that ran contrary to Sumter's, Pickens urgently requested from Greene some "regular troops."[41]

Greene acted quickly. On 16 May, the day after Fort Granby fell, he gave Light Horse Harry Lee his marching orders. "You will march immediately for Augusta as the advance of the Army which will move by way of Ninety Six. . . . You will report your arrival to him [Pickens] and cooperate with him until the army arrives. . . . Should the posts surrender you will take special care that none of the Stores are plundered." Greene's concern with the latter point is also indicated in two letters to Pickens: "Great care should be taken to preserve the Stores for the use of the public if you succeed. As this may be a delicate point with you on account of the exorbitant claims of the Militia, I have given Lt Col Lee particular orders on this subject and I beg your acquissence there in." Greene also ordered Lee to "Perform the March as soon as you can without injury to your troops." On the same day he wrote to Pickens welcome news: "Lt Col Lee will be with you in about five days and will bring with him a field piece."[42]

5

A "Judicious and Gallant Defense"

"Your Early Arrival at Augusta Astonishes Me"

Fearing that he might encounter either a detachment of Lord Rawdon's force or one from Ninety Six, Lee requested that Greene leave with him Captain Edward Oldham's Maryland company of foot. Greene refused, as he had already detached to Lee Major Pinketham Eaton's battalion of North Carolina Continentals and a 6-pounder field piece. Eaton, who would serve gallantly, had been a colonel with the North Carolina militia at Briar Creek and was wounded there. Lee marched on 17 May.[1]

In his memoirs Lee wrote that he feared that the commander of Ninety Six, Lieutenant Colonel John Harris Cruger, "in consequence" of Lord Rawdon's abandonment of the Back Country, might himself abandon Ninety Six and "hasten to Augusta; giving up South Carolina to save Georgia." Lee, therefore, pushed men and horses hard in order "To reach Pickens before Cruger could reach" Augusta. (Cruger stayed at Ninety Six.) Relieving his "fatigued infantry by occasionally dismounting his dragoons and mounting his infantry," Lee's Legion covered the seventy-five miles to Augusta in two days, not the five days estimated by Greene, and "reached the vicinity of" Pickens's camp on 18 May. Major Eaton with his North Carolina infantry and the field piece arrived early the next morning, and on that day Lee entered Pickens's camp. Of this feat Greene wrote, "Your early arrival at Augusta astonishes me. For rapid marches you exceed Lord Cornwallis and every body else. I wish you may not have injured your troops."[2]

The Augusta area was defended by three forts: Fort Galphin (Fort Dreadnaught to the British), Fort Grierson, and Fort Cornwallis. Only the last was a true fort, the others fortified houses. Fort Galphin was located about twelve miles southeast of Augusta at Silver Bluff on the South Carolina side of the Savannah River. In 1776 the pioneering American naturalist William Bartram described Silver Bluff as a "very celebrated place; it is perhaps thirty feet higher than the low lands on the opposite shore.... this steep bank rises perpendicular out of the river" and "extends a mile and a half or two miles on the river, and is from an half mile to a mile in breadth, nearly level." There sat the fortified plantation house of the Rebel Indian trader George Galphin. Among warehouses, slave quarters, and other buildings sat Galphin's two-and-one-half-story stout brick plantation house surrounded by a brick wall. Given Galphin's political loyalty, the British had confiscated his property. Slave boatmen bringing supplies to the Augusta garrison in their narrow, thirty-to-forty-foot dugout canoes made of rot-resistant cypress had been forced by Rebel militia to seek safety at Fort Galphin and off-load their cargo. The fort therefore contained arms, ammunition, other supplies, and the annual gifts for the Creeks and Choctaws. Colonel Thomas Brown, in command at Augusta, had detached to Fort Galphin Captain Samuel Rowarth and a company of King's Rangers to guard the supplies and Indian gifts. Rowarth had about forty-seven officers and men, Tory militia, armed boatmen, and some other armed slaves: almost 200 men.[3]

Lee and Pickens decided that Lee should first move against Fort Galphin while Pickens and the militia maintained the siege of Augusta. Pickens reported to Greene that on the afternoon of 19 May the Legion infantry and one troop of Legion horse, all but one company of Colonel Samuel Hammond's militia regiment, "and what of Colonel William Harden's" militia regiment that was with Pickens marched for Fort Galphin. The detachment was commanded by Captain John Rudulph of the Legion. Yet in his *Memoirs* Lee takes credit for being at Fort Galphin and directing the operation. By then, however, he may have forgotten that in a letter to Greene of 22 May 1781 he wrote that Rudulph, "by the judgment & vigor of his operation compelled a most obstinate garrison to surrender," sent Greene a copy of Rudulph's report, and recommended this "meritorious officer" to Greene's "particular attention." Although the following narrative is based on Lee's account, he got his information from Rudulph. Lee was not there. It was Captain Rudulph's operation from start to finish.

Lee described it as a "forced march, with a detachment of infantry mounted behind his dragoons." He recounted a "scorching sun," and "For many miles

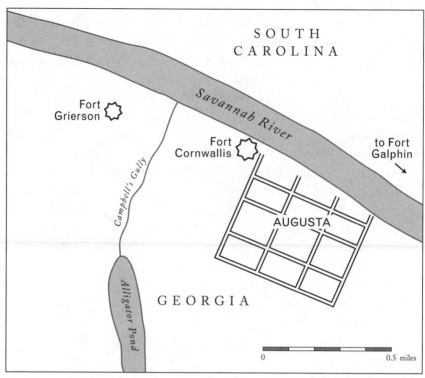

Second Siege of Augusta, 18 May–5 June 1781 (based on a map by Steven J. Rauch)

not a drop of water" available. The little force halted in "pine barrens which concealed them and skirted the field surrounding the fort." On the 21st Rudulph ordered the mounted militia to dismount and feign an attack on the fort from the "opposite direction." He reckoned that Rowarth was ignorant of the presence of the Continentals and hoped that most of the garrison would leave the fort to attack the militia, which would immediately retreat. Part of the Legion infantry would then rush into the fort while the rest, supported by the dragoons, would shield the militia by getting between them and the pursuing British.

It is one of the oldest tricks in the book of tactics—and it worked in textbook fashion. Upon the militia's appearance, Captain Rowarth and most of the garrison galloped out of the fort in pursuit. The militia ran. Captain Rudulph and his detachment of Legion infantry rushed across the open field into the fort and quickly subdued the remainder of the garrison. Rowarth soon surrendered to the force protecting the militia, although some of his riders got away. Rudulph lost one man to heat stroke. Rowarth had three or four men killed. It was a cheap victory with splendid results: a treasure trove of badly needed powder, lead, and other supplies. The historian Edward Cashin believed that "without the stores captured at Fort Galphin the subsequent Battle of Augusta could not have been fought." The operation is another example of a successful combined operation of regulars and irregulars: precisely what Nathanael Greene was aiming at when he wrote, "We must Endeavour to keep up a Partizan War."

Lee was ecstatic. "Savannah can be taken," he wrote to Greene: "10 days will do." Greene wisely decided that goal "must rest for the present" and ordered Lee to rejoin the main army "the moment the Post is reduced at Augusta." After congratulating Lee as well as Captain Rudulph and the officers and men who had followed him in the dash to the fort, he turned to the ever present and vital subject of supplies. "The Stores taken I have given General Pickens power to distribute as he may think best calculated to answer the just claims of the Militia and the good of the service at large. If you have appropriated any part of the Stores to the use of your Corps, which I hope you have not, as it will increase prejudicial jealousies, let the things received be part of the continental proportion." This was of a piece with Greene's ongoing efforts to smooth the relationship between Continentals and militia in order to be assured of the continued cooperation that had worked so well between Lee and Marion at Fort Watson and Fort Motte. To Pickens he wrote with regard to the stores, "I submit the whole matter to your discretion and leave you to make such a distribution as you may think will be best calculated to answer the just claims of the Militia and afford the Most effectual support to the service. You know the distress of this Army and the necessity there is for laying a foundation for a permanent opposition to the enemy in his quarter, and the Stores which may be necessary for those purposes." He then informed Pickens that eight wagons were on their way to pick up stores and ordered him to provide an escort.

Pickens replied on 1 June that the eight wagons had been loaded and sent off the previous day and that another fifteen wagons had arrived and would leave as soon as he could provide an escort. As there was a "considerable quantity of Salt which is a heavy Article," more wagons were needed. But in one respect he was disappointed. "The Arms we got at Fort Galphin being for the Indian trade are very indifferent." He informed Greene how he had divided the stores taken at Fort Galphin: one-third for the Continentals; one-third for the South Carolina militia; and one-third for the Georgia militia. Arms, ammunition, rum, and salt were set aside "entirely for the publick Service." In addition, "A Chest of Medicines was Sent with the eight wagons. They are much in demand, and no Such thing to be had in the country."

The space given above to the unglamorous subject of supply and transport amid the fighting and dying is meant to drive home once again the truth that without the sinews of war campaigns come to a grinding halt.

"We Have Now Got a Method That Will Put an End to the Rebellion in a Short Time"

Captain Rudulph and his men rested overnight. The following day, 22 May 1781, they were on the march again, recrossed the Savannah River, and rejoined the main force on a hill northwest of the town within view of the forts at Augusta. With Lee and Pickens was that fierce Georgia militia leader Colonel Elijah Clarke. All three men were familiar with the Tory commander at Augusta: Lieutenant Colonel Thomas Brown. Lee had sent ahead Captain Joseph Eggleston and his dragoon troop with orders to get a message to Brown informing him that Continental troops had arrived in the area, that General Greene was besieging Ninety Six, and therefore he should consider surrendering. Brown, however, refused to acknowledge the message. He thought it had come from Elijah Clarke, whom he had met before in battle and loathed.[4]

Thomas Brown (1750–1825) was made of stern stuff. On 2 August 1775 this young immigrant from a distinguished Yorkshire family underwent a day of terror that would have broken many a man. At a friend's house in South Carolina, just across the Savannah River from Augusta, he faced alone 100 Sons of Liberty who demanded that he declare for the Revolution. He refused and they rushed him. He pulled his pistols. One misfired. With the other he shot an attacker in the foot. The mob wrestled his pistols from him. He unsheathed his sword and "kept them at Bay for some time" until he was hit so hard in the back of the head by a rifle butt that his skull was fractured. The blow would leave Thomas Brown with headaches for the rest of his life. And the Rebel mob was not through with him. They tarred his legs and held his feet over burning wood. He lost two toes and could not walk well for three months. The Rebels thereafter referred to him as Burntfoot Brown. With knives they cut off his hair and scalped him here and there. Then they put him in a cart and paraded him through town, which brings to mind the tumbrils of the French Revolution. Thomas Brown, however, was not beheaded. According to the Rebels he recanted and pledged to use his influence to persuade opponents of the Revolution to desist. If so, it was a ploy. As soon as he shook off the dust of Augusta he once again took up the Royal cause and became one of the Rebels' most capable and implacable foes.[5]

On 14 September 1780, caught at Augusta between columns of Rebel militia commanded by Colonel Elijah Clarke and Major Samuel Taylor, Brown led a bayonet charge with his King's Rangers that drove Clarke's force from a stout stone building that was an Indian trading post known as the White House. There Brown took his stand: his King's Rangers in the house, Creek warriors in earthworks they dug around the perimeter. Brown was wounded in both thighs but remained on duty and in command. They ran out of water. Brown set the example for quenching their thirst by drinking his own cold urine. For food they ate raw pumpkins. They survived and fought on. On 18 September Lieutenant Colonel John Harris Cruger came within sight of Augusta with a relief force from Ninety Six, about 300 provincial regulars from New York, New Jersey, and South Carolina. Elijah Clarke's command had been reduced to about 200 men as undisciplined militiamen wandered off in search of plunder and to visit family and friends in the area. As Cruger advanced, Brown's Rangers left the White House and joined the assault, bayonets once again at the ready. Clarke and his men had no choice but to run. Many did not make it and were taken prisoner. Now began events that added to the hatred and bitterness on both sides that already consumed the Carolina and Georgia Back Country.[6]

There were at least twenty-nine prisoners taken by the provincial units. The Indians had also taken prisoners. Thirteen of the prisoners had at various times been captured in the past and paroled. The rule of parole was explicit. Breaking parole, that is, returning to the fighting before being exchanged, was punishable by death. Colonel Cruger wrote to Nisbet Balfour that he had no doubt the prisoners "will be roughly handled, some very probably suspended for their good deeds." And one of his officers wrote to a friend, "We have now got a method that will put an end to the rebellion in a short time—by hanging every man that has taken protection and is found acting against us." The officer was wrong, of course. His "method" guaranteed thirst for vengeance.[7]

There was no trial. The thirteen men who had broken parole were hanged from an outside staircase of the White House. Hugh McCall, an early historian of Georgia, claimed that many prisoners were turned over to the Indians. He wrote that the Indians "formed a circle and placed the prisoners in the centre, and their eagerness to shed blood spared the victims from tedious torture: some were scalped . . . others were thrown into the fires and roasted to death." McCall gave as his sources British officers who were eyewitnesses and "exultantly communicated it to their friends in Savannah, Charleston, and London, where it stands upon record in the papers of the day." Whether the story is true is relevant for historical accuracy, but quite irrelevant with regard to perception at the time. British patrols scoured the lands north of Augusta in pursuit of Clarke and to mete out retribution for rebellion. The Wilkes County courthouse and 100 Rebel homes in the county were burned. Livestock and other property were plundered. Guilt by blood was considered a crime. The families of the men who had followed Elijah Clarke were told to either leave Georgia within twenty-four hours or take an oath to the Crown.[8]

All this would be neither forgotten nor forgiven. Just as Tories were infuriated by Rebel atrocities and sought retribution, Rebels joined them in the long, dreary cycle of blood revenge. Thus eight months later, following the fall of Fort Galphin, as Light Horse Harry Lee and his regulars joined the partisans of Andrew Pickens and Elijah Clarke, many a Rebel militiaman poised to attack the forts at Augusta knew exactly what he would do if he could get his hands on Burntfoot Brown.

"The Old Field Was Strewed from One Fort to the Other"

Lee described Augusta in his memoirs as "situated on the southern bank of the Savannah River, in an oblong plain, washed by the river on the east and covered by deep woods in the opposite direction." Marshes and gullies cut the plain. Founded in 1736 at the falls of the Savannah River, Augusta was one of the most important towns in America. This backwoods entrepôt dominated the enormously profitable Anglo-Creek trade in the skins of the whitetail deer, and before the outbreak of the American Revolution was of major importance in relations between Indians and whites in the Southeast. In 1781 the town had about eighty buildings and a few hundred people. There was barely a town center among homes and farms dotting the landscape. Dominant among structures was a line of merchants' fortified trading houses that ran a dozen miles or more toward Creek country. Since Elijah Clarke's failed attack in September 1780, the British had built Fort Cornwallis, an earthen fort described by Lee as "judiciously constructed, well finished, and secure from storm." It was located 200 yards northwest of town and about 100 yards from the Savannah River. From Fort Cornwallis the defenders had clear fields of fire all around. West of Fort Cornwallis what Lee described as a "rivulet" flowed from Alligator Pond through a deep cut called Campbell's Gully into the Savannah River. About three-quarters of a mile across the gully was Fort Grierson. Among the seven or eight buildings inside a stockade was the fortified house of Colonel James Grierson, garrisoned by 112 men of the Georgia Loyalist militia. Brown's overall strength, including Colonel Grierson's command, was 236 provincial regulars of the King's Rangers, about 131 Tory militia, 300 Creeks, Cherokees, and Chickasaws (not all fighting men as some had families with them), and 200 slaves (not known if any were armed), for a total of 867.[9]

One wonders why Brown decided to defend Fort Grierson. Campbell's Gully was between the two forts, and he could not support Grierson from Fort Cornwallis as it was beyond firing range. If he still thought he was facing only militia, one can understand his decision. But as noted previously some of the men from Fort Galphin who had ridden out to pursue the Rebel militia had escaped and presumably made it to Fort Cornwallis. Had they not warned Brown that the Continentals had arrived? And Captain Eggleston of the Legion had sent a message to Brown informing him of the "near approach of part of Greene's army." Brown as we know thought the message was from Clarke, so it is possible that he did not believe that Continentals were present. In the end, what Brown knew and why he decided to defend Fort Grierson remain unknown.[10]

Lee and Pickens outnumbered Brown by 651 men: 468 Continentals and 1,050 South Carolina and Georgia militia. As with Brown's numbers, these are best estimates though probably close to the mark. Although the Rebels were superior in numbers, Brown was in a strong defensive position in Fort Cornwallis with ample supplies and ammunition. Lee was right when he informed Greene that only his 110 Legion infantrymen were "in any sort calculated" for "sieges and storms." In his memoirs Lee took credit for surveying the scene, deciding to attack Fort Grierson first, and "Communicating" it to Pickens and Clarke, who agreed. Perhaps, though Lee had a habit of claiming to be the originator of plans and ideas when in some cases origins lay either with another or were a group decision. In any event, on 24 May the Rebels attacked in force.[11]

The assault began with a cannonade from a field piece that had been positioned the night before. Pickens and Clarke with their militia attacked from the north and west. Major Samuel Hammond of South Carolina then led his militia forward. Every second man carried an axe to cut through the stockade surrounding the house. Major Pinketham Eaton, his North Carolina Continental battalion, and Major James Jackson with Georgia militia attacked from the south. Lee led his Legion infantry, supported by Captain Ebenezer Finley's Continental artillery with a 6-pounder, from the southeast to a position where he could either support Major Eaton if necessary or block Brown should he attempt to go to the relief of Fort Grierson. Captain Joseph Eggleston and his Legion horse took a position south of Fort Cornwallis, his assignment to intercept Brown if he tried to attack Lee. As the attack went forward, Brown sallied a little ways out of Fort Cornwallis with two field pieces to assist Grierson. An artillery duel ensued between Brown and Lee, but Lee wrote that it had "very little effect on either side."[12]

The issue was never in doubt. Grierson and his 112 men saw the hordes advancing on them and decamped. They fled the house, scrambled over the stockade, and ran for their lives under cover of the riverbank in a desperate attempt to reach Fort Cornwallis. Grierson with a few followers made it. Others, Pickens reported, "escaped in the Woods." But they left behind about thirty dead comrades and some forty-five taken prisoner. Samuel Beckaem, a Rebel militiaman of Georgia, was there and later wrote that "the old Field was Strewed from one fort to the other" with dead Tories. Unable to help, Brown retired inside the gates of Fort Cornwallis. Pickens reported to Greene that "During the action Capt Armstrong of the Legion drove the enemy's outposts from the town, and took possession of their redoubts, thus we are fully masters of the Country & Town and have circumscribed Colonel Brown to one fort." Lee recalled in his memoirs that "our loss was trivial, a few wounded, fewer killed. Unhappily among the latter was Major Pinketham Eaton, of North Carolina. . . . He fell gallantly at the head of his battalion at the moment of victory."[13]

Greene, who was then investing Ninety Six, congratulated Pickens but reserved most of his letter to the subject of the supplies taken at Fort Galphin. He was also anxious that Pickens and Lee wrap up the Augusta operation quickly. "We are pushing our approaches here with all possible diligence and wish you to effect the reduction of the enemies remaining post as soon as you can." That would not be as soon as Greene wished.[14]

"It Is My Duty and Inclination to Defend This Place to the Last Extremity"

The siege of Fort Cornwallis began with an eighteenth-century formality that strikes us today as quaint. The ranking Tory officer who had been taken prisoner after the fall of Fort Grierson requested of Pickens and Lee that medical supplies to treat the wounded and not available in the Rebel camp be procured from Fort Cornwallis. Brown's failure to accept the message sent to him earlier by Captain Eggleston was considered an insult by the Rebels, and they were not willing, Lee wrote, to once again "expose the American flag to contumely." They were, however, "disposed" to "obey the dictates of humanity," and therefore placed the officer on parole and permitted him to enter Fort Cornwallis and return with Brown's reply. The officer carried with him a letter from Pickens and Lee complaining about the treatment afforded Captain Eggleston's letter. Brown replied with a "very polite" letter along with medical supplies. His explanation for refusing to acknowledge Eggleston's message made it clear that he thought it was from Elijah Clarke, but the "extraordinary change in force opposing him" made it possible for him to engage in a civilized manner with his foes. Lee recalled that he and Pickens "were very much gratified that, while obeying the claims of humanity, they should have produced a renewal of intercourse, without which the contest drawing to a close would not be terminated but by a painful waste of human life." Men would continue to die, of course, but Lee meant not from a "spirit of hate and revenge," and he stressed those "noble feelings of humanity and forgiveness which ought ever to actuate the soldier." Cynics might scoff. But given war as part of the human condition, Lee's war-making was usually better by far than the barbarous rages that wracked the Back Country.[15]

During the siege of Fort Motte, Lee had found comfortable quarters in the farmhouse where Rachel Motte had taken refuge while Marion made do under the heavens. At Augusta he availed himself of the "mansion-house of a gentleman who had joined the enemy," fit quarters for a Lee of Virginia, "while Brigadier Pickens occupied the woods on the enemy's left." Tools taken at Fort Galphin and collected from neighboring farms were used to dig trenches. The men began at the riverbank, where they had cover, and aimed at Fort Cornwallis's left and rear. Lee and Pickens wanted to bring their 6-pounder to bear on the inner workings of the fort, but there was no high ground in the vicinity. Lee, however, had witnessed the effectiveness of Maham's tower at the siege of Fort Watson, and it was agreed to take that approach.[16]

Thomas Brown, seeing the trenches coming closer, decided to act. Lee described what happened. On the night of 28 May, Brown sallied, "fell upon our works on the river quarter at midnight, and, by the suddenness and vigor of his onset, drove the guard before him." But Captain George Handy and Legion infantry in support charged with bayonets and "after an obstinate conflict, regained the trenches, and forced the enemy to take shelter in the fort." Fearing further attempts by Brown to disrupt the siege works, Lee relieved the Legion infantry of all duty except protection of the works. It was a decision well taken. The next night Brown sallied again on the river quarter. The fight raged for a long time as men fought hand to hand, until Captain Michael Rudulph, "by a combined charge with the bayonet, cleared the trenches, driving the enemy with loss to his stronghold."[17]

On 30 May the timbers and other materials necessary to build the tower had been assembled at the point of construction, 150–200 yards from Fort Cornwallis. That night work began "under cover of an old house to conceal our object from the enemy. In the course of the night and ensuing day we had brought our tower nearly on a level with the enemy's parapet, and began to fill its body with fascines [long bundles of sticks tied together], earth, stone, brick, and every other convenient rubbish, to give solidity and strength to the structure." While this work went on, the trench behind the fort was "vigorously pushed" ahead with the intention of ending at the tower.[18]

Thomas Brown was not a commander to watch this mortal threat rise without attempting to destroy it. Nor were Pickens and Lee derelict in their preparations to thwart such a move. The militiamen guarding the trenches in that area were doubled. Captain Handy's Legion infantry was brought from the river quarter and stationed in support of the militia, while the late Major

Eaton's North Carolina battalion, now commanded by Captain Robert Smith, took its place. Along with Captain Handy's unit, Captain Rudulph's infantry was also detailed to protect the lines, and "one company of musketry was exclusively applied" to the defense of the tower.[19]

They had not long to wait. Brown attacked relatively early on the night of 29 May. To mask his real goal, part of his attacking force drove on the trenches in the river quarter, but there Captain Rudulph and his men gave them a "warm reception." While this fighting was going on, Brown "with the *elite* of his garrison, fell upon our works in his rear." Pickens's militia put up a stout defense. But they were without bayonets and Brown's bayonet-wielding King's Rangers finally forced them from the trenches. Whereupon Captain Handy left one company at the tower and with his main body of Legion foot "hastened to support the militia, who very gallantly united with the regulars, and turned upon the successful foe." Lee described the contest as "furious," and one can imagine the shouts, curses, and shrieks as cold steel found their targets. The "Marylanders under Handy carried the victory by the point of the bayonet." We have no figures of losses, but Lee wrote that "Upon this occasion the loss on both sides exceeded all which had occurred during the siege."[20]

On 31 May Pickens and Lee sent Brown a summons to surrender, reading in part, "Sir, The usage of war renders it necessary that we present you with an opportunity of avoiding the destruction which impends your garrison." Brown replied, "Gentlemen, What progress you have made in your works I am no stranger to. It is my duty and inclination to defend this place to the last extremity."[21]

The old wooden house behind which the Rebels had begun the building of the tower was still standing, and Lee admitted that he made a mistake in allowing it to remain, for if it caught fire the tower might be consumed in the blaze. He stated that Brown had noticed the proximity of the house to the tower and was "determined" to burn it. To counter the tower, and perhaps to bombard the house and set it afire, Brown had by then built a "platform in one of the angles of the fort opposite to our Maham tower." There Brown placed two cannon and began firing. The bombardment, however, neither stopped work on the Maham tower nor set the old house on fire. By 1 June the tower was finished and overlooking Fort Cornwallis. During the day the 6-pounder was hauled to the platform atop the tower and readied for firing. The following day Captain Finley was ready to answer Brown's cannonade, "which had been continued without intermission." Before noon on 2 June Brown's two cannon had been "dismounted from the platform, and all the interior of the fort was racked, excepting the segment nearest to the tower" and the trenches protected by piles of dirt.[22]

His direct assaults foiled, his artillery rendered useless, Brown hatched a scheme to plant a spy within the Rebel ranks to sabotage the tower by setting it afire. A Scottish sergeant of artillery in Brown's ranks, possessing according to Lee's amusing description "all the wily sagacity of his country," pretended to desert. Questioned by Lee, he maintained that the tower "if improved" would eventually "force surrender." To date, however, he told Lee that "the garrison had not suffered as much as might be presumed; that it was amply supplied with provisions and was in high spirits." In answer to another question, the sergeant said that he knew the location of the garrison's magazine containing its supply of powder. If the Americans used red-hot cannon balls they might blow up the magazine. Although it would be quite difficult to produce such balls, as the Rebels did not have a furnace, it was suggested in any event that the sergeant should be admitted to the tower and help aim the 6-pounder. He appeared reluctant to do that, fearing if retaken by his former comrades he could end on a "gibbet." Lee assured him of his complete safety, plied him with food and drink, and the sergeant agreed to help and was admitted to the Maham tower. But Lee had second thoughts. It was midnight and he was about to sleep, but when he reflected on what had occurred and the "character of his adversary he became much disquieted" and ordered the Scottish sergeant taken from the tower and kept under guard.[23]

If the tower could not be destroyed, Brown intended to inflict unexpected harm to the besiegers elsewhere. "Before Lee's quarters and the fort stood four or five deserted houses; some of them near enough to the fort" for riflemen to fire "from their upper stories." Pickens and Lee had them in mind for riflemen to cover an assault on Fort Cornwallis. At daybreak Brown sallied and "set fire to all but two of the houses." Of the two one was large enough to accommodate a number of riflemen. Pickens and Lee pondered on Brown's reasons for not setting those houses afire but could not come up with a satisfactory answer. They did notice that Brown's men were engaged in digging a sap outside the fort.

Meanwhile, Nathanael Greene was growing impatient. As early as 22 May, before he knew of the fall of Fort Galphin, Greene informed Lee that he had found the British post of Ninety Six "better fortified and garrison much stronger in regular troops than was expected," and "I beg you to accomplish your business at Augusta ... as soon as possible." On 26 May, following the fall of Forts Galphin and Grierson, Greene expected Fort Cornwallis to surrender "every Hour." The following day he wrote a correspondent that he expected the surrender of the "Main fort today at farthest." By 29 May he hoped it would "fall in a few Days," and that same day he wrote to Lee congratulating him on his progress but also informing him again that he wanted Lee to join him "as soon as the Post is reduced at Augusta." He wrote Pickens on the 29th, also congratulating him but stressing that he wished Pickens to "effect the reduction of the enemies remaining post as soon as you can." On 1 June he again wrote to Pickens, "I hope before this reaches you Augusta will be ours." Coupled with his nagging letters, earlier Greene had sent his aide Major Ichabod Burnet to "consult" with Pickens with regard to the distribution of stores. Burnet, however, had another mission, revealed in a letter of 1 June from Lee to Greene. Lee had been told by Burnet that Greene needed him and his Legion to complete the "present business" at Ninety Six. Whereupon Lee described how "the strength of this post, the uncommon inertness and disorder of our assistants [the militia], the inferiority of our regulars in point of number, & the judicious conduct of the enemy will render the issue of these operations later than you can wish or expect." He hoped to "finish the matter" by the 2nd or 3rd of June and promised to "not pass by any favourable opportunity." Pickens wrote the same day that they were pushing the issue "with what expedition we can." He admitted "our progress is but very Slow," but the immediate reinforcement of "two hundred regular troops . . . would greatly facilitate the reduction of this Post." Brown, he stressed, was better provisioned than originally thought, and though the militia was better armed than previously they were "far from being Well Arm'd." Greene replied two days later that he could not spare troops, that reinforcements for Augusta would have to await the "arrival of the troops now on the march from Charlotte who are expected in either to morrow or next day."[24]

Pickens and Lee had made a decision to assault the fort at nine o'clock on the morning of 4 June—without waiting for the promised reinforcements. It is reasonable to speculate that this decision was not easily taken. There was, of course, the possibility of failure and all that implied. They may also have feared a massacre if the 1,000 or so militia got inside Fort Cornwallis on the heels of the small complement of regulars. The rules of eighteenth-century siege warfare were clear. The garrison commander would not be dishonored by surrendering if he had no choice. But if he refused and the fort was taken by storm, all involved had to be aware that butchery might ensue, especially if the attacking troops took heavy casualties and got out of control and sought revenge. And the rules had in mind disciplined regulars. But in the case of Fort Cornwallis, undisciplined, revenge-minded militia were part of the equation: men whom Light Horse Harry Lee claimed "[exc]eed Goths & Vandals in their schemes of plunder murder & iniqu[ity]." Nevertheless, under pressure from Greene to end it, probably impatient themselves over Brown's stubborn defense, Pickens and Lee decided to storm Fort Cornwallis.[25]

Most of the fire from the 6-pounder mounted on the tower was directed at the parapet facing the river. From that direction the Legion infantry, including those who had been guarding the tower, would assault the fort. To assist them by keeping enemy heads down along the parapet, picked marksmen from Pickens's militia had previously been sent to the larger of the two houses standing. It was also closest to the fort. The mission of the officer in charge of the marksmen was to ascertain how many riflemen the windows and other openings would accommodate. The officer carried out his instructions, then left with his men and reported to Pickens. It was planned that before daybreak on 4 June the officer would reenter the house with the allotted number of marksmen. All was ready for the 9:00 A.M. assault.[26]

Then, at three o'clock on the morning of 4 June, "we were aroused by a violent explosion," wrote Lee, shattering the "very house intended to be occupied by the rifle party before daybreak. It was severed and thrown into the air thirty or forty feet high, its fragments falling all over the field." Thus was explained why Brown had set the other houses afire; thus was explained the sap pushed outside the fort to the destroyed house. Brown had obviously predicted that Pickens and Lee would use that house to post riflemen, and may have heard them during their reconnaissance but not when they left. A long fuse had burned along the bottom of the sap to the cache of explosives placed there.[27]

Despite partial success, Brown realized from the bombardment and other signs that Pickens and Lee were preparing to storm Fort Cornwallis, and he would have been just as aware as they of the awful consequences that could follow. Pickens wrote to Greene that their 6-pounder overlooked the parapet at a distance of about 150 yards and was firing into the "enemy's post." He also reported that many deserters and "a Number of half Starved Negroes" had "come out." The day before, 3 June, Pickens and Lee had sent Brown another request for his surrender. Brown held off replying until 4 June, when he sent an officer out under a flag of truce with a message that included terms of surrender he could accept. Negotiations ensued and 5 June was designated as the date of surrender. According to Lee, Brown wanted the 5th because the 4th was the king's birthday. The most important term agreed upon was for Brown and the other officers of the King's Rangers to receive parole and be sent to British-held Savannah. The Tory militia and the Rangers' rank and file would be considered prisoners of war.[28]

"A Georgia Parole"

And so it was in the wild backwoods of Georgia that an extraordinary formal scene took place. Pickens and Lee agreed that "The judicious and gallant defense made by the garrison entitles them to every mark of military respect." Under the terms of capitulation, therefore, the garrison marched out at noon on 5 June "with shouldered arms and drums beating" and stacked their arms. Not Lieutenant Colonel Thomas Brown, however. He was Pickens and Lee's chief concern. He was in mortal danger, and they knew it. Captain James Armstrong of the Legion was ordered to take Brown into protective custody inside Fort Cornwallis and escort him under guard to Lee's quarters. "This precaution was indispensable," Lee wrote, "as otherwise the laurels gained by the arms of America would have been stained by the murder of a gallant soldier, who had committed himself to his enemy on their plighted faith." According to Pickens, one man, undoubtedly of the militia, "insulted" Brown—probably a shouted remark—"and was for some time confined for it." Once they met, Brown told Lee that the Scottish sergeant had indeed been sent by him to gain entrance to the tower and set it on fire. Brown requested his release, which Lee granted and the sergeant "with joy rejoined his commander." Brown and his officers were officially given parole. That did not, however, guarantee their safety.[29]

Early the following morning, 6 June, Lee broke camp to march for Ninety Six. Pickens and his men would remain behind until enough wagons were collected to transport supplies to Ninety Six. Brown and his officers also left, bound for Savannah under the protection of Captain Armstrong and Legion infantry. Lee's orders to Armstrong were "to continue with Lieutenant-Colonel Brown until he should be placed out of danger." His fears were not misplaced. The Rebel militia captain, Tarlton Brown, confided in his memoirs that he and others followed the escort, looking for a chance to kill "Burntfoot" Brown. Captain Armstrong, veteran of many a fight, later stated that the danger encountered on the march to Savannah was the most he had ever experienced. But he succeeded in his mission. Thomas Brown and his fellow officers were delivered safely downstate to their comrades in arms.[30]

The King's Rangers' rank and file were also in danger. Pickens was "fully persuaded that were they to march for Savannah, they would be beset on the road," and if Greene agreed thought it best to send them to Charleston via Ninety Six. Thus he ordered Major Samuel Hammond's regiment and 1st North Carolina Regiment to escort the prisoners across the Savannah River and "march them to Ninety Six."[31]

Tory militiamen were not so fortunate. Rank and file were locked in a cellar in the house of Colonel James Grierson. Colonel Grierson and Major Henry Williams of the Wilkes County Loyalist militia were confined somewhere upstairs. On 7 June Pickens reported to Greene "a very disagreeable and Melancholy affair which happened yesterday in the afternoon." There are minor discrepancies in the accounts of what happened, but all agree on the central point. Major Williams tried to take cover among the rank and file in the cellar but was shot through the shoulder by one Andrew Shulus. Colonel Grierson was murdered, shot down in cold blood by a Georgia militiaman, James Alexander, who then rode away in plain view of other Rebels. After the war Thomas Brown charged that Grierson was murdered in front of his children. A Rebel militiaman, Micajah Brooks, wrote in his pension claim that the motive for Grierson's murder was the poor treatment of Alexander's father, who had been held as a hostage in Fort Cornwallis, and leaving an "aged Mother, Sisters and brothers . . . to starve." Dr. Thomas Taylor, a Tory surgeon, blamed Light Horse Harry Lee for failing to protect Grierson. Taylor had taken water to Grierson that morning and wrote that "some of the miscreants about bestow'd on us both the most bitter curses." He claimed that Grierson feared for his life and asked Taylor to appeal through Thomas Brown to Lee for protection, and that Brown's intercession failed. "Putting a man to death in cold blood," Taylor wrote, "is very prettily nicknamed giving a Georgia parole."[32]

Nathanael Greene was furious. In a proclamation dated 9 June he declared that the murder of Grierson and wounding of Williams was "Such an insult offered to the Arms of the United States, as well as an outrage committed upon the rights of humanity deserves the most exemplary punishment." He offered 100 guineas to anybody who could "discover & secure the perpetrator of this horid crime," and he promised to "treat all persons as murderers that shall be guilty of like conduct in the future." As with the murder of James Dunlap, backwoods *omertà* descended once again. The reward was never claimed, and James Alexander was never brought to justice.[33]

After a look at Greene's efforts once again to establish law and order in the Back Country, we will move on to his only siege of a fortified British post and its culmination in a bloody hand-to-hand fight between Americans.

6

Surrender Is "Inadmissible"

"Stop the Progress of Private Murders and Plundering"

James Grierson's murder was another reminder of the passions sweeping the Back Country. Not that Nathanael Greene needed reminding. The reader will recall from chapter 4 his letter to John Rutledge, exiled governor of South Carolina, declaring the urgency of reestablishing civil government. That urgency extended to Georgia. Even while occupied—and frustrated—with the stubborn defense of Ninety Six, Greene put into motion efforts to bring Georgia under civil control. On 1 June Light Horse Harry Lee had written Greene of the "necessity of civil government in this state & the propriety in raising at any expense the quota of regulars for its defense." The day before Fort Cornwallis fell Lee wrote that "If you do not take on yourself to govern this state, till civil government can be introduced, you will loose all the benefit from it, which your exertions & the public cause have claim to." This is from the letter quoted earlier in the previous chapter in which Lee described the Georgia militia as "Goths & Vandals in their schemes of plunder murder & iniqu[ity]. All this," he continued, "under the pretence of supporting the virtuous cause of America."[1]

Greene knew all this and had begun his efforts to bring order to the Georgia Back Country before Lee's first letter on the subject. He had written on 29 May to Colonel Elijah Clarke, who was then with Pickens and Lee at Augusta, of the need to establish in Georgia a force "upon the most permanent and economical plan." The regiment would be similar to a Continental regiment and the troops would receive the same "pay and Clothing" as

Continental soldiers. Clarke would have the authority to appoint officers and command the regiment until a governor was functioning and should make his "pleasure" known. Both voluntary enlistments and conscription were acceptable, whatever was the most "efficatious mode." Greene stressed that an "arrangement of the Georgia Militia is absolutely necessary for the protection of the good people in that State." Pay "attention to that business," Greene wrote. Shortly thereafter, he sent Joseph Clay (1741–1804) to Augusta to "collect as many of the Militia and Negroes as you can and employ them in demolishing the works on the Savannah River. I also wish you to take such measures as may most effectually stop the progress of private murders and plundering" and "to consult with the principal Officers in the Militia service and with them concert a plan for forming the Militia . . . upon the best footing for opposing the enemies future attempts for getting possession of the interior Country." The English-born Clay had been a prominent merchant in Savannah and the Southern Department's paymaster general since 1777. The historian Edward Cashin described Clay as Greene's "mentor in matters pertaining to Georgia."[2]

Back Country savagery was not restricted to Georgia. The area north of the Saluda River in South Carolina was described by the historian Robert Stansbury Lambert as a "center of loyalism," which made it a target for Rebel raiders. A man named John Larkin was sent by people living near Perkins Ford on the Saluda to report to General Greene, who was still besieging Ninety Six, "the great distress they are in from the savage conduct of a party of Men belonging to" Colonel LeRoy Hammond's militia regiment. On 5 June Greene replied to "The Inhabitants Upon the Saluda," expressing "my abhorrence and detestation of such a practice" and promised to do all in his power to "restrain and check such violences." He then offered a way for Tories to help themselves. "Those that have been in the British interest and by their past conduct have rendered themselves obnoxious to their Country have now an opportunity in part to atone for their past conduct by joining the American Army and manifesting by their future conduct a sincere repentence for what is past as well as a desire to promote the true happiness of their Country in future." Greene sent Larkin with a letter to Andrew Pickens with the message that violence could only be visited upon inhabitants if "they are found in Arms." Civil government when reestablished was the proper court to hand out punishment to Tories if merited. But "The Idea of exterminating the Tories is not less barbarous than impolitick; and if persisted in, will keep this Country in the greatest confusion and distress." Then, in a finely wrought sentence, he challenged Pickens to share the responsibility for putting an end to barbarism in the Back Country. "The eyes of the people are much upon you, the disaffected cry for Mercy, and I hope you will exert your self to bring over the Tories to our interest, and check the enormities which prevail among the Whigs in punnishing and plund[er]ing as private avarice or a bloody disposition stimulates them."[3]

Greene was not alone in reporting plunder and murder in the southern Back Country. In a letter received from William Sharpe, a delegate to Congress from North Carolina, Sharpe noted that Greene's "picture of the miseries of the inhabitants of the southern States" was "well founded" and "confirmed by every account" Sharpe had received. He agreed with Greene that "a permanent body of troops, at least equal to the collective force of the enemy" was required before "hope of recovering and defending" the southern states was tenable.[4] Nor was destitution and homelessness restricted to the white inhabitants of the Back Country. In contrast to the Low Country, there were relatively few slaves in the Back Country, but the ones who were there suffered along with the whites. A particularly plaintive example was recorded by Lieutenant Adam Jamison, deputy commissary general for the Southern Department. On 30 May five wagons from Augusta loaded with supplies arrived at Ninety Six. Among the plundered supplies Jamison "found two Naked female Negroe's, Aged from appearance, one Eight, & the other Six, being Sisters. Upon Enquiry, None of the Men who drove the Waggons acknowledge a right to them, or could render any account how the Negro's came in their Possession, which Induced Me to take them into Custody. On Examining the children next Morning, they told me their Masters name was Johnston, & that the said Waggoners came to their Mrs House (the Master being absent) & brought them off. They don't know where they Lived." Their fate? To borrow the words of the editors of the Greene Papers, "It is not known what became of the girls."[5]

Turning once more to Georgia, on 7 June Greene wrote again to Elijah Clarke, praising the "high reputation you have very deservedly acquired by your bravery," which "induces me to" prevail upon you "to use your influence to restrain two very capital evils which rage in this Country. . . . I mean private murders and plundering." If they did not end "very soon, I shall be obliged to exercise great severity and inflict capital punishment on such offenders which I will most assuredly do if they do not desist."[6]

Greene was obviously determined to stop those "two evils which prevail in all the Southern States . . . plundering and private murders." But he did not have enough men to patrol the countryside, intercept raiders, and protect inhabitants while fighting a war. Thus his reaching out to Clarke and Pickens to join him in establishing law and order. He also decided about this time that the dreadful situation in Georgia required faster action than could be supplied by a legislature. Indeed, it would take far too long to even gather a legislature. After consulting with a few Georgians, including Joseph Clay, Greene decided that the most practical approach was to form "a Council to consist of five or seven of the most considerable charactors of the State whose orders would have the force of Laws." He stressed that the members of the council had to be men in whom the people had confidence. "Appointing a Councel, raising a body of regular State troops, forming, arming, and arranging the Militia generally and destroying the enemies fortifications should be the first objects of the peoples attention."[7]

Greene's attempts to bring a measure of law and order to a ravaged land were largely unsuccessful. Hatred and bitterness were too deeply imbedded for quick relief. And all the while his immediate and pressing concern lay before him: Ninety Six, the last British post in the South Carolina Back Country.

"A Flourishing Part of the Country" and "the Water Is Very Good"

Ninety Six was established at least by 1737 as a trading post on the Charleston Path from the lower towns of Cherokee country that lay beyond. The accepted story for its name, long repeated, is that it was thought to be ninety-six miles from the Cherokee village of Keowhee, but the distance was probably closer to eighty miles. Ninety Six was 175 miles from Charleston.[8]

Two provincial British officers were much taken with the country surrounding Ninety Six. Lieutenant Anthony Allaire of the American Volunteers wrote in his diary in 1780 that it contained "about twelve dwelling houses, a courthouse, and a jail. . . . situated on an eminence, the land cleared for a mile around it, in a flourishing part of the country, supplied with good water, enjoys a free, open air, and is esteemed a healthy place." In the summer of 1780, a surgeon serving with the American Volunteers, Dr. Uzal Johnson, repeated much of what Allaire had written, and also noted that "the Water is very good."[9]

Lieutenant Colonel John Harris Cruger (1738–1807) was in command at Ninety Six. Cruger was rich, well-born, able, and tough. A former chamberlain of New York City, Cruger was of a prominent family that had been in America since the late seventeenth century. His grandfather John, who became a wealthy merchant, was either of Danish or German birth. His grandmother, Maria Cuyler, a Dutch woman, was also of an affluent New York merchant family. Our John married another well-born New Yorker, Ann De Lancey, daughter of Oliver De Lancey. Oliver served with the British during the war, became a provincial general, and raised De Lancey's Brigade. His son-in-law, John Harris Cruger, became commander of 1st Battalion, an example of nepotism not always being a vice. A man who knew Cruger described him as "a

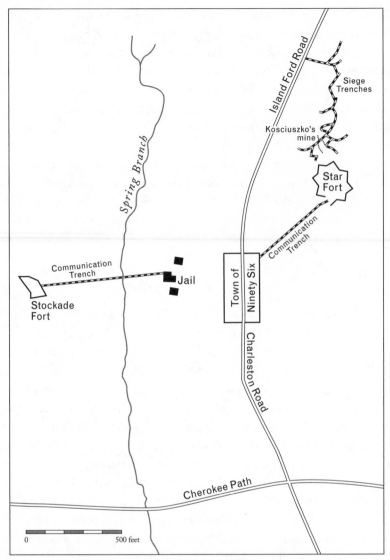

Siege of Ninety Six, 22 May–19 June 1781 (based on a map by John Robertson)

finished gentleman in all his conduct and treated the inhabitants with much civility, punishing his men for abuses committed and restoring to the owners plundered property." A thorough eighteenth-century gentleman Cruger was, but as Nathanael Greene would discover, also a skillful and stubborn opponent who would spurn a demand to surrender.[10]

In the period between Allaire's and Johnson's descriptions and Greene's arrival, the defenses had been strengthened, first by Colonel Cruger and then by a British military engineer, Lieutenant Henry Haldane. Haldane immediately observed that the safety of the water supply, the Spring Branch west of town, was vital. A provincial officer, Lieutenant Colonel Isaac Allen, commanding 3rd Battalion, New Jersey Volunteers, wrote to Cornwallis on 19 December 1780 that "the works are extensive but in want of water." We should keep this in mind as our story progresses.[11]

A British officer described the town as "about 100 yards square, with Block House flankers." It was surrounded by a stockade. A ditch encircled the stockade. The excavated dirt was thrown against the walls, forming a parapet ten to twelve feet high. The purpose of the dirt parapet was to withstand cannon fire up to a 12-pounder. Thirty yards beyond the ditch an abatis completely surrounded the Town Stockade.[12]

To further protect Ninety Six, a large earthen redoubt was built about 200 yards north of the town facing the Island Ford Road, from which an enemy army was likely to appear. It was called the Star Fort from its eight salients. The fort was about eighty-five feet across. It was a controversial design in the eighteenth century because it could not hold as many men and cannon as more conventional designs. From the salients, however, defenders could pour deadly enfilading fire upon assaulting troops. The design of the Star Fort was laid out on an acre of ground by Lieutenant Haldane before he left. The work was then done by Cruger's men and slaves. The Star Fort was also surrounded by a ditch that varied in width from twelve feet on the west to thirty to forty-five feet on the north and east. It was probably five feet deep. From the ditch a glacis, or bank, sloped until it blended with the terrain. Beyond the glacis an abatis ringed the entire structure. Nathanael Greene estimated the height of the parapet as "near twelve feet." Since parapet measurement usually began at the bottom of the ditch, this meant that the Star Fort's parapet was about seven feet above ground level. Sandbags were prepared in case it was necessary to raise the height of the parapet. At its base the parapet was approximately twenty-five feet thick. Above that it is estimated to have been about ten to fifteen feet thick. Inside the fort there was certainly a banquette, or firing platform, at least three feet above the base, three feet wide, and four and one-half feet below the top of the parapet. For this was an age when the average male height was five feet, five inches. A gun platform was erected in the northernmost salient for a cannon to fire over the parapet.[13]

A communications trench measuring about 135 yards long, three and one-half feet deep, three to five feet wide at the top, and two feet wide at the bottom ran from the rear of the Star Fort to the northeast corner of the Town Stockade.[14]

There remained the protection of the Spring Branch, the small stream that was Ninety Six's water supply. The stream ran through a ravine west of town.

Also to the west, about ninety-one yards from the Town Stockade, was the jail, which was seventy-six yards from the Spring Branch. It was stoutly built of brick, three stories high, and measuring thirty-four by forty feet: a very defensible building. To strengthen the position even more, a V-shaped, seventy-foot-long earthen redoubt was built around the west side of the jail above the Spring Branch ravine. A communication trench two to three feet wide and two to three feet deep ran directly from the jail to the Spring Branch.[15]

The third component of Ninety Six's defense lay 200 yards from the jail across and overlooking the Spring Branch ravine. Along with the fortified jail, the Stockade Fort's purpose was to protect the water supply. Nathanael Greene described it as "a strong stockade fort with two block Houses in it." It was built on the site of an older fort that had seen fighting earlier in the war. It was about 100 feet by 200 feet, shaped similar to an obtuse triangle "with the top salient leaning in a northwesterly direction." Along the south, west, and northeast ran a ditch about eight to ten feet wide and three to four feet deep. The dirt from the ditch was used to create a parapet about twelve feet thick against the stockade. A swivel gun in the salient covered the western and southern parapet and ditch and could be brought to bear to protect the Spring Branch. An abatis may have surrounded the entire Stockade Fort, but no archaeological evidence of it has been found. A communications trench led down to the Spring Branch.[16]

Cruger's garrison consisted of northern provincial regulars and South Carolina Tory militia: the 165-man 1st Battalion, De Lancey's New York Brigade, Major Joseph Green commanding; the 253-man 3rd Battalion, New Jersey Volunteers, Lieutenant Colonel Isaac Allen commanding; and 856 men from six Tory militia regiments. Cruger had three brass 3-pounders but only one fully trained gunner. He offered to allow the Tory militia to leave before the Rebel army arrived. They would have none of that. They turned their horses loose in the woods and cast their lot with the garrison. Cruger assigned the defense of the Star Fort and Town Stockade to his New York and New Jersey regulars. The militia was assigned to the Stockade Fort across the ravine. A subaltern's guard was posted in the jail and its redoubt.[17]

This was the force and defensive network that confronted Nathanael Greene and his army of 908 Continentals from Maryland, Virginia, and Delaware, and 66 North Carolina militiamen, when his little army arrived at Ninety Six on the morning of 22 May and laid siege.[18]

Should Greene have besieged Ninety Six? He knew by two intercepted letters from Balfour and Lord Rawdon to Cruger that the latter had been ordered to abandon Ninety Six and join Thomas Brown at Augusta. Never receiving Rawdon's orders, Cruger stayed put. Armchair generalship is often dubious, but it has been suggested that given his knowledge of Rawdon's intentions, Greene's goal of driving the British from the Back Country would have been better served had he bypassed Ninety Six and joined Lee, Pickens, and Clarke at Augusta, with overwhelming numbers quickly forcing Brown's surrender. He could then have turned his combined force in the direction of Ninety Six, sent Rawdon's letters to Cruger under a flag of truce, and waited to see if Cruger would carry out Rawdon's orders. If Cruger did obey those orders, Greene could allow him to proceed unmolested to the Low Country, thus achieving a bloodless victory and completing the expulsion of British forces from the Back Country. But that would have added sizable numbers to Rawdon's force. The what-ifs of history, however interesting they may be, do not count, so let us focus on what actually happened.[19]

"One of the Best and Neatest Draughtsman I Ever Saw"

Although Greene had no experience in siege warfare, it is hard to believe that a man as widely read in military history as he was did not know the basic concepts of siege operations as described and executed by the master of that particular art of the soldier, Sebastien le Prestre Vauban (1633–1707), marshal of France. In the seventeenth century the great Vauban wrote the bible of siege warfare, *A Manual of Siegecraft and Fortifications,* and the French were its leading practitioners. If Greene was unfamiliar with Vauban and his methods, which is doubtful, he had with him the chief engineer of the Southern Department, the Polish patriot Colonel Thaddeus Kosciuszko (1746–1817), who had been trained in France. Kosciuszko's expertise was in demand in America, where there were few if any formally trained military engineers.[20]

Like many European nobles, Kosciuszko was fired with passion for the American cause. Upon his arrival in America in 1776 as a volunteer, Congress appointed him a colonel of engineers. He was involved for a short time on the river defenses of Philadelphia. There he met and became good friends with Major General Horatio Gates, and when Gates was transferred to the Northern Department he took Kosciuszko with him. Gates praised the young Pole as an "able Engineer, and one of the best and neatest draughtsman I ever saw." The latter accomplishment almost certainly came from a year's study developing his natural ability at the Royal Academy of Painters and Sculptors in Paris. Kosciuszko worked in a subordinate position on the defenses of Fort Ticonderoga in northern New York State, and during the American retreat to Saratoga he served with distinction by placing obstructions along the line of march to impede the British pursuit. At Saratoga, under Gates's command, he did important work in preparing fortifications on Bemis Heights and other

Thaddeus Kosciuszko, 1746–1817; oil painting by Jacob Ruys. (Courtesy Independence National Historical Park Collection)

areas. In 1778–1779, Kosciuszko, as chief engineer of the Middle Department, improved the defenses of West Point. His work there gained the approval of George Washington, with only minor alterations.[21]

In 1780 Kosciuszko was transferred to the Southern Department to serve under his good friend Gates, but by the time he was ready to assume his duties Greene had succeeded Gates. Greene kept him on and Kosciuszko served as chief engineer of the army during the rest of the Southern Campaign and successfully completed his initial assignments. On 3 December 1780, the day he took command in Charlotte, Greene ordered Kosciuszko to undertake a "most minute survey into the State of the Rivers" and ordered his chief engineer to survey the Catawba River upstream from "Mill Creek below the forks up to Oliphant Mill." Accompanied by Captain John Thompson, a veteran of Sumter's campaigns and Kings Mountain and a native of the Catawba country, Kosciuszko carried out his assignment quickly and presented Greene with a detailed report. This was obviously the source of Greene's knowledge of the Catawba that surprised and impressed General William Lee Davidson of North Carolina.[22]

Because of the lack of subsistence in the Charlotte area, Kosciuszko's next assignment was to find a camp for the main army east of Charlotte on the Pee Dee River and describe the countryside surrounding it. The engineer also carried out this assignment promptly and to Greene's satisfaction. Receiving the order on 8 December, he returned on the 16th with his report, and by the

26th the army was at its new camp. Six days later Greene ordered Kosciuszko to Cross Creek (modern Fayetteville), North Carolina, to obtain "tools suitable for Constructing a number of boats" for the army and to "make all the dispatch the business will admit." He was engaged in this task when Greene began his retreat through North Carolina with Lord Cornwallis in pursuit, and on 1 February Kosciuszko was recalled to the main army.[23]

On 22 May 1781, the day Greene's army appeared before Ninety Six, Kosciuszko had served the American cause well for almost five years. But his work had been restricted in the North to preparing defenses against enemy assaults and in the South to surveying rivers and topography and building boats for Greene. At Ninety Six, however, he was faced with a situation in which he had no firsthand experience: siege warfare.

The first step in eighteenth-century siege operations was to dig a trench parallel to the works you intended to besiege. The trench, known as the first parallel, was always dug out of range of the enemy's artillery and sallies by infantry. Redoubts for artillery were built in front of the first parallel. Zigzag approach trenches vertical to the enemy's works would then be dug and a second parallel trench opened. Following more zigzag approach trenches, the third parallel trench was dug just outside the enemy's works. As the digging proceeded, artillery to batter the enemy's defenses and open them to an infantry assault was steadily moved forward to each parallel and protected by earthen redoubts. The third parallel presaged the infantry assault. All this occurred under counter-bombardment and night sallies by the defender's infantry. It was slow, tedious, dangerous work.

On the night of 22 May, Greene, Kosciuszko, and Greene's aide, Captain Nathaniel Pendleton, reconnoitered so close to the Star Fort that they were spotted and fired upon. That same night Greene ordered fleches, V-shaped earthworks, for artillery built near the Star Redoubt. The next day Cruger's artillery bombarded the works. That was followed up by a nighttime sally of bayonet-wielding provincial regulars led by Lieutenant John Roney of De Lancey's Brigade. They destroyed the works, killed many of the working party, captured their tools, and carried back to the Star Fort Lieutenant Roney, who had received a mortal wound during the brief clash. According to British sources and Greene's first biographer, the works were built only 70 yards from the Star Fort, although Kosciuszko maintained that they were 150 yards away. Whether 70 or 150 yards is irrelevant. The Vauban method is quite clear: the first parallel and works for artillery must be built beyond enemy artillery range and beyond the ability of infantry to sally. One must therefore ask why the trained engineer and the commanding general widely read in military affairs blundered? Kosciuszko blamed the setback on the inexperience of American troops in siege warfare as well as their beginning the digging with the "night far advanced." Inexperienced they were, no doubt of that, but there can also be no doubt that the misjudgment that led to the destruction of the works and lives lost belonged to Kosciuszko and Greene, not the troops. Why they made this elementary mistake remains inexplicable.[24]

The upshot of their error in judgment was to begin again the next night 300 to 400 yards from the Star Fort, behind a ravine—which they should have done in the first place. According to Kosciuszko, it was 300 yards' distance and done in order "to acquiented [acquaint] the men of the proceeding and of the nature of the work with less danger." Here he implies that the other ranks were responsible for the first night's disaster, which is nonsense. Other sources placed the distance at 350 to 400 yards, but that is of little matter. On the morning of 24 May artillery was brought forward to the new works. Kosciuszko wrote, a "few shots firing to the Town and Star redoubt with great effect, Alarmed the Enemy prodigious[ly]." How he came to this dubious conclusion is unknown.[25]

There occurred about this time an incident that is also part of the eighteenth century mode of warfare. Colonel Cruger's wife, Anne De Lancey Cruger, and the wife of Cruger's deputy, Major Joseph Green, were living in the farmhouse of a Rebel militia officer, Colonel James Mayson, three miles west of Ninety Six. Mayson had several young daughters, and prior to the American army's arrival Cruger's officers had been in the habit of visiting under the pretext of paying their respects to Mrs. Cruger. General Greene learned of this during his approach to Ninety Six. Light Horse Harry Lee wrote that Greene "tranquillized the fears of the ladies, and, as they preferred continuing where they were, he not only indulged them, but placed a guard detail at the house for their protection."[26]

Meanwhile, the war continued. Digging in the Carolina red clay went slowly. Kosciuszko described the "Nature of the Ground" as "very hard," resembling "Soft Stone." On the night of 27 May a battery was constructed 220 yards from the Star Fort, with the zigzag approach trenches 30 yards beyond. All that night and the next the men digging were subjected to enemy fire. Three days later the second parallel was half finished at 150 yards. The British sallied that night, "but with small effect," Kosciuszko wrote. Yet he admitted that "Three or four men of both side were killed," which means a desperate struggle in the dark of night as bayonets, musket butts, entrenching tools, fists, knees, feet, perhaps teeth, found their mark. According to Kosciuszko, "the militia now began to come very fast from the adjacent Countys, which gave oportunity to upon [open] the Trenches against" the Stockade Fort protecting the Spring Branch water supply. On 3 June General Greene's adjutant, Colonel Otho Holland Williams, sent a letter to Cruger to "demand an immediate surrender." Cruger replied, "my Duty to my Sovereign renders inadmissible at present." The next day Greene ordered arrows soaked in pitch shot flaming from muskets with a view to ignite the shingled roofs of the town. That night Cruger countered by having his troops remove the roofs, and at the same time troops in the Star Fort sallied and destroyed a mantlet (moveable shelter) used to protect Kosciuszko's sappers. Greene's answer was another artillery barrage.[27]

"The Chief Supply of Water"

On 7 June a triumphant Light Horse Harry Lee and his Legion arrived at Ninety Six, adding another 150 men to Greene's army. Lee had with him the provincial regulars taken prisoner at Augusta. What happened next deeply angered Colonel Cruger. The American officer escorting the column of prisoners mistakenly "took the road nearest to the town," Lee wrote, which brought both captives and captors under Cruger's artillery. Cruger believed it was done deliberately to mock him and his garrison, and though it endangered the prisoners he ordered his gunners to fire upon the column. No injuries resulted, but the Rebel officer was "severely reprimanded by" Lee "for the danger [to] which his inadvertence had exposed the corps."[28]

The approach trenches continued to be dug toward the Star Fort, but with Lee's arrival a second element was added to the siege. Lee claimed that he was appalled that little effort had been made to cut the enemy's water supply. He wrote in his *Memoirs,* "The enemy's left had been entirely neglected, although in that quarter was procured the chief supply of water." There is no record of a discussion on this matter between Lee and Greene or with Kosciuszko, but one certainly occurred, and Lee can never be accused of withholding his opinions on any subject. Greene immediately "directed" Lee to begin operations against the Stockade Fort. Colonel Cruger, now threatened on both sides, reacted violently. Nightly sallies from the garrison were described by Lee as "fierce and frequent, directed sometimes upon one quarter and sometimes upon another," as Cruger's men attempted to "carry our trenches; and to destroy by the spade whatever he might gain by the bayonet." The attacks failed in their intent, but in addition to death and injury the noise of these encounters meant sleepless nights on both sides as men clashed with all the savagery that hand-to-hand combat entails.[29]

Lee's arrival and his obvious intent to take the Stockade Fort overlooking Ninety Six's water supply brought that vital resource to the fore. At some point, probably after Lee's appearance, Colonel Cruger ordered a well dug in the Star Fort. Laborious digging ended at twenty-five feet and found—a dry well. There was no water. Men would have to sneak by way of the two- to three-foot-deep communications trench some 167 yards from the Town Stockade to the Spring Branch and bring back water for both troops and civilians. And the Spring Branch was within "pistol shot of the American pickets," a British officer wrote. He described the men chosen for this perilous duty: "naked Negroes . . . their bodies not being distinguishable in the night from the fallen trees with which the place abounded."[30]

Kosciuszko's sappers, meanwhile, had been digging a tunnel, which forked into two tunnels, meant to end under the rampart of the Star Fort, where a mine would be detonated to blast an opening for assault troops. Upon Greene's instruction, 150 pounds of powder for the operation had been sent from Augusta by Andrew Pickens. Two days after Lee's arrival, on the night of 9 June, Kosciuszko was inspecting the tunnel. The British, "in the apprehension that something extraordinary was carrying on in the enemy's works," sallied in two detachments and began bayoneting sappers. One detachment found the tunnel opening. Kosciuszko got away but not before being bayoneted in the buttocks, which a British officer lampooned as an "inglorious wound" upon "the seat of honour."[31]

By 12 June Lee's trenches were well advanced toward the Stockade Fort. Lee recalled, "We now began to deplore the early inattention of the chief engineer" to concentrate on cutting the enemy's water supply. Lee maintained that access to the Spring Branch could and should have been cut earlier, thus forcing Cruger to surrender. He prevailed upon Greene to allow an attempt to set fire to the Stockade Fort and thus deprive Cruger of protection of his water supply on that side. On the 12th a "dark, violent storm came on from the west, without rain." A sergeant and nine privates from Lee's Legion infantry carrying two pine torches went forth on this "hazardous enterprise." Hoping to divert the defenders' attention, Lee's artillery, which he had brought from Augusta, opened up with a barrage. At the same time, activity before the Star redoubt signaled that an assault would take place on that side. Taking advantage of what cover there was, crawling on their bellies when there was none, Lee's men closed on the Stockade Fort. The sergeant reached the ditch before the rampart. His men were close behind. He was in the act of lighting his torch when he was discovered and shot to death. Five of the privates were also killed while the survivors ran for their lives and gained the safety of Lee's lines.[32]

"I March This Night and Have Great Hopes of Saving Cruger"

On 3 June, six days before Kosciuszko felt the sting of a British bayonet, Lord Rawdon reported that a fleet from Cork, Ireland, consisting of "62 sail" arrived off Charleston and two days later landed "3rd, 19th, and 30th

Regiments, a Detachment from the Guards, & a considerable body of recruits, the whole under the command of Colonel [Paston] Gould of the 30th." A marine officer aboard the fleet described the arrivals as "compleat & in good Health." By then Rawdon was so ill, probably with malaria, that he apologized to Cornwallis for dictating two letters to his Lordship instead of writing personally. He had been told that "I could not outlive the summer in this climate." Word of his condition had spread to the Rebels. Major Hezekiah Maham, of Maham's tower fame, reported that Rawdon was "Very Sick." Yet possessed of an inner toughness, firmly resolved to relieve Ninety Six, young Rawdon persevered. "I am by no means now in a state of health fit to undertake the business upon which I am going, but as my knowledge of the country and my acquaintance with the inhabitants make me think that I can effect it better than any person here, I am determined to attempt it."[33]

But this required reinforcing the troops he had led from Camden with some of the new arrivals, and on this point military bureaucracy and personality clashes intervened. Rawdon and Colonel Balfour had made clear to Colonel Gould that Lord Cornwallis had given them powers to decide which part of the reinforcements were necessary "for the safety of the Province at this particular juncture." They decided "that Two complete Regiments" were required. Colonel Gould balked. "We have had the most miserable trouble with Gould," Rawdon wrote. Gould was apparently a decent chap, "well disposed to make matters easy." But he was under the influence of Lieutenant Colonel Alexander Stewart, commanding 3rd Foot, of whom Rawdon wrote, "The case is Stewart has too high an opinion of himself to conceive that he ought even indirectly to give way to me, a Provincial colonel." This was not an isolated problem with the British Army in America. Both Rawdon and Stewart were regular British Army officers, but Stewart's regular rank trumped Rawdon's provincial rank of lieutenant colonel. (How fascinating if minutes had been kept of this clash, or a diarist had been present.) Finally, a solution was found. The entire reinforcement would remain in South Carolina, but Colonel Gould "allowed" Rawdon to take the elite flank companies—light infantry and grenadiers—of all three regiments on his march upcountry. Combined with his own force, that meant Rawdon would have "near 1,800 infantry," almost 750 more than Greene's regulars. And ill as he was Rawdon was probably delighted to leave small-minded military bureaucrats behind him. He wrote to Cornwallis on 7 June, "I march this night and have great hopes of saving Cruger."[34]

General Greene learned of the reinforcement fleet shortly after its arrival. But the news did not come from either of his two chief informants, Thomas Sumter and Francis Marion. He apparently learned of it before they did. Greene called it "private intelligence" received, which was a notice in the

Royal Gazette of Charleston. Greene made clear to Sumter and Marion that he wanted them to oppose any effort by a relief column marching for Ninety Six. "Should the enemy attempt to penetrate the Country," he wrote to Marion, "I beg you to collect all the force you can and join General Sumter without loss of time and give the enemy all the opposition you can until we form a junction with our collective force it being my intention to fight them, and I wish them to be cripled as much as possible before we have a general action." On the same day, 10 June, he wrote in similar fashion to Sumter, and a few days later he urged Sumter in case Rawdon's troops "advance [to] fight them every day, so as to retard their approach as long as possible. Washington's and Lee's corps will join him in this [n]ecessary business." By "Lee's corps" Greene meant the cavalry. The Legion infantry would remain at Ninety Six with Lee and concentrate on taking the Stockade Fort and cutting the town's water supply.[35]

But would Sumter be able to carry out such a mission? He was still suffering from the grievous wound suffered during the big fight at Blackstock's in November 1780, when he defeated Banastre Tarleton. His biographer wrote that he was "struck in the right shoulder by a ball that passed through and carried away a splinter of the backbone before lodging." Sumter had been out of action until 9 February 1781. Even though since then he had led the failed raid down the river systems described in chapter 2, he was still not fully recovered. He wrote to Greene on 11 June, "I am unfortunate enough to find that My Indisposition in Creases So fast as Not to have any hopes, from the Nature of it, to be able to Remain with the Troops Many days longer; I Shall in deavour to hold out until you are so Disengaged as to take Measures in consequence of my Withdrawing." Greene replied on 13 June, "distressed at the increasing pains in your wound." As we know, the relationship between the two men was fragile. But Sumter was the head of the South Carolina militia and commanded the allegiance of too many for Greene to do without his services. He proceeded to stroke the Gamecock. "I cannot think of you leaving the service without the greatest pain. Few people in any Count[r]y know how to command and fewer in this than is common. It will be of importance to the public good that you continue to command if you are unable to perform active service, for you may continue to direct if not execute. Your name will give confidence to our own people and strike terror into the enemy." The final sentence was certainly correct. We do not know if Sumter really meant to retire, but in any case he would continue in his fashion to execute as well as direct.[36]

Even though Greene repeatedly urged Sumter and Marion to prepare to confront Rawdon should he march upstate, he also expressed the hope that Rawdon would be deterred by a French fleet sailing to the Carolina shores. To Sumter he wrote as late as 12 June, "But I can hardly persuade myself yet that they will venture out thus far into the Country, at a time when the second Division of the French Fleet is certainly on the coast, and probably near Charles Town." Rawdon had somehow learned of Greene's belief that a French fleet was approaching. On that basis he first decided not to march into the Back Country. But he soon changed his mind, and in the same letter in which he announced his intention to save Cruger he informed Cornwallis that "the town and lower districts are safe against any French force." A French fleet would eventually appear, not at Charleston that summer but in October off the Virginia capes. That, however, is another story.[37]

Greene was also concerned with other matters at this time, befitting a commander who must also see to important matters of state and the daily administration of his army. The Spanish had declared war on Britain in June 1779, although not as an ally of the United States, for Spain's only interest in the American rebellion was the chance it gave them to recover lost territories from the British and pick off British colonies in the West Indies. The Spanish establishment detested revolutionaries. In August–September 1779, the Spanish field commander, General Bernardo de Galvez, captured the British forts on the east bank of the Mississippi all the way to Natchez and forced the British Navy from the lower Mississippi. He took Mobile on 12 March 1780, and on 10 May 1781 captured Pensacola. When he learned of this latest Spanish coup, and while pondering on Lord Rawdon's intentions, Greene took time to write General Galvez on 12 June, congratulating him on his success and offering "every possible exertion" to facilitate the Spanish capture of Savannah. In doing this, Greene was following Congress's instructions to cooperate with the Spanish. There is no record in Greene's papers that Galvez ever replied to the American's overture, or that the letter even reached him. In any event, Spanish interests lay in the Mississippi Valley, the Gulf Coast, Florida, and the West Indies. Galvez had bigger prizes in mind than a provincial American city.[38]

On the same day Greene wrote to Lieutenant Edmund Gamble, commissary at Salisbury, North Carolina, on a homelier but to the army far more important matter. After commenting on the "great difficulty" in getting supplies from the North, he instructed Gamble to use artificers among the militia to make leather cartouche (cartridge) boxes, which the soldiers needed to carry their ammunition efficiently and keep it dry. He ordered Gamble to use "every exertion" to "forward the business" and "set about it immediately." A matter of constant concern was raised by Greene in another letter of the 12th to Governor Abner Nash of North Carolina: "Once before I mentioned to your Excellency the absolute necessity of furnishing this Army with forty or fifty good Dragoon horses. I beg leave to repeat the application and to observe it is impossible to give protection to the Country without a large Cavalry."[39]

As Greene tended to other business, digging and nightly clashes on the approaches to the Star Fort continued as the Rebel army inched closer to the outer defenses. Matters downstate, in the meantime, were not going as Greene wished. Sumter had issued contradictory orders to Marion. On the 13th he ordered Marion to leave his "heavy baggage, and march with all possible expedition on towards 96, so as for our whole force to act together if requisite." The next day he informed Marion that he had "received accounts that the enemy are not moving upwards" and advised Marion "to halt, until this matter can be clearly ascertained." Yet on the very next day it "appears probable" that Rawdon was advancing. Marion, therefore, should "move higher up the river, in readiness to cross, if the enemy continue advancing." Sumter had also written to Greene of the "enemy advancing & Giving out that that they are Going for Ninty Six." He believed they were near Orangeburg. This prompted Greene to immediately summon Pickens and all the men he could gather to join him at Ninety Six and also to send word to the Georgians, Colonel Elijah Clarke and Major James Jackson, to do the same. One of Greene's aides, Major Ichabod Burnet, ordered Captain John Rudulph, who commanded Lee's cavalry, to immediately join Lieutenant Colonel William Washington and his 3rd Continental Light Dragoons and "act with" him. Greene informed Washington that Rawdon was moving "in force" to relieve Ninety Six, and ordered his cavalry commander to gain the "ridge road" between Orangeburg and Ninety Six and with Sumter and the Legion horse "harrass" the enemy and "impede their march." Then came startling news from Sumter. One of his colonels, Charles Myddelton, reported that Rawdon's force had not moved toward Orangeburg. It was just a small party of Tories. Sumter, therefore, canceled his march upstate, and if the information turned out to be true, "I shall this evening pursue my former intention, that is to March Downwards with my Whole force Which is about Six hundred horse and Two hundred foot. I beg you will not be apprehensive that I may be out of place by this Movement. I shall make a point of being with you in time if the enemy Shoud advance." It has also been asserted that another reason for Sumter's rearward movement was his fear that Rawdon's real objective was Sumter's headquarters, supply depot, and armory at Fort Granby. Whatever the case, Colonel Myddelton's intelligence was erroneous. Rawdon's goal was Ninety Six, and he was on the march. By the time Sumter realized this and turned around, his slow pace guaranteed that he would never get to Rawdon's front.[40]

Francis Marion, in the meantime, on the 16th was at Rock's Plantation on the Santee River, about three miles downstream from Nelson's Ferry and about forty miles southeast of Orangeburg. He was at a standstill awaiting further orders from Sumter. In his letter of that date to Greene, Marion did not mention Rawdon's force. He was more concerned that if he left "this part of the country," provisions south of the Santee would be lost to the enemy. He had sent Colonel Peter Horry to "Quell" the Tories on the Pee Dee. He intended to send Major Maham downriver to deal with Tories at various locations. Marion felt that if he remained where he was he could defeat any enemy attempt to gather provisions. Given the date of his letter, his location, and his deep, ongoing reluctance to operate with Sumter, it is obvious the Swamp Fox would be of no assistance to Greene.[41]

A snafu had also developed with Captain Rudulph and Lee's Legion cavalry, which had been ordered to join Washington's dragoons and act with Sumter. Rudulph apparently misread his orders and "delayed his march," Greene wrote to Sumter. "He is now ordered to march and join [Lieutenant Colonel William] Washington with all possible dispatch." Greene also informed Sumter that he expected Elijah Clarke and James Jackson to join him "with the Georgians." Twelve hours elapsed until Greene's letter reached Captain Rudulph, who immediately marched. Rudulph came within twenty-four miles of Orangeburg yet failed to find either Washington or Rawdon's column. He did find out that Rawdon had left Orangeburg on 15 June, and "marched for Ninety Six via Juniper Springs," at the fork of the Augusta and Ninety Six roads. This prompted Rudulph to turn around and head for Ninety Six. He and his men "rode all night to get dow[n] & now almost all day to get back[.]" Captain Rudulph was "amazed" not to have heard from Washington.[42]

Wherever Washington was and what he was doing, one Rebel unit managed to clash with Rawdon's column. But it did not go well. According to Sumter, Colonel Charles Myddelton, with some 200 riders, came up with Rawdon's rear guard and engaged "about 200 mounted infantry." It was a trap. Rawdon reported that he had enticed Myddelton "within reach by a prospect of cutting off our foragers." Sumter wrote, "At the Same time their Cavalry Charged him in flank and Rear, & Soon broke him to pieces." Colonel Myddelton returned to Sumter's camp with only forty-five men. Rawdon reported that four officers and twenty to thirty men were killed. The rest, wrote Sumter, "Dispearced," which we may interpret as riding for their lives. Thus the British demonstrated that they, too, could use a classic guerilla tactic against their partisan foe. On their march upcountry, the only enemy Rawdon's reinforcement of regulars, fresh from Ireland in their heavy woolen uniforms, really had to worry about was the terrible heat and humidity of the Deep South in high summer.[43]

While Rawdon's troops tramped on their way to the far Back Country, at Ninety Six Greene's sappers pushed the approach trenches closer to the Star Fort and came under increasing fire from the defenders. To counter this, Greene ordered a log rifle tower built similar to those used at Fort Watson and Augusta. Thirty feet high, thirty-five feet from the British defenses, it was completed on 14 June and immediately "did great execution," a British officer wrote. The defenders raised the height of the parapet another six feet with sandbags and attempted to destroy the tower with hot shot. But without furnaces to heat the shot, the attempt failed. The riflemen in the tower were so effective that British cannon were removed from their firing platforms during the day and used only at night.[44]

Sometime between 12 and 14 June Cruger learned that Rawdon was indeed on his way. There are various stories on how he gained this knowledge and whether the messenger was a man or a woman, but all agree that a lone rider walked his (her?) horse through the Rebel camp, onto the open field outside the British defenses, as local people often did. At the right moment the rider galloped hard for the Town Stockade and made it safely, waving aloft Rawdon's letter as the gate was flung open. This dramatic event and the news received would have increased Cruger's resolve to continue his stout resistance.[45]

It also put additional pressure on Greene to bring the siege to a close with Cruger's surrender. The approaches were within a few feet of the Star Fort's ditch. But the main tunnel for the mine was not finished and time was growing short. Convinced that Rawdon's object was the relief of Ninety Six, knowing that the Anglo-Irishman was drawing nigh with a superior force, despairing that Sumter and Marion would join him, Greene was left with two alternatives: suspend the siege and get out of Rawdon's way, or mount assaults on both the Star Fort and the Stockade Fort. Light Horse Harry Lee maintained that Greene was initially "averse" to an assault "and probably would have decided on the safe course, had not his soldiers, with one voice, entreated to be led against the fort." The soldiers, Lee continued, "could not brook the idea of abandoning the siege without one bold attempt to force a surrender," and "This generous ardor could not be resisted by Greene." Given Lee's habit ranging from exaggeration to concocting tales, one's initial reaction to his claim is doubt. Colonel Kosciuszko, however, also wrote of the "ardor" of the troops, and once the decision had been made a "number of Officers and soldiers" volunteered for the assault. It would be an all-American fight, not a British national on either side.[46]

At either 9:00 A.M. or noon (sources differ, but does it really matter?) on 18 June 1781, 1st Maryland and 1st Virginia, Lieutenant Colonel Richard Campbell commanding, stormed the Star Fort. The forlorn hope was led by Lieutenant Isaac Duval of the Maryland Line and Lieutenant Samuel Selden of the Virginia Line. Pioneers were in the van with axes to chop through the abatis. The troops rushed into the enemy's five-foot-deep ditch. On their heels were men carrying long poles with hooks at the end to grab and tear down the sandbags on top of the parapet. Riflemen in the tower kept down the heads of the defenders with incessant firing. Inside the ramparts New York and New Jersey provincial regulars awaited their countrymen with bayonets and spears, while some delivered galling enfilading fire through apertures that had been made among the sandbags. While the forlorn hope tried to clear the way, the main body behind them remained in their lines and poured in a continual fire by platoon volleys. Then Major Joseph Green of New York, commanding in the Star Fort, made the key decision of the day.[47]

From the sally port in the rear of the fort two detachments of thirty men each entered the ditch: New Jersey Volunteers commanded by Captain Peter Campbell; New Yorkers from 3rd Battalion, De Lancey's Brigade, Captain Thomas French commanding. Dividing into two parties, they double-timed in opposite directions around the fort. When they came upon the Rebel forlorn hope they pushed bayonets against the Marylanders and Virginians, now beset from two directions. A melee ensued: shouting, cursing men, the clash of steel upon steel, howls as bayonets found their mark. Lieutenants Duvall and Selden were wounded. Selden, trying desperately to pull down sandbags, was hit by a musket ball in his right wrist that "shattered the bone of the limb nearly to the shoulder." Caught between cold steel on each side, ripped by crossfire from the apertures in the ramparts, the forlorn hope tried desperately to hold its ground. General Greene would write to Samuel Huntington, "Never was greater bravery exhibited than by the parties led by Duval and Selden." But it was more than human flesh could endure. The survivors of the forlorn hope withdrew.[48]

Meanwhile, Lee's operation against the Stockade Fort had gone very well. That noble warrior Captain Robert Kirkwood of the Delaware Line commanded the assault. In his journal he reported that the garrison "held out about an hour, but then left it in our full possession." It was a wasted effort. Greene realized that the assault on the Star Fort had failed and ordered a withdrawal of both forces. At sunrise the following day, 19 June, a dejected army, defeated for the third time, broke camp and marched away. It was all over at Ninety Six.[49]

Two matters remained to be dealt with. Amid the joy of the garrison and the gloom of the besiegers a matter of honor between eighteenth-century officers and gentlemen was observed. The guard detail Greene had placed to protect Mrs. Cruger and Mrs. Green was left at its post when the army departed. After Colonel Cruger learned of Greene's withdrawal, he gave the detail a safe-conduct pass so they could rejoin their retreating comrades. And some hours later, Light Horse Harry Lee recalled, Mrs. Cruger hailed a Rebel officer commanding a detachment of light troops that had been "absent some days" as it passed by the farmhouse. The officer and his men were unaware that Greene's army had left and were headed for the old camp. But Mrs. Cruger told the officer "what had happened, and instructed him to overtake the retiring general."[50]

The other matter was grim. It was not over for Lieutenant Samuel Selden of 1st Virginia. The terrible wound to his right arm meant amputation. In those days, in place of modern anesthetics, strong men held the patient down when the surgeon took up the saw. Selden waved them off. As the surgeon was about to begin his grisly work on the bone, Selden held his right hand with his left, "his eyes fixed steadily on it; nor uttered a word till the saw reached the marrow, when in a composed tone and manner he said, 'I pray you Doctor, be quick.'"[51]

Greene's only siege had ended disastrously. Who was to blame?

7

A Bravura Performance

"His Blunders Lost Us Ninety Six"

Light Horse Harry Lee blamed Kosciuszko for the failure. His comments quoted in chapter 6 on neglecting to cut the water supply strongly suggest this. In a footnote in his memoirs Lee left no doubt. "Kosciuszko was extremely amiable, and, I believe a truly good man, nor was he deficient in his professional knowledge, but he was very moderate in talent—not a spark of the ethereal in his composition. His blunders lost us Ninety-Six; and General Greene, much as he was loved and respected, did not escape criticism, for permitting his engineer to direct the manner of approach. It was said, and with some justice, too, that the general ought certainly to have listened to his opinion, but never ought to have permitted the pursuit of error, although supported by professional authority."[1]

The case for Kosciuszko's advising Greene to concentrate on the Star Fort rests on two arguments made by the chief engineer. One held that the Star Fort was the strongest part of Ninety Six's defense system, dominated all the other works, and therefore had to be dealt with first. With regard to the water supply, Kosciuszko wrote that the decision to concentrate on the Star Fort was buttressed "very much by the inteligence broud [brought] that the Enemy had Waills [wells] in every work and Could not be distressed been [by being] Cot of from the spring which could be effected by taking possession of the small redoubt [Stockade Fort]." Greene's first biographer, William Johnson, reinforced Kosciuszko's argument by relating what a member of Greene's military family (probably Otho Williams) related to him. Johnson was told that "the project of cutting off the water had been well weighed and considered, and rejected on mature consideration. There was not a doubt entertained of the practicability of obtaining water by digging in almost any part of the enemy's works. The country was so level and the crown of the hill so little elevated above the bed of the rivulet, that there was no room to doubt this." During the siege of 1775 by Tories, Rebels had found water by digging a well forty feet deep through hard clay inside the Town Stockade. There is no record of such an attempt in 1781, and Cruger's attempt to find water by going twenty-five feet deep inside the Star Fort came up dry. He had to send naked slaves out at night to fetch water from the Spring Branch. Kosciuszko's biographer admits the possibility of Greene's receiving wrong intelligence and Lee's being right. Yet he could not resist scoring Lee by writing, "But it was much easier for Lee to decide the question *post factum,* than for Greene to weigh accurately before he attacked."

One may also ask why Greene did not suspect the crucial nature of the Spring Branch when people were seen going to it for water early in the siege, even before slaves were sent out at night, and why measures were not taken to prevent passage to the source. A teenage partisan at the siege, Thomas Young, wrote many years later that "we could see them very plain when they went out to a brook or spring for water." Acting on their own, Young and "old Squire Kennedy (who was an excellent marksman)" with their rifles "took our position, and as a fellow came down to the spring, Kennedy fired and he fell; several ran out and gathered round him, and among them I noticed one man raise his head, and look round as if he wondered where that shot could have come from. I touched my trigger and *he* fell, and *we* made off, for fear it might be *our* time to fall next."[2]

All of this raises a question. Who was the source of the intelligence that each work had easily available water? It was almost certainly local. Recall from chapter 6 that Lieutenant Henry Haldane, who had laid out the defenses of Ninety Six, immediately observed that the safety of the water supply, the Spring Branch west of town, was vital. And also recall the words of Lieutenant Colonel Isaac Allen of the New Jersey Volunteers: "the works are extensive but in want of water." Their knowledge of the water situation was based on their own observations, but also certainly on local knowledge. Could it be that Greene's inaccurate intelligence came from local people thought to be friends but in fact King's Friends who well knew the vital nature of the Spring Branch but led Greene astray? Although this is pure speculation, the question is intriguing.

And what of Lee's statement that Kosciuszko was "very moderate in talent"? Here the first night's work lends credence to Lee's charge. How could a trained military engineer make such an elementary mistake as recommending the beginning of works for a battery within not just easy range of the enemy's artillery but close enough for infantry to sally, put the bayonet to the sappers, destroy the works, and carry off the entrenching tools? Which we know is precisely what happened. The answer can only be ineptitude.

Greene never blamed Kosciuszko for the failure. In fact, in his Orders of 20 June he thanked the Pole for his efforts, which "would have gained infallible Success, if time had admitted of their being completed." He was probably right that Ninety Six would have fallen given enough time, but that is another "if" of history that need not detain us. Indulging in his habit of blaming others for his defeats, Greene put the onus on Sumter and Marion for failing to gain Rawdon's front, delaying him, and then joining the main army, enabling Greene with increased numbers to intercept Rawdon before he reached Ninety Six and fight him. In his report to Samuel Huntington on the failure of the siege, he wrote that he had detached all of his cavalry "with orders to General Sumter to collect all the force he could and keep in their [Rawdon's] front, and by every means in his power retard their march. Either from bad intelligence or from the difficulty in collecting his force he permitted the Enemy to pass him at the Congaree before he got his troops in motion; afterwards he found it impracticable to gain their front." Although a restrained statement, he let his feelings slip a little in the same letter: "it is almost impossible to draw the militia out of one District into another." A Sumter champion, the South Carolina historian Edward McCrady, admitted that "inaction" by the Gamecock was a factor in Rawdon's unopposed march, although he allowed that it was "caused by his exhaustion from his wound." Both McCrady and Marion's biographer, Hugh Rankin, noted that Rawdon's line of march initially seemed to threaten Fort Granby: Sumter's headquarters, supply depot, and armory. "General Sumter," McCrady wrote, "had remained there . . . until he had ascertained that Lord Rawdon on the 15th had passed Orangeburgh." In private Greene threw aside restraint. In 1811 Andrew Pickens recalled that "The night the siege was raised at Ninety Six, I asked Gen'l Greene if he knew the cause of their [Sumter and Marion's] not harassing the enemy, or their not joining the army. He was much irritated, and expressed himself in a manner I had not heard him before or after."[3]

With regard to militia being unwilling to serve outside their various districts, once again we must remind ourselves that almost all of these men were small farmers whose families lived in isolated circumstances, often in areas where Tories also lived, thus their understandable reluctance to go too far away in perilous times. There were particular occasions during the Rising when militia did campaign far from home. Examples are Georgians and South

Carolinians going as far as northern North Carolina during Cornwallis's pursuit of Greene; Georgians and Over Mountain Men engaging in South Carolina at Musgrove's Mill and other actions; Over Mountain Men participating at Kings Mountain, and in 1776 going as far east as the coast during the failed British attempt to gain a foothold in Charleston Harbor. But on all those occasions British armies were not on the march in the districts in which the various militia units lived, and the frontier over the mountains was relatively quiet. So with Rawdon on the march, which would have encouraged Tories, militia looked first to the safety of their families. Yet we can also sympathize with Greene and his frustrations, for there are times when the greater good demands an extra measure of sacrifice.

Greene did not raise the issue with Sumter in any of his letters of this period, but he was candid in a letter of 25 June to Francis Marion. He would have fought Rawdon had the militia rallied to him, "But being left alone I was obligd to retire. I am surprised that the people should be so averse to joining in some general plan of operation. It will be impossible to carry on the war to advantage or even attempt to hold the Country unless our force can be directed to a point, and as to flying parties here and there they are of no consequence in the great events of war." As to the latter argument, Greene once again seemed not to appreciate the efforts of the partisans in waging guerilla war. At this point in the campaign, however, he was right that it was time for militia commanders to stop acting independently and work with Greene on a "general plan of operation." For "if the people will not be more united in their views they must abide the consequences for I will not calculate upon them at all unless they will agree to act conformable to the great plan of recovering all parts of the Country and not particular parts."[4]

Greene also directed part of the blame for his failure to take Ninety Six upon the governor of Virginia, Thomas Jefferson, and the officials of that state. He had asked Jefferson as early as 23 March to send him 1,500 militiamen. Jefferson replied on 30 March that the council had ordered out half the number Greene requested. But in early May the situation in Virginia changed when Cornwallis marched northward from Wilmington and invaded the state. Virginia officials then canceled Greene's reinforcements and ordered the militia to remain in the state. On 27 June a deeply disappointed Greene wrote to Jefferson that "The tardiness, and finally the countermanding of the Militia ordered to join this army has been attended with the most mortifying and disagreeable consequences." He claimed that their absence had "obliged" him to raise the siege of Ninety Six, and that if the militia had been present the post could have been taken in four days. "For want of the militia the approaches went on slow and the siege was rendered bloody and tedious."

Whether Greene was right that the Virginia militia could have made the difference will never be known. But after paying "high respect ... to the prerogatives of every State" and "with all due deference the propriety of your Excellency's order," Greene once more got to the heart of the matter that bedeviled relations between states and Continental forces throughout the war. "No general plan can ever be undertaken with safety where partial orders may interrupt its progress; nor is it consistent with the common interest that local motives should influence measures for the benefit of a part to the prejudice of the whole." Although he accepted the "prerogative of a Governor" to call out the militia to defend the state's inhabitants, Greene the nationalist then invoked an authority that most state officials would stoutly reject: "But those who are ordered out upon the Continental establishment are only subject to the orders of their [Continental] officers." It was a problem that would not be settled during the Revolutionary War, or afterward during the Confederation period of the new republic.[5]

"I Therefore Resolved to Withdraw the Garrison"

While Greene moved slowly away from Ninety Six, on 21 June, to the jubilation of the garrison, townspeople, and refugees, Lord Rawdon's relief column marched into Ninety Six. At first Rawdon had no intention of chasing Greene in the hope of bringing him to battle, but when he received intelligence that the American army was only sixteen miles away he changed his mind. Leaving behind his baggage, even the soldiers' packs, Rawdon marched on the night of 22 June. Greene wrote that Rawdon's pursuit "had a terrible effect upon the Country, the well affected were flying with their Families in all directions," bringing to mind once again the plight of civilians fleeing the clash of armies in our own time. But the long march from Charleston in the torrid climate, then fast marching in pursuit of Greene, took its toll on Rawdon's men. Forty miles from Ninety Six at the fords of the Enoree River, Rawdon was aware that "Our troops were by that time so overcome with fatigue that I was obliged to halt. Greene, continuing his march across the Tyger and Broad Rivers, left me no further prospect of getting up with him."[6]

Rawdon returned to Ninety Six. The town and garrison were almost out of "stores and provisions," and Rawdon thought "it impossible to furnish it with the necessary supplies. I therefore resolved to withdraw the garrison." He gave Tories in the district a choice. He called together the leading men and proposed that if they would unite and defend the district against Rebel partisans, he would leave a "small party" to assist them. He also promised to send detachments on occasion "in proportion to the force Greene might at any time" move into the district. Families who desired to leave the district could take up residence on abandoned plantations within British lines in the Low Country. To give the people time to think about the choices offered, and also "to provide for the removal of such families" who chose to depart, Rawdon "left the more active part of my force with Lt Colonel Cruger and marched with 800 foot and 60 horse to Congarees."[7]

During his initial march to Ninety Six, Rawdon had written to Balfour that a strong force should be sent to Orangeburg "as a provision against any sinister event." Colonel Gould then agreed to release 3rd Regiment of Foot (Buffs), commanded by Lieutenant Colonel Alexander Stewart, the officer Rawdon thought had "too high an opinion of himself." While Rawdon was still at Ninety Six, Stewart notified him that "he was considerably advanced on his way." This news convinced Rawdon to leave the strong force with Cruger and march with the smaller force and feint a move against Greene's supply depot at Charlotte, thus forcing Greene to fall back there. "Thro' some misapprehension," communications from Charleston stopped Stewart's march and ordered him to withdraw to Dorchester. Rawdon believed Greene had become aware of this and meant to encircle him when he arrived at Orangeburg. Making forced marches, Rawdon reached the Congarees on 1 July.[8]

The Army Will March to "Intercept Lord Rawdon"

Greene indeed wanted to fight Rawdon again. But for that he needed reinforcements. Three days after marching away from Ninety Six, he wrote to Colonel Isaac Shelby, one of the leaders of the Over Mountain Men across the Appalachians in what is now East Tennessee. The Over Mountain Men were ferocious fighters. They were among the Back Country and frontier force that had defeated provincial regulars at Musgrove's Mill, and later again joined with their Back Country comrades to win the pivotal Battle of Kings Mountain. A Tory at that battle who saw them up close during the fighting later described them as appearing "like so many devils from the infernal regions . . . as they darted like enraged lions up the mountain." Relying on Shelby's "zeal and patriotism," Greene asked him to join the Southern Army "in a few days with 1,000 good riflemen well armed and equipped for action." He believed that Shelby had enough "influence" to bring this about. The land where the waters ran west, however, was the cutting edge of the frontier, where the danger of Cherokee attacks ever lurked. Shelby answered on 2 July that the number of men Greene had requested would leave the frontier "greatly exposed" until a treaty could be made with the Cherokees, whose leaders would not be ready for negotiations until 20 July. The harvest, "just now on hand," was another obstacle. Nor could he count on men from the neighboring Virginia mountains, who "are just about to march" against Cornwallis. And a "great number" of the "best men" from the frontier were in Georgia with Colonel Elijah Clarke. But Shelby wanted to help "our suffering friends" in South Carolina. He was also concerned that if British fortunes rose in the Carolinas and Georgia it would prompt "our old inveterate enemies the Cherokees" to attack the frontier settlements. He therefore promised to make the "utmost exertions" to join Greene with the men who could be spared.

One month later Shelby wrote that the treaty with the Cherokees had been concluded, and with 700 "good rifle men well mounted" he was on his way to join the Southern Army when he learned from Andrew Pickens that the British were retreating to Orangeburg and possibly Charleston. The expedition therefore had been suspended. The reason was the refusal of the militia to undertake the mission. For "in those times," wrote William Richardson Davie, it was "absolutely necessary" to explain to the militiamen what was intended and obtain their approval. Both Shelby and his co-leader, Colonel John Sevier [pronounced severe] made this clear in separate letters to Greene. Shelby wrote of "That distance being so very great for us," and Sevier cited "the Unhealthy Season Approaching & the Circumstances of Our Militia Not admitting of a Long tour," the march had been postponed "untill the fall season." Maddening to Greene, of course, but there was nothing he could do about it.[9]

Greene also tried his luck (I use the word deliberately) with the important leader of the Salisbury, North Carolina, militia district, Colonel Francis Locke. He requested that Locke join him with 800 or 1,000 "good militia," and added, "This is absolutely necessary as all the troops coming from the Northward have been halted in Virginia to oppose the enemy in that quarter." He asked for a reply "as soon as possible." If Locke replied, the letter has not been found. Five days later one of Greene's aides, Captain William Pierce Jr., wrote from Charlotte that following Greene's orders he had instructed Locke to join the Southern Army. He continued in a sarcastic vein: "The sentiments of the People seem favorable, they wish you success, and talk of joining you with as much composure as the Councils of our Country do in establishing a plan for raising the Continental Army. They talk of turning out in large numbers and boast of the great exploits they intend to do, but as they are Militia. . . ." (Pierce's final sentence mirrors the opinion of Tory militia by British Ensign John Wilson during the 1779 Georgia campaign and quoted in the Prologue: "whose promises are often like their Boasts.") On 1 July Greene wrote Locke again and stressed the urgency of the situation. "Let me beg of you therefore to march to our assistance as large a reinforcement as possible and I doubt not that we shall drive the Enimy into Charles Town." Greene also sent a

French volunteer, Colonel François Lellorquis, Marquis de Malmedy, to Salisbury, probably to hurry things along. Malmedy reported astounding news: Colonel Locke "has furloughed his militia at home." Because of Greene's request, however, he ordered them out again, and in seven days he promised to have 800 men at Charlotte. That did not happen. On 10 July Malmedy was puzzled why Colonel Locke had not marched on 4 July as he had promised. In fact, when Malmedy "urged him again" to get in motion, it turned out that Locke had yet to order the colonels of the counties in his district to assemble their men. But, of course, he would do so immediately.[10]

By the end of the month, long after Locke and his men were needed, Greene wrote an icy letter to the militia commander. "I am not a little surprisd after the repeated order of Government [Greene meant Governor Thomas Burke of North Carolina] and the several pressing applications I have made to you for a reinforcement of Militia from Salisbury District to find at this late period by information from different quarters that none are on the march. The people must be lost to every sense of duty and to their own safety[,] if they have been properly warned, not to obey the summons, and if they have not been legally warned you must have been criminally negligent." Locke replied on 10 August. He admitted that Greene had criticized him "(with very good reason)" but insisted that he could not force the colonels "of other Counties, or even this County to do as I would fain have them do." North Carolina militia would eventually join the Southern Army, but Locke himself would not arrive until after Greene's last major battle, and then for only a short time. Greene should not have been surprised by this development. During the Race to the Dan in early 1781, Andrew Pickens wrote him that the Salisbury militia "are continually deserting, and no persuasion can prevail with them." He considered them "among the worst men" he had ever commanded.[11]

Nor would Greene receive help from elsewhere, his pleas to militia leaders for naught. He wrote to Lee on 24 June, "It is next to impossible to draw the Militia of this Country from the different parts of the State to which they belong. Marion is below, Pickens I can get no account of, and Sumter wants to make a tour to Moncks Corner, and all I can say to either is insufficient to induce them to join us." And then he added, "Every body seems engaged in moving their families, which is attended with great inconvenience at this time." Yet with two opposing armies on the move, and with Rebel and Tory bands meting out retaliations that often descended into barbarism, what could one expect? The failure of the South Carolina militia to rally to Greene's army confirms our earlier observation that militia in time of peril have what is for them a higher obligation: the safety of their families. And

Greene's comment about Pickens was unfair, for at the time the militia commander was following Greene's orders to lead the army's baggage train to safety. Pickens was also concerned for the safety of his own family, who with their personal belongings were with him. He then made a bold decision. His home was only twenty miles from Ninety Six. Yet he proceeded to make a strong symbolic statement that the army could protect people by sending his family home. Writing just after the war, the historian David Ramsay believed Pickens's action "saved the country in the vicinity from depopulation and the army . . . from sustaining a great diminution of their numbers, by the desertion of the militia to take care of their families."[12]

At the time that he abandoned the siege of Ninety Six, Greene was also much concerned that in his opinion the British had attained a superiority in cavalry. His keen appreciation of the vital importance of cavalry in the South is once again revealed in a letter to George Washington written two days after the army left Ninety Six. "My fears are from the Enemys superior Cavalry. To the Northward Cavalry is nothing from the numerous fences but to the Southward a disorder by a superior Cavalry may be improved into a defeat, and a defeat into a route." On 1 May, nearly three weeks before the siege of Ninety Six had begun, Greene wrote to Baron von Steuben ordering all the dragoons in Virginia "fit for duty" to join him, for his own dragoons are "much broke down." The next day he reminded Governor Abner Nash of North Carolina that "In my last [13 April] I requested a number of Cavalry horses[;] the service is so severe our horses are almost wore out. The Enemy have a great superiority in the field."

Greene and Cornwallis were as one on this issue. "Without good cavalry we can do nothing in this country," his Lordship had written back in 1780. Draft horses to pull wagons were also critically important. In that earlier letter, Greene had asked in addition for "a couple of hundred" draft horses to replace those "that are dayly failing by hard service in collecting provisions." Yet several weeks later it appears that no draft horses had been sent. Greene's quartermaster, Colonel Edward Carrington, wrote to his deputy, Colonel Nicholas Long of North Carolina, for 200 "at least," for "Our Draught Horses are failing us fast, from excessive service," and "I beg you" to supply only "such as are strong, & perfectly fit for service."

To augment his cavalry, Greene had long wanted to authorize one of Marion's militia officers, Major Hezekiah Maham, whom Lee held in high regard, to "raise of a Corps of horse." But in the absence of South Carolina's governor, John Rutledge, under whose authority the militia operated, he had put it off. Given his view of the situation, however, with the enemy "endeavoring to increase their Cavalry," Greene decided to act on his own. He sent Maham a "Lieutenant Col Commandants" commission and authorized him to raise and equip a corps of 160 enlisted men to serve for one year and to be paid "not less" than Continental cavalry, which was $8⅓ per month—when they were paid, which was seldom if ever. He apparently wrote a similar letter to Colonel Peter Horry, another of Marion's officers. Horry readily agreed but wanted it understood that even though he would be commanding militia cavalry, he insisted upon retaining his prized Continental rank as an infantry officer, to which Greene assented. Maham and Horry would later engage in a feud that drove Greene and Marion to distraction.[13]

It must be noted that in his memoirs Lee indirectly contradicted Greene's claim that the enemy's cavalry was superior. Although Rawdon had, "during his repose in the lower country, contrived to strengthen himself by a newly raised corps of horse under Major [John] Coffin, he did not . . . derive any material good from this accession of force." During Rawdon's temporary pursuit of Greene described earlier, "no attempt was hazarded against" the American cavalry acting as Greene's rear guard. Lee claimed that the rear guard, "conscious of its superior cavalry, retired slowly, always keeping the British van in view." Lee added in a footnote that Coffin's corps "was badly mounted—small meager horses being the only sort procurable. The best officers and riders, thus mounted, cannot stand tolerable cavalry, much less such as then occupied our rear."[14]

So who was right? Greene was right in his continual quest for good dragoon horses. Cavalry was crucial in the South and the service was hard. Lee, on the other hand, was noted for mounting his men well. Although the cruel privations undergone by the Southern Army were real for both men and horses, on occasion Greene was prone to exaggeration. Whoever was right on which cavalry was superior, a dramatic event with regard to horses would soon occur.

Despite his desire to fight Rawdon, Greene wrote to Lee on 25 June that Lee and Sumter should move into the "lower country," that Lee could act as his "judgment may direct," and that "The Southern Army will move towards the Wateree and prepare to take post upon the high hills of Santee." Six days later he changed his mind. For Lee had written him on 30 June that Rawdon had left Ninety Six and "is on his march to the Congaree (Fort Granby)" with fewer than 500 men. Lee's informant was a Tory officer who had mistaken Lee's troops for the British and was captured. The next day Greene wrote to Francis Marion, "We shall march . . . towards the Congaree in the morning." Greene's "last intelligence was that Lord Rawdon was moving towards the Congaree with only 400 Men. If so he may be defeated with great ease. Dont spare any pains to collect your force as it is my determination to give the enemy battle the moment I can collect our force." At 3:00 A.M., 2 July, the Southern Army marched to "intercept Lord Rawdon."[15]

"A Commander of Such Talent, Constancy, and Resource"

Rawdon in the meantime had left Ninety Six on 29 June. "I arrived at Congarees on the 1st of July, having made forced marches in hopes of surprizing a corps of militia at that place." According to Lieutenant Colonel William Washington, who was in the area with his dragoons, Rawdon arrived "last Night about 11 O'Clock" at "the Fort below Friday's Ferry," that is, the site of old Fort Granby, which Lee and Marion had taken earlier in the year. He estimated Rawdon's force at 1,000 to 1,200, which was too high. Rawdon paid a price for fast marching in the stifling heat. Fifty men died of heat exhaustion on the way. And instead of the corps of militia he had hoped to surprise, "I soon learned that the enemy's light troops were in our neighborhood." It was Captain Joseph Eggleston and a detachment of horse and foot from Light Horse Harry Lee's Legion and North Carolina. Eggleston independently confirmed that Rawdon had more men than the 500 Lee had reported to Greene, and he came very close to the mark with a figure of 870, 10 more than Rawdon had reported to Cornwallis. Lee himself was thirteen miles from Rawdon. He ordered Eggleston with thirty dragoons to join with a previously assigned reconnaissance party of infantry, under Major John Armstrong of North Carolina, and proceed during the night, to "gain the forage country & to seek an opportunity for striking at the enemys foragers." Eggleston deployed "in a secret and convenient position" two miles to Rawdon's front. The next morning, 3 July, Rawdon's cavalry came out to forage. Lee's report to Greene was gleeful. Eggleston's scouts saw "the main body of the British horse" approaching. Lee correctly implied that the British were enticed: "the enemy presuming on a militia prize pushed on with vigor." They "were met with great gallantry, & were in a few moments entirely defeated, & pursued to the picquets of the [British] army." Lee reported that three officers and forty-five privates, their horses, arms, and accouterments, were captured, and only "one man escaped." The "Enemys superior Cavalry" evaporated. With only minor discrepancies, Rawdon confirmed Lee's version of the action. "On the 3rd, our cavalry having contrary to express order gone out by themselves to forage, they suddenly found themselves surrounded. . . . Two officers and forty dragoons with their horses and appointments fell into the hands of the enemy without any loss on their part."[16]

Rawdon seemed to be in peril. Without a cavalry screen, he could not keep enemy cavalry at a proper distance to avoid annoyances or mask his intentions.

He wrote that "I clearly saw the enemy's design." If he meant that he expected Greene to come up on his rear, he was right. Greene wrote to Colonel Washington on the day when Rawdon lost most of his cavalry that he was marching to the Congaree via Winnsboro, where he would leave his baggage train so the troops can "move rapidly." He wanted Washington and Lee to stop Rawdon from "receiving reinforcements or crossing the Congaree." But Rawdon did not have to cross the Congaree River, for his march had taken him south of the river to old Fort Granby. Congaree Creek was the physical barrier confronting him. But Rawdon was up to adversity. He reacted immediately after his cavalry vanished. Congaree Creek was two miles from his position. It was "broad," he reported, "in most parts deep, and the banks difficult." Lee had maneuvered skillfully and was positioned on the opposite bank of the creek. He had destroyed the bridge and felled trees across the ford. Rawdon reached Congaree Creek at noon. He believed his "approach was unexpected" by the Rebels because of the "violent heat." A "few ineffectual shots" failed to stop the British: "we threw over a body of infantry . . . the enemy immediately dispersed and left us at liberty to clear the fords without interruption." Rawdon then continued his march south in the direction of Orangeburg.[17]

"The whole evening," Lee later wrote, "was spent in rapid movement." Although Rawdon was across Congaree Creek, Lee was "confident . . . of being immediately joined by Sumter, Marion, and Washington, when a serious combined effort would have been made to stop the progress of the enemy." None of them appeared, however, "nor," Lee wrote, "was any communication received from either." At nine o'clock that evening, Rawdon stopped for the night, as did Lee. At first light Rawdon was on the move again. As his van appeared, Lee withdrew, still on Rawdon's front, still hoping to rendezvous with Washington and the partisan bands. Some thirty miles from the Congaree Lee took a position behind Beaver Creek. In Lee's estimation, "here was the last point where the junction was practicable." Reinforcements not appearing, Lee had to turn away from Rawdon's front, and the intrepid Anglo-Irishman continued his march unmolested to Orangeburg, where he hoped to meet Colonel Stewart with 3rd Foot (Buffs).[18]

Francis Marion was the only one in a position to either stop or delay Stewart's march. He wrote to Greene on 7 July that he would move on Stewart and attempt "to do something to him or at least prevent him from Joining Rawdon." He also informed Greene that one of his detachments had taken prisoners who told them that Rawdon's troops were "so fatigued they cannot possibly move," and that three regiments were "going to Lay down their Arms & they believe they will today if they are orderd to March." Marion had received faulty intelligence. Despite the fifty men who had collapsed and died under heat beyond their imaginations, their comrades persevered and kept marching. Soldiers gripe continually. That is a given of military life. But with rare exceptions, when ordered to move on they do so, cursing, grumbling, often hating their officers . . . but they move on, as Rawdon's men in their woolen uniforms did through the terrible ordeal of the Deep South in high summer.[19]

Meanwhile, Marion as promised moved on Stewart. Unfortunately, he took the wrong road. He marched at 1:00 A.M. on 8 July, scouts out to warn of danger. He was on the road usually taken by those on their way to Orangeburg. Stewart, however, for reasons unknown, took a little-used road parallel to Marion's, and like ships passing in the night without running lights both forces continued on almost undisturbed. Stewart did lose three wagons loaded with rum and wine to Peter Horry's detachment, which probably discomfited officers and men more than the heat. In his report to Greene, Marion repeated his earlier assertion that Rawdon's troops were ready to "Lay down their Arms . . . most of them was Exceedingly Discontented."[20]

Heat and hunger affected horses as well as men and led to assignments not being carried out as Greene had ordered. Marion wrote on 10 July that he could not join Greene as he was forty miles from Beaver Creek and his horses were worn out for "being two days without forage or grass." Andrew Pickens had horse problems, but he was also distracted by events in the far Back Country. He had been instructed by Greene to watch Cruger at Ninety Six and discover his intentions. Pickens reported on 6 July that his horses were "much worn down from the long march" and were "intiarly unfit to perform the service of discovering the enemys movements or even to gett out of their way should they prove too powerfull for us." But he had sent a detachment back to the area around Ninety Six "to make discoveries and if possible to find out the movement and intentions of the enemy." On 10 July he wrote that Captain Joseph Towles, whom he had sent to gather intelligence, had just returned with his report. Cruger's wagons were "Loaded with the Baggage, & the horses Geer'd" as of 1:00 P.M. on the 9th. A Rebel spy had entered Ninety Six the next day and actually talked to John Harris Cruger. The British would march "this morning." Pickens promised to do everything possible to harass Cruger, but his horses were "Reduced by the heat" and "want of Furrage." Yet he pursued Cruger to about forty miles west of Orangeburg, until he received reports "that very strong parties of Indians and Tories was Murdering the Frontier Inhabiters," and "haveing but a Dull Prospect of doing Cruger much Dammage for sundery Reasons, I march'd to the relief of them settlements."[21]

Greene himself had gone ahead of the army on either 4 or 5 July "with a proper escort to form an opinion to what point it will be best to move the troops to." General Isaac Huger was left in temporary command while

Greene joined William Washington's dragoons to scout the countryside. He wrote a letter to Huger on 7 July that arrived the following day. The letter has not been found, but it confused Huger as well as Greene's aide, Captain William Pierce Jr. Pierce wrote to Greene that day, "We are at a loss for a full construction of your letter." Greene's adjutant, Colonel Otho Holland Williams, who was with the army, wrote on the same day that "In consequence of your Letter" to Huger "the army march'd last night" and arrived at Howell's Ferry on the Congaree "about 11 oClock and have been crossing ever since in three Small Canoes and a very Old Flatt which just now sunk. We have got the Flatt on shore and the Artificers are about repairing her." Once across, "The army will march immediately to Bever Creek." Williams was obviously nervous in Greene's absence. He admitted ignorance about the geography of the area and the locations and movements of Lee and Washington. And of Greene. "But where you are, or where you expect to pick up Col Stewart I have no intelligible idea." He finished with a plaintive plea. "I wish you cou'd rejoin the Army before it comes into any critical circumstance."[22]

Greene was back with the army by at least 9 July. Rawdon was then in Orangeburg. He sent orders to Cruger to join him as quickly as possible. The day after his arrival Stewart joined him with 3rd Foot (Buffs). On the same day Rawdon learned that Greene had crossed the Congaree and "was advancing against us." Greene was now ready to fight. As Otho Holland Williams put it, "A junction of the whole formed a very respectable little army." For at long last Greene had been "joined by Generals Sumter and Marion with about 1000 Men composed of State Troops and Militia," whereupon "we began our march on the 11th to attack the Enemy at Orangeburg." On 12 July Greene came "within four miles of Orangeburg," Williams wrote, "where we halted, and lay the 12th instant from about nine o'clock in the morning till six in the afternoon." The troops were issued rum "To refresh themselves and prepare for Action."[23]

Reconnaissance of Rawdon's position was then conducted by Greene himself at the head of the cavalry of Lee and Washington and accompanied by his senior officers. Greene's inspection "was made with great attention and close to the enemy," Lee wrote, for without cavalry Rawdon was unable to keep the reconnaissance party at a distance. That, however, put Rawdon in good stead, for it led to close appraisal of his deployment. Four days later, his memory fresh, Otho Williams wrote that Greene found Rawdon's position "materially different from what it had been represented. The ground is broken, and naturally strong, from the Court-house (which is two stories high and built of brick), to a bridge four or five hundred yards distant, the only pass over the Edisto within many miles." After the war, Lee recalled that Rawdon had stationed infantry in the courthouse, which Greene described as "not inferior to a good Redoubt." Lee also remembered "several other houses commanding the river, to the southern banks of which he [Rawdon] could readily retire uninjured should he think proper to avoid battle until Lieutenant-Colonel Cruger should join." A second obstacle, as Lee noted, was that the American cavalry, "from the nature of the ground and the disposition of the enemy, could not be brought to take its part in the action," and thus Greene would lack "an essential portion" of his army. Williams also pointed out that Cruger, with his own garrison and the rest of Rawdon's force, was marching to join Rawdon. Lee wrote that Cruger was "daily expected." As for Rawdon, he had prepared for battle. Being without cavalry, he deployed to force Greene into a "direct attack" by "throwing both our flanks upon the" North Fork of the Edisto River.[24]

Nevertheless, some of Greene's officers recommended attacking. But according to Lee the majority were against it. So was Greene. He wrote to Thomas McKean, the new president of the Continental Congress, "Could we have got them out into the open Country we could have cut them to pieces in a few minutes. But secured on one side by an impassable River, and covered on the other by strong buildings little was to be expected from an attack." He also knew that Ninety Six had been evacuated, which "was one great object of our Manouvre." He decided to detach Lee's cavalry to join Sumter and Marion on an operation against the lower posts "in hopes to force the Enemy in Orangeburg to retire into the lower Country for the protection of those posts." So instead of attacking, Greene wisely deployed to offer Rawdon an opportunity to attack him. Just as wisely, Otho Williams wrote, Rawdon "declined the opportunity." That evening Greene withdrew, "so rapidly," Rawdon reported, "that under the cover of his light troops he had secured his passage back across the Congaree before I was apprised of his retreat."[25]

Greene marched north on his way to the High Hills of Santee, described by a South Carolina historian as a "salubrious and delightful region." The High Hills, where grain was plentiful, were about 200 feet above the north bank of the Santee River and stretched some twenty miles south of Camden. There Greene would establish a camp of repose "to refresh the army," which had been either engaged with the enemy or in motion since shortly after the Battle of Guilford Courthouse in mid-March. It was just as well. The army was worn out. One example should suffice. Captain Robert Kirkwood's Delaware Continentals, detached to Lee's cavalry at the siege of Ninety Six after Lee arrived from Augusta, between then and leaving the vicinity of Orangeburg had marched 313 miles in enervating heat. And food was scarce in the vicinity of Orangeburg: "never did we suffer so severely as during the few days' halt here," wrote Lee. The troops were often reduced to living on what nature provided, as described by Lee in his inimitable style.

Rice furnished our substitute for bread, which, although tolerably relished by those familiarized to it from infancy, was very disagreeable to the Marylanders and Virginians, who had grown up in the use of corn and wheat bread. Of meat, we literally had none; for the few meager cattle brought to camp as beef would not afford more than one or two ounces per man. Frogs abounded in some neighboring ponds, and on them chiefly did the light troops subsist. They became in great demand from their nutritiousness; and after conquering the existing prejudice, were diligently sought after. Even the alligator was used by a few; and, very probably, had the army been much longer detained on that ground, might had rivaled the frog in the estimation of our epicures.[26]

The evening after Greene marched away, Cruger arrived in Orangeburg, bringing with him the "loyalists of the Ninety Six District." It was the usual sad column of refugees, laden with all the belongings they could bring with them. Left behind were hearth and home, where they had endured backbreaking labor to establish themselves in a new country. At least 800 men of the Ninety Six brigade of militia were with Cruger, and some were accompanied by their families. They had decided to seek a "situation where they would be secure against the savage cruelty of the rebel militia." As our story progresses, however, we should remember the rest of Rawdon's sentence: "after which the men proposed to embody and make incursions into the disaffected settlements."[27]

It had been a bravura performance by young Rawdon, who was ill with malaria throughout the operation. "Fortunate it was," wrote Sir John Fortescue, historian of the British Army, "that a commander of such talent, constancy, and resource as Rawdon had been at hand to take charge of the scattered posts in Carolina after Cornwallis's reckless abandonment of them, and to bring at any rate a great part of them into Charleston." Now, however, we must take leave of this twenty-six-year-old soldier, for "the total failure of my health obliges me now with great regret to make use of the leave of absence which the Commander in Chief had the goodness to grant me at the beginning of the year." Francis, Lord Rawdon, later 1st Marquis of Hastings and 2nd Earl of Moira, would go on to an illustrious career and in India become one of the builders of the Second British Empire.[28]

It is now time to consider an operation by another commander and decide whether he deserves plaudits or censure.

8

Dog Days

"Push Your Operations Night and Day"

At Ninety Six Greene once again had been bested tactically. Yet once again he was the strategic victor. The last British post in the far Back Country had been evacuated. Writing to Cornwallis in early June, before his march upcountry to the relief of Ninety Six, Rawdon had laid out his new plan. "By making the Congaree our frontier and transplanting our friends from the Back Country to the rich plantations within that boundary whose owners are in arms against us, I think we may with few troops secure and command a tract which must in the end give law to the rest of the province." That plan was now in shambles. A Rebel raid in strength to within fifteen miles of Charleston, to be described shortly, did profound psychological damage to the royal cause. And many of the refugees from the Ninety Six District, the backbone of Tory strength in the distant Back Country, ended up not on "rich plantations" but in displaced persons camps.[1]

While Greene marched from an area of little food to find a camp of rest and repose in the High Hills of Santee, Thomas Sumter was also in motion. He led not only his brigade but, for the first time in the field, Marion's Brigade and Light Horse Harry Lee's Legion cavalry. Sumter's mission, Greene wrote, was "to attack their [British] lower posts at Moncks Corner and Dorchester ... by which we were in hopes to Force the enemy at Orangeburg to retire into the lower Country for the protection of those posts." Sumter had earlier contemplated such an expedition, and Greene at that time had ordered Marion to "call out all the force you can and cooperate with him in any manner he may direct." Greene had informed Lee of Sumter's plan and given him discretion to act as his "judgment may direct," with all that implies. That took place prior to Greene's decision to pursue Rawdon. Now, however, with Greene and the army definitely headed for the High Hills of Santee, Sumter's expedition began. Greene sent him off with an eighteenth-century pep talk: "push your operations night and day. . . . tell Colonel Lee to thunder even at the gates of Charlestown. I have high expectations of your force and enterprise. Nothing can deprive you of complete success but the want of time."[2]

Sumter was described by his biographer as the "nominal head" of the expedition. Given the cast of characters, that is an excellent description. Until then, Marion had treated joining forces with Sumter like avoiding the Black Death. Added to this toxic mix, Sumter and Lee disliked each other. The Gamecock began his march on 12 July with between 1,000 and 1,100 men and one field piece served by veteran Continental gunners. The field piece will become a key part of our story. All were mounted: the militiamen of Sumter and Marion and Lee's Legion horse. The raid was given the name Dog Days Expedition in 1855 by the South Carolina writer William Gilmore Simms in *The Forayers, or, The Raid of the Dog-days*. The dog days comprise the period from about 3 July to 11 August, before the rise of Sirius, the dog star, and is described by the *Oxford English Dictionary* "from ancient times as the hottest and most unwholesome period of the year." The primary target was the British post at Monck's Corner, about thirty-two miles from Charleston, where 19th Regiment of Foot, Colonel James Coates commanding, was stationed. The 19th, about 600 strong, was one of the newly arrived regiments from Ireland. The men had never seen action but they were trained and under the usual strict discipline. Coates had been reinforced by about 150 mounted South Carolina Rangers. The post was located at Biggin Church, the nickname for the parish church of St. John's, Berkeley. Sumter later reported "Church Walls three Bricks & one half thick" and the position encircled with two rows of abatis.[3]

Sumter got in motion in the vicinity of Orangeburg. It was approximately sixty-six miles to Monck's Corner. The situation called for keeping his force together and marching rapidly to Monck's Corner to surprise 19th Foot by descending on Biggin Church so quickly the British would be prevented from evacuating the post and getting away. Given his numbers, Sumter did not have to worry about small enemy forces, and he could have sent out a few small reconnaissance parties to make sure that Rawdon did not move suddenly in his direction. Instead, Sumter chose to take his time and weaken his command by dispatching too many large detachments on various assignments. Three days after he marched he wrote Greene that Colonel Hezekiah Maham, whom he had "Detach'd, as a party of observation," reported British reinforcements, including "all the Horse they could possibly collect," perhaps 150, at Monck's Corner. Maham's report together with the "large Detachments I have out occasions me to move wt the greatest causion & all the Allacrity in my power." (How one moves with caution and alacrity simultaneously is an interesting question.) Lee's cavalry, followed by some 200 riders commanded by Colonel Wade Hampton of Sumter's Brigade, was well ahead of the main body and ever closer to Charleston. According to Sumter, Hampton "was to have fallen in the Rear of Colo Lee near Dorchester," which was about nineteen miles from Charleston. After leaving a "Strong observation Detachm't" at Four Holes Bridge, Hampton went "in quest of Colo Lee" but could not find him. (With regard to the "Detachm't" at Four Holes Bridge, Sumter may have meant one commanded by Wade Hampton's brother, Colonel Henry Hampton, as he wrote in his letter of 15 July to Greene.) Sumter claimed that Lee either told or sent word to Hampton that he would contact him at Goose Creek Bridge, some sixteen miles below Monck's Corner and about eighteen miles from Charleston. Hampton rode there, took the bridge without opposition, and the next day surrounded nearby St. James Church on Goose Creek during Sunday services and captured the entire congregation, many of whom were Tories. He paroled the Tories but kept their horses. Sumter wrote, "after Colo Hampton's waiting there sometime and being altogether disappointed by Colo Lee; he procedded down," that is, toward Charleston. Wade Hampton was closing in on the "Neck," the narrow isthmus between the Ashley and Cooper Rivers that connects Charleston to the state beyond. At the northern end of the isthmus was a well-known tavern, Quarter House, only some 5.6 miles from Charleston's gates. Sumter reported that Captain William Reid, leading Hampton's advance of twelve men, "discovered some British Dragoons drawn up at Quarter-House; upon which he made so Gallant & Spirited a Charge as broke them; & being follow'd by the main body, they kill'd wounded & took the whole saving two." Sumter did not mention that the eighteen British Dragoons were convalescents who were preparing to flee Quarter House. Hampton had one man killed, Captain John Wright, and after the British surrender the commander of the convalescents, Lieutenant David Waugh, was killed, probably in retaliation. Hampton also burned two schooners, probably at Strawberry Ferry, one loaded with indigo, and took another thirty-odd prisoners. Some of Hampton's men then proceeded down the Neck to within two miles of Charleston's gates. The alarm sounded in the city, whereupon Hampton "thought it prudent" to withdraw. Sumter implied that it was all Lee's fault, that it was Hampton's being detained at Goose Creek waiting for Lee to appear that warned the enemy of his approach. This seems far-fetched. The British had certainly been warned of Hampton's proximity before he tarried at Goose Creek. The detachments he had sent all over the countryside could not have been missed and unreported. Sumter's dislike of Light Horse Harry colored his report. (As noted above, the feeling was reciprocated.) In a withering sentence, Sumter wrote to Greene, "Colo Lee was to have taken the Dorchester Rout[,] have done what he cou'd there, & proceeded down to the Chars Town Gates, but he altogether failed in this business."[4]

Not true. Near Dorchester Lee had captured "all the waggon horses" of Rawdon's supply convoy and four wagons. Three were empty, but one was "laden with ammunition for artillery." The post at Dorchester was either "broken up," as Lee put it in his memoirs, or abandoned by its garrison. Lee sent a small detachment "below the Quarter-house in the Neck," with the hope that being near Charleston would lead to an "advantageous stroke." Alas, "none of the usual visits to the Quarter-house took place" that day, "nor was even a solitary officer picked up in their customary morning rides." Lee did not embellish his minor victories, labeling them and the actions of the other detachments as "trivial successes"—except for Wade Hampton's, whose achievements were described by Lee as "the most important."[5]

Sumter had also sent out other detachments "to Approach and Attack the Enemy," and "large Detachments to prevent the Enemy getting further Succor, & to throw every Impediment in their way shou'd they Attempt to retreat." He was ready to move with his main force and the artillery piece when on 15 July he "recd Accounts that the Enemy were at Murray's Ferry, in consequence of which I Detach'd 300 this morning," but now "I am informed they are gone again." He was then at a place called The Rocks on the Santee River, some twenty-five miles from Monck's Corner. He wrote that had it not been for the Murray's Ferry report he would have been on the march.[6]

"It Was the Most Daring Thing I Ever Heard Of"

On Sunday 15 July, Sumter sent Colonel Peter Horry of Marion's Brigade on a reconnaissance mission to gauge the British position and strength at Monck's Corner and "also," Sumter wrote, "to destroy Wadboo Bridge and force a picquet they had thereat." The picket was probably at Biggin Bridge, and an attempt by Colonel Horry to dislodge it failed. Wadboo Bridge crossed a creek of that name and was on the British avenue of retreat from Monck's Corner. Its demolition was assigned to Major Hezekiah Maham. Although Sumter thought Maham had carried out his mission, the damage done to Wadboo Bridge was superficial and would be easily repaired by the British.[7]

As Horry's force approached Biggin Church the following day, 16 July, the British cavalry "came out in force and full charge." Sumter reported that the veteran partisan commander Colonel Edward Lacey "broke the Enemy's charge with the Rifelmen of his Regemt." Then, by Sumter's own admission, Colonel Coates outmaneuvered the Gamecock. Sumter tells how in clear detail. "After this Scirmish Colo Horry discovered the Enemy advancing in force. In Consequence of which he retreated to fall in with me. I was then approaching: but when informed of this I thought it adviseable to retrograde a little to a defile which I had left in my rear, & await their coming up, it being a very advantageous position; but to my Mortification it turn'd out to be a covering Manuever for they avacuated in the Night." How ironic that Sumter, known for his aggressive tactics, on this occasion allowed Coates to steal a march on him by being cautious.[8]

It was 3:00 A.M. on the 17th before the Rebels discovered that the British had flown the coop, and that was only because they spotted flames consuming Biggin Church and British supplies and baggage, almost certainly left behind to allow fast marching. A British officer wrote, "On the march we lost every atom of Baggage we had. All the Officers baggage, Mens Tents, Knapsacks, Blanketts etc. etc. were all burnt, destroyed or pillaged."[9]

During the night Coates led his men southeast to the partially damaged Wadboo Bridge, which the British repaired and crossed, then destroyed again, and kept marching eastward in the general direction of Charleston. "We marched all that night," wrote Captain David John Bell of 19th Foot. Sumter arrived at Biggin Church an hour after sighting the flames. He had no idea of Coates's location. In his memoir Lee blamed this on the militia who had failed to render Wadboo Bridge impassable, and compounded their error by not remaining on the ground to oppose a crossing as well as inform Sumter of Coates's route. Sumter sent out scouts in every direction, "many of whom are perfectly acquainted with the ground & Neighborhood for Miles round." When Sumter was informed of Coates's route, he wrote to Greene, "I . . . shall parsue Instantly." In the van as he marched were Lee and his Legion cavalry, Colonel Wade Hampton with Sumter's cavalry, and some of Marion's mounted partisans. With regard to the last, according to Sumter, "Marian's Brigd diminished fast from the time I left you. When we overtook the Enemy, he had Scarcely 100 left." But Sumter's decision to leave the field piece behind in the interest of speed was a far more serious matter.[10]

There now ensued a chase of eighteen to twenty miles from Biggin Church to Quinby Bridge. According to Lee, three miles from Quinby Bridge the pursuers spotted what Lee described as Coates's rear guard of some 100 infantrymen with baggage wagons. Captain Colin Campbell commanded. Captain Bell portrayed the detail as numbering about sixty, "part of the Rear Guard, Sick Stragglers, etc. etc." Lee ordered his cavalry to take "close order" and detached Captain Eggleston with one troop to the left to "turn the enemy's right." The British deployed for battle. Lee's bugler sounded the charge and the Legion cavalry supported by Hampton's and Marion's militia horse "rushed upon them with drawn swords at full gallop." As they bore down on the British line the horsemen could hear the order to fire. But the sight facing the raw recruits of 19th Foot, the solid line of horses galloping at them, hooves drumming the ground, raised sabers, shrill yells of riders ringing in the air—it was all too much for men who had never seen battle. Lee wrote that the British infantrymen, "without discharging a single musket, threw down their arms and begged for quarters." The charging horsemen reined in, quarter was granted, and neither side suffered casualties in what could have been a bloody melee.[11]

Leaving the prisoners guarded by some militia horse, Lee rode on with his cavalry down the road toward Quinby Bridge. But Captain Campbell, no doubt mortified at the craven behavior of his troops, had ordered them to again take up their arms. Lee had not gone far when a courier reached him with the news. Light Horse Harry immediately returned to deal with the situation. Writing many years later, Lee maintained that all of this took place out of sight and sound of Colonel Coates and the main body of 19th Foot, and that Colonel Coates did not know that he was being pursued. Yet Captain Bell, writing about three weeks after the action, stated that it took place "within three hundred yards of the Regiment." Bell's statement trumps Lee's recollection. Meanwhile, in Lee's absence Captain John Armstrong with the first section of Legion cavalry arrived at Quinby Bridge, where he found 19th Foot on the other side of Quinby Creek. Lee wrote that the British had partially dismantled the bridge and were waiting for the rear guard to cross before completing the destruction. Lee also maintained that though Armstrong sent word back of his location, he did not inform Lee that he was at the bridge. Lee apparently assumed Armstrong was in open countryside. Lee sent his adjutant to Armstrong and "warmly reminded him of the order of the day, which was to fall upon the foe without respect to consequences." In an oft-repeated story, Lee then followed up with a rousing description of the "brave Armstrong putting spur to horse" and with his section galloping across the partially dismantled bridge, sending loose planks flying into the river. He then claimed that Lieutenant George Carrington's second section followed Armstrong by leaping over the chasm to join his comrade and engage the enemy. Lee's account reads like a boy's adventure novel of my youth.[12]

In his report to Greene four days after the action, Sumter makes no mention of planks flying beneath the hooves of charging horses or daring riders leaping a chasm, but he was generous in his tribute to Armstrong: "Further that the Charge made by the Gallant Capt Armstrong of Colo Lee's Corps ... was thro' their whole line of March, in which he lost 2 dragoons killed." And as if anticipating Lee's future fiction, he added, "this Adroit Exploit needs no colouring." Sumter implied that Lee also failed on this occasion: "Had the whole of the Cavalry gone thro' with its Charge, it's most probable that they wou'd have Captured the Enemy." That we can never know and is probably an exaggeration. But Lee's performance was not stellar. Four days after Sumter's initial report, Greene contradicted Lee's *Memoir* in his report to the president of the Continental Congress. Greene wrote that Lee had been "informed that the Enemy had crossed Quinby Bridge and were in a Lane with their Artillery. Lee sent forward an order to the Legion to halt, but before the order could reach the advanced Corps Capt Armstrong had passed the Bridge; which the Enemy were endeavoring to take up, and was charging their line."

Greene continued. "He drove them from their Artillery but the Musquetry beginning a heavy fire obliged him to file off, into the Woods not having advanced up to the Lane. He had two Men and 4 Horses killed, and Major Mayham [Hezekiah Maham] who was with the advance had his Horse killed under him." Greene also paid tribute to Armstrong and his men: "Nothing can equal the gallantry of this troop." Captain Bell of 19th Foot, who witnessed the action, agreed with Sumter and Greene. After crossing the bridge "a little after daybreak ... we thought ourselves safe & took a little rest, but about nine O'Clock a party of Rebels galloped over the Bridge in the face of our Field Piece, rode through the Regiment & wounded two Men: it was the most daring thing I ever heard of: one of them made a stroke at the Colonel which he turned of[f] with his Hanger [short sword]. McPherson instantly brought him down ... with ... a plain common Muskett Shot." As usual, Lee told a good story, but Armstrong's feat did not need embellishing. Sumter got it right when he wrote, "this Adroit Exploit needs no colouring," which makes one wonder whether Lee gushed about Armstrong's feat in Sumter's presence.[13]

"I Will Never More Serve a Single Hour under You"

Despite the drama of Armstrong's charge, the preliminary action at Quinby Bridge was minor in contrast to what happened next. On the British side of Quinby Creek was Quinby Plantation, also referred to as Shubrick's. There Colonel Coates deployed his regiment. Sumter described "Their position ... [as the] most Advantageous that cou'd have fallen in their way, lodged in a long line of Houses on an Emminence," whereas "my troops had some of them small coverings such as fences & a few small Houses." The British Captain Bell described the situation of the houses as on "a very commanding Height." Today one looks in vain for that "commanding Height." Given Low Country topography we can interpret it to mean a slight rise in the ground. Now Sumter's decision to leave his field piece behind came into play. Marion noted in his letter to Greene that the houses had "Clay Walls which was very Difficult to penetrate without a field piece (the one we had was sent back from the Church) and where Our Cavaldry Could not possibly act." The situation called for infantry if an assault was to be made on the strong British position. Lee and his cavalry played no further part in the fighting.[14]

On 18 July Sumter came up and from five o'clock in the afternoon until sunset, a period of about three hours, directed the action. He had about 1,100 men against Coates's 350. True to form, against an enemy that Sumter himself described as being in a strong defensive position, he ordered his troops forward. Marion reported his part of the action to Greene. "[I] was Orderd to Advance with my Brigade on the Left." He described the ground he advanced over as "intirely open." About fifty yards from the British position, Marion's men took what little cover they could behind a fence and delivered "a very heavy fire." Coates's men, from "shelter in and behind the houses," fired upon Marion's line "from the stoop of the Houses & through the doors windows & Corners." For the action at the plantation, Marion reported to Greene that he had five men killed and ten wounded. Eight days after the battle, in a letter to Greene, Sumter blamed Marion for his own losses. "Genl Marion . . . Suffered Considerably by Soposing the enemy Could Not fier upon his men when Moving up in a Certain direction." Yet he did allow that Marion "Soon found his Mistake" and "had his men brought of[f] in Good order & behaved Well upon every occasion."[15]

On the right Sumter sent forward Lieutenant Colonel Hugh Horry with his regiment, also over open ground. Horry lost a captain and three privates killed and a captain and five privates wounded. Horry was also unable to close with the enemy.[16]

According to Marion, Sumter sent his own brigade up the middle, between Marion and Horry, and Sumter's letter of 25 July to Greene confirms that. The regiments right to left were commanded by Colonels Charles Myddelton, William Polk, Thomas Taylor, and Edward Lacey. Sumter's Brigade had some cover. As described by Sumter, it "Possessed & acted under Cover of the Negro cabins & fence." His men were then "within forty yards of the enemy." Sumter reported seven killed and twenty wounded in his own brigade.[17]

Heavy fire continued for some time. Captain Bell described it as being "kept up with great Spirit on both sides for about forty Minutes. I never saw more regular firing at a field day than was ours." Sumter wrote of a "calm and well directed fire ... kept up for an hour." After that period of forty to sixty minutes, apparently sniping fire continued until sunset. Their ammunition exhausted, the Rebels then had to withdraw. The lack of their field piece, left behind at Biggin Church under the command of the veteran Continental gunner, Captain Anthony Singleton, was sorely felt. The only tactic left to them was to charge across forty to fifty yards of open space against men firing from behind good cover. They were not about to do that again. Sumter tried to put a good face on his failure. He had a "Design of Renewing the attack in the Morning," for Captain Singleton "was Coming up with the field piece" and "I Could have Got powder ball Sofficient." He maintained that with the field piece the enemy "Could have been Subdued in twenty minuets." But "we was within Twenty four miles of C. Town," he wrote, implying that British reinforcements might appear. That, however, was not the real reason why he could not renew the attack.[18]

Sumter's command was falling apart. Throughout the ranks men seethed with anger over the botched attack, many feeling that they had been sent into action without a chance of success, that comrades had been needlessly killed and maimed. Lee and his Legion cavalry had not taken part in the assault, and strangely he did not comment on it in his memoirs. But the editor of the 1869 edition, his son Robert E. Lee, stated that his father had forgotten to describe the attack, which failed "in consequence chiefly of Sumter's failure to bring up his artillery." How could Lee have forgotten such a dramatic episode? In any event, Lee decamped. In addition to his proximity to Charleston, Sumter reported that "Col Lees Marching off in the Morning, at Once Determind me to Retreat." Many of Marion's men also left. "Genl Marion has but few men With him the Remains breaking off." This plus Lee's departure was no surprise, given the poisonous relationships involved. But the blow that stung was the reaction of a longtime Sumter lieutenant. Sumter wrote that the departure of so many of Marion's men "furnished a pretext with my Brigade that they ought to go home also—Some has taken this Liberty." By this he may have meant Colonel Thomas Taylor, who had been with the Gamecock since the early desperate days following the fall of Charleston. Taylor was an imposing figure, "six feet, one inch high," his son reported, "& finely proportioned, with a eagle eye & ruddy countenance." Those eagle eyes must have been flashing and his "ruddy countenance" darker than usual as Taylor sought out his commander. Taylor's son told the historical collector and editor Lyman Draper a tale that has come down generation by generation in the Taylor family to the present time. His father "found Gen. Sumter sitting cooly under the shade of a tree—& said, 'Sir, I don't know why you sent me forward on a forlorn hope, promising to sustain me, & failed to do so, unless you designed to sacrifice me. I will never more serve a single hour under you.' "[19]

"Alas, the Execution Failed"

Continuing his campaign to stroke the Gamecock, Greene was fulsome in reply to Sumter's first report, extolling the "gallantry of the troops," lamenting that "the exertions had not been crowned with more deserved success," extending his "particular thanks to the officers and men," and assuring Sumter that the "advantages" gained "reflect honor upon your command." The next day he expressed his true feelings to Andrew Pickens. "Had not General Sumter detached his force too much and had he not mistaken a covering party for an advance of an attack he would have taken the Garrison at Monks Corner amounting to near six hundred Men." To Lafayette two days later he wrote, "Our late movements below did not fully answer my expectations. Never was a better opportunity afforded an officer than General Sumter had." Although at Quinby Plantation, Greene continued, "the militia and State Troops behaved with a degree of gallantry which would have done honor to veterans," the "want of artillery which had been left behind" enabled the enemy to maintain "their post until our people spent all their ammunition and was obliged to retire." Sumter's admirer and champion, the South Carolina historian Edward McCrady, harking back to the terrible wound inflicted at Blackstock's and from which his hero was still suffering, wrote, "Probably Sumter was not in a physical condition to have undertaken this expedition." That is a fair statement. A little less than three weeks before the Dog Days Expedition began, after discussing Sumter's situation with Colonel William Polk, who commanded a regiment of ten-month men under Sumter, Greene wrote to the Gamecock, "Colo Polk informs me your health is getting worse, and your Wound more troublesome." McCrady, however, added, "But who besides himself could have led it?" Nathanael Greene had an answer to that. Greene reserved a corner of his mind to store disappointments, and a little over a month later he was still stewing over the lost opportunity. He wrote to his old comrade, the victor at Cowpens, Brigadier General Daniel Morgan: "Had you been with me a few weeks past, you would have had it in your power to give the world the pleasure of reading a second Cowpen Affair. General Sumter had the command. . . . But alas, the execution failed. . . . The expedition ought to have neated us 600 men, and the chance was more than fifty times as much in our favor, as it was at Tarlton's defeat. Great Generals are scarce; there are few Morgan's to be found."[20]

There is little to be gained speculating whether Sumter could have taken the garrison at Monck's Corner had he not misread Coates's maneuver, or what would have happened had Morgan been in command. Let us concentrate instead on what actually happened. Sumter did not execute well. Nor did Lee. Yet Sumter's expedition had forced the British to give up their post at Monck's Corner, only thirty-four miles from Charleston. Wade Hampton— and Light Horse Harry if we can believe him—had raided to within a few miles of Charleston's gates. All this only a little over a year since Charleston had fallen, an American army taken into captivity, and a victorious British Army marching into the Back Country to establish strongpoints and British rule. Britain's soldiers in South Carolina were well aware of what all this meant. Lieutenant Colonel Nisbet Balfour, commanding at Charleston, spelled it out for Sir Henry Clinton. Sumter's strike into the Low Country, "the great force of the enemy, especially of cavalry, in which we are vastly deficient, and the general revolt of the province will, I conceive, even with the present force, circumscribe any future positions we may take." Thus with the Dog Days Expedition Thomas Sumter attained something in common with Nathanael Greene: tactical failure, strategic advance.[21]

Greene Must Have Been Appalled

At the time he was bemoaning Sumter's flawed raid, Greene was also increasingly involved in a matter that he would pursue in tandem with military planning. We read in chapter 6 of his efforts to introduce law and order and civil government to the Georgia Back Country by appealing to Colonel Elijah Clarke, sending to the state his personal representative, Joseph Clay, and urging Georgians to establish a government without observing constitutional niceties. In his camp of repose in the High Hills of Santee, he once again took up this vital issue. And in doing so revealed further evidence that his gifts ranged beyond the military arts to adroit maneuvering in political affairs.

In January 1781, Greene informed Congress that he had appointed a physician, Dr. Nathan Brownson, purveyor for the hospital department in the South, "untill the pleasure of Congress can be known, or a more perfect arrangement takes place." The purveyor was responsible for procuring all medical supplies, including hospital stores. Brownson traveled to Philadelphia, arriving in late March, and delivered the letter. Five days later Congress appointed Brownson deputy purveyor general. Dr. Brownson was a Georgian, and while in Philadelphia was in contact with the Georgia delegates to Congress, who would have been anxious for news of their state from a firsthand source. A subsequent event suggests that serious discussions took place between Brownson and the delegates. On 26 April 1781, a little over a month after Brownson's arrival in Philadelphia, the Georgia delegates wrote Greene expressing their uneasiness with the "irregular situation" among Georgians. Their opposition to the British being "equal to any," has "given tone to some of the most brilliant actions in that department upon the small scale." Yet lacking "order and direction," the state loses the "credit of their exertions." Then the delegates got around to how they meant to fix things. To "remedy these evils, and to render their endeavors more useful," they had "invested" Dr. Brownson with a "Brigadier General's commission, and given instructions for uniting our people under his command." Greene was requested to "give the measure efficiency, by approving and protecting it." Why the Georgia delegates thought Dr. Brownson qualified to command the Georgia militia is unknown, but it is well known that in all ages legislators are often prey to strange notions.[22]

Greene must have been appalled. What would be the reaction of veteran militia leaders like Elijah Clarke, whose ferocious performance at Musgrove's Mill had been so admired by Isaac Shelby; and John Twiggs, whose riflemen had wrought death and destruction upon 63rd Foot at Blackstock's; and James Jackson, who had performed heroically at Cowpens? How to deal with this delicate situation? The delegates' letter reached Greene about 16 July, delivered by none other than newly minted Brigadier General Nathan Brownson. A few days intervened before Greene replied to the letter, and we may safely speculate that in the interval he and Brownson had some very thorough and candid conversations. On the 18th, Greene replied that "I am a little apprehensive the military charactors in that State will not readily subscribe to the propriety of Doctor Brownsons appointment." That was putting it mildly. "But," he continued, "I will write them on the subject as I believe I have their highest confidence." On 24 July, Greene wrote to Colonels Clarke, Twiggs, and William Few, the last not actively leading troops at that time, but he had in the past. Greene added an ironic touch by having the letter delivered to the colonels by Brigadier General Brownson. After informing them of Brownson's appointment, he commented on it in a manner that subtly cast doubt on the delegates' action. "His abilities to discharge the duties of the appointment are no doubt unquestionable and the reasons offered for the measure must have their influence. I can only say that it is highly probable that the present struggle will continue for a long time and the sooner the whole force of the State can be brought into order and directed to one point the greater the probability of the States feeling security from her Military exertions." He then neatly handed the problem over to the colonels. "A head to all the business is necessary[;] who this ought to be your own feelings must determin." We can be sure that Greene knew exactly what their feelings were and what they would do. To Joseph Clay, who was acting for him in Georgia, Greene was even more suggestive. "Mr Brownson is coming to Georgia with an appointment of Brigadiers. Should you think it will promote the public service and the military characters will be content therewith you will pave the way for his exercising command. But should it be likely to produce discontent, I suppose it will be laid aside."[23]

It was indeed laid aside. A compromise was reached. Dr. Brownson was elected governor; John Twiggs was appointed brigadier general of the Georgia militia. At the end of August Governor Nathan Brownson wrote Greene congratulating him on the "reestablishment of civil Government in this state" and thanked him for the "effectual aid" he "lent the good people of this state in accomplishing so important an object."[24]

They Cared Not a Whit about America

While dealing with the Brownson affair, Greene changed his mind about setting up a government in Georgia by extraconstitutional means. In late July he wrote to Joseph Clay.

> When we lay at 96 I recommended to your State appointing a Council for the better government of the people. Since then I have got some intelligence through Congress from Europe which renders it of importance to establish Civil Government upon the Constitutional plan. I am not at liberty to go into an explanation, but you may depend upon the necessity and advantage of the measure. And as to what some people proposes of taking advantage of the present time to reform the Constitution, rely upon it there is nothing more injudicious. It will throw everything into confusion and finally the people will agree on nothing. A Legislature is necessary to give you political existence not only in America but in Europe much more than here.[25]

The reason for this sudden about-face lay in more than distance between Europe and Nathanael Greene's little army of ragged, smelly regulars and partisans, and it would profoundly affect his strategy. It was spawned in a world of splendid palaces and elegant drawing rooms whose perfumed denizens believed in their God-given right to rule and cared not a whit about America. Their concerns were the balance of power in Europe and the effect the American Revolution was having on it as well as the danger a republican revolution might present to Europe's monarchical system of government. All this became especially apparent after France allied itself with the American Rebels and declared war on Britain. The cast of characters began with Maria Theresa, empress of Austria and the Holy Roman Empire, and the mother of the doomed Marie Antoinette of France. Maria Theresa loathed revolutionaries. She was also, as the historian Richard B. Morris pointed out in his brilliant work, *The Peacemakers,* "obsessed by the horrors of war" and "convinced . . . that her ally, France, could not sustain a long war against England." On 15 May 1779 she offered her services to end the war by mediation. The son who would succeed Maria Theresa upon her death the following year as Joseph II observed to the British ambassador in Vienna, Sir Robert Murray Keith, "The cause in which England is engaged is the cause of all sovereigns who have a joint interest in the maintenance of due subordination and obedience to law in all the surrounding monarchies." Could he have been any clearer about the necessity of defending monarchy? Stoutly supporting both mother and son was the Machiavellian diplomat Prince Wenzel Anton von Kaunitz-Rietberg, head of Austria's chancellery and minister of foreign affairs, of whom Professor Morris wrote, "Kaunitz would have no truck whatsoever with revolution or revolutionaries." Pressing Austria's case at the court of Versailles in official meetings with the French foreign minister and a tete-à-tete with Marie Antoinette was the veteran old-school diplomat, the Austrian ambassador Comte deMercy-Argenteau, connoisseur of fine wines, elegant living, and the charms of Rosalie Levasseur, a celebrated operatic star.[26]

Well before Maria Theresa's mediation proposal, American representatives were roaming Europe seeking recognition, but except for Benjamin Franklin in Paris they were getting nowhere. John Jay met frustration in Spain, though he did stoutly resist giving up American claims to the Mississippi and Western lands. When the American William Lee, assigned by Congress to plead the American case in Berlin and Vienna, arrived in Vienna in 1778, he was snubbed, refused an audience with Maria Theresa, and treated with disdain by Prince Kaunitz in "several icy interviews." Lee was astute enough to note that the court in Vienna was "infinitely more insulting to *France* than America, because the thick heads look on the business as a matter entirely between *England* and *France,* leaving the other [America] totally out of the question."[27]

Nor did William Lee have any luck in Berlin. Prussia's brilliant monarch Frederick the Great had no intention of offending Britain by recognizing the United States. Going way beyond his brief, Lee suggested that Frederick become a mediator. That, too, was out of the question, as Frederick was then trying to persuade France to drop Austria as an ally and join Prussia in an alliance with Russia. What did he care about America?

In that vast, expansionist country to the east and north of Prussia, the supreme sensualist of her age played her own game. Catherine the Great's morals shocked the stiff-backed British ambassador, Sir James Harris, but her twenty-one lovers—with the exception of two—"played no significant role" in furthering Russia's interests, which was her main concern. Although unwilling to commit herself on the American matter, Catherine's approach to the issue was summed up neatly by Frederick the Great: she wanted, he observed, "to have a finger in every pie." She certainly did not want Britain humbled to the point where France would become the primary European power. Complementing her governing style was her cunning chancellor, Count Nikita I. Panin, a master of masking his opinions. Panin's influence was then being replaced by Catherine's former lover Prince Grigori Aleksandrovich Potemkin, whose interest lay not in America but in Russia's expansion into the Muslim lands to the south. At the same time he was friendly toward Britain and harbored an intense dislike of France.[28]

In 1779, however, France had no interest in mediation. Although Britain probably wanted a graceful way out of the war, it scorned mediation if it included discussion of independence or the presence of American Rebels at the negotiating table. The hot-tempered British ambassador to the Netherlands, Sir Joseph Yorke, put it bluntly and succinctly: "unless any of our mediators offers to disavow Independancy of America I would send them all packing and fight it out." The key player in Paris, the sometimes cautious, at times incautious, French foreign minister, Comte de Vergennes, had been equally blunt and succinct in December 1777, four months before France took the fateful step of entering into the American alliance and declaring war on Britain. He wrote to his ambassador in Madrid, Comte de Montmorin de Saint-Herem, "Take for your motto M. le Comte, and have it adopted where you are: *Aut nunc aut nunquam* [Now or never]." About a year and a half later, spring 1779, with Maria Theresa about to offer mediation between England and France, Vergennes would have none of it. After all, France had a new ally. In April 1779, France and Spain signed the Convention of Aranjuez, becoming allies in the war against Great Britain. Mediation was out of the question. (As mentioned earlier, Spain did not become an ally of the United States and had no interest in furthering the American cause.)[29]

Yet during the course of 1780 Vergennes's earlier optimism faded. France was growing war-weary. Far more serious was a situation Vergennes had ignored in the euphoria that so often embraces war makers when they roll the dice. Vergennes had been running the war, both the French and American efforts, on what amounted to a credit card: big loans with high interest rates. And the bills were coming due. France's fiscal situation was perilous. Vergennes was ready to consider mediation, and by 1781 he wanted it. Various proposals floated through European courts. One of the most outrageous, and nightmarish, was put forward in St. Petersburg by Count Panin. Instead of dealing with the Continental Congress, the mediators would accept only American representatives chosen by their respective state assemblies. Prince

Kaunitz in Vienna pounced on the proposal. Another plan proposed a triple division of North America: Canada back to France, the southern states kept by England, the northern states "declared a free republic." These schemes and others died aborning and bring to mind Rebecca West's observation on international politics: "Clumsy gestures based on imperfect knowledge," which we in the twenty-first century know all too well. By the spring of 1781, however, Vergennes had zeroed in on the plan that was presented to the Rebels.[30]

"A Claim Totally Inadmissible on Our Part"

On or about 18 July, Nathanael Greene received letters from Philadelphia written in late May and early June by members of the Continental Congress. A letter of 3 June from Samuel Huntington, president of Congress, informed Greene that "we have received authentic Advice" that Joseph II of Austria and Catherine the Great of Russia "have offered their Mediation between the Belligerent Powers, which was embraced with apparent eagerness on the Part of Great Britain, and will probably be accepted on the Part of France and Spain, and we are called upon by our Ally to prepare for negotiations as soon as possible." Greene also received a copy of a circular letter that Huntington had written to the governors of the states. Comte Vergennes, while seeking mediation to end the war, remained steadfast in favor of independence for the United States—but a truncated America, for Vergennes was considering a truce during mediation under a principle of international law known as *uti possidetis* (as you possess). This meant that once the truce went into effect each side would keep the territory it held when the guns went silent. That raised the possibility of Britain demanding a peace treaty giving it permanent possession of South Carolina and Georgia. And in fact Vergennes was "prepared to yield" Georgia and, incredibly, "even . . . the American-held portion of South Carolina."[31]

The mere suggestion of a mediated peace treaty, especially one based on *uti possidetis,* chilled American politicians and soldiers. Huntington's circular letter to the governors pulled no punches. He urged them to supply "provisions, men, and money" for the purpose of "driving the enemy from their present possessions in every part of these states, but at all events, to confine them to the Sea coasts; in order to give as little room as possible to the enemy's claim of uti possidetis, which will undoubtedly be most strenuously claimed by them in the course of the negotiation—a claim totally inadmissible on our part." Huntington meant the news to be kept secret but forgot to include that instruction, so he wrote the next day that the "Intelligence is of a Nature that ought to be kept secret" and that Congress requested "that effectual Measures may be observed to prevent Copies of Extracts of the Letter of the 1st Instant from being taken or published." Did Huntington really believe that such momentous news could be kept secret? Congress then was as leak-prone as it is today. Several letters of delegates in May and June of that year mention the danger of *uti possidetis.* And the intelligence was trickling down. A Virginia militia officer, Colonel Samuel McDowell, was well informed. On 25 July he wrote to another militia commander, Colonel William Campbell, that a "congress of several great powers in Europe is to meet to settle the war ... America will be included in the treaty." He urged that "we ought, if possible drive off the enemy or pen them in as small bounds as in our power. Hold what we possess will be strongly insisted on in the treaty."[32]

Greene was also adamant about rejecting *uti possidetis.* On 18 July he wrote to John Mathews of South Carolina, chairman of a standing committee of Congress to correspond with the commander of the Southern Department:

> I am fully agreed with you in opinion that it is bad policy to hold up an Idea of giving a part of the United States to save the rest and am determin to support the whole if possible, as you will see by the measures I have been pursuing.... I wish an attempt could be made to establish Civil Government in South Carolina. The Inhabitants of Georgia are making the attempt. If Governor Rutledge is still at Philadelphia, I wish he would not delay a moment in coming here. All the Gentlemen of influence should return to this Country to assist in correcting all the irregularities prevailinyg, and try to keep the hopes of the people alive.[33]

The possibility of European mediation based on *uti possidetis* is the key to understanding Greene's military and political strategy. It was two-pronged: push the British as close to the coast as possible while at the same time, by establishing civil governments in Georgia and South Carolina, showing the world that America, not Britain, governed those states. Earlier his push for civil government had been focused on establishing law and order and ending murder and plundering. That was still an important goal. But now it was even more urgent in order to forestall decisions made in distant lands that threatened to deny the American revolutionaries what they were determined to have.

Battle being the other prong of his policy, Greene and his troops could not tarry long in their pleasant sanctuary in the High Hills of Santee. Lord Rawdon may have given up command, but the British field army was still out there and at some point had to be dealt with.

9

The "Confidence and Good Opinion of Those in Power"

"The Civil and Military Are Mutually Dependent on Each Other"

On 16 July Greene's little army had arrived at its new camp of repose in the High Hills of Santee at James's Old Field on Midway Plantation, two days before Sumter's foray into the Low Country ended in mutual recriminations. One of Marion's officers thought it "a beautiful spot." In a letter to Governor Thomas Burke of North Carolina, Greene wrote that "The Army has suffered incredible hardships; and requires a little relaxation." For as Light Horse Harry Lee reminds us, this period of rest was "the first experienced since Greene's assumption of command," a period two and one-half weeks shy of eight months. But if Sumter's expedition failed, as "soon as they [the troops] are a little refreshed," Greene informed Burke, "and our force and the hot season permit, I shall make another effort to get the enemy from holding any of the uper Country."[1]

Another paragraph in the letter to Burke is of interest in any judgment of Greene. "Should your excellency think proper to take the field I shall be happy to cooperate with you in any measure calculated to promote the happiness and security of these states. While the war last the civil and Military are mutually dependent on each other and the most perfect good understanding is essential to both; and I beg your Excellency to be perswaded that it will be my constant endeavor to deserve the confidence and good opinion of those in power." Those final words bear repeating: "the confidence and good opinions of those in power." They once again place Greene as one with his chief,

George Washington, in recognizing and supporting the primacy of the civil power, a critical concept of governance that would spare the new nation the ambitions of military adventurers.[2]

Never at a Loss for Proposals and Advice

The main army was joined in the High Hills by Light Horse Harry Lee and his Legion. They too needed a rest. Lee wrote that "The troops were placed in good quarters, and the heat of July rendered tolerable by the high ground, the fine air, and good water of the selected camp. Disease began to abate, our wounded to recover, and the army to rise in bodily strength." Never at a loss for proposals and advice, Lee wrote to Greene on 29 July, speculating that Lord Cornwallis, still in Virginia, "will take route for Wilmington." He proposed that if Greene sent his cavalry to rendezvous with Lafayette's command, then in Virginia opposing Cornwallis, "it is not improbable but an advantageous action might take place, before the British army could reach their fortified town." In truth, nobody knew what Cornwallis was up to, and it might be suggested that neither did his Lordship. Greene as usual was ahead of Lee. Seven days before Lee's proposal Greene had written to Lafayette that "If Lord Cornwallis should cross James River and push into North Carolina, you will follow him." Left unwritten was the obvious: that in such a case Greene would at the least detach a unit to join Lafayette. But he did not think such a move by Cornwallis "probable," and if his Lordship "continue to prosecute his operations in Virginia, you will not detach any of your force this way." In response to Lee's letter, Greene informed Lee that he had already instructed Lafayette with regard to Cornwallis's movements. In the same letter, Lee had included several proposals dealing with reorganization of the militia and South Carolina state troops. Greene replied that he had already made such attempts, and then recited facts of life to his young cavalryman. With regard to militia, in a well-wrought sentence he pointed out that "it is difficult to make their men see their true interest where it is opposed to their present ease." Then, referring to the situation with Thomas Sumter, he wrote, "I wish it was practicable to get the State troops to join the Army; but be assured it would prove so fully my opinion of a certain person, to give such an order, as not only to prevent further exertions, but even opposition; and it is uncertain how far disappointed ambitions may lead a man." Given his close-up observation of Sumter Lee certainly knew this.[3]

Lee also reminded Greene of the necessity of ending "the ways of murder & robbery in Georgia," and that "Your proclamation will be necessary in Georgia to check the licentious appetite of the people." This was a repeat of his admonitions delivered during the siege of Fort Cornwallis at Augusta, while Greene was besieging Ninety Six. Surely Lee was aware of the efforts Greene had made to establish law and order and civil government in Georgia. And did he really believe that a proclamation issued by Greene would be worth the paper it was written on? People paid no attention to proclamations, whether American or British. Greene did not issue one, and he also reminded Lee of the efforts he had made on behalf of Georgia.[4]

Lee had headlined that letter with a general piece of advice that he enclosed in quotation marks: "Depend only on your own measures." Greene replied, "Your advice is very proper to depend on my own measures." He then reminded Lee, "but they extend to Virginia. If you mean I ought to depend on my own force here I think it would not be right, as it is by no means certain what effect the Northern operations will have upon the Southern."[5]

Lee was not through. His fertile mind came up with "an idea that the enemy's post at Haddrells Point might be struck at advantageously." But Haddrell's Point was in the extreme Low Country, beyond the city of Charleston, to the southeast and across Charleston Harbor from Sullivan's Island, deep in enemy territory. Four months later Francis Marion reported that the post was strongly protected by abatis. To raid Haddrell's Point would be a ride not only long and dangerous but debilitating on men and horses in the very middle of the hot, sickly season. Greene wisely rejected Lee's proposed raid. "I have no great opin[ion] of the affair at Hadrales Poi[nt] and at this time I should no[t] chuse to have your Corps low down in the Country, or muc[h] fatiged.... Orangburgh I th[ink] a better object. You are at liberty to go down yourself for inquiry."[6]

In his *Memoir* Lee included a description of what Greene planned to do at that time: Greene "determined, first to liberate North Carolina by carrying the garrison of Wilmington." But North Carolina had not been reconquered by the British and was not in need of liberation. Cornwallis had only marched through the state and then abandoned it after the Battle of Guilford Courthouse to chase his siren song in Virginia, leaving behind Major Craig's small force at Wilmington on the coast. Civil government had been in the hands of the Rebels since 1775. There was a substantial Tory minority in the state, especially in the eastern portion, and they would temporarily demonstrate their strength in an affair to be described later in the narrative. But any real danger to North Carolina passed with Cornwallis's pyrrhic victory at Guilford Courthouse. According to Lee, after his victory at Wilmington, Greene would return to South Carolina, "pass into the enemy's country south of the Congaree, and compel him to give it up." Having accomplished the second stage of his plan, Greene would "hasten to Virginia with the *elite* of his force, uniting to it the army of Lafayette, and once more to face Lord Cornwallis." Lee's fairy tale continues with details of his being ordered in readiness and sending out a secret reconnaissance party to gain information and boats for the passage of the Cape Fear River. The plan was abandoned, Lee wrote, when Greene was informed by Washington that a French fleet would appear on the coast in the fall, and Greene thereupon decided to concentrate on the liberation of South Carolina and Georgia. The only contemporary evidence of Greene's interest in Wilmington at this time is in a letter of 12 August to Governor Burke of North Carolina. And it was specifically restricted toward "routing the Enemy from Wilmington" in order to discourage the Tories, "but my force and situation has put it out of my power." If Greene felt that he could not confront the 300-man British garrison at Wilmington, what chance would he have had of routing the British in South Carolina, and then hastening to Virginia to once again take on Cornwallis? It is quite probable that in conversations in camp between Greene and Lee various scenarios were discussed, probably at Lee's urging. But we can be quite sure that Nathanael Greene would not have seriously entertained such a cockamamie idea as outlined by Lee. Contemplating all this, one is drawn to the conclusion that when Lee wrote this many years after the war his imagination was working overtime.[7]

Lee left Greene's camp with his cavalry on 5 August, apparently assigned to gain intelligence of what the British were up to and to engage targets of opportunity. He wrote Greene three days later that he had suffered "much toil" with "very little success." With sixty of his men he had attacked a thirty-two-wagon convoy escorted by 300 troops. The enemy cavalry and van were handled easily, but Lee was repulsed by infantry that stayed "regular and cool." Cornet Carrington with twelve men had captured twenty prisoners near Orangeburg but lost seventeen of them when they were attacked by sixty Tories. Lee believed that the British "will advance up the Congaree," and then of course advised Greene how to handle the situation. "If you was to retrograde to Campden or a little beyond it I believe it would induce them to venture farther into the country. Perhaps you may find it convenient to make this manouvre, when you are in readiness to pass the Wateree." Greene declined Lee's advice. He replied the next day that he was "not of opinion that a retrograde movement will induce the enemy to cross the river; nor do I believe they will fight us if we cross; but they may." He was right in the first half of sentence, wrong that the British would not fight if he crossed the river. When he broke camp later in the month he did head north toward Camden, but for reasons entirely unrelated to Lee's belief, which will be discussed in the next chapter.[8]

Lee persisted. On 10 August he proposed to cross the Congaree, "& may probably reach Chs Town gates." He requested an immediate answer, and if

Greene approved, to send him the Legion infantry. This was not a good idea and at the very least borders on irresponsibility. To risk one of the army's most valuable units on a reckless scheme? To campaign in debilitating heat in the middle of the malaria season? This did not smack of the prudence Lee usually displayed. Greene would have none of it, writing "I wish you not to go below." Alluding to Lee's earlier proposal that he maneuver to bring the British to battle, he patiently explained his situation to young Lee, the crux of it being that he needed reinforcements before seeking a fight.[9]

"Gen'l Sumter Has Pla[y]ed the *Old Soldier* with Me"

At least Lee was in the field and active, even if his brain was overactive with schemes. Thomas Sumter, on the other hand, was personally inactive yet actively troublesome. On 25 July 1781 he ordered Captain William Ransome Davis to proceed to Georgetown with a detachment of state cavalry "to secure all articles of property belonging to the enemy" and all persons hostile to the interests of the United States. Davis should seize indigo, salt, hospital stores "& all other articles suitable & wanted for the army . . . except so much as may be necessary for family use." Although Sumter was Marion's nominal superior, he was poaching on Marion's district in a town in which Marion had always shown a special interest and where his officer commanded. Four days later Lee informed Greene of what Sumter had done. Greene replied that Sumter's action "I think to be wrong but it is too late to prevent it." Marion took it philosophically, writing to Sumter that it "may Interfere with my Command but I suppose I must Submit." During the first week of August 1781, Sumter temporarily retired to his plantation near Charlotte, North Carolina. It is fair to assume that his physical condition plus strenuous activity during the Dog Days Expedition required a rest from campaigning. But there may have been another reason for his presence in North Carolina. The depot of his commissary of captures was in that state, and it was time to distribute booty. His biographer Anne King Gregorie wrote, "It seems likely that Sumter's presence would have been necessary, especially as traditions of the country say that he always secured his share of the spoil." He would not return to the field until October, and then only under orders.[10]

At the same time as he withdrew to North Carolina, Sumter decided to withdraw his men from the field. Colonel William Henderson (1748–1788) of the Ninety Six District had temporarily assumed command of the brigade after the Battle of Blackstock's and Sumter's incapacitation. Later Henderson would for a time command the South Carolina state troops Sumter had raised. On 14 August Henderson wrote Greene, "With expectations of

Seeing at least four or five hundred men fit for the field, I came to take command of the *Brigade of State Troops,* but I find Gen'l Sumter has pla[y]ed the *old Soldier* with me, for I have not been able to Collect quite Two hundred fit for action, and they in a most Shatter'd condition" (italics Henderson's). He had no sooner closed this letter when he followed it up with a short letter enclosing a memorandum of instructions from Sumter "that Realy Serprises me. That I Should Come here for no other purpose but to furlow a parsel of Troops & that When the Enemy is at Our Very Doors; & there horses To be Guarded by militia No Readier a way to Dismount the men Could be Devised." Sumter's memorandum directed Henderson to move the troops three to five miles to a bluff "where there is good water." Their horses were to be sent to a swamp where, Sumter specifically instructed, they were to be guarded by "Militia, which Shall serve them as a Tour of duty." The rest of the troops were to be given a "respite from service" until 1 October "& many of them fourloughed home from time to time as the servic[e] will permit," and he added that Henderson should "apply to Gen' Greene for that purpose." Henderson asked for Greene's opinion.[11]

Greene was astounded. He replied, "It would be little less than madness to grant the indulgences General Sumter requires." He could not fathom Sumter's "reasons for such an extraordinary measure . . . nor can I conceive how he could think of taking such a step without consulting me or obtaining my consent for the purpose." Such a move would leave the country "open to the enemy to ravage and the Cont[in]ental Army exposed to any attack" while Sumter's militia "are at home on furlough." Greene went on to state frankly the wide difference of service between regulars and irregulars, bringing into the open an ever-present, underlying tension. Besides the harm Sumter's measure would do to the Cause, "granting such extensive indulgences to an order of men who have more than five times the pay of Continental Soldiers who are confined to the field from one years end to the other forbids the measure. A comparison of service, must give great discontent to" regulars to see the militia "who took the field but yesterday, at liberty to go home and see their friends, while those of the Continental Army are rigidly confined to their duty." It was not true that the Back Country militia had taken "the field but yesterday," and it was unfair of Greene to make such a charge. As was made clear in the Prologue, the militia had kept the flame of resistance alive during the grim months following the fall of Charleston and surrender of one Continental Army and overwhelming defeat of another, and thus laid the essential foundation on which Greene would build. One has to question whether Greene appreciated the vital nature of the militia's earlier contribution. But in clearly stating the difference between conditions of service experienced by regulars versus the militia, and the deep resentment that might occur in the event of a mass furlough of militia, Greene was right. Sumter's instructions to Henderson were irresponsible. With a British army remaining in the near Back Country, this was no time to go home and relax with family and friends. Greene wrote to Henderson, "You will not furlough a man or officer unless for some particular reasons and you will give positive orders to have the whole collected as fast as possible, and every man at home called to the field as soon as may be, who are not employed as Artificers." There was one problem with Greene's determination that Sumter's Brigade remain in the field: malaria running rampant within at least a 100-mile radius of Charleston. At least one historian has claimed that Greene at the time did not realize "what a southern summer could do to the health of his troops."[12]

Act "as You May Think Proper"

Yet Francis Marion not only remained in the field deep in malaria country but was active and cooperative as well. On 10 August Greene sent Marion a letter from Colonel William Harden (1743–1785), who commanded troops of Marion's Brigade assigned to the deep Low Country south of Charleston. The courier could not find the Swamp Fox and had brought the letter to Greene's camp in the High Hills. Harden reported that a British foraging party was active between the Edisto and Combahee Rivers. A captured letter from the Charleston commandant, Nisbet Balfour, revealed that "*Not one Dragoon is here,* being most usefully *employed to the Southward getting Provisions Rice* etc." (italics Balfour's). By 15 August Colonel Harden reported that the British were still at Combahee Ferry, a little less than fifty miles south of Charleston, waiting for boats, although Greene had written earlier to Lee that "Schooners were taking off the Rice." Harden stated that "what rice they cant get away with [they say] they will burn." He needed help, and Greene ordered Marion, if practical, to go to Harden's assistance. Once again Greene displayed his willingness to give wide latitude to subordinates sent on detached missions. He gave Marion permission to act "as you may think proper," for "you are best acquainted with the natural difficulties attending the attempt and must govern your self accordingly." These instructions mirrored those given to Greene by Washington when the Great Virginian gave Greene command of the Southern Department. Yet true to form Greene also felt the need to remind the Swamp Fox of what Marion knew: that it was "of the greatest importance to check the enemy ... for if they are permitted to pursue it with impunity theyll soon possess themselves of all the rice of that country and totally dispirit the militia." Marion could not set out immediately due to movements of large bodies of the enemy near his position but promised to notify Greene when he did move "Southward." By at least 18 August Marion knew from Harden that "the People this way seems to be discouraged as we have not force Enough to do any good." By 20 August Marion felt that he had better move soon, reporting that Harden's militia was "Dispersing" and was at half strength. He planned to leave behind a small force to convince the enemy that he was still in his usual haunts with his brigade. According to William Dobein James, Marion sent Captain George Cooper with "mounted militia . . . to the neighbourhood of Dorchester and Monk's Corner, to create a diversion there." Two days later Marion set out "with about two hundred picked men," wrote James, "by a circuitous route and forced march of at least one hundred miles, crossed the Edisto, joined Harden and approached the British."[13]

The day after he marched Marion arrived at Round O, about forty-five miles west of Charleston. He had expected to rendezvous there with Colonel Harden, "but found him very sick, & his troops not collected." After resting men and horses on the 24th, Marion marched to Horse Shoe, directly south of Round O. On the 26th he detached Colonel Hugh Horry to the Chehaw River, "where I was informed was three schooners taking on rice with a Guard of thirty men but unluckily they heard of my Approach & went down the river the day before." That night he was joined by 150 men under Colonel William Stafford, who commanded the militia of St. Peter Parish south of Charleston, and 80 men commanded by Colonel Harden's son, Major William Harden Jr. Marion was now 400 strong. On the 27th he kept moving south. "I crossed the great Swamp" at the head of the Ashepoo River and camped "South of Godfrey Savana." He was now within five miles of British and allied forces. He sent out parties to reconnoiter. They found the enemy posted in a position "too strong to make any Attempt on them." He estimated enemy strength at 180 Hessians, 150 British, 130 "Toreys," and 80 horse of the Queen's Rangers. Nevertheless, he resolved to engage despite being outnumbered.[14]

The next few days were taken up with maneuvering and minor skirmishing between patrols. On 30 August, some twenty-five miles west of Charleston, Marion set up an ambush "in a thick wood Within a mile of Parkers Ferry within forty yards of the road which the Enemy must come." Marion instructed his officers, then deployed his forces and waited. It was not until sunset when about 100 Tories from the ferry approached Marion's ambuscade. He intended to let them pass and wait for bigger game, but one of Marion's men was spotted: "Challenged, not Answering," the Tories opened fire, whereupon Marion could not restrain his men from returning fire, which prompted the Tories to turn and "spur" for the ferry. Marion sent a "few horse after them" and they were chased across the Edisto River. The noise of the encounter brought British cavalry, who were on their way, to the rescue at "full speed." The enemy horse "received the fire of the whole Line Running The Gauntlet." British infantry appeared "& a heavy fire" ensued. Then Rebels referred to by Marion as "some Villains" "Cryed out" that the British were outflanking them on the right "& penetrating the wood" and they broke and ran. While Marion and other officers were trying to rally them, the British took the opportunity to "carry off" their field pieces and wounded "& retreated on a trot, Leaving twenty men and twenty three horses Dead on the Spott." The Rebels immediately took over the road and remained three hours, "but my people having been without provisions for 24 hours I retired two miles to refresh them." A detachment sent to follow the enemy, "who lost no time passing the river," found forty dead and wounded horses along the road, all but three good dragoon horses, a serious loss for the British. A civilian the British took at the ferry and kept with them for "some miles" told of "fifty men being badly wounded & many other which I think cannot be Less than Eighty in the whole." Marion must have taken special pleasure in news that Major Thomas Fraser commanding Queen's Rangers "had his horse killed and his whole Cavalray rode over him & is greatly Bruised."[15]

Marion probably underestimated his success and the British loss. Twenty-five-year-old Connecticut-born Quartermaster Stephen Jarvis of the Queen's Rangers, who took part in the action, labeled it "our sad disaster." He described a perfect ambush, "men and horses falling before and behind," as Fraser's cavalry "charged over this long causeway" and "received the most galling fire ever Troops experienced. . . . We only saw the flash of the pieces [as] the enemy was so complete hid from view. . . . We lost one hundred twenty-five killed and a great many wounded. . . . All our Artillery was killed or wounded before they could bring their guns to bear upon the enemy."[16]

In his report to Greene, Marion praised Colonels William Stafford, John Ervin, and Hugh Horry, who "behaved like the Sons [of] Liberty." But he was disgusted by the performance of Colonel Harden's son and Major Cooper. He maintained that had they done their part the British cavalry "must have been Destroy'd or taken," but Major Harden "never fired a gun" and Major Cooper was never "in sight," thus one-third of Marion's force did not take part in the action. This episode brought to a head a serious problem in the militia organization of the Charles Town District. Major Harden's father, Colonel William Harden, though he had led several successful forays against the British, was not well thought of. Governor Rutledge wrote to Greene about a week after Marion's expedition that "Harden, though a very worthy brave Man, keeps up no discipline or Authority" over his men. "He just lets 'em do as they please." Several days later he wrote to Marion that he intended to replace Harden, and eventually he chose Colonel Joseph Barnwell. But Colonel Harden refused to step aside. Harden and Barnwell "can't settle the affair of command," Governor Rutledge complained. Nor could he: "I cd not give it to Barnwell with[out] affronting Harden, & perhaps disgusting many of his Friends." Meaning, of course, that it was a political as well as a military problem. Marion tried to stiffen operations by staying through 31 August "to give some orders to Colo Harden, & put that part of the Country in a better and more regular way of doing their Duty." But the issue of command in the Charles Town District remained unresolved.[17]

Marion left Harden on 1 September, and upon his return to his usual haunts he would be thrust quickly into the maelstrom of a major battle.

Juggling Responsibilities

Greene's ability to juggle many responsibilities is seen in his continuing attention to civil government, gauging the effect of European mediation on his campaign, laboring on the administration of his army, and attempting to gather reinforcements for the coming battle. To the French volunteer the Marquis de Malmedy, who was in Salisbury, North Carolina, trying to gather, equip, and send on reinforcements, Greene wrote that had they arrived when needed he could have "ru[i]ned Lord Rawden and may still if he attempts to keep the uper Country; and we can keep the Militia of the South states together, which is very difficult and I fear not possible." General Mordecai Gist in Maryland had written earlier to Greene that a Maryland detachment of 400–500 and 100 from Delaware would march in "a few weeks." Explaining difficulties in supplying the men with clothing and equipment, Gist gave vent to his "Chagrin and mortification" with "public bodies" that have "neither inclination or capacity to direct, nor ability or integrity to execute, Yet arrogate to themselves the power of governing military movements." Greene replied that he was confidant Gist would surmount the difficulties and march "as early as possible." He also stated that the Maryland troops with him were short of officers, thus a "sufficient number of officers" was needed quickly. When the Maryland and Delaware troops finally marched, however, they would join not Greene but Washington's army in Virginia. Close to home, he wrote to Colonel William Henderson of Sumter's Brigade and Andrew Pickens with regard to drafting militia for one year's service. He wanted 400–500 men from Pickens for this purpose, to be commanded by Henderson. Pickens himself would eventually join Greene, but with only 280 men. The search for reinforcements never ceased—fruitlessly more often than not.[18]

"Manufactures" under Colonel Nicholas Long had been established in North Carolina to produce supplies for the army, but "good Artificers" (craftsmen of various skills) were needed for those establishments. Greene wrote to General Jethro Sumner, the ranking Continental general in North Carolina, urging that such men be recruited from the militia already in service. One of the "Manufactures" was in Salisbury, where Major George Davidson, commissary of hides for the Southern Department, was engaged in the vital task of making shoes and boots. To correct the distribution system, Greene instructed Davidson not to deliver shoes or boots to any officer without express orders from either the deputy clothier general, Captain John Hamilton, or Greene himself. Greene directed Hamilton to inventory all "public" clothing at Salisbury and Oliphant's Mill and to send all the overalls, hunting shirts, and shoes found to the army. All other "public" clothing was to be properly secured and a record made and sent on. Before returning to camp to report, Hamilton was to go on to Peytonsburg, Virginia, and examine and ensure the preservation of clothing located there. Greene's aide, Captain Nathaniel Pendleton, instructed Major John Mazaret to gather lead and paper at Salisbury and Oliphant's Mill in order to make cartridges in Charlotte, and to advise General Greene how many cartridges could be made. Thus along with the high dramas of skillful maneuvers and desperate battles, Greene, his aides, and supply and transport officers continued to be assiduous in their devotion to the homely but crucial task of supplying the army.[19]

Late that summer good news arrived from Georgia. Greene's previous efforts to establish civil government in that state bore fruit when the Georgia General Assembly convened on 17 August at Augusta. His finessing of the Nathan Brownson affair paid off on the same date when the Assembly officially elected Brownson governor.[20]

"Heroick Fortitude and Christian Resignation"

While Greene wrestled with the crucial needs of reinforcements and supplies, he also had to deal with a cause célèbre, another burden on an overburdened commander. Colonel Isaac Hayne (1745–1781) was a planter and Low Country militia commander, a Rice King, therefore a member of the South Carolina establishment. Besides his Hayne Hall Plantation of some 900 acres on the Pon Pon River, about twenty-eight miles west of Charleston, he owned nearly 9,000 acres, perhaps more, throughout South Carolina and neighboring Georgia. Hayne was captured by the British either in Charleston or elsewhere when the city fell in May 1780. To avoid confinement on the prison hulks in Charleston Harbor, he took British "protection, and acknowledged himself a subject of his Majesty's Government" and went home to Hayne Hall on parole. Hayne would maintain that he was bound by his oath only as long as the British could protect him, and if the Rebels took control of the area where he lived and therefore the British could not protect him, he was released from his oath. The British rejected that reasoning and considered him a traitor. But the legalities of the affair need not detain us. The upshot was that in the summer of 1781 Hayne was once again captured after he led a raid against British forces. The day after the judgment of a court of inquiry, Lord Rawdon, in one of his last acts before leaving for England, and the Charleston commandant, Colonel Nisbet Balfour, sentenced Hayne to death. On 4 August 1781 Hayne was taken from his cell. In view of thousands crowding the streets of Charleston, exhibiting in the words of his lawyer "Heroick Fortitude and Christian Resignation," Hayne walked to a place outside the city lines. When the executioner attempted to put a cap over his eyes, Hayne took the cap from him and pulled it on himself. He was then hanged by the neck until he was dead.[21]

The Rebels were outraged. Eight days after Hayne was hanged, Greene wrote Colonel William Henderson, "Should you take any british officers keep them close prisoners until you hear farther from me on the subject. I shall explain my self more fully to you in a few days." He gave the same order to Lee but was more forthcoming. He explained that he was waiting until the Rebel prisoners at St. Augustine, Florida, who were being released, were safe on friendly territory, "After which I will avow my intention of giving no quarter to British officers if they persist in this practice, and mean to retaliate on the first person I take." Strong words, but note the phrase "if they persist in this practice." Greene was hedging on his threat of retaliation. Pressure, however, would grow to respond in kind.[22]

On 20 August all of Greene's Continental officers signed a letter requesting him to "retaliate in the most effectual manner." While in Camden preparing to march Greene wrote Colonel Balfour in Charleston that given the "cruel and unjust execution of Col Hanes . . . I mean an immediate retaliation unless you can offer some things more to justify the measure." On the same day he wrote a proclamation announcing that it was his "intention to Retaliate for all such inhuman insults, as often as they may occur," although he delayed issuing it until after the return of prisoners from St. Augustine. Balfour's reply defended Hayne's execution and issued an artfully phrased threat that was certainly not lost on Greene. "Having said thus much, & holding those in Public Situations above the dread of menace, I shall not tell You of the many American Officers who, in different parts of the Continent, are now in our power, nor remind you, that Britain will loudly claim retribution for the Blood of her Officers, when causelessly shed." Over a month and a half passed after that exchange before Greene requested an order from both Washington and Congress, for he did not "think myself at liberty on a matter of such magnitude" and was "ready to execute whatever may be thought adviseable." Washington's answer introduced a voice of sanity into the Hayne affair and was probably the reply Greene wanted. "I really know not what to say on the subject of retaliation. Congress have it under Consideration, and we must await their determination. Of this I am convinced, that of all Laws it is the most difficult to execute, where you have not the transgressor himself in your possession. Humanity will ever interfere and plead strongly against the sacrifice of an innocent person for the guilt of another." A silly congressional motion to exact revenge on the person of Lord Cornwallis following his surrender at Yorktown was considered but not acted upon. There would be no retaliation.[23]

"It's Impossible for Us and Them to Inhabit One Contry"

An ongoing and far more serious problem than the Hayne affair faced Greene throughout South Carolina. Andrew Pickens, who had been ordered to shadow John Harris Cruger on his march from Ninety Six to join Lord Rawdon at Orangeburg, reported that he had "pursued Colonel Cruger near as Low as the Rocky Spring and Detach'd parties as low as Indian Head." He had taken "three Brittish prisoners, some Tories, & a number of Families," but "the old Men, Women & Children we pass'd on to the British Lines." This prompts us to imagine the anguish of families as they were separated, men of fighting age held as prisoners while women, children, and elders were sent on to relative safety. Pickens not only favored such a policy of sending noncombatant family members from the Ninety Six District to the British, but also recommended that it be pursued on a larger scale. He gave several reasons for his thinking on this issue. First, it was British policy to evacuate the district. Second, if allowed to stay, Tories would become spies "to our Prejudice." A third reason was retaliation for the British policy of driving Rebel families away unless they swore fealty to the Crown. But since it was British policy to evacuate Tories from the district, the Rebels would be doing their enemies a favor, thus "we heap Coals of Burning fires on our Enemies by Rewarding them with good for Evil." Then, however, Pickens stated a reason that stands alone in its starkness and once again labels the conflict a bitter civil war between Americans. "And Lastly, it's impossible for us and them to Inhabit one Contry, and Live together in peace, at one time." In his reply Greene contradicted Pickens's recommendation to send the Tories away. Instead, he believed it in "our interest to encourage the return of the Tories; and I wish you to give them all the encouragement in your power; and afford them all the protection you can." Yet by 31 August it had become unofficial policy in the Ninety Six District "to order off the families & dangerous connections of such as are now within the British or lies out of the British lines."[24]

In chapter 7 we left Pickens breaking off his pursuit of Cruger's column of troops and refugees in order to return to the Ninety Six District upon receiving news of Indian raids. The raiders had come in two parties, about seventy in one and "one Hundred said to have been in Another." They had left by the time Pickens arrived, to find not as much damage as reported. "They burn'd but few houses," Pickens reported, though there had been plundering. Pickens and his men were relieved, and certainly surprised to find that the raiders "were under such Restrictions that they murdered neither women nor children." The absence of such atrocities was a rare occurrence on the frontier, whether the raiders were Indians or their white enemies, and Pickens paid tribute to Tory "Officers and men who Exerted themselves for that purpose." But he planned to remain on the frontier because "the settlements are much alarmed as a number of Tories have lately gone into Indian Country." For though Rawdon had abandoned the last British post in the far Back Country, and many Tory families had elected to go with Cruger, there were diehards among them who refused to give up the struggle and had sought sanctuary among the Cherokees. Pickens identified one of them as "Bill Cunningham," who had led about forty Tory riders on the frontier raid and was pursued by a militia unit commanded by Major Fields Purdue, which killed five of Cunningham's men and retook some slaves and horses. Cunningham was of a murky background filled with contradictory evidence. He had taken the Rebel side early in the war but soured on the Cause, though he remained in South Carolina. Following the British reconquest in 1780, he joined a Tory militia unit as a private. He would return from his lair in Indian country to raid again in early August of 1781, when his band killed eight Rebels and picked up sixty recruits. After further raids in September and early October, Cunningham was in Charleston by 23 October. There we leave him for the time being. For we will meet William Cunningham again.[25]

"Plunder . . . I Almost Dispair of Totally Suppressing It"

Meanwhile, Greene's efforts to quell plundering were not going well. It had become a major problem throughout most of South Carolina now that the British had been driven from much of the Back Country. And Rebels were the major perpetrators. On 25 July Andrew Pickens reported that the Tories who had stayed in the Ninety Six District "are giving up very fast," although

a "number" of them "have gone into the Indian Country." Pickens had organized 100 men from Colonel Robert Anderson's regiment "for the purpose
of Defending the Frontiers," and another 100 of Colonel LeRoy Hammond's
regiment to protect against any incursion by the Tories at Orangeburg to raid
the "lower settlements on this side Saluda." The Tory threat, however, was not
his main problem. "That spirit of Plunder, so general among our own people, seem to be the greatest Difficulty we Labour under at present. I almost
Dispair of totally suppressing it notwithstanding my best Endeavours." And
much of the plundering descended into criminal acts. Some had moved their
families to the "Remote parts" of North Carolina and Virginia, and many
"seem to make a Trade of Carrying off Every Thing Valuable out of this Contry." The never-ending subject of remounts was a specific concern. "The Loss
of our Horses Distress us in a particular manner." And the thieves did not
play favorites: "Either the property of friend or enemy," Pickens added.[26]

Lower down, in the country around Friday's Ferry, the situation was also
deplorable. Colonel Wade Hampton reported to Greene that "The Situation
in which I found This neighborhood . . . is truely to be Lamented. Almost
every person that remain'd in this Settlement after the army marched, seems
to have been combin'd in committing Robberies the most base & inhuman
that ever disgraced man kind." Colonel Thomas Taylor had preceded Hampton by a few days and "had apprehended a few of the most notorious offenders," whereupon the "most Timid" among them grabbed their plunder and
fled for North Carolina and Virginia. Hampton then revealed an alarming
development: "the more daring . . . of this Banditti" apparently threatened
"distruction by murder etc to those who might presume to call the conduct
of them, or their accomplices in question." Hampton acted quickly and decisively. Gathering a "few of the State troops and those of the milita who had
spirit, or inclination enough to engage them . . . we have secured all of these
wretches that can be found." Those not caught, "finding matters were likely
to terminate against them," fled northward. Hampton referred the problem
to Greene for his consideration, and observed that in his opinion a statewide
operation should be mounted against plundering. Greene received Hampton's letter the next day and replied immediately. "I have always dreaded this
evil more than any other. . . . no person must be allowed to take property, of
any kind" without "written instructions" that only "General" officers should
issue and field grade officers execute. Echoing Pickens, he stressed "particularly horses" (italics mine). Offenders should be sent to the "main Army for
tryal [by?] a Court composed of the officers of the Militia State and Continental Troops. The tryals to effect life or lesor punishments according to the
nature of the offense."[27]

Official sanction against plundering under any circumstances came shortly after this exchange. Governor John Rutledge (1739–1800), long exiled from his native state, returned to South Carolina about the first of August and took up quarters at Greene's camp. On 5 August he issued a proclamation forbidding "all persons from plundering, taking, or holding the property of others under any pretence, or for any cause whatever," and those holding plundered property were ordered "immediately to restore such property to the owners." Justices of the peace were ordered to resume their duties and bring to account all accused of plundering "or any other criminal offense." Military officers were ordered to assist the justices "as they may require." Fine words they were and long overdue. They did not, however, stop plundering. Indeed, Rutledge's proclamation was worth about as much as the proclamations British officers were so fond of issuing. Even Greene's threat to execute plunderers failed to stop them.[28]

"I Would Sooner Cut Off My Right Hand"

Greene and Governor Rutledge had known each other since December 1780, when Greene had arrived to take command of the Southern Department. With Cornwallis in hot pursuit, they had shared dangers and travails during the army's desperate race over wretched roads across the width of North Carolina. On one occasion, probably after the Battle of Guilford Courthouse, Greene and Rutledge sought shelter from the weather in a building "little better than a hovel" and "occupied one bed." During the night Greene accused Rutledge of being a "very restless bedfellow." Rutledge denied it and said Greene was the culprit, which Greene denied. Whereupon they searched the bed and found that a hog, disliking the weather as much as the men, had joined them.[29]

Major General Nathanael Greene and Governor John Rutledge would work hand in glove toward the establishment of civil government and the liberation of South Carolina. Greene's sensitivity to the premier position of the civil side in their relationship was made dramatically clear in a letter of admonishment to Light Horse Harry Lee, who had taken it upon himself to arrange the purchase of "a quantity of indigo for the purpose of procuring clothing" for his Legion. Greene wrote Lee that it would be "derogatory to Government for individuals to take a measure of that sort without the order of the Governor." He stressed that though Rutledge was "a man of great liberality," he must "be treated with every degree of respect and attention." He acknowledged that Lee's "anxiety" for the Legion and his "zeal for the service are truly laudable, but they must be bounded by considerations of a higher

John Rutledge, 1739–1800;
oil painting on wood by
John Trumble, 1781. (Yale
University Art Gallery)

nature," and he was therefore certain that Lee "will be no less attentive to the harmony of the State [than?] to the interest of your corps." Lee wrote an abject letter of explanation and apology in which he assured Greene that "It is impossible for me even to think of any act which can disturb the mind of the governor." Given the harmony between Greene and Rutledge and the latter's importance to the Cause, we should know more about this Rice King.[30]

Rutledge's father, also John, immigrated to South Carolina from Ireland in 1735. He was descended from an English family that crossed the Irish Sea in the 1650s following Cromwell's conquest of Ireland. John's brother Andrew had preceded him and took the easy path to success by marrying a wealthy widow. When John senior arrived fresh from Ireland he followed suit, marrying Andrew's stepdaughter, fourteen-year-old Sarah Hext, and thereby came into possession of Sarah's two plantations and two houses in Charleston. The father sent our John to England to be educated. In 1754, at age fifteen, young John was admitted to Middle Temple to study law, and in February of 1760 was called to the English bar. He sailed for home later in 1760, was admitted to the South Carolina bar in January 1761, and wasted no time in making a name for himself. In a case that was certainly the talk of the town, he was retained by Mary Cooke to sue a merchant, William Lennox, for £7,000 for repeatedly breaking promises to marry her. The trial was held in November 1761. The twenty-two-year-old lawyer's "eloquence astonished all who heard him." Mary Cooke was awarded £2,500 in damages. John received a substantial and well-earned fee of 100 guineas. His legal reputation established, the young attorney was on his way to bigger and better things. His contemporary, the historian David Ramsay, wrote that Rutledge, "instead of rising by degrees to the head of his profession . . . burst forth at once the able lawyer and accomplished orator. Business flowed in upon him. He was employed in the most difficult cases, and retained with the largest fees that were usually given." Rutledge's biographer agreed with Ramsay's assessment. He was later described by one of his law clerks as "a Man of quick apprehension, sound Judgment much sagacity, and ready eloquence."[31]

John Rutledge was soon caught up in the emerging conflict between the mother country and the colonies. He was elected to the Commons House of the Assembly in the same year as his dramatic legal victory. There he defended "local rights and privileges of the Commons House against royal officials." In 1765 he was one of South Carolina's delegates to the Stamp Act Congress in New York City. He was twenty-six, the youngest of the twenty-seven delegates. As the dispute grew more heated, so did Rutledge's stance. He did not, however, initially favor independence, neither after fighting broke out in 1775 at Lexington and Concord in Massachusetts, nor when in the same year the Rebels by force of arms overcame Tory resistance in the Back Country—where, we might add, John Rutledge had extensive land holdings. When the South Carolina firebrand Christopher Gadsden declared for independence from Great Britain, Rutledge accused him of speaking treason and announced that he "was willing to ride post day and night to Philadelphia, in order to assist, in re-uniting Great Britain and America."[32]

Yet he also favored establishing a new government for South Carolina, for royal officials had fled and London was unwilling to negotiate the widening differences between mother country and the colonies. On 26 March 1775, South Carolina's General Assembly elected Rutledge president and commander in chief of the state. His first major crisis came in early June 1776 when a British armada appeared off Charleston Harbor. The British were bent on a naval and ground reconnaissance in force that ended in shambles. Their main target was the fort on Sullivan's Island in the harbor. Major General Charles Lee, an experienced though eccentric British officer turned American Rebel, whose inflated reputation had not yet burst, had been sent by the Continental Congress to command the Southern Department. He felt strongly that Fort Sullivan could not be held and insisted that it be abandoned. Whereupon John Rutledge revealed his mettle. He wrote to the fort's commander, General

William Moultrie, "General Lee wishes you to evacuate the fort. You will not do so without an order from me. I would sooner cut off my right hand than write one." Little wonder that during his presidency and later as South Carolina's first governor, John Rutledge would be known as the Dictator.[33]

When the final break with the mother country came, with the Declaration of Independence, Rutledge opted for the Rebel cause. The British invasion of 1780 sent him into exile. Now, thanks to the Back Country militia he considered a "pack of beggers," and to Nathanael Greene and the Continental Army, he was back and wasted no time in partnership with Greene to do what was necessary to establish civil government. On 6 August, the day after issuing his proclamation against plundering, Rutledge wrote to the South Carolina delegates to Congress that he had "issued Commissions of the Peace" and appointed qualified "Magistrates, for each District." He wanted to issue special commissions of "Oyer & Terminer" (authorizing judges to hear criminal cases), but there were no judges or an attorney general available, and he urged those outside the state "to come on, immediately." He would postpone issuing the commissions "untill their Arrival," but if they tarried he would be forced "to make Temporary Appointments to these offices." Convening a legislature was vital: "having the Legislative, as well as Executive & Judicial, Authority operating in its full and proper extant . . . Wd have a great effect, on our affairs particularly abroad"—here echoing Greene and the danger of European intervention. He postponed issuing writs of election because it would be "ungenerous to exclude our worthy Friends lately held prisoners in St. August[ine] & C-harles Town." But he urged the delegates and others in Philadelphia who were members of the last Assembly "or are of weight and influence in the Country, to come hither, with the utmost expedition." Rutledge committed to reimburse travel expenses "by means of Indigo which I hope to be able to send soon to Philadelphia."[34]

Rutledge was harsh, even vindictive, toward Tories, and his severity extended to men who refused to serve in the militia. He instructed Francis Marion that the only reason for a leave of absence was sickness. Any man who refused to serve "must be deemed an enemy and taken prisoner and sent to the British . . . must not be permitted to return, and shall have their property confiscated." Militiamen who engaged in plundering "any persons" should be "prosecuted as felons." Those going to Charleston "or the enemy without a permit from you or an officer" must be treated as spies "and suffer accordingly." Women who went into Charleston or to a British post "without leave, must not be permitted to return." He stressed that "Severe examples must be made of all negroes," and any who "aid or assist" the enemy "shall suffer death." Since the British had sent wives and families of Rebels out of the state,

Rutledge ordered Marion to "send into the enemy's lines the wives and families of all such men as are now with or adhere to the enemy." He claimed that "I lament the distress which many innocent women and children may probably suffer by this measure," but justified it on the "principles of retaliation."[35]

Nor had Governor Rutledge forgotten or forgiven those who had taken protection under the British while he and others were fleeing from Lord Cornwallis's troops. He had a list of those men. For following the surrender of Charleston to General Sir Henry Clinton in May 1780, 210 residents of the city signed an address dated 5 June to Sir Henry and the British naval commandant, Admiral Marriott Arbuthnot, that is so craven it is embarrassing to read today. They tendered "our warmest congratulations on the restoration of this capital and province to their political connexion with the crown and the government of Great Britain; an event that will add lustre to your excellencies characters, and, we trust, entitle you to the most distinguishing mark of the royal favor." They finished this contemptible litany by entreating "your excellencies interposition in assuring his majesty, that we shall glory in every occasion of manifesting that zeal and affection for his person and government, with which gratitude can inspire a free and joyful people." All 210 took an oath of allegiance to the Crown and pledged their support of the British cause. Their reward was restoration of their rights as Englishmen. Men who refused to submit were taken from their families and shipped to St. Augustine for confinement. No doubt some of the signers were Tories from the start, opposed to revolution and the severing of ties to Britain, but others simply put property before honor. For men such as John Rutledge, who had kept the faith and soldiered on, the latter were beyond the pale. Consider his reaction to the following.[36]

When it came to Rutledge's attention that a "Mr. W," who had signed the address to Clinton and Arbuthnot, was actively engaged in trading in Georgetown, then under Rebel rule, he was incensed. "I really am amazed at the impudence of these people to dare after such an atrocious act, to come out and reside amongst us without making their application to proper authority and knowing whether they would be received or not, as if they had really been guilty of no offense whatever . . . though they have acted in a most criminal manner." Rutledge did not "desire to have any of them with us, and will not receive any of them. . . . Every one of us should lose all of his property for such infamous conduct." He ordered Marion to have "Mr. W, taken and sent up to me under appropriate guard." He should also confiscate the property "he has with him . . . money, goods, negroes, boats . . . whatever," and send it all to Rutledge. Any other property Marion found should be sold and the money considered public funds.[37]

While Governor Rutledge was lending his considerable influence to establishing civil government in South Carolina, Nathanael Greene, among his myriad responsibilities, was once again involved in an unpleasant duty that all commanding officers sooner or later must face: meting out military justice.

"Expressing himself in a Disaffected manner in the presence of the Soldiers," Sergeant John Hadley had also spoken in words "Disrespectful" of his commanding officer, Lieutenant Colonel John Eager Howard, as well as "frequently saying in presence of the Soldiers, he would never endeavour to injure the Enemy." It would be fair to state, therefore, that Sergeant Hadley had had it with the war. Greene had also had it with Sergeant Hadley. On 5 August a court-martial presided over by Howard found him guilty of such statements and sentenced him to death. (Modern legal minds will be shocked at Howard's presence on the court, a clear conflict of interest.) General Greene approved the sentence and ordered Sergeant Levi Smith to execute Sergeant Hadley by having him "Shot to death." Nathanael Greene was a bookish man, the most cerebral of his fellow generals. Yet he also had within him the hardness necessary to men who would win wars. To drive home to the army what could be expected of such transgressions, Greene ordered that the troops "are to be under arms and attend the Execution." No time was wasted. The following day, 6 August, before silent ranks of his fellow Continentals, Sergeant John Hadley was "Shot to death" between 6 and 7 P.M. Following his execution, the troops were "immediately" given "good dry straw to Sleep on."[38]

There were more executions that summer. A court-martial on 27 July sentenced to death Joden Roziers of the North Carolina Line for desertion, joining the "Tories & bearing arms against the United States," and "Passing thro' Camp with a Fictitious Name"; and on 3 August James Ballet and John Barrett of the Maryland Line for "Desertion & Bearing arms against the United States." Greene approved the death sentences. On 10 August between 5 and 6 P.M., the three men were "hang'd by the Neck until he be Dead" by Sergeant Robert McCorkle.[39]

Desertion coupled with joining the enemy and bearing arms against the United States and then being captured invariably meant court-martial and the death sentence. If you were a regular, at least you got a trial. Militiamen of either side, when caught by their former comrades, were often immediately hanged from the nearest tree. Simple desertion and other crimes by regulars brought flogging into play. An earlier court-martial of a private who stole bacon from a home near the camp and threatened one of its occupants resulted in 100 lashes. The court that heard Sergeant Hadley's case also dealt with several desertions. Two men received fifty lashes each and one had his term of service extended. A soldier who was a chronic deserter and forged his colonel's name was given 100 lashes. Another, a thief as well as a deserter, lost his musket and stole three blankets, a pair of shoes, and a knapsack. He was given 100 lashes and ordered to "make Restitution for the things stolen."[40]

What a harsh age, modern readers might say, and they would be right. It was a brutal age. Children were hanged for theft, women lashed for plundering, chattel slavery accepted as a centuries-old part of the human condition. (We should keep in mind, however, that the twentieth century was far more destructive worldwide, and these early years of the twenty-first are not promising.) But leniency was not an unknown concept to the hard men who led eighteenth-century armies. In another court-martial of 3 August a forage master who had failed to forward a "boatload of Corn," which thereupon spoiled, was acquitted because the court judged that he was guilty only of "an error in judgment." A soldier taken prisoner at the surrender of Charleston in May 1780 was convicted of "joining the enemy" and bearing arms against the United States, and though sentenced to death the court recommended mercy because he had not had a chance to escape. Greene accepted the court's recommendation and remitted the sentence.[41]

"Charles Town Is the Greatest Object to the Southward"

In the meantime events were developing elsewhere that would directly affect Greene's Southern Campaign. On a strategic level his correspondence at this time was permeated with his hope that a French fleet would appear off the coast for a joint naval-ground operation to drive the British from Charleston. He had been informed in a letter from the French minister to the United States, Chevalier de la Luzerne, delivered by Governor Rutledge upon the latter's arrival from Philadelphia, that a French fleet was indeed sailing to the mainland from the West Indies. The questions to which no American knew the answers were its precise destination and whether it would cooperate in joint operations with the American army. From Greene's reply to Luzerne, he obviously believed the fleet would cooperate, but as Luzerne's letter has not been found we cannot know whether Greene read more into it than was justified: that the fleet would be available for joint operations against Charleston. George Washington made the same assumption with regard to New York City. He had long yearned to retake the city, from which he had been driven by the British in 1776 in humiliating fashion. He wrote to Greene on 1 June with news of his conference in Wethersfield, Connecticut, with Comte Rochambeau, commander of the French Expeditionary Force of 5,500 troops stationed at Newport, Rhode Island. Although Rochambeau was never enthusiastic about attacking New York City, they had "finally determined," wrote Washington, "to make an attempt on New York . . . in preference to a southern operation." Washington hoped that the French fleet of twenty-eight sail under Comte de Grasse, carrying another 3,470 troops, would take part.[42]

Greene replied to Washington on 6 August. He agreed that "New York as a place of Arms, and from the importance of its harbour, command of supplies, as well as its situation to harass and distress our people, may be considered by far the greatest object upon the Continent, and in my opinion every effort should be made for its reduction in preference to all others." By then Greene assumed that de Grasse was bound for New York. After the city's capture, "I should suppose that the whole French fleet might enter the Chesapeak," and thereby "greatly contribute to the speedy surrender of the enemy." But he was quick to note that "Charles Town is the greatest object to the Southward," and "if the operations cannot be carried on in Virginia and here at the same time I think Charles Town must have the preference as the greatest object." In a follow-up letter the next day, Greene hoped "the fleet will stay to compleat the reduction of Charlestown and New York," and did not mention Virginia.[43]

The fleet under Admiral de Grasse would appear, but not off either New York or Charleston. As early as 28 May, Comte Rochambeau had written to de Grasse that "There are two points at which an offensive may be made against the enemy: Chesapeake Bay and New York. The southwesterly winds and the state of distress in Virginia will probably make you prefer Chesapeake Bay, and it will be there where we think you may be able to render the greatest service." On 14 August Washington, to his initial fury, learned that de Grasse had chosen the Chesapeake, where on 2 August Cornwallis had begun establishing a base at Yorktown. Recovering quickly from his intense anger and disappointment, Washington rendezvoused with Comte Rochambeau, and on 21 August the 7,000-man Franco-American army—more than half French—began its march to Virginia. The ensuing Yorktown campaign was a masterpiece of timing, cooperation, and what every successful general needs—good luck. Yet in his letter of 7 August to Washington, Greene was "afraid the french will run off to West Indies, after staying with us a few weeks, and leave the business unfinished." De Grasse would stay considerably longer than a few weeks, and his participation was the key ingredient in ensuring the end of Lord Cornwallis's American adventure.[44]

Of immediate concern to Greene, however, was the British field army in South Carolina. It had to be dealt with, and that would lead to the bloodiest battle of the Southern Campaign.

10

"We Obtained a Complete Victory" (Greene) "I Totally Defeated Him" (Stewart)

"You Know the Object; Therefore Be Prepared"

The army broke camp on 23 August. The time of repose was over. It was time to seek the enemy. Time to fight.[1]

Greene had written two days before to Light Horse Harry Lee: "You know the object; therefore be prepared." The object was the last British field army south of Virginia. Lord Rawdon, broken in health, had sailed for England two days before Greene broke camp. Prior to that, on 16 July, Rawdon had turned over "command on the frontier" to Lieutenant Colonel Alexander Stewart (1739–1794). Stewart had been a soldier for twenty-six years and had served in Germany during the Seven Years' War. This was his first American posting. It was Stewart who had provoked Rawdon's ire by arguing against releasing any of the newly arrived reinforcements to Rawdon for the relief of Ninety Six. "He has too high an opinion of himself," Rawdon wrote then. Another British officer, Major James Wemyss, described Stewart as a "brave officer, rather of indolent habits, and a little too fond of the bottle." Nor do Stewart's fawning and boastful letters to Lord Cornwallis speak well of his character. Those flaws, however, as interesting as they are, do not speak to his competence in battle, of which at this point we know nothing.[2]

Stewart lay south of Greene, only some fifteen miles away at McCord's Ferry. But after Stewart established his post, Greene informed Thomas McKean that "The great Rains that fell ... rendered it very difficult crossing the Rivers." The swamps between the two armies were "so full of Water that, there was no possibility of passing, the Water being up to a Horses Belly for miles together

in the low ground," so "that we cannot cross the Wateree here." Greene therefore marched north toward Camden, to come at Stewart in a roundabout way.
There were other good reasons for doing so. Supplies and reinforcements from
northward, should the latter miraculously appear, would come by the Camden
road, and that "road being good, and the passage of the river easy, I thought
that would be, all things considered the best route."[3]

The plan to attack Stewart did not originate with Lee, although one might
be led to believe it given his repeated urgings that Greene should bring Stewart to battle. Greene had made it clear on more than one occasion that he
was awaiting reinforcements before taking the offensive. Three days prior to
the army's breaking camp and marching toward Camden, Lee advised Greene
that if he were across the river "you would be convenient for action, & would
weaken your enemy by his desertion." Desertion by British regulars was by
no means certain, and we can be sure that Greene was well aware of the value
of location, and perhaps irritated by Lee's incessant harping. He replied the
day before marching. "Was our force as I could wish, or had it b[een] for
some time past[,] Mr. Stewart should not have lain so long quiet. I am fully
sensible of the advantages you hint at, nor have I been unmindful of them.
But arrangements and reinforcements have been wanting nor are they by any
means in that forwardness I could wish but we will make the most of them.
Have your Legion as strong as possible to second the attempt; for depend
[on?] it, we must have victory or ruin, nor will I spare anything to obtain it."[4]

While preparing the army for its march to Howell's Ferry on the Congaree River, Greene ordered that the sick and lame (ex-GIs of my generation
will recall our sergeants bellowing at morning formation, "Sick, lame, and
lazy, fall out!") would remain in Camden and that "a Sufficient number of
Women, particularly those that have Children must be left as Nurses." One
of his aides, Major Edmund Hyrne, wrote to Captain Edmund Gamble,
quartermaster at Salisbury, that Greene wanted arms and cartridge boxes for-
warded "with all possible dispatch." It was unlikely that there were any arms
to send. Greene wrote to Colonel William Henderson that he intended to
link up with him to attack Stewart, provided Henderson and Pickens had
the number of troops Greene expected. Although he was at the start of a
major movement against the enemy, Greene expressed pessimism in a letter
to Lee: "the tardiness with which every body moves who were expected to
join us almost makes me repent that I have put the troops in motion." The
North Carolina regulars expected four days before might take another "four
or five days to come." In chapter 7 we quoted Greene's requests that Colonels
Isaac Shelby and John Sevier join him with their Over Mountain Men and
their answers. By 1 September he had received Shelby's reply of 3 August and

Sevier's of 6 August, explaining why they were not marching eastward. In his replies of 1 September Greene swallowed his disappointment and praised their "Mountain Militia, formidable to their enemies and zealous in the service of their Country," and urged them to raise 1,000 to 1,200 "good Militia to join us at farthest by the tenth of next Month." He had heard nothing from Pickens and feared he would not arrive with the numbers he hoped for, nor did he believe Henderson would be able to do much better.[5]

Greene was in one of his down moods. He concluded the letter to Lee, "You know I never despair, nor shrink at difficulties, but our prospects are not flattering." He was prone to periods of gloom, and given the enormous disadvantages under which he operated this should come as no surprise. A small, unpaid, ill-equipped, poorly clad, often hungry army. His main supply line stretching hundreds of miles northward. Militia crucial to success imbued with a here today, gone tomorrow mentality and a passion for plunder and blood revenge. And the land itself: harsh, semi-wild even in the Low Country, barbarous in the Back Country. Some commanders would have been broken by all this. Greene just complained, got it off his chest, and persevered. Students of the campaigns of General Andrew Jackson never fail to marvel at his indomitable will to push ahead no matter the odds. Greene was no less indomitable. He was just quieter about it.[6]

The army left Camden on 27 August. Although Greene did not know it, three days later Admiral de Grasse's French fleet of "28 Ships of the Line and a Number of frigats" and carrying 3,470 regulars arrived at the mouth of Chesapeake Bay, the first arrival for the upcoming Franco-American Yorktown campaign. Greene would learn of this about two and one-half weeks later in a letter from Lafayette—another reminder in our era of instant messaging of slow eighteenth-century communications. On the same day de Grasse arrived, Greene was at Howell's Ferry on the Congaree River, awaiting boats. Crossing the river, moving steadily toward his prey, by 1 September he bivouacked on Beaver Creek near Orangeburg, where the British army had been camped. Light Horse Harry, still detached from the main army, reported that on the night of 31 August the British Army had encamped at Eutaw Springs on Eutaw Creek, a short tributary of the nearby Santee River. Eutaw Springs was about thirty miles east of Orangeburg and fifty-four miles north of Charleston. Still full of advice, Lee suggested that Greene position the army at Richardson's Plantation in the High Hills of Santee, which would be "more convenient for the reception of Congaree supplies," and for "any offensive movement." Lee was unaware that Greene was already south of the Congaree. Steadily, the army moved on, and Stewart was unaware that Greene was stalking him.[7]

As he was closing in on Stewart, Greene wrote to the president of the Continental Congress, enclosing Marion's report of his expedition to assist Major Harden and stating that Marion merited "the highest encomiums for his good conduct, Judgment, and personal bravery." He sent Marion a letter congratulating him and his command "for their gallant behavior" and informing him that he would forward Marion's report to Congress. He also urged Marion "to form a junction with us as soon as possible" for the looming battle with Stewart. His aide Captain Nathaniel Pendleton wrote the same day to Andrew Pickens that Greene wanted him to march "this evening" to join the army and to bring cattle, for "the Army is entirely without Beef." Pickens answered that he would march on the evening of 5 September but cattle in the area were scarce, although he would send men to look for some.[8]

Stewart was very much in the dark as to Greene's whereabouts. In his report to Lord Cornwallis, he stated that he had withdrawn from Orangeburg to Eutaw Springs because of his dire need of supplies and his reluctance to weaken his command by sending a strong escort to meet and protect a slow-moving supply convoy coming from Charleston. He had moved to get closer to the convoy. Yet he still lacked intelligence of Greene. It was not for lack of trying, but the Rebels had rendered intelligence-gathering "impossible by waylaying the bypaths and passes through the different swamps and even detained different flags of truce which I had sent on public business on both sides."[9]

Battle Strength of the Armies

Greene and Stewart each claimed to be outnumbered. Greene wrote that "our numbers were greatly inferior to theirs." Stewart reported that "with not 1,200 fighting men I beat between four and five thousand." Historians have come up with various numbers but the consensus of all except two has the armies at about equal strength, ranging between 1,800 and 2,400. In fact, Stewart was outnumbered, although he certainly fought more than 1,200.[10]

Stewart probably fought with 1,793 effectives. On the morning of the battle, 8 September 1781, Stewart's return "before the action at Eutaw" showed 3,030 officers, noncommissioned officers, and rank and file. On detached duty were 255 while 566 were sick in hospitals and 106 men listed as "sick in camp." That left him with 2,103 effectives. That figure, however, is lowered by the absence of 310 officers and men, as described in the next paragraph, giving Stewart a final total of effectives in the battle at 1,793. Some soldiers were assigned as "Bat Men and Baggage Guard" but no numbers were given so they must be ignored. Yet also dated 8 September we have a "Return of

Troops under Lieut-Colonel Stewart in the Action at Eutaw Springs" stating that only 1,396 officers, noncommissioned officers, and rank and file actually fought in the battle. So where did those 397 men go? I believe we can take Stewart's second 8 September return with a large dose of salt.[11]

Because the British were short of bread, another return of that morning accounted for the 310 officers and men sent out early as a rooting party to gather sweet potatoes from neighboring plantation fields. The detachment broke into small groups to carry out the task. Writing some thirty years after the event, Lee claimed that when Greene's advance met a British reconnaissance patrol "the rooting party . . . hastened back to the British camp, upon first fire, and therefore escaped." Lee was certainly mistaken. Otho Holland Williams reported that "the whole fell into the hands of the Americans." He was probably referring to an incident recorded in the daily journals of two officers of the Delaware Regiment. Captain Robert Kirkwood and Lieutenant Thomas Anderson used almost identical language regarding one action with part of the rooting party and agreed on the number involved and their fate. Captain Kirkwood wrote, "Coming within three miles of the Enemy's Encampment, we overtook a Rooting Party of 60 men Coming in with Potatoes, most of whom were either Killed, wounded or taken." There is no mention in American sources of other small groups from the rooting party coming into contact with Greene's forces. Stewart reported to Cornwallis that the rooting party did not return "till the action was over," which indicates that the survivors may have laid low during the battle.[12]

With regard to Stewart's stated strength in the battle, a caveat must be added for consideration. The day after the battle British prisoners were marched to McCord's Ferry on the Congaree River via Rebecca Motte's house, where Governor John Rutledge was staying. He wrote that "A British officer, Prisoner, tells me, they had 2000—all Regulars."[13]

Greene's strength in the battle also depends on which returns we accept. Continental returns dated 25 July and 5 August, including foot, horse, and gunners, total 1,745 of all ranks. But each was issued over a month before the battle—and it was the sickly season. On 4 September, four days before the battle, Greene ordered field returns of each corps "to be made immediately." In 1822 Greene's biographer, William Johnson, who had those returns at hand, gave the "rank and file" of Greene's regulars at 1,256. With regard to the militia, an August 25th return of the North Carolina militia under Colonel François, Marquis de Malmedy, listed its strength at 204 fit for duty. But writing the day after the battle, Governor Rutledge estimated Malmedy's command at "abt 180." Also writing on 25 August, Colonel William Henderson, commanding South Carolina state troops, reported to Greene that he had 370 men, "one-third of whom are unarmed," and noted that they are "very Sickly" and he had been "exceeding ill of fever" but hoped "it is about leaving me." Governor Rutledge, however, gave Henderson's strength as "abt 200 State Troops (in the Action)." It is unclear from his text if Johnson had actual returns for the militia and state troops. He gave their number as 842. But according to Governor Rutledge, again writing a day after the battle, militia and state troops numbered about 1,020. I accept Johnson's figure of 1,256 Continentals and Rutledge's of 1,020 irregulars, for total American strength at the battle of 2,276. Thus overall Greene outnumbered Stewart by 843, and Stewart's regulars outnumbered Greene's by 537.[14]

Tension would have begun to build in the American camp. On 6 September Greene ordered the troops to put their arms "in the most perfect Order as there is the prospect of our coming to Action with the Enemy." On the morning of the 7th he ordered the troops to draw one day's provisions, cook them, take a jill of rum (enough to wet one's whistle but not enough to cause troops to stagger in the ranks), and prepare to march. Marion "joined us," Greene wrote, "on the evening of the 7th at Burdell's Plantation, 7 miles from the Enemies Camp." Pickens had already arrived. Their presence meant more planning to insert the new troops into the order of battle. At 8:00 P.M. further orders were issued to the troops: the army would march at four o'clock on the morning of 8 September to "Attack the Enemy." With ornate nineteenth-century prose, Greene's first biographer has the general "Wrapped in his cloak, and canopied by the Heavens, with his head pillowed on the root of a shady china-tree, the general passed that night in slumbers, undisturbed by anticipation of the bloody scenes of the following day."[15]

Spirits Aroused, the Army Marched On in Line of Battle

They marched as they would fight, in Greene's customary manner, learned from Brigadier General Daniel Morgan, whose masterly lesson in tactics, fighting a set-piece battle with a combination of regulars and militia at Cowpens the previous January, was lost on George Washington but taken to heart by Nathanael Greene. Morgan had fought a defensive battle ending in a counterattack. At Eutaw Springs Greene would fight offensively but with the same order of battle.[16]

Four battalions of militia, two from South Carolina, two from North Carolina, formed the front line. They were commanded by two generals and a colonel. One South Carolina battalion was posted on the right under General Francis Marion, "who," Greene reported, "also commanded the front line." In the center were the two North Carolina battalions commanded by

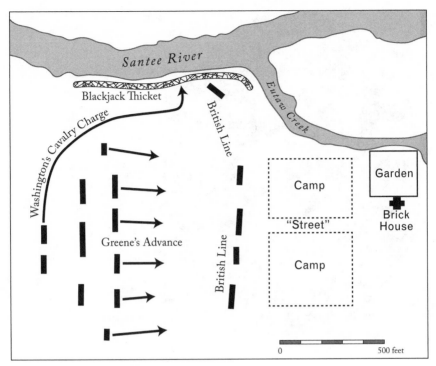

Battle of Eutaw Springs, 8 September 1781

the Marquis de Malmedy. General Andrew Pickens commanded the second South Carolina battalion, which was posted on the left. Two 3-pounders, Continental Captain Lieutenant William F. Gaines commanding, advanced with the front line. Upon reaching Stewart's main force, the militiamen of the front line would be the first to fight.[17]

Three brigades of regulars made up the second line: on the right three battalions from North Carolina commanded by veteran officers, Lieutenant Colonel John Baptist Ashe, Major John Armstrong, and Major Reading Blount, and in overall command another veteran, Brigadier General Jethro Sumner; two battalions of Virginians in the center commanded by Major Smith Snead and Captain Thomas Edmunds, overall command exercised by Lieutenant Colonel Richard Campbell; from Maryland two battalions on the left, Lieutenant Colonel John Eager Howard and Major Henry Hardman commanding, Colonel Otho Holland Williams in overall command. Joining the second line were two 6-pounders under the command of Captain William Brown.[18]

In advance were Lee's Legion on the right and Lieutenant Colonel William Henderson's South Carolina state troops on the left. Henderson was in overall command of the advance, his immediate subordinates Lieutenant Colonels

Otho Holland Williams,
1749–1794; oil painting
by Charles Willson Peale.
(Courtesy Independence
National Historical Park
Collection)

Wade Hampton, Charles Myddelton, and William Polk. Upon meeting the British main force, the advance was to retire upon the flanks of the front line. General Thomas Sumter was not present, but his men of the state troops would fight that day not only in concert with but in the manner of regulars, a deployment that Sumter had claimed would not work. Assigned to the reserve were Lieutenant Colonel William Washington's 3rd Continental Dragoons and the faithful Captain Robert Kirkwood and his Delaware Continentals. According to Otho Williams, the army marched in four columns.[19]

About 6:00 A.M., two hours after Greene's army left camp, two North Carolina conscripts who had deserted entered Stewart's camp with the news that the Americans were nigh and marching to attack. Stewart sent Major John Coffin (1756–1838) with 140 infantry and 50 cavalry "in order to gain intelligence of the enemy (as none could be collected by spies)." Coffin, a Massachusetts shipmaster turned soldier, had on his own joined the British assault on Bunker Hill in 1775 and displayed such courage that he was given a commission as an ensign in the British Army. Upon marching three miles and coming within sight of the American van, Coffin charged. Otho Williams believed that he did so out of "ignorance of its strength, and the nearness of the main army." Greene reported that the "Infantry of the State Troops kept up a heavy fire and the Legion" infantry, Captain Michael Rudolph commanding, "charged them with fixed Bayonets," whereupon "they fled on all sides, leaving four or five dead on the ground, and several more wounded."[20]

Coffin's appearance convinced Greene that Stewart with his main force was not far behind, and he decided to deploy both his first and second lines from column into line of battle. Before issuing that order, however, he paused for a tradition common to eighteenth-century armies and that Greene on this occasion especially adhered to in order, Otho Williams observed, "to have time for his raw troops to form with coolness and recollection." By "raw troops" he meant that the Carolina militia, though hardened as they were to partisan fighting, for the first time would engage in a formal, open-field battle in which opposing lines would approach each other in formation and without cover until they were firing at close range. Greene, therefore, "distributed the contents of his rum casks," before ordering "his men to form in the order for battle." Williams described it in fancier language in a letter to a friend: "we halted and took a little of the Liquid, which is not unnecessary to exhilarate the Chimiral Spirits upon such occasions." Spirits aroused, the army marched on in line of battle.[21]

Stewart had no choice but to stand and fight. "Finding the enemy in force so near to me," he reported to Cornwallis, "I determined to fight them as from their numerous cavalry a retreat seemed to me to be attended with numerous consequences. I immediately formed the line of battle with the right of the army to the Eutaw branch [Creek] and its left crossing the road to Roache's Plantation, leaving a corps on a commanding situation to cover the Charleston road and to act occasionally as a reserve."[22]

"The Militia Fought with . . . Spirit and Firmness"

While the British formed, the Rebels marched on, but not over open fields. Greene reported that "All the country is covered with Timber from the place the Action began to the Eutaw Springs." As Otho Williams observed, "being in woods," the lines had to move slowly to preserve order. But the "woods were not thick, nor the face of the country irregular; it undulated gently, presenting no obstacles to the march, although producing occasional derangements in the connection of the lines."[23]

When the militia met British pickets two or three miles from where the action with Coffin took place, they were ordered to keep firing as they advanced. The pickets were driven back. About 9:00 A.M. the militia came upon the British main force arrayed in line of battle. The dying time about to begin, officers on both sides, from cornets to generals, were with their men.[24]

The militia faced formidable fighters. All but 3rd Foot were veterans of vicious partisan fighting as well as set-piece battles: 63rd Foot, 64th Foot, a small detachment of 84th Foot in reserve, and the New York and New Jersey regulars who in savage hand-to-hand fighting had repulsed Greene's frontal assault at Ninety Six. Third Foot (Buffs) was one of the reinforcement regiments of recruits that had arrived only three months before. Instead of following the usual practice of assigning key battlefield commands to British officers, Stewart placed in command of his main line of resistance Greene's nemesis from Ninety Six, that stalwart New York City Tory Lieutenant Colonel John Harris Cruger, whom Stewart would later praise for his "conduct and gallantry during the action." Colonel Stewart also made two other decisions. On his right flank, almost at a right angle to his front line, in a thick stand of scrub oak known in South Carolina as a blackjack thicket, he stationed Major John Majoribanks (pronounced marshbanks) with the elite grenadier and light infantry flank companies of 3rd, 19th, and 30th Foot. Majoribanks's command was about 300 strong. Stewart's third decision was also made before the fighting started, as explained below.[25]

Otho Williams described "the ground on which the British army was drawn up" as being "altogether in wood; but at a small distance in the rear of this line, was a cleared field, extending west, south and east from the dwelling house, and bounded north by the creek formed by Eutaw Springs, which is bold, and has a high bank thickly bordered with brush and high wood." The latter was the blackjack thicket where Stewart had stationed Major Majoribanks and his flank companies. The British camp, with its tents laid out in a military manner, occupied part of the open field. The dwelling house mentioned by Williams was situated on a knoll behind the British right flank. It was a stout, two-story brick building "with garret rooms," impervious to small-arms fire, and commanding the entire open field. There were outbuildings, including a barn, to the left of the house. A palisaded garden extended from the house to the high bank of Eutaw Creek. Stewart's third decision concerned the house. He gave Major Henry Sheridan a standing order: "upon the first symptoms of misfortune" (to use Otho Williams's words), Sheridan with a detachment of New York Volunteers was "to take post in the house to check the enemy should they attempt to pass it" by covering "the army from the upper windows."[26]

Twenty-nine years after the battle Captain Lieutenant William Henry Gaines, commanding the two 3-pounders (known as grasshoppers) marching with the militia, recalled in a letter to Light Horse Harry Lee that about thirty minutes before the American front line came upon the enemy, Greene ordered him "to push forward down the road and to attack the enemy wherever I should find him." To protect Gaines from the possibility of a cavalry attack, Greene placed under his command "a Lieutenant and twenty-two" infantrymen. "I considered mine a forlorn hope," Gaines wrote, "and was happy to believe in the General's confidence in me by this instance of the honor conferred." He and his men quickly left the army behind by "nearly or quite a mile . . . when I received word from you that a body of the enemy were in rapid march and close upon me, upon the left." That is a very interesting statement. By "you" Gaines meant Lee, and we must ask: what was Lee, who should have been with his Legion advance on the right, doing elsewhere on the field? Lee "advised me to prepare immediately for action." Gaines declined, for "my orders were peremptory to march until I should see the enemy. While in hasty march and in conversation with you the enemy appeared." As he was leaving, Lee told Gaines that " 'I will endeavour to send a regiment to your relief.' " So as the action started Lee established a pattern of roaming the battlefield, giving orders to officers not under his command, and prepared to direct other units to where he saw fit.[27]

"In a few seconds Gaines engaged . . . with my little grass-hoppers and twenty-two fine fellows of the infantry." Otho Williams described the artillery duel as "bloody and obstinate in the extreme." Gaines let the British advance to "within twenty-five paces" before opening up with "canister shot," which "I relied upon altogether, the distance being too near even for the use of grape." But by "repeated firing the straps which covered the trunnions of one of my pieces gave way, and recoiled several feet from the carriage." Gaines immediately had the straps put back in place in order to give the appearance that the gun was operable, but it was "no longer fit for service." And "in a few minutes . . . the same misfortune attended the other piece." This came, however, as the British "gave way, and were pursued and cut to pieces" on the right by a "gallant little corps" of cavalry, "about twenty in number." Of the enemy, he wrote, "About one hundred and sixty lay before the mouths of the artillery."[28]

Meanwhile, advancing on the British line from the west, the Rebel militia did something they were thought incapable of doing. Marching in line of battle with drums beating, they began firing on the British and Tory regulars facing them. The British returned fire. Greene reported that "a most tremendous fire began on both sides from right to left." The militia, he wrote, "fought with a degree of spirit and firmness that reflects the highest honor upon this class of Soldiers." He also paid tribute to Generals Marion and Pickens and Colonel Malmedy, who "conducted the troops with great gallantry and good conduct." Another witness to this maelstrom was Otho Williams, who described the fighting even more vividly. "It was with equal astonishment, that both the second line and the enemy, contemplated these men, steadily, and without faltering, advance with shouts and exhortations, into the hottest of the enemy's fire, unaffected by the continual fall of their comrades around them." Thus we have come full circle from Greene's lament four years earlier: "To march over dead men, to hear without concern the groans of the wounded, I say few men can stand such scenes unless steeled by habit or fortified by military pride." Another Rebel militiaman echoed Greene when recollecting an earlier battle where "the dead and wounded lay scattered in every direction over the field," and noted: "however, by custom, such things become familiar." Some fifteen months of savage partisan warfare had hardened men to accept such scenes—provided they were well led. Williams attributed their behavior to their trust in Francis Marion and Andrew Pickens. One of Marion's men was his drum major, a slave named Jim Capers. His pension application stated that "he received four Wounds, Two cuts upon the face, one on the head with a sword & one with a Ball which passed through his left side, killing the Drummer immediately behind him." Capers was freed after the war. William Griffis was bayoneted at Kings Mountain, received a severe head wound at Guilford Courthouse, and at Eutaw Springs a ball "perforated his body by reason of which he has even now [1836] to wear a truss." Two of his brothers served with him at Eutaw Springs. Both were killed in action.[29]

The militia continued to stand fast and deliver their fire. Greene later wrote to Baron von Steuben that "The gallantry of the officers and the bravery of the troops would do honor even to the arms of his Prussian Majesty." On the British line John Harris Cruger, his fellow officers, and his troops were equally gallant, and upon the ranks of the Rebel militia Cruger's remaining artillery continued "vomiting destruction." At last, Otho Williams wrote, they "began to hesitate." Malmedy's North Carolinians wavered first. Greene noticed and ordered General Jethro Sumner and his newly raised North Carolina Continentals to plug the hole left in the center by Malmedy's militia. It was done and the fight raged on. In his report Greene paid tribute not only to Sumner's raw recruits but also to the British veterans. The North Carolinians "fought with a degree of obstinacy that would do honor to the best of veterans," keeping up a "heavy and well directed fire, and the enemy returned it with equal spirit, for they really fought worthy of a better cause, and great execution was done on both sides." But in its turn, Sumner's brigade began to give way. The British noticed and the troops on the left could not be restrained. It was bayonet time—nineteen inches protruding from a five-foot musket. Without orders—"by some unknown mistake," Stewart wrote—they charged, the troops shouting as they shortened the distance between them and the Rebels. For meeting cold steel, the militia of Marion and Pickens had neither the training nor bayonets of their own. They "yielded, and fell back," wrote Williams, but we can be certain that the withdrawal was not as orderly as his words imply, while the British troops in pursuit, sensing victory, were probably in some disorder, or "deranged," as Williams put it. It was a moment made for the regulars to intervene.[30]

"Let Williams advance and sweep the field with his bayonets," Greene ordered. Whereupon with drums rolling the Continental brigades shouted and advanced against the British left, which began to withdraw. At forty yards the Virginians delivered a volley. This was followed by Lee, leading his Legion infantry, wheeling against the exposed British left flank and delivering its own volley in a "destructive enfilading fire." The "British left wing," wrote Otho Williams, who watched from astride his horse as he commanded the American attack, "was thrown into irretrievable disorder." The center and right of the British line was still holding fast. But the fugitives of the left ran into and through them and they "began to give way from left to right." The Maryland Line then delivered its own volley. All along their line British resistance began to crumble. Lieutenant Colonel Henderson on the American left flank was seriously wounded and Lieutenant Colonel Wade Hampton commanding the state troops assumed command and led them in a charge that took "upwards of 100 prisoners," Greene wrote. He added that Colonel Washington brought up the reserve on the left and charged "so briskly with Cavalry and Captain Kirkwoods Infantry as gave them no time to rally or form. Lieutenant Colonels Polk and Middleton who commanded the State Infantry, were no less conspicuous for their good conduct than their intrepidity; and the Troops under their command gave a specimen of what may be expected from Men naturally brave, when improved by proper discipline," the latter comment perhaps meant as a dig against Thomas Sumter, who had raised the state troops. These men, Williams observed, were "in the most exposed situation on the field," for in addition to what faced them they were receiving flanking fire from Major Majoribanks's command in the blackjack thicket. "Never was the constancy of a party of men more severely tried," wrote Williams. Although matters were going well all along the front, it was obvious that eventually something had to be done about Majoribanks.[31]

First, however, it was time to turn the British front-line retreat into a rout. Otho Williams believed that at such a juncture "Cavalry are the military means in rendering disorder irretrievable," and that "the Legion cavalry might have been turned upon the British left with very great effect." They were in position to do so, and their infantry was in position to provide support. "Why this was not done," Williams wrote, "has never been explained; we can only conjecture . . . one or both of two causes that existed on that day. Col. Lee was generally absent from [his cavalry] during the action, and bestowing his attention upon the progress of his Infantry; and Captain Coffin" with his Tory cavalry was on the scene and according to

Williams "probably" outnumbered Lee. It is obvious, however, that Williams thought it worth the effort.[32]

Major Majoribanks and his 300-strong flank companies on the far right, ensconced in the blackjack thickets, stood fast and remained a threat not only to the state troops but also to the exposed flank of the Maryland Line as the regiment advanced. According to Otho Williams, Greene ordered Washington to charge the British right along with Wade Hampton's state cavalry and Kirkwood's infantry. Otho Williams described Washington's reaction to Greene's order. "Had he had the good fortune to have taken on Kirkwood's Infantry behind his men, all would have gone well; to have been detained by their march, would have been inconsistent with his general feeling." Stripped of its gentle language, Williams was really stating that Washington blundered. Ever the dashing cavalryman, he "galloped through the woods," leaving Kirkwood and his vital infantry component far behind while leading his dragoons into disaster. Majoribanks's men were safe inside the blackjack thickets, impenetrable to cavalry. Washington's blunder was made clearer in a statement by John Eager Howard. "The absurdity of cavalry charging infantry in a thick underwood, was shown at Eutau." Failing to dislodge Majoribanks, Washington ordered his dragoons to follow him along the thickets to reach the British battalion's rear. This maneuver exposed the troopers to close-range British musketry. "A deadly and well directed fire," wrote Otho Williams, "wounded or brought to the ground many of his men and horses and every officer except two." The ground was strewn with dead and wounded men and horses, the latter thrashing and screaming in their agony. Riderless horses galloped over the field. Trooper John Chaney recalled that "Washington jumped his horse into the midst of the enemy." His horse was killed and Washington was pinned beneath it, bayoneted in the chest, and taken prisoner. British soldiers emerged into the open to bayonet wounded and unhorsed riders. Lieutenant Gordon and Cornet Simmons escaped to continue fighting. Colonel Wade Hampton gathered to him the survivors of Washington's dragoons. When Kirkwood and his Delaware infantry arrived with bayonets at the ready, Majoribanks led his men down the creek bed, hidden by its high bank, and took positions in the palisaded garden next to the house and behind the bank of Eutaw Creek.[33]

Washington's disastrous charge did not appear to have had a negative effect on the advance of the American infantry. A rout was on. It was obvious that for the British the "first symptoms of misfortune" had arrived, thus high time for Major Sheridan to execute Colonel Stewart's standing order to barricade his detachment of New York Volunteers inside the house and prevent the enemy from passing. If we can believe Light Horse Harry Lee's memoirs, some of his Legion infantry led by Lieutenant Lawrence Manning were hot on the heels of Sheridan's New Yorkers as they took possession of the house. "One of our soldiers actually got half way in," Lee wrote, "and for some minutes a struggle of strength took place—Manning pressing him in, and Sheridan forcing him out. The latter prevailed, and the door was closed." Lieutenant Manning used prisoners his men had taken as shields as he withdrew, "the enemy in the house sparing him rather than risking those with him." Can we believe this tale of derring-do? With Lee one is often never quite sure, but he tells a good tale.[34]

Otho Williams tells a slightly different story. He describes a rout. "The whole British line was now flying before the American bayonet," and many prisoners were taken. He corroborates Lee's tale to some extent, agreeing that the Legion infantry "was very near entering the house pell mell with the fugitives." He does not mention a struggle in the doorway between Manning and Sheridan, instead stating that "It was only by closing the door in the face of some of their own officers and men that" Sheridan and his New Yorkers "prevented" Lee's infantry from entering the house. But he does agree that as they withdrew the Americans used British prisoners as shields.[35]

Meanwhile, where was the rest of the American infantry? The Marylanders and North Carolinians and Virginians? Why had they not joined the Legion infantry in the chase across the field? Otho Williams, who was there and in overall command of the Marylanders, gave one answer. "The retreat of the British army lay directly through their encampment, where the tents were all standing." The American infantry officers proceeded through the British camp into the open field, where they were exposed to intense fire from the house, especially from the upper windows, and suffered grievously. The surgeon of 1st Maryland reported that 1st Lieutenant James Ewing "recd Seven Wounds & nearly all his Men were Killed and wounded." And that paragon among regimental commanders, Lieutenant Colonel John Eager Howard, was seriously wounded when a musket ball broke his collarbone. Yet he "could not be prevailed on to leave the Field altho Suffering under a painful wound for many hours." But according to Williams, the temptations of the camp proved too much for most of the other ranks. He stated without equivocation that the camp "presented many objects to tempt a thirsty, naked and fatigued soldiery to acts of insubordination." The tents also provided "concealment" from the New York Volunteers who were delivering a "galling and destructive fire" upon the officers, who "found themselves nearly abandoned by their soldiers." Williams concluded: the troops, "dispersing among the tents, fastened upon the liquors and refreshments they afforded, and became utterly unmanageable."[36]

His account has been challenged with an argument that the troops were indeed held up in the British camp but not for the reason given by Williams.

There could have been little food, this argument goes, since Stewart had been reduced to foraging for sweet potatoes to feed his troops, and as for liquor, there could have been little rum in the camp as the casks were in the supply wagons in the rear. Thus the obstacles in the camp were the tents themselves, especially the ropes and stakes that held them up. It is true that for troops advancing in line of battle formation the camp would have presented an obstacle. But as a well-known eighteenth-century British military manual states, camps were laid out with wide spaces "called *streets*" (italics the manual's). They ranged from fifty-nine to ninety-nine feet, for unencumbered passage. Depending on the size of the force, there could be several streets, with a main or grand street being wider than the others. The officers managed to get through the camp without a problem, almost certainly by following the "*streets.*" Is it not reasonable to assume that they would have ordered the troops to deploy into columns in order to avoid the tents and their ropes and stakes and follow the "*streets*"? And can we simply dismiss Williams's testimony as "inaccurate"? He not only was there, in command of the Maryland Line, he was a man of high character whose reports of various actions in the Southern Campaign are of great value. I see no reason not to accept Williams's explanation of why all or most of the soldiers did not follow their officers through the British camp. He is supported by the pension application of James Magee, who served at Eutaw Springs. He testified fifty-one years later that "the British were driven beyond their baggage, when our men commenced rummaging their tents, drinking rum etc etc which the enemy discovering, came back upon us, & drove us back into the woods." Of course, pension applications must be used very carefully given the lapse of time and the faulty memories of old men. But an episode like this is of the type that is well remembered. The irony of all this is that even had the troops not stopped in the camp to plunder but passed through, they would have been just as easy targets as their officers were.[37]

With the American infantry attack stalled, Major Majoribanks on the British right, and Major Coffin with his mixed force of cavalry and infantry on the left, emerged to take advantage of the situation. Greene noticed these movements but was unaware that his infantry, which he meant to dispose of Majoribanks, was looting the British camp. To deal with Coffin he sent his longtime aide, Captain Nathaniel Pendleton, with orders to Lee to repulse Coffin. Pendleton's report of what happened is clear and direct.[38]

> When Coffin's Cavalry came out, Gen. Greene sent me to Col. Lee, with orders to attack him. When I went to the corps Lee was not there, and the order was delivered to Major Egleston, the next in

command, who made the attack without success." Pendleton continued, "The truth is, Col. Lee was very little, if at all, with his own corps after the enemy fled. He took some dragoons with him, as I was informed, and rode about the field, giving orders and directions, in a manner the General did not approve of. Gen. Greene was, apparently disappointed when I informed him Col. Lee was not with his cavalry, and that I had delivered the order to Major Egleston.

One of Andrew Pickens's officers, Colonel Samuel Hammond, said in his account of the battle that "my regiment was attached to Colonel Lee's." Hammond claimed that Lee could not be found where he belonged because he was attempting to take over command of the Virginia Continentals after their commander, Colonel Richard Campbell, was mortally wounded. Campbell's officers thought otherwise and an argument ensued. In Lee's absence, Major Eggleston led the Legion charge against Coffin and was repulsed. There can be no guarantee that Lee would have succeeded where Eggleston failed, but at the very least the charges of Captain Pendleton and Colonel Hammond indicate that Lee was pursuing personal glory at the expense of his duty. Their accounts, in conversation long before being put down on paper, would have circulated throughout the army, and Lee was aware of wagging tongues. Eutaw Springs festered over the years, and in his memoir Lee described the order carried by Captain Pendleton as "unfortunate and unauthorized" and the reason for the "turn in this day's battle." He added that Greene "never issued such orders." Surely the statements of Pendleton and Hammond outweigh Lee's version.[39]

Greene had meanwhile ordered his artillery under Captain William Brown forward in an attempt to neutralize the destructive fire coming from the house. The guns included his two 6-pounders and two 6-pounders captured when the British front line was routed. But in the open field beyond the British camp, having pushed too close to the house, the gunners were ripe targets for Sheridan's New York Volunteers firing from upstairs windows. Their entire fire was directed upon the gunners, and "very soon," wrote Otho Williams, "killed or disabled nearly the whole of them." It was then, Williams wrote, that Major Majoribanks sallied from the palisaded garden and seized the four 6-pounders and dragged them to the protection of the house. This statement is supported by Captain Lieutenant William Gaines, whose 3-pounders had broken down earlier in the fighting. "We shook hands as he [Brown] passed, and to my utter astonishment he returned in a few minutes without his pieces. . . . a small party from the house" had spotted the guns coming forward and "concealed themselves in the weeds until the pieces were in among them, when they showed themselves" and opened fire. Three of Brown's lieutenants were wounded, one mortally, and two sergeants and "two or three" gunner's assistants killed. According to Gaines, "the six pounders were taken without having fired a shot." And the gallant Majoribanks was not through. Otho Williams stated that Majoribanks was joined by some of Sheridan's men who left the house and charged the American infantry "among the tents, and drove them before him." Colonel Stewart, who was much given to tooting his horn, reported to Cornwallis that "When our left gave way, in rallying it I was obliged to expose myself much. The moment I had got the line in order, I placed myself at their head and charged the enemy, the flank battalion at the same time charging them in flank. They gave way in all quarters and their infantry never stoped till they got behind a swamp seven miles from the field of battle, leaving us entierly masters of the field." To his credit, however, he also wrote, "to Major Majoribanks and the flank battalion under his command I think the honour of the day is greatly due." (Majoribanks would suffer a mortal wound in the action.) Otho Williams described the end quite differently. "The American army, however, soon rallied, after reaching the cover of the wood, and their enemy was too much crippled to venture beyond the cover of the house." The brick house at Eutaw Springs had saved the British, playing a role similar, although on a lesser scale, to the stone house at Hougoumont, defended by British and German troops thirty-four years later at the Battle of Waterloo. The brick house was, as Wellington said of the Hougoumont house, "admirably situated."[40]

Greene decided that it was time to disengage. Sergeant Major Seymour reported that the troops "were so far spent for want of water, and our Continental officers suffering much in the action, rendered it advisable for General Greene to draw off his troops." The Americans were also running short of ammunition. Greene wrote that "The want of cartridges and the strength of the enemy's position prevented me from pushing our advantage farther." But the casualty rate among American officers and sergeants in this battle certainly was an important reason prompting Greene's decision. It was staggering: either fifty-five or fifty-six officers and forty sergeants killed or wounded. Among the wounded was Brigadier General Andrew Pickens, shot in the chest. John Eager Howard's son wrote of his father's "severe wound which kept him in ill health for several years, and from the effects of which he never entirely recovered." Greene reported that there was "no water nearer" than Burdell's, from whence the army had marched that morning. One wonders, however, why he did not avail himself of water nearby. Francis Marion's biographer and comrade in arms, William Dobein James, wondered the same, and wrote, "Plenty of water might have been procured, in Eutaw creek, some hundred yards from the battle ground; and why the retreat was not conducted there, or to the Santee River, distant a mile, this author is at a loss to discover: unless it was that Greene's force was scattered up the road, and he wished to concentrate it. It was not from dread of the enemy." Eutaw Creek was too close to the British to conduct a large-scale procurement of water, but James's suggestion of the Santee River seems a reasonable alternative. Yet Otho Williams agreed with Greene: "he withdrew his army to Burdell's, seven miles distant," because "At no nearer point could water be found adequate to the comforts of the army." Greene reported that "I left on the field of Action a strong Picquett." Williams corroborated this, adding that it was under the command of Colonel Wade Hampton. Colonel Stewart, on the other hand, denied the presence of a picket and maintained in one of his letters to Cornwallis that Greene's letter (to McKean) is "full of lies."[41]

"We obtained a complete victory," claimed Nathanael Greene to Governor Thomas Burke of North Carolina. "I totally defeated him," boasted Alexander Stewart to Cornwallis. Was the truth somewhere in between? A drawn battle, perhaps? No, that would be the easy way out. The truth is that the British were once again the tactical victors. Although Stewart did not "totally" defeat Greene, when one breaks off the fight and withdraws seven miles from the battlefield, leaving the enemy in possession of the better part of it, one cannot claim victory. And a strong picket does not constitute possession of the field. A picket is a body of soldiers posted to warn of an enemy's approach. Despite his character flaws—his fawning letters to Cornwallis help to reveal them—Stewart had proven to be a sound battle captain. Besides his key decisions made before the battle that were described earlier, he kept his nerve when all seemed lost and successfully counterattacked. Yet in what may have been his finest hour as a soldier he lost 84 killed, 351 wounded, and 257 missing (captured, really), almost 38 percent of his army. He could not risk another battle, whereas according to Otho Williams "it was Gen. Greene's intention, to renew the action the next day." This despite losing 139 killed, 375 wounded, and 8 missing: just shy of 23 percent of his force. (Captain Robert Kirkwood gave a return of 130 killed, 355 wounded, and 40 missing, a fraction over 23 percent.) The Rebels had fought the good fight, had lost, yet Greene was ready to fight again. But it was not to be. The following day Stewart began a retreat that, in the months following, did not end until the last British field army south of Virginia eventually entered British lines outside Charleston, unfit to remain in the field for major combat, never more to reappear except as raiding parties to obtain food and forage. So the continuing debate as to who won and who lost descends to mere quibbling. Otho Williams put it best some 233 years ago: "the best criterion of victory is to be found in consequences."[42]

Nathanael Greene had once more lost a battle, had once more won the strategic victory.

11

High Drama on Cape Fear

"Chagrin and Ill Humor Pervaded the Detachment"

Alexander Stewart claimed that he "remained all that day and the next" at Eutaw. But Marion reported that Stewart met a reinforcement of 300 men commanded by Major Arthur MacArthur on the morning of 9 September, the day after the battle, "about two miles above Ferguson's Swamp" and that "They Immediately turned down the road & Crossed that Swamp, & is now there halted." Greene knew that British reinforcements were marching to join Stewart, and he had detached Marion and Lee, wrote Otho Williams, "to watch the line of communications between the Eutaws and Fairlawn," the latter in the village of Monck's Corner. Lee and Hezekiah Maham had gone to the "Enemy's front." Prisoners had been taken: twenty-four British and four Tories, among them fourteen dragoons captured by "Six men of Lee and Maham." But Marion also reported that his horses "are so tired they cannot scarcely move."[1]

Marion wrote again on 11 September from a position near Stewart's bivouac. His riders then numbered "no more than" 100 men. In the late afternoon he received a message from Lee and Maham, who had encountered a British force of 300 infantry and about 15 cavalry "going down," that is, toward Charleston. Marion assumed they were on their way to meet reinforcements, and he was right. More of that later. There had been a skirmish, with Lee and Maham suffering two horses killed and two men wounded. Marion ordered them to rejoin him and await Greene's orders. The skirmish, however, was somewhat more complicated than that, given the two diametric accounts that have come down to us.[2]

In his memoirs Lee wrote that he assigned Captain Joseph Eggleston with a troop to attack the column's flank while Lee "moved along the road to force the enemy in front." Once Eggleston was in position, "the charge was sounded, and the cavalry rushed upon the enemy." But the wood through which Eggleston and his troop charged "was thickly set with black jack. It became more difficult as you came nearer the road." The British officer commanding the rear guard gave Eggleston a "warm reception," then fled, abandoning "several wagons." Lee admitted that Eggleston and his men were "roughly handled." Eggleston's horse was killed and his clothing and equipment "pierced" by five rounds. Lee described the action as "an unexpected issue, and which would not have taken place had not the wood arrested his progress." Really? Are we to believe that both Lee and Captain Eggleston, who were at Eutaw Springs and knew what happened to William Washington when he encountered blackjack thickets, committed the same error? Lee did not describe his own action, if there was one; he merely wrote that his "squadron was very little injured, having none of the impediments to encounter, which accidentally interfered with Eggleston." He described the action as a success that "turned out to be useless, for the miserable wounded supplicated to be permitted to proceed." Lee wrote that he magnanimously agreed, collected his own wounded, and rejoined Marion.[3]

Another memoirist who was at the same action disagreed. In the previous chapter we quoted Colonel Samuel Hammond's criticisms of Lee for his performance at Eutaw Springs. He now criticized Lee's actions on 9 September in even more heated fashion. Hammond claimed that the British infantry numbered only fifty or sixty and were marching in front of and behind "several wagons" and all the American prisoners from Eutaw Springs, including Colonel William Washington. When the British spotted Lee's force, the infantry deployed in front of the wagons. "We were halted," Hammond wrote. "Colonel Lee gave orders to Capt. Eggleston to charge with his troops and *take the escort*" (italics Hammond's). The rest of Lee's force formed in reserve. "Eggleston charged the enemy breasted by their bayonets and covered by their wagons." Although Hammond did not mention firing, the British may have fired one, perhaps two, volleys. And the horses would not have galloped into the massed bayonets, for in that respect horses are "smarter than people." Eggleston "lost several brave men, with a Sergeant of great merit, and was compelled to retreat in disorder. We saw this with great concern, but expected the attack would be immediately renewed successfully; but, to our amazement, a retreat was ordered. Chagrin and ill humor pervaded the detachment; Col. Maham and myself requested Col. Lee's permission to make an attempt with our own commands, and pledge ourselves to take upon *ourselves* the responsibility of the attack. We were peremptorily refused" (italics Hammond's).[4]

If Eggleston had encountered blackjack thickets, surely Hammond would have mentioned them. It seems more likely that Eggleston charged down the road. Once again we have reason to doubt Lee's story.

"The Condition of the Wounded Was Deplorable"

Three days after the battle Greene with the main army was at Martin's Tavern near Ferguson's Swamp, twelve miles from Stewart. The following day he ordered the troops to be ready to march back to Eutaw Springs on the 13th. Perhaps his withdrawal was recognition that he was not going to be able to catch Stewart. More likely, it may have been due to intelligence from Marion of the arrival on 12 September of General Paston Gould and 30th Foot at Stewart's bivouac at Colleton House near Monck's Corner. Upon his arrival, Gould took command of the army. He wrote to Sir Henry Clinton on 30 September reporting on his movements after arriving at Stewart's bivouac. He stated that it was not until 14 September that he had intelligence of Greene's presence at Martin's Tavern, but we know that Greene had returned to Eutaw Springs the previous day. Gould reported that he marched against Greene on the 16th, "with design to bring the Enemy to Action, or force them to cross the Santee." He informed Clinton that "Upon the first intelligence of our Movement Greene quitted his position and retired hastily to the Santee," crossed, and either "destroyed" or "concealed" the boats on the opposite side. Yet Greene had withdrawn three days before Gould marched: a minor impediment to a general seeking to pad his performance. In any case, Gould retraced his steps, as he was unable to cross the Santee without boats. He had also received news that a French fleet was somewhere "on the Coast, and the uncertainty of its destination," which led him to the decision that it would not be "adviseable to be at too great a distance from Charles Town in the Event that this Province should prove to be their Object." He therefore informed Clinton that he would fall "down gradually towards Monck's Corner."[5]

By 16 September Greene was once again in a camp of repose in the High Hills of Santee. It was just as well. The effect on the rank and file of the bitter fighting at Eutaw Springs and its heavy toll of dead and wounded officers and sergeants dictated a rest before the army gathered itself and set out again to drive the British closer and closer to Charleston's gates.[6]

The plight of the wounded was pitiful. In the eighteenth century, to be among the wounded after a battle was to descend into hell. In his pension application, Josiah Culbertson wrote that "I had seen the hospitals in

Philadelphia, Princeton, and Newark and would prefer dying in the open air of the woods." Even before the Battle of Eutaw Springs, Dr. James Browne had informed Greene that the hospitals were without medicines and supplies. And we should not let the use of the word hospital by contemporaries mislead us. The wounded would be lucky to have the shelter of a tent. Greene's aide, Captain William Pierce, recommended the establishment of a commissary "at the Hospital," with "two or three trusty Soldiers to assist him in procuring fresh Provisions, such as Chickens, Ducks, Mutton & to make soup and such things." There was no coffee, tea, or sugar, and "the Wounded are also very much in want of wine." Pierce wondered if it would all right to commandeer "a certain proportion of the inhabitants about Martin's and Monck's Corner." Otho Williams's description of the plight of the wounded was far more vivid and also reveals that wounded officers outranked enlisted men in care.[7]

> The condition of the Wounded was deplorable. We found them without necessaryes, some of them scarcely attended, and others wholly neglected; many had their wounds animated with fly blows [eggs of flies nesting in flesh], and all together they exhibited one of the most humiliating and distressing Scenes I ever beheld. Their moans indicating pain, want and despair impressed the Spirits of every humane Spectator with that pathetic sorrow which inclines to inactivity and despondence. I interested myself as much as possible for their relief but had not means to alleviate their misery. Doctr Brown left us with only one young Surgeon and I'm informed rode towards Coll Thompsons[.] Most of our wounded officers who were all well attended went that way.

There was little that Williams could do except gather the wounded in one location, place them in the care of two lieutenants, and "leave them two or three Days Provisions with an issuing commissary." But as the water in the that location "is not good . . . I hope you will order measures to be taken for removing them."[8]

"You Can Have No Idea of the Consternation Which Seized the Country"

While the Rebels and the British maneuvered and fought in the South Carolina Back Country, events occurred in North Carolina that were of little if any consequence to the overall Southern Campaign but by their dramatic nature—one in particular—either shocked or elated contemporaries and are therefore worthy of discussion. The events were dominated by three striking personalities.

Since the overwhelming defeat of a Tory force at Moore's Creek Bridge in February 1776, southeastern North Carolina had been more or less controlled by the Rebel state government. Although areas of the Back Country were thrown into turmoil in early 1781 by the passage of American and British armies as Cornwallis pursued Greene, and in March of that year by events leading to the Battle of Guilford Courthouse, once Cornwallis withdrew to Wilmington on the coast the Rebels remained firmly in control in the Back Country. The same cannot be said of the swamps and longleaf pine forests of the southeastern part of the state. "This country," wrote the British Major James Craig, who was there, "is in a glorious situation for cutting one another's throats."[9]

In chapter 1 we covered the occupation of Wilmington and its immediate environs in February 1781 by a small British force commanded by Major James Henry Craig (1748–1812), a strong personality described by a contemporary as "very short, broad and muscular, a pocket Hercules, but with sharp, neat features, as if chiseled in ivory. Not popular, he was hot, peremptory, and pompous ... clever, generous to a fault, and a warm and unflinching friend to those whom he liked." To which we might add, to those whom he did not like, namely Rebels, a harsh and unforgiving foe. Craig was thirty-three years old, a veteran of Bunker Hill in 1775, where he was severely wounded; of the Canadian campaign of 1776, in which he had played a key role at Trois-Rivières in turning back the American invasion; and as a captain in the 1777 Saratoga campaign, where he had so impressed General John Burgoyne on several occasions that he promoted him to major. He was wounded at least twice that year, once seriously. Craig would go on after the war to a distinguished career in the French Revolutionary and Napoleonic Wars; the conquest of the Cape Colony from the Dutch; divisional commander in Bengal; by 1801 Lieutenant General Sir James Craig, Order of the Bath; and cap his career, 1807–1811, as captain-general and governor-in-chief of British North America, where he was given special responsibility for Lower Canada (much of Quebec Province). Although he excelled in preparing Canada for an expected American invasion, his political acumen came nowhere near matching his military prowess, and it was in Quebec, especially when dealing with the French majority, that Craig revealed his belief in the superiority of British society over all others. He was tone deaf to "social and cultural differences." To Craig, the American populace was either for or against the British cause, and those who refused to swear allegiance to the king and join the Loyalist militia could expect no mercy.[10]

As described in chapter 1, Craig was unable to resupply Cornwallis at Cross Creek because of the activities of Rebel militia along the Cape Fear

River. Nevertheless, his presence at Wilmington gave heart to the Tories of southeastern North Carolina. For the first time since their disaster at Moore's Creek Bridge in 1776, they dared serious resistance against their oppressors. The Rebels were "very Loth to go Against the British," wrote a militia officer in February 1781, and were engaged against the local Tories, for they feared to "leave their Families Exposed to a set of Villains; who Dayly threatains their Destruction." And if Tory bands were hard pressed they could withdraw to Wilmington. One band, reported a Rebel leader, when threatened sought refuge in Wilmington, then "being well armed and equipt for war made a sally out into their old stronghold . . . and made a stand." Craig added to Rebel woes by sending out raiding and foraging detachments of his own troops. In April British infantry stormed a house holding sixteen Rebels. One British soldier was "slightly wounded," reported Craig. Of the Rebels, "all fell by the bayonet." Craig's continued presence in Wilmington coupled with his harsh tactics and raids by Tory and regular forces kept what had been a relatively peaceful, albeit repressed, countryside in turmoil.[11]

The Rebel governor of the state, the "witty and congenial" Thomas Burke (c. 1747–1783), was an Irishman born in County Galway. Describing years later his family's coming upon hard times, he wrote that "misfortunes reduced me to the alternative of domestic indolence dependence or an enterprising peregrination, and I very early made the choice of the latter." His peregrination took him in 1763 to Virginia, then to North Carolina, where he settled on a plantation near Hillsborough in the north central Back Country. A political radical, he was elected to the Continental Congress and involved himself in military affairs. Burke was strong-minded, and on one occasion tried to remove from the army General John Sullivan of New Hampshire on the grounds that he was "grossly incompetent." They traded insulting letters and their feud almost led to a duel. There was some truth in Burke's charge against Sullivan, but the general remained in active service. Thomas Rodney of Delaware thought that Burke "may Justly be stiled the ablest and most useful Member there at present." A good organizer and a man of enterprise, Burke was determined to move against the Tories.[12]

Burke wrote to Nathanael Greene that his first order of business would be to suppress Tory "violences and depredations." But he added that success in such an endeavor hinged upon eliminating Craig's force at Wilmington. Assuring Greene that he did not intend "any rash attempts on fortified places, with incompetent forces," he requested Greene's "opinion and advice." Although Burke did not ask Greene to send Continentals to assist in an action against Wilmington, in his reply Greene made sure Burke understood that such assistance was not possible. He agreed "that the best way of silencing the Tories is by routing the Enemy from Wilmington." But as he had previously made clear to Light Horse Harry Lee, although he had "long had it in contemplation to attempt something against Wilmington . . . my force and situation has put it out of my power." He offered Burke various pieces of advice and met two of his requests by allowing the Continental officer Colonel James Read to remain in North Carolina "to afford your Excellency every assistance in his power," and sending his chief engineer Colonel Thaddeus Kosciuszko "to afford you every aid you can wish." Otherwise, Governor Burke was on his own.[13]

Ironically, what Burke did not know was that Cornwallis had left an order with Major Craig that might have solved the Rebels' problem—provided it had been carried out. As noted previously, Cornwallis had ordered Major Nisbet Balfour in Charleston to send troop transports to Wilmington in case his Lordship decided to return to South Carolina. It is fair to state that Cornwallis never seriously considered returning. But before marching north he ordered Major Craig to remain at Wilmington to hold the town in the event that he did return and sail for Charleston. But if Cornwallis entered Virginia and joined forces with General William Phillips, Craig's orders were to use the transports to return his own command to Charleston, as he would no longer be needed in North Carolina. Thus when Cornwallis entered Virginia in late May, Craig's standing order to evacuate Wilmington went into effect.[14]

Craig, however, demurred, and presented a clear picture of a subject discussed in chapter 1: the demoralizing effect on Tories when British forces came, temporarily conquered, and left. On 28 May he wrote Major Balfour a candid letter.

> You can have no idea of the consternation which seized the Country on the arrival of the empty transports from the notion which immediately spread that we were going away[.] Had I remained as was first suppos'd only a few weeks for the supply of Lord Cornwallis's army, my going would not have been attended with such circumstances as it will now after here four months—Now it will add one to the many instances of this Kind which have rais'd a clamor against us . . . I am pretty confident even with what force I have I could encourage and support them so as to become masters of the Country and disarm the Rebels.[15]

Balfour and Rawdon approved Craig's plea that he remain in Wilmington. Subsequently, Craig learned that Cornwallis was displeased with Craig for staying so long, whereupon Craig expressed his "mortification" in an abject letter of apology to his Lordship. But Craig was right.[16]

"I Looked So Much like a Rack of Nothing but Skin and Bones"

A key part of Major Craig's operations was to capture Rebel leaders. On 30 July Craig wrote to Balfour that "One of my Tory parties under a Colonel Fanning, who is exceedingly active, surpriz'd a few days ago the whole heads of Chatham County, to the number of 36, who were assembled in the court house to draft men. He parol'd 24 but brought down 12 of the worst here." One of those twelve men observed to Craig that Fanning "had *beheaded the county*" (italics Craig's).[17]

David Fanning (1755–1825) came to be loathed by Rebels and their faithful chroniclers. But were the resourceful Fanning a Rebel leader he would have been celebrated throughout the Carolinas to our own times. As it was, his life during the war was an adventure tale writ large. Fanning's contemporaries passed down a description of a "man of fine pysique, small in stature, but very muscular and in early manhood very athletic." His complexion was described as "florid or sandy." He was probably of a "prickly disposition." Tradition has it that as a boy he was afflicted with a disease of the scalp known as "scaldhead" that rendered him bald, and to cover his baldness he thereafter wore either a silk skullcap or a wig. Yet his Canadian descendants, who maintain "a lively oral memory . . . were surprised and puzzled by the 'scaldhead' tradition." Another tradition maintains that after being orphaned young he was subjected to harsh treatment by his guardian. Why then did his daughter name one of her sons after that guardian, from whom Fanning learned how to run gristmills and sawmills? Based on Fanning's life we can accept that "His early training made him very self reliant, and caused him also to be exceedingly reckless and passionate." He was said to have been a "superb horseman and tamer of wild horses."[18]

Fanning's wartime experience, as related in his *Narrative,* is filled with deeds of derring-do, some of which seem far-fetched, but it gives us a vivid picture of life in a Back Country of hunters and hunted. He was almost certainly a Loyalist by conviction from the very beginning of the rebellion. Between 1775 and 1780, he largely led a life on the run in South Carolina, and in his *Narrative* regales us with Houdini-like escapes after being captured several times. How do we treat these tales? Improbable but possible? Let us leave it that David Fanning led a life of adventure worthy of the perils of heroes of fiction.[19]

He tells us that on one occasion he was found in the woods by a fourteen-year-old girl from a friendly family, who at first was afraid to come near him, for she thought him dead and now a spirit who stank. It was his undressed wounds that stank, and "I looked So much like a Rack of nothing But Skin and bones and . . . my Clothes all Bloody[.] my misery and Situation was beyond Explanation and no friend in The world that I could depend on."[20]

Friends succored him, he recovered, and his situation changed dramatically little over a year later, in May 1780, when Charleston fell to the British and the victor's columns marched into the Back Country. Fanning wasted no time in once again taking up arms for the king, even distributing the royal proclamation "through the country for upwards of 100 miles." He was at the Battle of Musgrove's Mill, and subsequently "fell in" with Major Patrick Ferguson's 1,100-man Tory force. But he was not with the doomed Scotsman when Ferguson was killed and his command overrun and destroyed by Rebel militia at the Battle of Kings Mountain in October 1780. The rising Rebel strength in South Carolina following that pivotal victory prompted Fanning to leave for North Carolina.[21]

There Fanning engaged in guerilla skirmishing with Rebel militia while Lord Cornwallis pursued Greene and finally engaged him at Guilford Courthouse in March 1781. Fanning remained to fight after Cornwallis abandoned the Carolinas for Virginia, because there remained at Wilmington Major James Henry Craig and his force of regulars, and their presence gave heart to the King's Friends. Chosen by his followers to lead them, Fanning made his way to Wilmington to receive Craig's blessing. On 5 July 1781, Major Craig issued a commission appointing Fanning "to be Colonel of the Loyal Militia of Randolph and Chatham Counties." He was two months shy of the coup that would make him famous down through the centuries and infamous to his enemies.[22]

"How Very Deficient We Are in the Military Sagacity and Diligence"

On 1 August Major Craig went on a rampage. Marching from Wilmington 330 strong—250 British regulars and 80 Tories—the following day he met a Rebel force of the same strength. According to Governor Burke, the Rebels under Colonel James Kenan were assigned to perform reconnaissance and to "Check their ravaging parties," by which he meant Tory raiders. But Kenan decided to fight Craig. Depending on the source, Craig made either a flank attack by cavalry and a simultaneous frontal assault by infantry, or a frontal assault by cavalry and an attack by infantry on the Rebel rear. Whatever tactic was used, the Rebels were sent flying. Governor Burke was disgusted. He wrote to Greene that it showed "how very deficient we are in in the Military Sagacity and diligence."[23]

Craig then headed for the old royal capital of New Bern, about eighty miles northeast of Wilmington. On the way he destroyed Rebel crops and burned and plundered their plantations. Plunder was not limited to slaves, horses, and valuables. One man reported that the British "robbed my house of our clothing." Craig's Tory allies increased from 80 to 400. A Rebel reported that the British were also "Enticeing Negroes to Desert their Masters and go with them." On 19 August Craig entered New Bern. Several ships were burned and over 3,000 bushels of salt destroyed. Given its vital importance to the life of humans and animals, the loss of the salt would have been keenly felt. Craig reported that "The universal cry among the common people is: 'We must conquer, submit or die. We cannot subsist without salt.'" Salt remained so scarce that in late October a bushel cost "fifty hard dollars," Craig wrote. Two days later he left New Bern and marched westward and laid waste everything in his path. While Craig marched and destroyed, Tory leaders including David Fanning raided elsewhere in southeastern North Carolina. Consternation swept Rebel ranks.[24]

But a glimmer of hope lay to the northward. Major General Anthony Wayne and his Pennsylvania Line had been ordered to reinforce Greene's army in South Carolina. Governor Burke and General Wayne were friends. Could not Wayne temporarily delay his march through North Carolina to oust Craig from Wilmington? Burke had good reason to be optimistic about Wayne's arrival. As early as 23 July the Marquis de Lafayette, commanding in Virginia, had informed Greene that under certain conditions he expected to send Wayne southward and had requested Burke to provide "subsistence and transportation" for Wayne's column. Burke wrote Greene on 31 August that he expected Wayne "hourly" and hoped he could remain in North Carolina "for a little time, in order that we may by one decisive[e] blow destroy the power of the Enemy in this State, and all their future hopes by an entire extirpation of the disaffected." Craig himself received rumors of Wayne's approach with 1,100 Continentals and had thereupon marched back to Wilmington. But Wayne was not approaching. Washington had ordered Lafayette to keep Wayne in Virginia until instructed otherwise. For something far more important than striking the British at Wilmington and quelling the Tory rising in North Carolina was in the offing.[25]

In his memoirs Light Horse Harry Lee asserted that Greene planned a secret expedition to take Wilmington and on 2 August had ordered Lee to "hold himself in readiness, with his Legion" and the Delaware and Maryland Light Infantry. There is no such order in the Greene Papers, but for security purposes it could have been an oral instruction. Letters that Greene wrote to Alexander Martin, Anthony Wayne, and Washington offer strong evidence that Greene did plan such an expedition. But Lee failed to mention that it was to be a joint operation with General Wayne and his Pennsylvania Line should Wayne march southward to join Greene. Washington's order to Lafayette to keep Wayne in Virginia would have been enough to prompt Greene to shelve the plan, although Greene informed Washington that it was Governor Burke's misfortune, to be described shortly, that led to his decision.[26]

Lee also added a dramatic tale to his story of the aborted Wilmington expedition. "Minute intelligence respecting the enemy and his defenses, as well as boats for passage of the Cape Fear River, remained to be procured before the expedition could commence." Lee wrote that he dispatched Captain Michael Rudulph "with a small party from the Legion infantry, to acquire the one and to collect the other." In the dark of night Captain Rudulph and his men stole out of camp, made their way through woods to the Pee Dee River, crossed it, "and approached with celerity the country south of the Cape Fear." Acting "with his usual diligence and caution," Rudulph carried out his mission to perfection and sent back a report "so favorable" that "The day was fixed for Lee's march . . . his final orders were made out." Then, Lee wrote, Greene was informed by Washington that a French fleet would probably arrive on the American coast in the fall, whereupon Greene cancelled the operation, as he believed that as soon as the British learned "of the probability of a visit from the French fleet, the garrison would be withdrawn from Wilmington." Captain Rudulph was recalled, "holding nevertheless secret his visit to Cape Fear."[27]

Lee once more lived up to his gift for storytelling, and it is tempting to believe that he made up the Rudulph tale. But the possibility of such a secret mission must be admitted, with the lack of documentation made necessary by the need for secrecy.

Returning to reality, Major Craig's march back to Wilmington revealed once again London's pipe dream that few Americans favored rebellion. As soon as his column passed through an area, Rebel militia hiding in swamps and forests emerged and sought blood revenge on their fellow Americans. In one incident eighty light horse caught up with a Tory band, "cut many of them to pieces, took several and put them instantly to death." Governor Burke, however, had given up on here today, gone tomorrow militia and resolved to raise a force that would remain in the field until, he wrote, "the business is completely finished." He aimed at raising two to three thousand militiamen for three months to operate against not only Tory militia but also Major Craig's regular force at Wilmington. Most of these men would have to be raised in the western districts. Burke, therefore, moved his government to Hillsborough in the Back Country. Meanwhile, David Fanning had gathered a force of a little over 1,200 Tories near Hillsborough. With him were Colonels Archibald McDugald and Hector McNeil. A Rebel force about 240 strong under General John Butler was forty miles away across the Haw River. Burke was aware of Fanning's presence in the area and wrote to Butler that the

Fanning-McNeil force "intend some stroke and I am fully persuaded that it is against you." Burke's conviction was the biggest mistake of his life.[28]

"I Had Previously Determined . . .
to Take the Rebel Governor Burk"

Given Major Craig's policy of capturing Rebel leaders, what bigger prize than Governor Thomas Burke? Fanning recalled, "I had previously Determined within myself to take the Rebel Governor Burk . . . and had a conversation with Major Craigg on the subject." According to Fanning, he feinted in the direction of General Butler's Rebel force, then marched for Hillsborough. He may have taken with him only 600 to 700 men. They "pushed on," Fanning wrote, "all that day and the following night." At seven o'clock on the morning of 12 September, Fanning burst into unsuspecting Hillsborough in three columns. Fifteen Rebels were killed, twenty wounded, and about two hundred taken prisoner, including several Continental officers, colonels among them, and seventy-one enlisted men. But the real prize was the capture of Governor Thomas Burke and his entire council. It appeared that Fanning had cut off the head of the snake.[29]

A careful historian of the entire affair, Algie I. Newlin, wrote that Fanning's force remained in Hillsborough for several hours and laid it to a "looting spree" that gained fresh momentum "with the discovery of a large stock of whiskey. . . . They yielded to no restraint and became a howling mob as they swarmed about the village, rioting and looting." It was sometime between noon and 2:00 P.M before the Tory column left Hillsborough, marching eighteen miles that day and night and eight miles the following day to Lindley's Mill.[30]

Colonel Hector McNeil commanded the advance guard of the long Tory column. Upon being informed that McNeil's security was lax, Fanning pushed ahead and joined the advance guard and confronted McNeil. Before the latter could answer Fanning's query on security, they were fired on. For General Butler, upon receiving news of the debacle at Hillsborough, had reacted immediately, gained Fanning's front, and set up a well-laid ambush. Butler's men, now about 300 strong, were positioned on the brow of a broad plateau overlooking the road approaching Lindley's Mill. The opening Rebel fusillade killed three men, including Colonel McNeil. Fanning's description of McNeil's death is brief and stark: he "Received 8 balls through him and five through his horse." A simultaneous attack was aimed at the rear of the column, where the prisoners were under guard. Fanning ordered the advance guard to retreat to where he had left the prisoners. Once they were secured, possibly in a Quaker meeting-house by the roadside, he planned an attack on the Rebels. There followed a vicious four-hour fight that ended when the Rebels withdrew. They suffered twenty-five killed, ninety wounded, ten captured—a casualty rate of just over 41 percent. Fanning lost twenty-seven killed, sixty too critically wounded to be moved, and thirty walking wounded, some 17–19.5 percent of his force. Fanning was one of the badly wounded: "at the conclusion of the Action I received a shot in my left arm which broke the bone in several pieces and the loss of Blood was so Great that I was taken off my horse and led to a secret place in the woods." Unable to continue, Fanning turned over the command to Colonels Archibald McDugald and Archibald McKay and Major John Rains and directed them to send a courier to Wilmington to inform Major Craig of their prize captive and their situation. Three men remained with Fanning, and within four days another seventeen would appear to assist in his care and security. It would take Fanning twenty-four days to recuperate enough from his wound that he could be lifted onto a horse. In his narrative he paid high tribute to the officers to whom he had turned over command of his little army. Pursued by General Butler, they marched 160 miles, did not lose one prisoner, and turned them all over to Major Craig, who had marched to meet them.[31]

It was left to the Quakers of the area around Lindley's Mill to do what they could for the critically wounded and bury the dead. Thirty-four of the corpses were laid in a mass grave.[32]

"Treating the Inhabitants Denominated Tories with Great Severity"

If the Tories and Major Craig believed that Fanning's coup would end Rebel resistance in North Carolina, they were badly mistaken. Governor Burke's plan went into action when the militia of the Salisbury District in the Back Country was called out by General Griffith Rutherford. In early October, about 1,150 strong, they marched eastward to take on not only the Tory militia of southeastern North Carolina but also Major Craig and his British regulars. They joined up with General Butler and his men and by mid-October encountered a force of 300 to 600 Tories at a place called Raft Swamp (near modern Red Springs, North Carolina), about eighty miles west of Wilmington. The Tories were routed after a sharp, running fight in which Rutherford used cavalry to great effect. That ended Tory resistance in the region. Rutherford then prepared to move on Wilmington.[33]

Reports had reached Nathanael Greene that Rutherford was "treating the Inhabitants denominated Tories with great severity driving them indiscriminately from their dwellings without regard to age or Sex and laying waste their possessions destroying their produce and burning their houses."

Following his oft-repeated policy of a mixture of firmness and mercy toward the disaffected, Greene treated Rutherford to a long lecture, stressing that "in national concerns as well as in private life passion is a bad councellor and resentment an unsafe guide." For "To detach the disaffected from the British interest is our true policy and this can be done by gentle means only; and such as remain stubborn and obstinate there is ways and means of bringing them to punnishment far more consistent with the dignity of Government." Rutherford denied the stories and Greene accepted, at least on paper, that the reports he had received were "groundless." Given Rutherford's reputation for "cruelty," however, as well as the consistent savage nature of the fighting between Rebel and Tory militia bands, in which retaliation was the rule not the exception, I believe we can accept the reports as true.[34]

Rutherford divided his force for the approach march to Wilmington. One hundred cavalry and 200 mounted infantry under Captain Robert Smith marched down the west bank of the Cape Fear River. Rutherford and the main force crossed to the other side of the river and advanced on Heron's Bridge, ten miles from Wilmington. There a British detachment had been stationed since early in the British occupation. Craig withdrew the troops. And there the matter rested for about a month. Heavily outnumbered, Craig could not march out to challenge Rutherford to battle. Rutherford on the other hand had no artillery and dared not send his horde against British regulars behind their defensive works. Captain Smith, goaded by his men, had tried that against a fortified brick house on Eagles Island across from Wilmington. Surrounded by an abatis, it was defended by fifty Tories and Hessian Jaegers. Smith's attack proved futile, and after an hour's fight he withdrew with one dead and several wounded.[35]

With the British unable to send out foraging parties, the food situation in Wilmington became grim. It has been suggested that perhaps that is why Major Craig expelled from the city all Rebel women and children, allowing these noncombatants "to carry with them nothing but" the clothes on their backs. According to some of the women, Wilmington's Tories opposed Craig's "inhuman edicts" and "with all their power strove to mitigate our sufferings." Whatever his reason, Craig on this occasion as well as during his scorched earth raids in the countryside revealed a cruel nature to match Griffith Rutherford.[36]

With Lord Cornwallis's surrender at Yorktown on 19 October 1781, there was no reason for the British to continue their North Carolina adventure. Craig was ordered to evacuate Wilmington, and on 18 November transports loaded with troops and Tory refugees sailed for Charleston. David Fanning was not among them. Upon recovering from his severe wound, he carried on the fight, even after Craig's evacuation of Wilmington. But by January 1782 he was negotiating a truce with the Rebel government. Truces came and went and were repeatedly violated by Rebels and Tories alike. Following a Rebel ambush, he carried out a final raid in the usual partisan fashion. Several Rebel officers, including Colonel Andrew Balfour of the Randolph County militia, were assassinated and their homes burned and plundered. But Fanning was growing "weary of the disagreeable mode of Living I had Bourne with for some Considerable time." One of his first steps in seeking a settled life was marrying sixteen-year-old Sarah Carr. Fanning arrived in Charleston in June 1782; Sarah followed. According to Marion's biographer, Fanning pestered General Alexander Leslie to give him a command and a "handsome reward" to bring him the heads of Marion and Greene. The story is lent weight by Greene's warning to Marion: "It is said that Fanning is determined to have you dead or alive therefore take care of your self." General Leslie rejected the proposal, and Fanning and Sarah eventually ended up in New Brunswick, Canada, in September 1784. He bought land, farmed, owned a gristmill and a sawmill, was elected to the provincial assembly in 1791. He and Sarah had three children, a daughter and two sons. Life was going well for the old partisan. Ten years later, however, David Fanning became the assembly's first member to be expelled as a felon. The previous year he had been convicted of raping one Sarah London and sentenced to death. He vigorously denied the charge, claimed it was politically motivated, and appealed to the governor for a pardon. He received the pardon but was banished from New Brunswick for life. He and his family went to Nova Scotia, where he once again prospered, grew old, and died in 1825, age seventy. His greatest exploit, the capture of Governor Thomas Burke, spread his name far and wide but was of no consequence to the outcome of the Southern Campaign.[37]

Following his capture and delivery to Major Craig, Governor Burke's Via Dolorosa continued. He was sent to Charleston, imprisoned on Sullivan's Island, and was eventually granted parole to live on James Island. But there he was at the mercy of newly arrived North Carolina Tories. When two men standing on either side of him were shot by snipers, one killed and the other wounded, he feared for his life and asked the new British commandant in South Carolina, General Alexander Leslie, for either a parole inside American lines or a safe place within British lines. Leslie did not answer him, and Burke therefore decided that the British had violated his parole. He escaped and made his way to Nathanael Greene's camp. He offered to return to Charleston if he were held under the same conditions as a Continental officer, but the British refused. Whereupon Burke left Greene's camp for North Carolina and resumed his governorship. Greene convened a court of inquiry to investigate the matter. In an age where personal honor among gentlemen was a sacred concept, the decision was devastating. For "it was the opinion of the Court and General Greene that the Enemy have legal claim upon you as a prisoner of war, that your leaving Headquarters before the matters could be settled or adjusted, and that your taking the Government under those circumstances is considered highly reprehensible in you and dishonorable to the State."[38]

In a hot-tempered letter to Otho Holland Williams, who had delivered the court's decision through William Richardson Davie, Burke defended himself and accused Williams of "overweening arrogance." But many in North Carolina, especially army officers, also felt that Burke had dishonored himself. He expected to be drafted to serve another term as governor. He was ignored and Alexander Martin, who had served as acting governor in his absence, was elected. A historian wrote of Burke, "Although impetuous, obstinate, and idealistic, few men of his time had greater impact on the evolving political developments." How sad then that this talented man, who could have been of good service to the new nation coming into being, left this world so early. He became seriously ill in October 1783. Embittered by his experience, separated from his wife, Burke died at his plantation the year the war ended, December 1783, "alone, unable to sleep, in physical pain and mental anguish and . . . Laboring under a Complication of disorders." He was thirty-six.[39]

And what do we make of the Carolina adventures of Major James Henry Craig? The original purpose of the British occupation of Wilmington, to supply Cornwallis's army, was certainly a legitimate military operation. As we know, that failed. How, then, do we judge Craig's continued presence and his devastating raids into the interior of southeastern North Carolina? To Nathanael Greene, Craig's "views were calculated to increase his own glory more than to improve his Masters interest." Yet in his critique of British policy, Craig's argument that the Tories would have been devastated had he left has, on paper at least, merit. But his campaign after his failure to supply Cornwallis, and his Lordship's departure for Virginia, was an exercise in futility that led to a savage Tory rising that provoked an equally savage Rebel response that in the end prevailed. His force was too small to permanently suppress Rebel activities, and his efforts to do so had no effect on the outcome of the Southern Campaign. When one contemplates those several months of terror, murder, arson, and plundering by British regulars and the militia of both sides, one hears not the jubilation of victors, but the shrieks of men being hacked to death, the crackling of flames consuming homes and belongings, and the lamentations of widows and orphans.[40]

12

"Like Goths and Vandals of Old"

"Sick and Unfit for Duty"

As southeastern North Carolina went up in flames, Greene continued to hope that the French fleet under Admiral de Grasse would sail south after its mission at the Chesapeake was finished and combine with Greene's army to force the British surrender of Charleston. Although Washington had warned him as early as 4 September that de Grasse "could not continue a long Time on the Coasts," Greene could not let go of the tantalizing possibility that de Grasse might relent. In his reply to Washington of 7 October he persisted. "One thing . . . in your Excellency's letter which gives me pain that is the stay of our Ally upon this coast can be but short. After your success against the Enemy in Virginia it will be a pity not to improve the opportunity for the recovery of Charles Town. The suffering of the Southern States claim every attention and I hope every exertion will be made for their relief." Greene continued his campaign to enlist de Grasse's fleet the following day in a letter to Lafayette. "Let me beg you if it is practicable to prevail with our good ally to prosecute the operations southerly."[1]

He also felt the need to have a personal emissary plead his case and sent both letters north by Light Horse Harry Lee. He wrote to Lafayette, "I have two things in view in sending him[;] one is to give the General full information respecting matters in this quarter and the other is to learn fully his intentions respecting a Southern expedition."[2]

While Greene waited and hoped, he planned operations to drive the British into Charleston. The long-awaited arrival of Colonels Isaac Shelby and

John Sevier with their Over Mountain riflemen was so much on his mind that he went to Charlotte "in hopes of meeting" Sevier. For Sevier was marching. He was already at Ramsour's Mill, North Carolina, about thirty-four miles northwest of Charlotte, and had informed Greene that "Our Troops are all Mounted & shall March with Industry." Sevier also reported that Shelby had rendezvoused with his men. He had some fear that Shelby would join his force to General Griffith Rutherford's in North Carolina, but believed he too would come on once he heard from Greene.[3]

In mid-October 1781 bad news arrived in a letter from Colonel Otho Holland Williams at the army's encampment in the High Hills of Santee. The hospital's physicians and surgeons were all "sick and unfit for duty" and the Southern Department's chief physician, Peter Fayussoux, "is severely attacked by a fever." The fever afflicting Dr. Fayussoux was malaria. "Several of our Soldiers are Dead," Williams continued, "and others are dying yit the number of sick does not decrease." So many wagoners were in the hospital that enlisted men were detailed to care for the draft horses. Malaria had taken such hold that "Battalions can scarce form Companies." But as for the few who were healthy, they "wear cheerful faces" and appear "too much accustomed to danger to be alarmed." Williams was also relieved on another score: cattle arrived "to Day" and flour was expected "every Day" following. He hoped "this dreadful Season will soon be over" and that when he wrote again it would be with more "agreeable intelligence." In a letter to the president of the Continental Congress, Greene's description of the plight of the wounded was graphic: "the little means we had . . . & the great numbers of our surgeons which fell sick in service, have left our sick & wounded in a most deplorable situation and numbers of brave fellows, who have bled in the Cause of our Country, have been eat up by maggots & perished in that miserable situation."[4]

To all this was added discontent in the ranks. Greene hinted at it in a letter of 18 October to his commissary, William Richardson Davie, in which he took Davie to task over the lack of that eighteenth-century necessity—salt. At the time the army had half a barrel. "I shall only observe that an Army which has received no pay for more than two years[,] distressed for want of cloathe, subsisted with spirits and often short in the usual allowances of meat and bread will mutiny if we fail in the article of salt; and besides . . . it would soon produce such a variety of diseases and complaints that the greater part would soon be transferred from field to hospital." If for the lack of salt the army was forced to "disband[,] the evil will rest at your door." The seriousness of the situation is highlighted by Greene's harsh words to a friend, confidante, and comrade in arms. Davie wrote before receiving Greene's letter that "a large quantity of salt" was at Edenton, North Carolina, but he had not the money to pay for it. Greene's retort implied that Davie was exaggerating the problem, that "many difficulties" are overcome by "proper exertions," "industry," and "patience and perseverance." In November Greene learned that twenty bushels of salt had left Salisbury for the army and fifty bushels were waiting for Davie to forward.[5]

Lack of salt was just one problem. Wrote the early historian David Ramsay, "a dangerous spirit made its appearance among the Maryland soldiers." They had many grievances and longed for home. According to Ramsay, they sent several petitions to Greene, "complained of want of clothing" and "that out of seven regiments there were scarce two hundred [men] remaining, and that they have never received any pay." On the night of 21 October "numbers were seen to go privately out of their camp with their arms etc." Alarm swept the officer corps. They ordered to the men to parade for roll call. As this was going on, a South Carolina soldier, Private Timothy Griffin, came on the parade drunk, and shouted, "Stand by it, boys. Damn my blood, if I would give an inch," and continued his tirade until Captain M'Pherson of the Maryland Line knocked him down. The following day Griffin was court-martialed for "encouraging mutiny and desertion" and sentenced to be "Shott to Death" that day. About 5:00 P.M., "in the presence of the whole army," Private Timothy Griffin of the South Carolina Line met his maker. The rank and file took notice and the crisis eased but the situation would continue to fester.[6]

Despite the travails of the army, Greene would have felt some measure of relief if he could have read a letter of 12 October from Nisbet Balfour to Lord Germain. The losses suffered at Eutaw Springs, plus "the smaller" losses "that from Climate as well as service are daily occurring," had "greatly reduced the Actual Strength of the Army Operating here."[7]

"Like Goths and Vandals of Old"

Although his main concern was the British Army in the Low Country, Greene was not unmindful of the security of the far Back Country. There were no British posts left there, no British regulars to contend with, and the Tories who stayed were cowed after the British withdrawal to the Low Country. But there was another menace. On 15 October Governor Rutledge wrote Greene asking if he wanted "the whole draught" of Pickens Brigade "to march down immediately," or if the Ninety Six regiments should stay to defend "agst the Incursions of Indians and Tories." The Tories Rutledge referred to were those who had taken refuge with the Cherokees in the mountains west of the Ninety Six District. Rutledge thought that Pickens's plan to deal with this problem might be "effected before the Men would be wanted" to join the main army. Greene's reply was emphatic. He asked Rutledge to inform Pickens "that it is my opinion the two regiments he mentions had best be employed for the protection of the frontiers," and he asked Rutledge to so instruct Pickens. "Our situation is far from being agreeable," he continued, "and there are strong reasons for an attempt to drive the Enemy into Charles Town but the support of the frontiers is indispensably necessary, and nothing on my part shall be wanting to enable them to stand their ground."[8]

The Indian danger to the frontier and Back Country was of long standing. The far frontier was west of the Appalachians in what is now East Tennessee, where Sevier and Shelby's Over Mountain Men lived. The Back Country, also thought of as a frontier, was east of the mountains in the western parts of North Carolina, South Carolina, and Georgia. Indians throughout the country knew that an American victory in the Revolutionary War would unleash hordes of land-hungry settlers who had no respect for treaties establishing lines between settlers and Indians. Thus from the beginning most had thrown in their lot with Britain, which had established the Proclamation Line of 1763 in the Appalachian mountains forbidding settlement west of the line without permission of the Crown. Not that the settlers had paid much attention to it. Nor did their leaders. George Washington, then actively engaged in land speculation, regarded it as a "temporary expedient to quiet the minds of the Indians." The Indian owners of the land and the white invaders were engaged in a brutal, no-holds-barred 300-year war for control of the continent. Like Egyptians and Assyrians and Greeks and Romans and Arabs and Vikings and Mongols and Aztecs before them, like Zulus after them, frontier Americans were conquerors, and they had the conqueror's self-confidence that their cause was just. Whether simple farmers or nabobs, they were obsessed with dreams of land and opportunity. They would have that land, they would have it any way they could take it, and if their manner of taking did not square first with British, then U.S. policy, so be it. They swarmed, valley by bloody valley, "like Goths and Vandals of old" wrote the Virginia planter William Byrd of the Scotch-Irish among them. For they had the "West in their eyes." In our time the settlers have been demonized by some writers. One claimed that "the worst representatives of the white man's society went into the wilderness first," which reveals generational chauvinism as well as aping the attitudes of the eighteenth-century eastern gentry. Not that there can be any doubt that the settlers were, in the words of a Creek who knew them well, of a "turbulent and restless disposition." A frontier wife gave her take on it to an English traveler in the early nineteenth century. "'It is all for the mere love of moving. We have been doing so all of our lives—just moving from place to place—never resting—as soon as we get comfortably settled, then it is time to be off to something new.' When asked why she did not finally refuse, she said, 'Oh, my dear, you don't know what it is to be married to a gadding husband.'" Whatever their reasons, they were like locusts, but unlike the insect variety they never went away.[9]

During the Revolution, the fighting on the southern frontiers began in July 1776 when the Cherokees, armed with 5,000 pounds of British powder and lead, rose in defense of their homeland. Henry Stuart, brother of John Stuart, British Indian agent in the South, had brought the ammunition to the Cherokees on twenty-one packhorses from Mobile. He and Alexander Cameron, British agent to the Cherokees, urged the Cherokees to wait and act in concert with a British offensive. But they should have known better than to supply the Cherokees with the wherewithal to make war and not expect them to put it to immediate use. West of the Appalachians, the Cherokee offensive succeeded in forcing scattered settlers to flee one valley, but they were repulsed elsewhere. The Cherokees were more successful east of the mountains, attacking the Back Country from Virginia to Georgia with musket and tomahawk, scalping knife and faggot. Cherokee war parties included Tories, in one case, reported a South Carolina Rebel, "about ninety Indians, and 120 white men." They "spread desolation all along the frontiers, and killed a great number. . . . Plantations lie desolate, and hopeful crops are going to ruin." In North Carolina people in two western counties abandoned their homes and forted up, as they said then. "About thirty houses burned and plantations destroyed hundreds of fields loaded with A plentiful harvest laid waste and destroyed, many cattle killed and horses taken away."[10]

Retribution was swift and terrible. That autumn of 1776, from Virginia and the Carolinas, powerful militia columns struck deep into Cherokee country, burning and pillaging towns, storehouses, and crops. No memorable battles were fought, only hopeless skirmishes, for the forces arrayed against them were too formidable for the Cherokees to seriously resist. The earth was scorched by the invaders. The Virginia column alone, Colonel William Christian commanding, reported that the Indians had left behind "horses, cattle, dogs, hogs, and fowl," and "between forty and fifty thousand bushels of corn and ten or fifteen thousand bushels of potatoes." The Cherokees, a mountain and agricultural people, were left to face winter without lodges or food. They were knocked out of the war for the next four years, and their disaster so discouraged their neighbors to the south, the Creeks, that their full strength was never brought to bear in service of the British cause. Creek reluctance extended to the other southeastern Indian nations. The explanation offered by John Stuart reminds us of the repeated complaints by Tories of British failure to support them, and is linked to that failure. He reported that "all the Southern Tribes are greatly dispirited, by the unopposed successes of the Rebells, and no appearance of any Support from Government to His Majesty's distressed subjects in the interior parts of the Provinces, or to the Indians who have engaged in His Majesty's cause."[11]

But by late 1780, with a British army in the Deep South and British agents among the Indians, the Cherokees took heart and planned to once more launch an offensive. Unfortunately for them, their plans became known and the Americans struck first. A force of 300 Over Mountain Men under Colonel John Sevier and 400 riflemen from the mountains of southwestern Virginia, Colonel Arthur Campbell commanding, swept through Cherokee country, killing and burning. Campbell reported to Thomas Jefferson that towns "in which were upwards of one thousand Houses, and not less than fifty thousand Bushels of Corn, and large quantities of other kinds of provisions, all of which, after taking sufficient subsistence for the army whilst in the Country, and on its return, were committed to flames or otherwise destroyed." The disaster of 1780 was also described the following year by the well-known Cherokee leader Raven, who managed to make his way to Savannah and speak to Thomas Brown, whose sufferings at the hands of Rebels and stout defense of Augusta were described in chapter 5. Brown was now the new British superintendent of Indian affairs in the South. Raven told him that "The Rebels from Virginia attacked . . . in such numbers last fall there was no withstanding them, they dyed their hands in the Blood of many of our Woman and Children, burnt 17 towns, destroyed all our provisions by which we & our families were almost destroyed by famine this spring." Raven also admitted that a delegation of chiefs had gone to Virginia "to make the Rebels believe the Nation meant Peace, but it was only to save the Corn upon the Ground & prevent our towns being burnt[.] when our Corn is made we will attack them with as much spirit as ever."[12]

A leading historian of Indian-white relations in the South during the war judged Raven's words as merely "attempts at maintaining prestige and acquiring supplies." It is certainly true that the Cherokees never again mounted an offensive to equal their failed effort in 1776. But in the fall and winter of 1781 and into 1782 the Ninety Six District remained in danger of raids by combined Cherokee and Tory bands, thus the necessity of Andrew Pickens and his brigade to forgo joining Greene and the main army and launch raids into Cherokee country. In late October a mixed band of Cherokees and Tories, all in war paint, attacked Gowen's Fort on the Pacolet River. After a brief resistance, the fort surrendered, with the promise that the occupants' lives would be spared. The leader of the war party, a Tory known only as "Bloody Bates," had lied. A massacre ensued: men, women, and children butchered.[13]

Pickens with two regiments struck back immediately. It was a short operation, lasting only eleven days. Pickens destroyed the beloved Cherokee town of Chota on the upper tributaries of the Chattahoochee River and villages nearby. Thirty warriors were killed, another thirty captured. The operation would not mark the end of raids and counter-raids, but for the time being Pickens and his men had brought some relief to the Ninety Six District—at least from the Cherokees to the west. In the absence of Pickens and his brigade, however, a new menace rode into the district from the east.[14]

The "Bloody Scout"

A South Carolina historian described William Cunningham "as being of lively, jovial disposition, open-hearted and generous, priding himself upon keeping his word, but of a quick and fiery temper." When the Revolutionary War began in 1775, Cunningham, nineteen at the time, joined the Rebels. His personal journey from the Rebel cause to Loyalism apparently began when he had a sharp disagreement with his superior over the terms of his enlistment, was arrested, placed in irons, and court-martialed. The court, however, acquitted him, and in 1776 he joined the massive American expedition against the Cherokees. In 1778 a Rebel killed Cunningham's lame and epileptic brother John and abused his father. Cunningham tracked down the murderer and killed him. He also is said to have declared that he would no longer serve the Rebel cause, yet as one historian has pointed out, he made no attempt to join hundreds of Back Country Tories who had linked up with the British in Georgia and East Florida in 1778 and 1779. It was not until 1780, when the British established a strong presence in the South Carolina Back Country, that William Cunningham enlisted in a Tory militia regiment. The British departure in 1781 from the Ninety Six District led him, now a captain, to flee with about forty followers to Cherokee country and set up a base in the Blue Ridge Mountains. He raided Rebel settlements in the Enoree and Saluda River valleys in early July. In early August he swept through the same area again. Eight Rebels were killed and sixty Tories joined his band. He continued to raid the South Carolina frontier in September and early October. But by 23 October Cunningham was in Charleston. From there he would return to his old haunts and conduct what came to be known as the "Bloody Scout."[15]

Newly promoted to major, in early November 1781 William Cunningham rode out of Charleston at the head of his militia regiment. His force

William "Bloody Bill"
Cunningham, c. 1790;
watercolor on paper by an
unidentified artist. (Greenville County Museum of
Art, Greenville, SC)

was one of several militia units that left the city separately and were to rendezvous in the lower Ninety Six District. On the way Cunningham camped
at the plantation of Christopher Rowe, about a mile south of Orangeburg.
Prior to that General Greene had become concerned with what he described
as "the Tories . . . getting troublesome and insolent in the neighbourhood
of Orangburgh, in the Forks of the Edisto, and even up as high as the ridge
towards Ninty Six." He therefore sent Thomas Sumter to take post there.
As Cunningham settled into camp, Sumter was marching toward Orangeburg. Part of his force under Major John Moore was scouting well ahead of
the main body. On 13 November, Moore came upon Cunningham's camp
and was defeated in the ensuing skirmish. Sumter was "at a loss to Conceive
What the Intentions of these Troops are unless to Counter" Greene's plan to
establish a post at Orangeburg. "I am altogether undetermined how to act,"
Sumter wrote. His hesitation may have been because "The Militia I have are
Trifeling Consisting of the Worst men and arms in the Brigade. Neither is
the State Troops equal to What I expected."[16]

Sumter need not have worried. Cunningham had no interest in either
him or what Greene might be planning for Orangeburg. He continued west,

intent on his deadly mission. Some of the other detachments turned back, but one under Colonel Hezekiah Williams also continued on. By the 17th, Sumter had identified the two commanders and their possible destinations. "They are said to be heading for Ninety-Six or the Indian nation." Sumter relayed his information to Pickens. Beyond Orangeburg Cunningham and Williams separated, the latter heading for the Savannah River, Cunningham to the Saluda. He would soon go into action, and South Carolina has never forgotten what ensued.[17]

Cunningham and parties he detached engaged in several actions during their forays in the Ninety Six District. Cunningham himself led about twenty-two engagements and he and his men killed some seventy-nine Rebels. Both Cunningham's and the detached parties burned and plundered on a wide scale. But it was two actions in particular that enraged the Rebels. The first took place when the Rebel Captain Sterling Turner and about twenty-one men were returning from an action against one of Cunningham's detached parties in which they had killed several Tories, including Captain Thomas Radcliffe. They stopped to rest near Cloud's Creek, a tributary of the Little Saluda River. There Major Cunningham came upon them with his main force, about 300 strong. Turner and his men sought refuge in an unfinished log house. Cunningham refused to discuss surrender terms because he knew that some of Turner's men had been responsible for the death of Captain Radcliffe. After an hour of exchanging fire, six men in the house had been killed and the Rebels ran out of ammunition. Turner then either surrendered or the Tories stormed the house. One Rebel escaped, another was spared because the Tories mistook him for one of theirs. Following the unofficial policy of taking no prisoners in Back Country partisan fighting, Turner and the survivors were killed, "most cruelly murdered and mangled," reported Colonel LeRoy Hammond to Greene. "The Captain's head was cut off and one Butler . . . was tortured with more than savage Cruelty[.] Both his hands were cut of[f] whilst alive and it is said many other cruelties committed on him shameful to repeat." Colonel John Purvis with his militia regiment was within twenty-five miles of Turner's defeat but "could not face the Enemy," Hammond wrote, "for want of Ammunition not having one round a man[.]"[18]

Major Cunningham then rode up the south side of the Saluda River. He burned Anderson's mill and a militia post, then crossed to the north side and went downriver, continuing to burn and loot. At Edgehill Plantation on Little River, Colonel Joseph Hayes and about forty men garrisoned a militia post. On 19 November Cunningham struck. Hayes and his men put up a stout fight but eventually were forced to surrender. It is claimed that Hayes had been promised in writing humane treatment by Cunningham. True or not, twelve Rebels were executed and Hayes and his second in command, Captain Daniel Williams, were hanged. But the Tories used the pole of a fodder stack as a gallows and it broke and the two men fell to the ground, still breathing. Whereupon Hayes and Williams were hacked to death with swords.[19]

Cunningham has been charged with several more murders and cruelties following the Hayes Station fight, but whether he was at all of them is a moot question. On 21 November he headed down country. And none too soon. The Ninety Six District brigade was gathering. Andrew Pickens was on his way back from Cherokee country. Colonel LeRoy Hammond had rendezvoused with Colonel Purvis and was following the raiders. But a shortage of ammunition was hampering pursuit. Hammond had earlier begged powder from Governor Nathan Brownson of Georgia and received powder and "12 dozen Muskett Cartridges." The Georgians had also come to the aid of South Carolina with reinforcements: one hundred to join the expedition against the Cherokee and sixty under Colonel James Jackson "to Co-opperate with" Hammond and Purvis. Hammond pressed Cunningham hard. His advance actually caught up with him but its numbers were too few to engage and the Tories escaped and continued their retreat. Hezekiah Williams, who had been operating in the area of the Savannah River, had joined Cunningham. In an attempt to confuse their pursuers, they sent John Crawford of Williams's regiment back to Long Canes. Crawford and his men looted and burned, destroyed a Rebel wagon train and strongpoint, took prisoners, then sought safety in Cherokee country. One of the prisoners was John Pickens, Andrew's brother. With the other prisoners, he was given to the Cherokees. The prisoners were executed. John's end cannot be precisely documented, but tradition has it that he met death by fire.[20]

Andrew Pickens in the meantime had taken charge of the pursuit. His force included militia under colonels Levi Casey and Le Roy Hammond and South Carolina state troops. About ten miles from Orangeburg, Cunningham and Williams led their men into the swamps of the Edisto River, where they established several camps. Pickens did not hesitate. On about 20 December he attacked the first camp, destroyed it, and killed its occupants, about twenty Tories. That action immediately prompted their comrades to decamp and scatter through the swamps. The Rebels pursued. Sumter reported to Greene that Pickens and his men were "Close at his heals but allways prevented Giting up with him by the Swamps." Most of the Tories, including William Cunningham, made it to Charleston. Thus the ignominious end of the Bloody Scout.[21]

The Bloody Scout did not have a military purpose. It was a barbaric exercise in revenge by men hardened by six years of turmoil and war who had been on the receiving end of terrorism by the Rebels and had lost their homes and lands forever. For let us admit that there were Rebels who equaled William Cunningham in savagery. Early in the war Colonel Benjamin Cleveland of North Carolina gave a Tory two choices: hang with his fellow Tory swinging nearby or cut off his own ears and never show his face again. The Tory asked for a knife, whetted it on a brick, cut off his ears, and, "with the blood streaming down his cheeks," vanished. Or Captain Patrick Carr, who boasted of killing 100 Tories with his hands, and on the night the victors of Kings Mountain hanged nine Tories from an oak tree, Paddy Carr gazed up at their dangling bodies, at the lights and shadows from pine knot torches dancing across their tortured faces, and proclaimed, "Would to God every tree in the wilderness bore such fruit as that."[22]

Had Britain won the war, had Americans thereafter gloried in being the brightest jewel in the crown, William Cunningham might have come down to us as one of the honored men who rejected independence and defended the Crown against the dastardly Rebels. But the British lost, the victors wrote the histories, and he became forevermore "Bloody Bill" Cunningham.

To "Shield Him from the Vengeance of the Inhabitants"

While William Cunningham was on his way to Charleston to prepare for his Bloody Scout, and Nathanael Greene and his little army continued to rest and train in the High Hills of Santee, a world-shaking event occurred at a small tobacco port in Virginia called Yorktown. On the afternoon of 19 October 1781 Lieutenant General Charles, 2nd Earl Cornwallis, whom Nathanael Greene liked to refer to as the modern Hannibal, surrendered his army to a Franco-American ground and naval force that had trapped him on a peninsula, steadily tightened the noose, and all the while brought his Lordship and his troops under an intense artillery bombardment, the biggest of the war. Yorktown was a calamity for the British cause, for it led to a weakening of the will of the establishment to continue the war. But in South Carolina and Georgia it did not end the killing, the tears of widows and orphans, the burning of homes and fields, and the desperate plight of Loyalist refugees— eighteenth-century displaced persons.[23]

Greene received the momentous news from Yorktown on the evening of 27 October from an unnamed source in Richmond, Virginia. He later learned the correct date of Cornwallis's surrender (17 October) from his quartermaster general, the unsung Colonel Edward Carrington, who was engaged in Virginia in the frustrating mission of collecting and forwarding supplies to Greene's army. Of special interest, indeed joy, to southerners was news that the terror of the Carolinas, Lieutenant Colonel Banastre Tarleton, had surrendered the British troops in Gloucester, across the York River from Yorktown, to the French. Light Horse Harry Lee was present at Cornwallis's surrender. In his memoirs he wrote that Tarleton told the French general to whom he surrendered of his "apprehensions for his personal safety if put at the disposal of the American militia," and it was therefore arranged that the French would take Tarleton into custody to "shield him from the vengeance of the inhabitants."[24]

Washington wrote Greene five days after the surrender on 17 October with official notification of Cornwallis's capitulation. Prior to that, two days following the surrender, he and Lafayette visited Admiral de Grasse on board his flagship, *Ville de Paris,* in order to thank the admiral for his great services, especially in preventing Cornwallis's relief, and also request that he remain in American waters for further combined operations. Lafayette remained aboard after Washington left and continued to press the American case. De Grasse agreed to an operation against Wilmington but was adamant that he could not linger long enough for an attack upon Charleston. As we know, the proposed Wilmington operation was rendered unnecessary when Major Craig evacuated the city, leaving no British troops in North Carolina. On 31 October Washington delivered a final answer to Greene's pleas that the French fleet take part in an attack on Charleston. "Every Argument and Persuasive had been used with the French Admiral, to induce him to aid the Combined Army, in an operation against Charlestown; but the advanced Season, The orders of his Court, and his own Engagements to be punctual to a certain Time fixed on for his ulterior operations, all forbid his Compliance; & I am obliged to submit." De Grasse's "ulterior operations" lay in the West Indies, and given his orders from France his presence there was overdue. The hurricane season had passed, the naval fighting season in the Caribbean had begun. For the French, Charleston's fate was of little consequence. The great prize awaiting them, if they could take it, was Jamaica and its sugar plantations. But there was some good news for a general whose army was not only small but about to shrink more with the departure of the Virginia Line, whose term of service would soon be up. While the bulk of Washington's army would return to the North, "The Reinforcement for your Department will commence their March in a few Days, under the Command of Major Genl [Arthur] St Clair [pronounced sinclair], and will consist of the Pennsylvania, Maryland & Virginia Continental Troops, including their Cavalry." As it turned out, with the exception of one small unit the Virginians, foot and horse, never left Virginia. St. Clair marched with only the Pennsylvania and Maryland Lines. How had this come about?[25]

"Hanging One and Whipping 73 of Them"

In 1780, Virginia passed a law to raise 3,000 men. But the British invasion of the state brought a quick change of heart. William Richardson Davie, stationed in Virginia to gather provisions for Greene, reported that the law was suspended in most of the state, and "where it has been executed, it has been attended with so much evasion as to produce a much less force than was expected." Some county governments "have by force actually prevented the execution" of the law. Two months later Edward Carrington informed Greene that the last act of the Virginia legislature before adjourning was to pass a law making impressment illegal. The only help Greene could expect from Virginia were about 400 Continentals at Cumberland Old Court House in Virginia under Colonel Thomas Posey, who were supposed to have marched with General St. Clair in November 1781. But the officers refused to march without pay and the soldiers followed suit. The post commander, Danish-born Colonel Christian Febiger (1746–1796), known as "Old Denmark," finally solved the problem the eighteenth-century way: "I gott rid of the . . . Detachment, after hanging one and whipping 73 of them," whereupon Posey's command finally marched on 14 February 1782.[26]

"His Bold and Judicious Display"

The British had given up the Back Country and established their forces in an arc some thirty-five miles from Charleston. This was an astounding turnaround. Following the fall of Charleston to the British in May 1780, their forces had marched into the Back Country without resistance and established posts from Camden to Ninety Six. At the same time Thomas Brown and his King's Rangers and Tory militia took control of Augusta. Yet since Greene's return to South Carolina in late April 1781, it had taken only six months to destroy the British strategic position and drive them back into the Low Country. And the absence of French forces to assist Greene in a final push did not deter him from continuing his combination of military actions and civil activity to claim command of almost all of South Carolina and Georgia. The Over Mountain Men led by Sevier and Shelby had finally arrived. Sevier joined Greene on 24 October and Shelby was with Marion by 2 November. Together they numbered some 300–400 riflemen. As welcome as they were, according to Greene's first biographer it was the knowledge that the Pennsylvania and Maryland troops were marching to join him that led him to attempt his "long wished-for purpose of driving the enemy into Charleston. This object was now become one of high importance, that elections might be held as generally as possible for members of the legislature, and civil government fully re-established." Thus the time of rest and recuperation following the Battle of Eutaw Springs was over. But due to the shortage of supplies, it was not until high noon, 18 November 1781, that the advance of the army, the North Carolina Brigade, broke camp in the High Hills of Santee and marched for Simmon's Ferry on the Wateree River. Once across the Wateree, Greene informed Marion, the army would cross the Congaree River and from there proceed "down as low as Four Holes . . . by slow and easy marches." Once there, Greene counted on Marion to cover his left.[27]

Ten days after departing the High Hills Greene left the main army at Thompson's Plantation under the command of Otho Williams. It was the start of an audacious but little-heralded operation. Thompson's was near where the confluence of the Congaree and Wateree Rivers formed the Santee. Upon the American army's crossing of the Congaree, the main British force, stationed at Monck's Corner, had withdrawn to Goose Creek. Taking with him all the cavalry—200 from Lee's Legion, 3rd Light Dragoons, South Carolina state troops—and 200 infantry from the Maryland and Virginia Lines, Greene marched on 28 November 1781 "in the most secret and expeditious manner to Dorchester," as he reported to Thomas McKean. The town of Dorchester, near the head of navigation on the Ashley River, was important to the British as it enabled them to cover the country south of the Edisto River and traffic to Charleston and also collect supplies. Defense works included an extant tabby fort dating from the French and Indian War and a new redoubt. It was nineteen miles from Charleston. Greene arrived at Dorchester on 1 December after "one of the most disagreeable marches I ever made; the swamps being full, the rivers high and the face of the country almost all covered with water." He had hoped to effect a surprise, but apparently local Tories informed the garrison of his approach the night "before our arrival."[28]

Lieutenant Colonel Wade Hampton commanded the American advance. Greene reported that Hampton "charged a party of the enemy . . . killed eight or ten, wounded fifteen or twenty more, took several prisoners, and drove the remainder over the bridge under cover of their fortifications. The Enemy's whole horse came out immediately after this, but were driven back with so much precipitation, as prevented their shewing their face again." To Sumter he wrote that the action "produced an evacuation of the place that night," and that all the British cavalry "had a narrow escape."[29]

But a Connecticut Tory in British service recalled an action not that one-sided. Stephen Jarvis (1756–1840) was serving with the provincial cavalry encamped a few miles south of Dorchester. "We had hardly taken up our ground before some of our Militia from Dorchester came running into Camp, some of them much wounded. A large body of the enemy had charged into Dorchester and surprised our Militia." Jarvis and his comrades were ordered to march to Dorchester, where he with "two Dragoons and a few militia" was ordered to "decoy the enemy, and bring them on, whilst Major Fraser, with the cavalry well disposed for an attack, kept some distance in my rear." Jarvis claimed that the tactic worked to perfection. The American cavalry was supported by infantry in the rear. After making "several feint charges," the American horse "at last charged me in earnest." Jarvis fled to where the British cavalry was obviously deployed to ambush the charging Americans: "when Major Fraser gave the word . . . we dashed in among them, and slashing work we made great havoc amongst them, cutting them down and taking many prisoners." Jarvis pursued a fleeing American officer along a footpath, but when he saw the American infantry attempting a flanking movement he "wheeled about" and warned Major Fraser, and "As we had no infantry to support us we were obliged to retire, which we did with a good many prisoners—how many we killed is uncertain—certainly several."[30]

Yet the new British commander in Charleston, Lieutenant General Alexander Leslie, in a letter of 3 January 1782 to Lord Germain bemoaned the quality of his cavalry: "my being entirely destitute of real Cavalry creates infinite difficulties, and obliges me to supply their place with mounted infantry, who from inexperience in that line must fight under every disadvantage." He added that "The great superiority of the enemy horse renders it impossible to procure any certain intelligence." Leslie, however, did not sit on his hands. Even before writing to Germain, in late December he reorganized the British cavalry, reducing the corps from eleven to two and put a Massachusetts Tory, Colonel Benjamin Thompson, in command. Thompson's exploits in the fighting around Charleston in 1782 will appear later in the narrative.[31]

Whatever the accuracy of Stephen Jarvis's recollections, which in part contradicted Greene's report, it was indeed a Rebel coup, and it had been accomplished with a detachment of just 400 soldiers. For General Leslie informed Sir Henry Clinton that with Greene's "army reported to be in his rear . . . during the night Colonel Stuart withdrew the post there, and fell back to the Quarter House," only 5.6 miles from Charleston. One of Greene's aides, Colonel Lewis Morris Jr., was a great admirer of his general, but his prejudice in Greene's favor does not tarnish his description of the achievement. Writing to his father, Morris stated that the army was "too small to dislodge" the British from Dorchester

> by regular movements and the common process: it could only be effected by one of those masterly maneuvers which mark the genius and character of a great officer at the head of a detachment, composed of a few infantry and the cavalry of the army. Genl Greene proceeded from the Congaree by secret marches to Dorchester and by his bold and judicious display finessed the enemy into a belief that the whole army was present. Impressed with that idea they destroyed their works and stores, and under cover of the night precipitately retired to the Quarter House upon Charlestown Neck—those at Goose Creek retired likewise, leaving us in quiet possession of the country. Thus have the abilities of the Commander seconded by a little army rescued a country from the hands of an Enemy always his Superior, and sometimes at least three times number.[32]

Even Stephen Jarvis admitted, "The next day the army retired below the Quarter House."[33]

General Leslie had more bad news for Germain. "It is with much sorrow that I am obliged to inform your Lordship of the almost total revolt of this Province, since our misfortune in Virginia many persons in whom we placed confidence have abandoned us, and those" who had remained loyal had been driven "with their families from their possessions, and deprived of every means of support, are become a burthen upon us, which tho' great, cannot with humanity be avoided."[34]

13

"They Would Make Good Soldiers"

"Nothing but the Sword Will Reclaim Them"

Greene did not tarry at Dorchester. It was not his practice to occupy with his Continentals sites from which the British had withdrawn for the simple reason that he did not have enough troops for garrison duty. Nor did he carry out his original intent to establish headquarters at Four Holes, where, he informed Thomas Sumter, "it would be very difficult to feed the army." He decided to move twenty-two miles from Dorchester to Round O and ordered Otho Williams to march the main army there.[1]

Sumter had returned to the field from his sojourn in North Carolina upon the express orders of Governor John Rutledge. On 17 September the governor assigned six regiments to Sumter's Brigade, one-third to join Greene and serve for two months under Greene's orders. They were to march on foot to Greene's headquarters and serve as infantry. The partisans must have been stunned. They were horsemen. They rode to war, occasionally fought on horseback. An attempt to dismount half of the Back Country partisans with Greene's army over a year before, prior to the Battle of Guilford Courthouse, to serve as much needed infantry, was largely responsible for "fast desertion," wrote Andrew Pickens. (Tory partisans felt the same, as Cornwallis had discovered: "this militia can be of little use for distant military operations, as they will not stir without a horse.") Yet Sumter, strangely passive, did not object. He was not well. Two days after receiving Rutledge's order he wrote Greene that "My present indisposition, renders me incapable of carrying the whole of your requisitions into Execution, being Scarce able to Sign my

Name, but rest assured that every thing in My Power shall be done to promote your designs." He had expressed similar promises before but had failed to follow through. By late September he was unable to mount his horse. Perhaps the arrival of the healthy season revived him, for a month and a half later he was in the vicinity of Orangeburg, where, as related in chapter 12, one of his detachments clashed with William Cunningham, bound for his Bloody Scout in the Ninety Six District. Sumter had then complained about the quality of his troops. Desertion was rife. Counting militia and state troops, on 14 November he had only 418 men under arms, and the order to dismount was no doubt at least partially to blame for Sumter's problems of troop quality and numbers. Thirteen days later he was down to 320 "effective men."[2]

Greene intended Sumter to occupy Orangeburg and Four Holes Bridge and prevent supplies from reaching Charleston. Because of the scarcity of forage at Four Holes, he suggested that Sumter should garrison it with dismounted infantry and feed them from provisions collected upcountry. He also asked Sumter to dismount most of his men and form a detachment of "about fifty of the best state cavalry" to be commanded by Colonel Wade Hampton, and explained his reasoning. "As the Enemy have no longer the command of the Country it is our interest to change the plan of the war and as subsisting a great body of horse is expensive as well as distressing, the sooner they can be lessened the better if it can be done consistent with the general security of the country." For the "nigher we get to Charlestown the less number of horses will be wanted." About two weeks earlier Sumter had numbered his cavalry at 110 riders and, unusually cooperative, offered to send them all to Greene, who accepted the offer.[3]

There was good reason beyond denying Charleston supplies to station Sumter at Orangeburg. In chapter 12 we quoted Greene as noting that the "Tories are getting troublesome and insolent in the neighbourhood." This was a marked change for the Orangeburg District. Until the late summer and early fall of 1781, the district had been largely spared the bloodletting that decimated other parts of the state. It was an intensely Loyalist district where, wrote the Tory Colonel Robert Gray, the inhabitants "enjoyed so much tranquility that many of the loyal refugees who came from Ninety Six as late as August and September [1781] stopped in the country at the distance of 100 miles from Charles Town & leased plantations."[4]

Beginning in August 1781 and over the next few months the situation changed dramatically with the return to South Carolina of Governor John Rutledge. As we have learned, he was not in a forgiving mood. You were either for or against the Rebel cause, and if the latter you had no place in South Carolina. In a letter to Marion he instructed that any man who refused to serve in the militia "be deemed an enemy . . . sent to the British . . . and must not be permitted to return." On 27 September he issued a proclamation offering, with certain exceptions, a "full and free pardon" to Tories who surrendered within thirty days of the proclamation date and served for six months in the Rebel militia. In the Orangeburg District the lukewarm among the King's Friends joined, the die-hards took to the swamps. As Sumter's biographer points out, even among the lukewarm "there was no real conversion and both Whig and Tory were now too much irritated to live together in peace. Many who had submitted took up arms against their new Whig allies and the long delayed civil war began in earnest in the Orangeburg District. The swamps were filled with armed men of both sides who dared not sleep at home."[5]

In the final two months of 1781 and into early 1782, Greene and Sumter corresponded about the Tories of the Orangeburg District, of whom Sumter wrote, "out lying parties through this country are Numerous and Troublesome." In one letter he informed Greene that his officers who had been out on combat missions "informs me that they think there is Not less than fifteen hundred persons of one Kind or other between this [Orangeburg] and the South Fork of the [Edisto] River . . . all Lying in deep swamps Close upon the banks of the river which they pass in an Instant either upon logs or by Swimming from one side to the other as occasion May Require." Sumter believed that "Nothing but the Sword will Reclaim them." Yet he promised Greene that he would do all he could to "enduce the Tories to with draw from the British," and he was true to his word. The Rebel pursuit of William Cunningham as he returned from his Bloody Scout filled the swamps of the Edisto with bands of armed men, which led to "Considerable Numbers" of Tories fleeing to Orangeburg "for Secourity." Sumter sent them to their former homes, but reported that "from the Temper of the people" and the feelings of their officers, "I fear Many of them Will be privately injured." Greene praised and encouraged him. "Go on with the good work of trying to bring them in, it will save the lives of so many people, and perhaps hereafter they will prove good Citizens." Governor Rutledge's proclamation offering pardons to Tories had expired on 27 October, but on 19 December Sumter reported that "Several have Surrendered" since then and "I shall Continue to Receive them." In a subsequent letter he explained that he did so because "It's drawing them from the British Interests; As Also Weakening the out lying Tories." By late December some 300 had "come in." For some Tories, however, conversion was only skin deep. In late December twenty men who came in subsequently disappeared and were now "entirely out of our way." Sumter immediately sent out a party to look for these "Elopers."[6]

Concentration on the fighting men of each side should not blind us to the sufferings of their families. A Sumter letter of 19 December 1781 reminds us that the distress of noncombatants in war zones, so common in our time, was ever present in the Deep South of those years. "The Number and Retchedness of the Women & Children Cant be Conceived. Utterly out of the power of Many to Move, or Subsist Much longer where they are."[7]

Although Greene wished to show the Tories "mercy," he agreed that if they remained "obstinate after all these favorable overtures they may expect to suffer all the miseries that war can inflict." His main effort, however, was devoted to reconciliation. He wrote Sumter, "Don't spare any pains to take off the Tories from the british interest; for tho we have great reason to hate them, and vengeance would dictate one universal slaughter, yet when we consider how many of our good people must fall a sacrifice in doing it we shall find it will be more for our interest to forgive than to persecute. This was always my opinion and if the war continues in this Country, unless we can detach those people from the British interest, we shall feel more inconvenience from them than from all the british Army: Indeed we do now." Then this man who wanted soldiers who could "march over dead men" and "hear without concern the groans of the wounded" revealed his innate humanity. "Besides the benefit . . . I think the measure more consistent with the principles and feelings of human Nature, and the practice of civilization."[8]

Greene was one of the few men consistently right on the tragedy of the civil war raging in the Carolinas and Georgia. According to David Ramsay, there were 1,400 widows and orphans in the Ninety Six District. The Rebel General William Moultrie believed that the civil war "destroyed more property, and shed more American blood than the whole British army." We can only wish that America of that time and place had produced a Goya to record forever the pain, the suffering, the anguish, the heartbreak of the "Disasters of War."[9]

As in the past, Greene's entreaties had limited success. Bitter feelings were too deep-seated among too many people. Later, in the far western Back Country, night riders and their method of dealing with Tories prevailed, as recalled in his old age by a man who had been a teenage Rebel partisan. They "commenced ferreting out the Tories, particularly the worst ones, and such as had been in the habit of plundering, burning and murdering. Those we called the 'pet Tories,' or neutrals, we never disturbed, but those that had been very troublesome, had to pay the piper." James Potter Collins "usually stood as the horse guard, or was posted in the yard, as sentinel, while the others were engaged in pulling down the house." But it appears that young James at least occasionally took part in punishing Tories, and where the avengers rode bedlam followed. Always setting out after dark, we would surround the house, one party would force the doors and enter sword in hand, extinguish all the lights ... and suffer no light to be made, when we would commence hacking the man or men ... threatening them with instant death. . . . Another party would mount the roof of the house and commence pulling it down; thus the dwelling house, smoke house, and kitchen if any were dismantled and torn down, at least to the joists. The poor fellows, perhaps expecting instant death, would beg hard for life, and make any promise on condition of being spared, while their wives or friends would join in their entreaties; on the condition that they would leave the country within a specified time, and never return, they would suffer him to live, and I never knew an instance of one that failed to comply, and numbers put off without any such measures being enforced. There was no property molested except the buildings ... and they were at liberty to do the best they could with everything but their lands; those they had to leave.[10]

According to Collins, "there were none of the poor fellows much hurt, only they were hacked about their heads and arms enough to bleed freely. Many of the worst went among the different tribes of Indians, some went down the Mississippi River about Natchez, and some to Spanish country, now Louisiana, others went to the frontiers of Georgia, and numbers to Tennessee and Kentucky; most of those who staid among civilized people became good citizens, good neighbors and men of respectability, many becoming very popular. I have seen many of them, years afterwards, that I knew well, but they did not recognize me, and I never mentioned it to any one." Most historical attention to the fate of Tories centers upon the tens of thousands who went into exile in Canada, the Bahamas, Britain, and elsewhere in the Empire. But James Collins's observations remind us that at least equal numbers and probably more either headed west or hunkered down where they lived and eventually once again became part of the social order.[11]

"They Would Make Good Soldiers"

By 7 December Greene was encamped at Round O. Two days later he wrote a letter to John Rutledge on a most delicate matter. Although he was expecting the arrival of reinforcements from the North under General St. Clair, the departure of the Virginia Line, whose time of service was drawing to an end, would leave the army with about the same number of regulars. Greene felt strongly that he needed more soldiers, and in his letter to Rutledge he carefully built a case for what he was about to propose. "From the preparations making in Charlestown for its defense, and from the measures taken to incorporate the Tories and embody negroes, as well as spirit up the Savages, it appears the Enemy have farther designs upon this country. It is difficult to tell what will be their plan; nor can we form an idea how far European politics may affect our operations here." If the British planned "offensive operations" and reinforced their army, then Greene would be forced to retreat unless he too received reinforcements. He then gave a hint of what he was aiming at. "Good policy would dictate therefore, that you should strengthen yourselves by every means the natural resources of the country will admit." Instead of immediately broaching the subject, however, he continued to build his case, noting that even if the British meant to hold only Charleston, the city was worthy of an increased force that "would oblige them to abandon it." Following another two paragraphs, one of which was devoted to whether the naval cooperation of the French that he had begged for was really needed, Greene got to the point.[12]

"The natural strength of this country in point of numbers, appears to consist much more in the blacks, than the whites. Could they be incorporated, and employed for its defense, it would afford you double security. That they would make good Soldiers I have not the least doubt and I am pursuaded the State has it not in its power to give sufficient reinforcements without incorporating them." He continued for another two paragraphs, the penultimate quite long, building his case. He was further "pursuaded, that the incorporation of a part of the negroes, would rather tend to secure the fidelity of the others, than excite discontent, mutiny and desertion among them." In return for their service, the black soldiers would be given freedom from slavery. He requested an early decision by the governor and his Council.[13]

There! The unthinkable was out in the open. When the war broke out in 1775, the black population in the Low Country was just shy of 60 percent to the whites, 40.2 percent (104,000 to 70,000). In the words of a leading historian of the Revolution, the Low Country "looked far more like the West Indian colonies of Barbadoes and Jamaica than like any colonies to the north." The whites were well aware that they were sitting on a powder keg, and early in the eighteenth century the term "internal enemies" came into vogue. Blacks had not been armed since the Yamassee War of 1715–1718. Governor Rutledge, who was still in the High Hills of Santee, did not answer until 24 December, informing Greene that he had been unable to convene the Council until "yesterday." The Council's decision was to refer Greene's proposal to the legislature, whose meeting was "near at hand." He also informed Greene that the last Assembly, held before the British invasion of 1780, had rejected arming blacks "almost unanimously." He softened his message by assuring Greene that if the new Assembly found it "expedient" to accept his proposal, it would be done.[14]

Greene had an ally, at first glance a most unlikely one, the dashing and doomed twenty-seven-year-old Colonel John Laurens (1754–1782) of South Carolina. He was a rabid revolutionary, writing in 1774 during the Stamp Act crisis: "I would wish my countrymen to speak out and to speak boldly. Their cause is the sacred cause of Liberty, in which no shifts or evasions should be used. I go further and say if we are not entitled to the Privilege which we contested for it is time now to procure it, which, if we cannot do peaceably, we must purchase it with our swords.... It would be base in us to submit. If we can be united to Great Britain upon no other terms, let us hasten a separation." Young Laurens also carried to extreme the sacred concept of honor so treasured by the eighteenth-century officer class. (It must be noted that his sense of honor did not extend to the wife and child he abandoned in England.) He arrived from Virginia on 28 November at the army's camp fifteen miles below Orangeburg, just a few hours after Greene had left with his flying column on the Dorchester operation. Besides being an interesting character, given the impact young Laurens would later have on Lee's Legion, we should know more about him.[15]

John Laurens, 1754–1782; miniature by Charles Willson Peale. (Courtesy Independence National Historical Park Collection)

"They Would Make Good Soldiers" · 273

John Laurens was to the manor born, scion of a great South Carolina Low Country family whose fortune was based on the slave trade. His father, Henry Laurens, had moral qualms over slavery, even though he had been South Carolina's second largest slave trader and owned some 300 slaves who labored on his Low Country plantations. His son's expensive education in London and Geneva was paid for with the profits of slavery. Yet John Laurens not only supported Greene's proposal to raise black regiments, he had made such an attempt earlier and even more radically wrote in 1776, "I think we Americans at least in the Southern Colonies, cannot with *a good grace* contend for Liberty, until we shall have enfranchised our Slaves."[16]

If he was a century and more ahead of his time and place with regard to slavery, Laurens was as one with his fellow Rice Kings in his attitude toward the mechanics of Charleston—a snob of the first order. In 1775, during the great debates in the city that led eventually to the state's separation from Britain, he wrote to his father from London,

> I must confess it gives me great concern to hear that some of our lowest Mechanics still bear great Part in our Public Transactions. Men who are as contemptible for their Ignorance, as they may be pernicious by their obstinacy, not but that I wish every Citizen to have a Voice, far be it from me when we are struggling against oppression, to make distinctions unfavorable to Liberty—but when such men as these take the Lead, it argues a Defect on the Part of abler Hands, and brings our cause into disgrace . . . perhaps it is necessary to tolerate such Presumption in order to preserve Harmony among ourselves. It will be the policy of Wisemen to guide these Upstart Patriots, & let them enjoy the opinion of acting from themselves.[17]

Before examining Laurens as a soldier, we should quote that paragon of courage and leadership in the American Civil War, Joshua Lawrence Chamberlain of Maine: "An officer is so absorbed by the sense of responsibility for his men, his cause, or for the fight that the thought of personal peril has no place whatever in governing his actions. The instinct to seek safety is overcome by the instinct of honour." As we review John Laurens's battlefield career prior to his joining the Southern Army, we will question whether he had a sense of responsibility for his men and have cause to wonder if he ever felt the rational person's "instinct to seek safety."[18]

Against his father's wishes John Laurens joined Washington's staff as a volunteer aide in 1777 and served gallantly if recklessly in major battles. He performed so boldly at the Battle of Brandywine that Lafayette remarked, "It was not his fault that he was not killed or wounded, he did every thing that was necessary to procure one or t'other." At the Battle of Germantown he "was shot through the fleshy Part of his right Shoulder" but soldiered on and took part in the failed and foolhardy scheme to set fire to the Chew Mansion, in which British infantry had taken a stand. Thus early in his military career he exhibited a behavior in battle that went beyond what was expected. He became an official aide-de-camp to Washington two days after Brandywine. At the Battle of Monmouth in the summer of 1778, Laurens was involved in fierce hand-to-hand fighting, had his horse shot from under him, and received a slight wound that did not prevent him from staying the course. Of his behavior as well as that of his good friend Alexander Hamilton, an eyewitness, James McHenry, wrote that "They seemed to court death under our doubtful circumstances, and tryumphed over it as the face of war changed in our favor." Laurens next served in Rhode Island, and in a major action maneuvered his detachment of light infantry with skill and, surprisingly, prudence. Nathanael Greene, who was there, reported to Washington that "its not in my power to do justice to Col Laurens who acted both the General and the Partizan. His command of regular Troops was small but he did every thing possible to be done by their numbers."[19]

The accolades he received for his performance in Rhode Island prompted Congress to commission him with the Continental rank of lieutenant colonel and also order Washington to give him a line command. To command your own regiment in battle was a prize to be treasured. Fame could follow. Yet it was upon this occasion that hot-blooded John Laurens revealed a sagacity that usually eluded him on the field of honor. He declined the promotion, for he could not, he wrote Congress, accept it "without injuring the Officers in the line of the Army; and doing an evident injustice to my Colleagues in the family of the Commander in chief," and "the latter are my seniors and from length of service as well as merit I humbly conceive have prior claims." His action and words so impressed Congress it passed a resolution that "highly" approved the "disinterested and patriotic principles" in his letter.[20]

In 1778 the British captured Savannah, Georgia, and the following year marched on Charleston. John Laurens's attention was immediately directed to the peril facing his native state. The previous year he had broached to his father the idea of raising a black regiment that he would command, but Henry, although generally sympathetic with his son's views on slavery, had a better understanding of the obstacles and persuaded him to desist. Now, however, with their state and city endangered, Henry Laurens not only sided with John, he joined with another South Carolina Rice King and delegate to Congress, William Henry Drayton, under normal circumstances his bitter political enemy, to gain congressional approval to arm slaves. Readers will recall that

Drayton was introduced in the Prologue as a man who disdained those he considered his social inferiors yet felt no compunction in allying with the *profanus vulgus* if it suited his purpose. Unlike Henry and John Laurens he suffered no pangs of conscience over slavery and probably viewed blacks as less than human. Again, however, his political aims overcame his personal beliefs, and he and Henry Laurens urged Congress to endorse the raising and arming by South Carolina and Georgia of "three thousand able-bodied negroes" commanded by white officers. Their reward after the war would be freedom.[21]

Congress for the second time offered John Laurens a lieutenant colonel's commission, and this time he accepted. After all, if he was to command a black regiment a proper military rank was necessary. Thus credentialed, Laurens set out for South Carolina. Upon his arrival in 1779 he found the state facing an emergency. The British commander in Georgia, General Augustine Prevost, had invaded South Carolina. Laurens rode immediately to the camp of General William Moultrie, who had set up a line of defense at the Coosawhatchie River. It was on this occasion that Laurens revealed that he was a perfect fit for Frederick the Great's observation that "Valour without wisdom is insufficient." Moultrie decided to withdraw to a more secure position and posted a rear guard at the river's main crossing point. By 3 May it was time to withdraw the rear guard, whereupon John Laurens, eager for fame, volunteered. Moultrie agreed and gave him 400 troops, among them 150 picked riflemen. Laurens's assignment was merely to escort the rear guard back to the new position. Hardly a mission to gain glory. So he disobeyed his orders and with his command and the rear guard crossed the Coosawhatchie to engage the enemy. The British occupied buildings overlooking his position. Laurens had paid them no attention. The British obliged him with musket and cannon fire, inflicting casualties. Laurens was wounded in the right arm and once again had a horse shot from under him. He turned over the command to Captain Thomas Shubrick with orders to stay a while and retired from the field. Now it was Shubrick's turn for insubordination, but in doing so he saved one-third of General Moultrie's army by quickly recrossing the river to safety. Laurens's excuse for the debacle, delivered to Moultrie, was "'Why sir, said he, your men won't stand.'" Moultrie was more than annoyed and in his memoirs delivered a succinct and accurate portrayal of Laurens. "Col Laurens was a young man of great merit, and a brave soldier, but an imprudent officer; he was too rash and impetuous."[22]

Laurens had presented the plan to arm slaves upon his arrival and it had been rejected. He now once again proposed it, this time in writing. Governor Rutledge also replied in writing. "I laid your Letter respecting the black Levies before the Council yesterday, but they adhere to their former sentiments on that subject." One of the Council members, Christopher Gadsden, rendered his opinion and undoubtedly that of his fellow members with brutal candor in a letter to Samuel Adams. "We are much disgusted here at Congress recommending us to arm our Slaves, it was received with great resentment, as a very dangerous and impolitic Step." But Laurens refused to give up. He had been elected to the South Carolina House of Representatives and in July 1779 he apparently introduced an amendment to a defense bill that would add slaves to both Continental and militia regiments. His defeat was massive. David Ramsay wrote, "The measure for embodying the negroes had about twelve votes: it was received with horror by the planters, who figured to themselves terrible consequences."[23]

Glory also remained ever on John Laurens's mind. At the Franco-American siege of Savannah in September–October 1779, he commanded the South Carolina Continental light infantry and dragoons. In the assault and hand-to-hand fighting that took place, he once more courted death, once more survived recklessness. During the British siege of Charleston in 1780, he disobeyed General Benjamin Lincoln's orders to avoid an engagement and ordered a bayonet attack on Hessian troops "in order to gratify my young officers," and then started an unauthorized artillery duel that resulted in the death of Captain Joseph Bowman of the North Carolina Continentals, "a valuable captain of Infantry." Yet Laurens wrote, "Upon the whole it was a frolicking skirmish for our young soldiers." Another officer correctly labeled it "a mere point of honor without advantage." He had again shown himself to be not only reckless with his own life but insubordinate and, unlike Joshua Lawrence Chamberlain, irresponsible with the lives of his soldiers. John Laurens was obviously unfit for troop command.[24]

Taken prisoner at the surrender of Charleston, he was paroled and languished for some six months in Pennsylvania until he was exchanged in November 1780. Congress then appointed this stripling, totally inexperienced in foreign affairs, minister to France with a mission to obtain a sorely needed loan, supplies, and a French fleet superior to the British in American waters. Laurens's biographer rated his mission a "middling success," and concluded: "Temperamentally unsuited for the often tedious work of diplomacy, Laurens conducted himself in a manner more befitting an officer leading a frontal attack on an enemy post. His lack of patience, tact, and reserve, essential qualities for a diplomat, might have fractured Franco-American relations had not Vergennes and the other ministers recognized a young man's inexperience and excused his indiscretions." Vergennes, accustomed to dealing with the shrewd and brilliant Benjamin Franklin, gave his verdict in a letter to the French minister to the United States: "I hope that no one will be sent back here."[25]

Laurens returned in time to rejoin Washington as an aide-de-camp and take part in the Yorktown campaign. He was a fluent French speaker and was able to help Washington persuade Admiral de Grasse to remain on station and block seaward reinforcement of or escape by Cornwallis. The death of another officer led Washington to give Laurens command of a battalion. On the night of 14 October 1781, Laurens led eighty men, undetected, to the rear of Redoubt No. 10. When Alexander Hamilton led his battalion on a frontal assault, at the same time Laurens and his men rushed into the rear. The outnumbered British and Hessians were quickly overcome, and the redoubt's commander, Major Thomas Campbell, was captured by John Laurens. His performance on this occasion cannot be faulted.[26]

Three days later Cornwallis called for a cease-fire while surrender terms were discussed. Washington chose John Laurens as the American representative while General Rochambeau called upon Lafayette's brother-in-law, Viscount de Noailles, to represent the French. Talks were apparently heated at times, but a document was produced and on 19 October Cornwallis signed. It was time for John Laurens to go home and finally realize his dream of going into battle with a black regiment behind him.[27]

Elections to the South Carolina legislature were held on 17 and 18 December. John Laurens was among those elected, and with regard to arming blacks as soldiers, he would act as Greene's point man with his fellow legislators. But that body would not meet until about a month later in the New Year. Greene's proposal would have to wait.[28]

Lee Wrote That He Was "Perfectly Recovered"

Greene had come up with a plan to cover all approaches to Charleston: Sumter would occupy Orangeburg and Four Holes; Marion the northeastern approaches between the Ashley and Cooper Rivers in the parishes of St. Thomas and St. Stephen; and Lee, if "he is but well enough to command," the country between the Ashley and Edisto Rivers. But malaria was a constant companion of both armies, and Light Horse Harry had been ill for some time with what was described as a fever and was certainly malaria. On 2 December Colonel Lewis Morris Jr. reported to Greene that Lee was "still very ill." Two days later, however, Lee wrote that he was "perfectly recovered" from his "indisposition." Greene then placed Lee in command of all the army's cavalry: Lee's own Legion horse and the 3rd Continental Light Dragoons, along with light infantry commanded by Major Joseph Eggleston Jr. His faith in Lee's acumen is revealed in his instructions. Although Lee's territory was between the Ashley and the Edisto, "if any Military object invites your attention in any other quarter you are not confind to this particular district but at liberty to improve it returning again as soon as you can." Lee's mission also included protecting the "Inhabitants from being plundered" by British raiding parties, "and more especially the Negroes from whom the enemy get all their best intelligence and who will be more or less useful to them as they are treated well or ill by us." Greene wanted Lee to "pay particular attention to this matter" and thus prevent contact between the British and slaves. In his memoirs Lee described what must have been oral instructions given by Greene. He directed Lee "to approach by gradual advances John's Island, and to place himself in a strong position within striking distance of it." Johns Island, about five miles south of Charleston, was an important part of the British defensive system. Cattle for the garrison were pastured there and forage for horses was available. Lee noted that from Johns Island "infantry might be readily transported by interior navigation to Savannah." (This route roughly followed today's Intracoastal Waterway.) Greene wrote that the "principal object of his attention" was to prevent raids from the island "as well as to inhibit the conveyance of supplies from the main[land] to the island." But Lee would soon conjure a proposed coup that went beyond static defense.[29]

"Your Insulted Friend, and Humble Servant"

While deploying his forces around Charleston, Greene was faced with a controversy in Georgia. As anybody who has served in either military command or a civilian supervisory role knows, the most difficult administrative problems revolve around people: their hopes, fears, jealousies, ambitions, disappointments, and that old human inclination to either poach or defend turf. Readers will recall from chapter 8 that the Georgia delegates to the Continental Congress had unaccountably appointed Nathan Brownson, a medical doctor without military experience, brigadier general in command of the Georgia militia. Correctly anticipating trouble over the delegates' foolishness, Greene adroitly managed a process that made Brownson governor while General John Twiggs became commander of the Georgia militia. But Twiggs and his fellow militia commanders must have been left with a sour taste even after Brownson ended up in a civil position. Thus the delegates' mischief added to the factionalism that had long run rampant in Georgia.[30]

A hint of trouble had come earlier in a letter of 30 October from Governor Brownson in which he accused General Twiggs of calling a council of war without informing Brownson and thereafter sending Greene a letter listing supplies the state needed. "Such irregularities," Brownson concluded, "will probably be continued or not as they are encouraged." Greene wrote Brownson that he had "written to General Twiggs to apply through your excellency for every thing in the Military department as application from different sources of Authority produces confusion in the supplies. I fancy he will not make another application but through you. If he should I shall refer to you again as I have not time to correspond with every officer and the Head magistrates of the States at the same time." He then wrote Twiggs on the same day and referred him to Brownson for an answer to his request for supplies. He also asked Twiggs to make future requests "through the Governor," for "public business is best conducted going through one channel." One would think that should have taken care of the quarrel.[31]

But on 7 December Greene wrote Twiggs that a Major John Eustace "has informed me of some little disagreement between you and Governor Brownson, I hope your zeal and patriotism will get the better of all those little incidents which arise from temper or accident." It was not, however, a little disagreement. In his letter to Twiggs, Greene wrote that it "is necessary that I should be informed from time to time how all Military matters are conducted." Furthermore, "when I wrote you … that applications for stores should be made through one channel I did not mean to discontinue a military correspondence." In other words, Twiggs was free to write Greene concerning military maneuvers and actions. About a week later Brownson reported to Greene that with regard to two actions, Twiggs's defeat of a party of Cherokees and an attack by Colonel James Jackson on the British post at the Great Ogechee Ferry, Twiggs had failed to send a report to Brownson. Adding insult to injury, Twiggs had also refused the governor's request that he do so on the grounds that his orders were to report both actions directly to Greene. Brownson added that he will "make no comment." But he was fuming, and two days later let it all out in a letter to Greene.[32]

"I am truly puzzled to know, what to think, of your late unaccountable treatment of me, and the state over which, I have the Honor to preside; could I believe you realy designed me the insult, your conduct has the appearance of giving, it would preclude all explanation or intercourse until a future day." He stated that when he left Greene's camp in the High Hills of Santee for Georgia, Greene had expressed "warm professions of esteem for me & your desire of supporting me," and he was not aware of any behavior on his part that "could have given just cause for a change of your sentiments or treatment of me," and therefore was "led to conclude, there must be some mistake or mistery in the business." But when Georgia "is in danger, you dare not trust me with knoledge of it, but communicate it to an officer who ought to act under my direction." Brownson's conclusion to his diatribe is most amusing: "I am, Your Insulted friend, And Humble servant."[33]

General Twiggs had learned of Brownson's original complaint and felt that he too had been impugned. In a letter to Greene Twiggs would "esteem it a singular favor if any matter has been mentioned which has in the least touched my reputation, that you will inform me." He believed that "my Zeal and patriotism for the good of the United States, has got the better of any little incidents which have arose from temper or accident. But was I tamely to submit, and not search for these Reporters, my Character would in a short time be so tarnished, as never to recover what they wish so unjustly to deprive me of. That we have Men of this Stamp among us I can assert with truth, how far they will be able to carry their diabolical Schemes into Execution future Events will determine."[34]

Greene answered Governor Brownson first. The printed letter in the Greene Papers is a little over two pages, single-spaced, and all but the last four lines have to do with the quarrel. It was a long lecture on the difference between the civil and the military. He pointed out that although Governor Rutledge presided in South Carolina, Generals Sumter and Marion sent their reports to Greene, and if they contained information "as are worthy his notice or concern the interest or security of the State I communicate to him." He was candid: "If General Twiggs is wanting in respect for you I cannot help it." Greene was "afraid Sir that party and faction is creeping in among you[,] for General Twiggs thinks himself no less injurd than you do."[35]

On the next day Greene assured General Twiggs that "no person has traduced your reputation with me." It "stands fair." He pointed out to Twiggs as well that "Some things are of a civil nature others of a Military. The latter is what I want to correspond with you upon." But he also stressed that "you should communicate to the Governor as well as to me all matters of an interesting nature whether civil or Military. It is a piece of respect due to him independent of the advantages arising from a free communication."[36]

Governor Brownson's term of office ended shortly thereafter. But it would not be the end of hurt feelings and indignation among others requiring stroking by Greene while the fighting went on and men died and civilians suffered the calamities of war.

From the North, however, a modicum of relief was nigh.

"All Our Out Posts Are Broke Up & Called In"

At high noon on 4 January 1782 Major General Arthur St. Clair (1736–1818), an ex-British officer of limited ability, marched into Greene's camp at Round

O with the long-awaited reinforcements of the Maryland and Pennsylvania Lines. As they would replace the departing Virginia Line, this would not leave Greene's army much stronger.[37]

St. Clair and his regiments had set out from Yorktown on 5 November 1781. Under St. Clair's overall command, Major General Mordecai Gist led the Maryland contingent and Major General Anthony Wayne part of the Pennsylvanian Line. The remainder of the Line—the whole once commanded by Wayne—were directly under St. Clair. Gist marched with his men, Wayne did not. For Anthony Wayne and Arthur St. Clair loathed each other, which is undoubtedly why Wayne chose not to accompany the army but set out with his aides three days after St. Clair's departure. He caught up and passed St. Clair in South Carolina's Waxhaws, below Charlotte and just south of the North Carolina line, and entered Greene's camp at Round O on 4 January, before St. Clair's arrival on the same day. Greene reported that St. Clair's column had been much reduced by "the length of the march, sickness, desertion, and those he left behind in charge of the stores." He noted that "The Virginia Line left us the same day he arrived, which leave our operating force little more than it was before."[38]

St. Clair remained at headquarters as Greene's second in command while Wayne was chosen to lead a small force to Georgia to give the Rebels, Greene wrote, "more effectual support than has been, hitherto, in my power." Greene's choice of Wayne to lead the detached command may have been done at least partly to keep him and St. Clair apart. It was reported that they had renewed their "old grudge" in a dispute of "much warmth" during the march south. If it did happen, it could only have taken place when Wayne passed St. Clair in the Waxhaws. Wayne left Round O on 11 January with about 100 men of the 1st and 2nd Continental Dragoons, an artillery detachment of a few gunners, some 300 mounted South Carolina state troops, and about 170 Georgia volunteers. Greene's orders to Wayne included his usual strong instructions to mitigate the "malignity and deadly resentments" between Rebels and Tories, "and put a stop as much as possible to that cruel custom of putting people to death after they have surrendered themselves prisoners." (Greene would not have been amused at the Rebel term for killing prisoners: "Georgia Parole.") Wayne was also to "Check" plundering "as much as possible, and point out to the militia the ruinous Consequences of that policy." If Wayne took the trouble to lecture the militia on the latter point, we can be sure that it went in one ear and out the other.[39]

A deserter from De Lancey's Brigade entered Wayne's camp on the South Carolina side of the Savannah River and gave the British strength at Savannah at more than 1,100 men. The news that he was substantially outnumbered did not faze Wayne, who crossed the river without incident and on 19 January entered Ebenezer, Georgia, eighteen miles upstream from Savannah. The British on the other hand vastly exaggerated Wayne's strength and makeup at "3000 Continentals Horse & Foot together." The royal governor James Wright wrote that "all our out Posts are Broke up & Called in & we Expect every Day to hear of the Main Body of the Rebel Army etc. having Crossed the Savannah River." He also reported that "a Party of Continental Horse have Shewed themselves at Different times & Places for 2 or 3 days past within 8 or 10 miles of Savannah." By 26 January Wayne informed Greene that he had "maneuver'd the Enemy out of" three posts "but in their retreat the British had destroyed "all the Grain & Forage . . . so that our whole dependence for the Essential Articles of bread & hard forage, is upon Carolina. I must therefore request your aid & influence upon this occasion." Wayne also urgently wanted something else: "a speedy reinforcement of *Veteran Infantry*" (italics Wayne's). Greene informed Wayne that he had "full Power" to draw supplies from South Carolina and outlined the method to be used.[40]

"*Veteran Infantry*," however, would await the arrival of Colonel Thomas Posey and his Virginia Continentals, some 400 strong, who had set out from Cumberland Old Court House east of Richmond on 14 February. Greene sent word to Posey to join Wayne. By the time Posey's column reached Salisbury, North Carolina, on 11 March, it had been reduced to 357 men. On that date Posey wrote Greene that many men were "entirely barefooted," and by 30 March he informed Greene's aide Major Ichabod Burnet that half his men were barefoot. Posey also reported that he was delayed by "a Violent spell of Wet Weather," resulting in "bad roads," and the need to impress "almost every mouthfull of Provision & Forage." After almost two months on the road, Posey's column marched into Wayne's camp at Ebenezer on 7 April.[41]

While Wayne made do in Georgia with the strength he had, planning proceeded for the first meeting of the South Carolina legislature since 1780. Governor Rutledge had wanted to meet in Camden, but Greene persuaded him to forgo Camden in favor of Jacksonborough, only about thirty-six miles from Charleston. He gave three reasons: the army could provide ample protection; "Provisions and forage are scarce at Camden, here there is the greatest plenty"; and the danger of a raid at Camden by a "body of Tories." (With regard to the latter point, did Greene have in mind David Fanning's raid at Hillsborough, North Carolina, in which Governor Burke and his council were taken prisoner, as described in chapter 11?) Rutledge and the Council agreed to the change. But later Greene received intelligence that a British reinforcement of 3,000 men was within "a day or two sail" of Charleston, and therefore the legislature "had better meet at Camden." Rutledge replied three days later that it was too late to contact the delegates in time. They would convene in Jacksonborough. It was just as well, for Greene's intelligence turned out to be false.[42]

Although deeply, and necessarily, involved in political matters, Greene never neglected military operations, and there had been brought to his attention before St. Clair's arrival an idea that had been fermenting in Light Horse Harry Lee's ever fertile brain.

14

Missions Impossible

"Most Unhappy of the Unhappy"

Lee had written to Greene on 11 December 1781 proposing an attack on the British force on Johns Island, south of Charleston. As noted above, the British used the island for forage and to pasture herds of cattle. Lieutenant Colonel John Harris Cruger, who had performed so well at Ninety Six and Eutaw Springs, commanded on Johns Island. Lee as usual promoted his plan in grandiose fashion, assuring Greene that "If Cruger could be taken which in my opinion is not the most hazardous, & the citizens would aid us, the town [Charleston] would fall." Not very likely, but Lee was no stranger to fantasy.[1]

Silence from Greene. Light Horse Harry, however, was not one to let drop a proposed coup in which he had the utmost faith. The following day, on the pretext that he had forgotten to inform Greene that the British had killed two hundred horses to save forage, he sweetened the reward he foresaw of a successful enterprise. "I must repeat my opinion that if Cruger and his command could be taken, that it would be in your power to oblige the enemy to give up Chstown or Savannah, or both." It was obvious that he had done some reconnoitering, for he claimed that "I can readily pass over to the island."[2]

All quiet at headquarters. Two days later Lee sent his general a short note. He had become impatient. "I have not heard from you but once, altho I have wrote four letters some of which made propositions of an interesting nature." He wrote again the next day, wondering if Greene had received his previous letters, even offering to give up command of the operation and act as "second on the occasion." This becomes clear when we learn of the involvement of that loose cannon, Lieutenant Colonel John Laurens. Had Lee recruited Laurens in order to add his influence in persuading Greene to approve the operation? They had certainly gotten together and discussed it, and ever eager for glory, Laurens wrote Lee that "No Lover was ever so anxious to hear from his mistress when he expected an assignation as I am to receive a letter from you." A note from Laurens to Greene was attached to a letter of 20 December from Lee to Greene. Laurens was anxious to be involved in a mission that "promises such important consequences." Lee's letter reported that "My attention is now wholly taken up with preparing for the enterprize against John's Island." He added that "If the enemy don't exceed 400, Laurens and myself will be adequate to the attempt provided you could assemble sufficient force to take a position to cover us."[3]

Greene finally replied on 21 December. He thought the prospect of success dim. "I am afraid you are too confident of your strength, and have too much contempt for the enemies." That it was to be an amphibious assault on an island filled Greene with dread. "I hate all Island[s] for Military operations when we have not command of the water." The British, he noted, could quickly move reinforcements from Charleston. The army was also short of ammunition and could not cover Lee until an adequate supply arrived. "But if after fully considering and attending to all these matters you are of opinion the enterprise is warranted and remain desirous of attempting it I will give you all the aid in my power and you have my consent to make the attempt." But he added, "Yet I think the thing may be overdone." He reminded Lee that failure and the "appearance of rashness" would be used against them "by our domestic enemies and afford our common enemy a great triumph." Greene was especially fearful of terrible "consequences" if "you get cut off" and the covering force "driven back." Finally, however, he paid tribute to Lee's judgment "and that of Col Laurens; and therefore I am willing to encourage whatever you think prudent to attempt."[4]

Greene's lukewarm approval was all that Lee and Laurens needed to press ahead. Both were lieutenant colonels but Laurens's commission was senior to Lee's and he therefore would be in overall command. In his memoirs Lee had either a memory lapse or deliberately described Laurens as "second in command." At the time, however, Lee was so anxious to proceed that he wrote Greene that "I have told him of my willingness to serve under him, so that no difficulty has arisen on this point." Light Horse Harry looked upon the attack on Johns Island as the climax of his brilliant career, immediately after which he expected Greene to follow through on "your promise of leave of absence" for Lee to return to Virginia. Despite Laurens being the commander of the operation, it was Lee's show, and unlike Laurens he was meticulous in planning and prudent in execution.[5]

He needed to be. As with any amphibious assault, it would be a hazardous operation, and the approach to Johns Island had obstacles unique to its environment. The island lay some five miles south of Charleston, separated from the mainland by the Stono and Wadmalaw Rivers. A tidal marsh was at one time between the headwaters of the Stono and the headwaters of the Wadmalaw, but in colonial days a channel called the New Cut was built to connect the two rivers as part of a series of coastal navigation improvements. The primary crossing of the Stono River to Johns Island was the Stono Ferry, north of the New Cut. British troops manned redoubts at the ferry landings on the mainland and the island.[6]

As there were no boats available, Lee had to find a ford, and for this he probably relied on local knowledge. Fording the Stono would be governed by the tides, for though traditionally called a river the Stono is actually a tidal channel. At ebb or low tide at the New Cut, "the depth of the water was not more than waist high," Lee wrote in his memoirs. The precise location of the ford Lee used has not been found, but it was probably at Goshen Point, about two miles southwest of Stono Ferry. Although Lee did not mention it, the marshes lining each side of the channel at the New Cut were on firm ground. This was important, for the bottoms of many South Carolina marshes consist of pluff mud, which is "shiny brown-gray, richly organic, and thick and sticky," and "it is very difficult" for men or horses "to walk for any distance in pluff mud."[7]

The British were also aware of the ford at the New Cut and had stationed two armed galleys, one above the ford, the other below, about 400 yards from each other, "as near to the ford as the channel would permit," Lee wrote. He also noted that the crossing could only take place "one or two nights in a month," because it was necessary that the ebb tide "should be nearly expended about midnight, the proper hour for passing to the island.... Besides, then the galley crews were most likely to be at rest; and we had sufficient time before daylight to execute our various arrangements."[8]

Lee carefully examined the routine followed by the galleys at night and convinced Greene that infantry could pass unobserved between them. Greene then gave permission to proceed—provided there was also a point where the cavalry could swim across. Lee remarked on the possible difficulty of finding a crossing place for the cavalry because of the "deep marshes which lined the shores." He had in mind the pluff mud described earlier. But after an extended reconnaissance, Lee's cavalry commander, Major Joseph Eggleston Jr., found an approach with a firm bottom. He then had two dragoons swim to Johns Island, find firm ground in the marshes, and insert stakes to guide the cavalry. This was reported to Greene and he gave the go-ahead. The date of the assault was set: the night of 29–30 December 1781.[9]

Then it was discovered that the British also had troops on James Island, just north of Johns, "contiguous," Lee wrote, to where he intended to operate. And Greene and the army were still at Round O, twenty-five miles away, not close enough to provide support. The operation was cancelled for that night but not forgotten. Meanwhile, General Alexander Leslie had described the redoubts guarding the Stono Ferry on the mainland side as a "ticklish post but commands the water communication." His standing order was to withdraw the troops from that position if the Rebels "come in force." Although there was no such movement by Greene, on the morning of 31 December the British evacuated the redoubts on the mainland and withdrew to Johns Island. Lee informed Greene that he was at a loss to explain the British movement unless it was the imminent arrival of St. Clair's reinforcements. Greene replied that he was "happy to hear" this "providing they don't fortify" on Johns Island, in which case Lee would have to abandon his plan. Greene added that he had "some thoughts of taking possession of those Islands with all our force as the most likely way of producing an evacuation of Charles Town as it will lead them to a belief that there is to be a naval cooperation shortly and our movements are preparatory to it." But he could not make a decision until he reconnoitered the area, and he still harbored the fear that Leslie might receive a "large reinforcement," in which case there would be no movement against the islands. British abandonment of the redoubts guarding the mainland side of Stono Ferry, however, led Lee and Laurens to once again plan to attack Johns Island.[10]

Sometime in December John Harris Cruger was succeeded in command on the island by Major James Henry Craig, fresh from his adventures at Wilmington and southeastern North Carolina. Cruger's troops were withdrawn and Craig took with him 82nd Foot, which he had brought with him from Wilmington, as well as new units. Leslie wrote to Sir Henry Clinton, "I have formed the Guards, 23rd. 33rd. 71st. and 82nd. into a corps under Major Craig." This statement is at first glance puzzling, because with the exception of the 82nd these units had marched north with Cornwallis and were lost at Yorktown. But in the same letter Leslie wrote, "I wait your excellency's orders relative to the small number of Lord Cornwallis' Army (Guards excepted)." It would therefore seem that Cornwallis had either left behind small detachments from these regiments, even though they were not listed in the "Return" of troops left with Rawdon, dated 15 January 1781; or, more likely, they were convalescents: wounded at Guilford Courthouse, left behind at Wilmington, and taken to Charleston by Craig. Craig's strength on Johns Island was either given or estimated at various times as between 400 and 550 men. It was Lee on 11 December who gave the estimate of 550, although on 20 December he implied a figure of 400. Five hundred and fifty is probably close to the mark, as General Leslie reported to Lord Germain that Craig had 600 men on Johns and James Islands, and most of the men would have been on Johns to protect the valuable cattle herds and other supplies.[11]

The arrival on 4 January 1782 of General St. Clair with the Pennsylvania and Maryland Lines allowed Greene to reinforce Lee and Laurens by giving them detachments from the Pennsylvania and North Carolina Lines. An experienced officer, Major James Hamilton of the Pennsylvania Line, commanded the new troops. The assault force now numbered about 700 men divided into two columns. Lee commanded the front column, Major Hamilton the rear column, Laurens in overall command. On 12 January Greene moved the army from Round O to St. Paul's Stono Church, some two miles west of Stono Ferry, close enough to support Lee and Laurens. That night the approach march by the attacking force began. According to Lee, in the beginning Laurens was with the rear column but later joined Lee and the front column. In his memoirs, Lee stated that Laurens was needed to supervise at the point where the soldiers entered the Stono, for Lee would be crossing with the front column. An officer with Hamilton's rear column, Lieutenant John Bell Tilden, noted in his journal that at midnight "we marched rapidly for Stono River." Near the tidal marsh Lee called a halt. The troops dropped their knapsacks and the officers left their horses. Before moving on Lee directed every officer "to take special care to march in sight of his leading section, lest in the darkness of the night a separation might happen." He reported that just before entering the marsh officers and men removed boots and shoes to prevent or at least reduce the noise of splashing as they waded toward the Stono. They probably tied them around their necks, because they would need them once they reached the opposite shore. January in South Carolina can be harsh, frost not unknown at that time of year. The average temperature was 37 degrees and the average water temperature about 50 degrees. The troops "moved very slowly," Lee wrote, "every man exerting himself to prevent noise." The van under Major John Rudulph reached the bank, their bare feet numb. Without hesitation they entered the cold dark waters of the Stono and waded through the night. At the head of the main front column Lee ordered a halt and sent a staff officer back to make sure that the "sections were all up." Lee was exhilarated as he listened to the "sentinels from each galley crying 'all's safe' when Major Rudulph with the van was passing between them." He later wrote in his inimitable style, "Every heart glowed with anticipations of splendid glory." Then—the staff officer returned with astounding news.[12]

The rear column, Major Hamilton's Pennsylvanians and North Carolinians, 400 strong, was missing. John Laurens with guides and some staff officers immediately went in search of Hamilton and his men. "Hour after hour passed," Lee wrote, with frequent messages coming back from Laurens, the information always the same: the rear column had vanished. The hour grew critical, for the ebb tide had been replaced by the beginning of the flood tide. The waters of the Stono were rising, and Rudulph's van was on the opposite shore. Lee made the only decision possible, and he made it just in time. He sent a sergeant across the river to recall Rudulph. Lee described the return march. "Rudulph found the water, which had not reached the waist as he passed, up to the breast as he returned. Nevertheless, every man got back safe; the tallest assisting the lowest, and the galley sentinels continuing to cry 'all's safe.'"[13]

Back on solid ground the troops built big fires to dry their clothes and warm themselves. Greene met Lee there and commiserated with him on the failure. And at daybreak who should appear but John Laurens with the lost rear column. He had at last found the errant force and "returned with it to our baggage-ground, most unhappy of the unhappy." In his memoirs Lee ascribed the failure to simple error and the darkness of the night, as there was no moon. Greene, however, reported that Hamilton's guide had deserted him "the moment he was most essential," and that, "together with his not moving exactly at the same time as the first Column did," led to the rear column's getting lost. Lieutenant Tilden maintained that they would have surprised "the enemy . . . if we had had good guides."[14]

Lee was crestfallen and as usual indulged in hyperbole. "Thus was marred the execution of an enterprise surpassed by none throughout our war in grandeur of design, and equaled by few in the beneficial effects sure to result from its successful termination." He went on at some length on what might have happened had the operation been successful, even going so far as to claim that Georgia would have been lost to the British because the loss of Craig's command on Johns Island would have forced General Leslie to recall the garrison from Savannah to help defend Charleston. Even Greene believed that "we mist the great object of the enterprise," which would have been the defeat, perhaps capture, of Craig's force as well as the taking of the abundant cattle and other supplies on the island.[15]

A "mist" opportunity? Or a fortunate escape from, at the least, a sharp repulse, at the most, disaster? Lee and Laurens and Greene seemed to believe that victory was certain had all the troops gained Johns Island. But Major Craig's force was not that heavily outnumbered, and they comprised seasoned soldiers. Moreover, Craig was a tough and very able officer. He had stationed a picket within a mile of the ford, and a second picket two miles away. His camp was on the eastern end of the island three or four miles from the second picket. Lee's plan was to subdue the first picket before the alarm could be spread, then evade the second picket on his march to Craig's camp. If soldiers from the first picket got away, Eggleston's cavalry would be in place to intercept them. Lee admitted that the ground where the British were encamped favored Craig, as one of the many ditches common in the "cultivated grounds in South Carolina near the sea" was about 100 yards in front of the camp. Thus Craig had plenty of room to deploy his infantry upon the approach of the Rebels. Lee hoped to surprise Craig before he could deploy but also admitted that "The chance of surprising him was not encouraging." A reasonable analysis of the proposed adventure is that there were too many ifs in the plan: if the first picket could be quietly subdued; if the cavalry could intercept pickets who got away; if the second picket could be evaded; if Craig could be surprised, the last probably impossible according to Lee. The upshot is that the lost column may well have saved Lee, Laurens, and Greene at the least embarrassment and at the worst a possible debacle. In any event, half of their goals came true. The next day, after learning about the Rebel attempt, General Leslie ordered Major Craig to evacuate Johns Island, taking with him the cattle and supplies. Apparently, Leslie thought the Americans would try again. He admitted to Clinton that the foray was "well concerted," yet was certain that they could not have captured Craig's force. But "very little was to be gained by their defeat, which must have been partial, and so many circumstances concurring to induce me to prevent the attempt, that I ordered the Island to be evacuated." Craig crossed the Stono to James Island and took position "near to the four redoubts previously . . . constructed."[16]

"People in General Returned to Their Senses"

On 17 January 1782, four days after the failure at Johns Island, the South Carolina legislature met at Jacksonborough. A hamlet thirty-five miles from Charleston, it was described by Lieutenant William Feltman of 1st Pennsylvania as containing "four or five tolerable good frame houses and a number of smaller houses." Life for the legislators would not be tedious in those humble surroundings. Lieutenant Feltman temporarily hobnobbed with the Carolina elite, mounting Governor Rutledge's "Guard in town, where I had the pleasure of spending the afternoon and part of the night with the Governor and a number of the members of Assembly, and half a dozen of very agreeable ladies; had plenty of good Maderia wine and spirits, which a few days ago came from Charleston." (Trading with the enemy?) In the vicinity were rice plantations with a "number of very elegant buildings close to our encampment—the inhabitants very polite and genteel. Balls almost every evening." In case the British should attempt mischief, Greene's army bivouacked on the plantation of Colonel William Skirving, on the Charleston road about four miles from Jacksonborough. This event should also be much heralded. A little over a year and half before all had seemed lost. Now South Carolina civil government was back in business and the would-be conquerors were back where they had started: cooped up within their lines at Charleston, their army reduced and sickly, provisions and supplies dwindling.[17]

Greene, on the other hand, ever pessimistic about British intentions, had not abandoned his hope to augment his strength by drafting slaves into the army, their reward freedom after the war. And now his keen ally was strategically placed. John Laurens had been elected to the legislature and proceeded from the misadventure at Johns Island to Jacksonborough, where he hoped to convince the other lawmakers of the necessity of such a drastic step. Laurens had written to Greene on 28 December, "It appears to me that the Governor & Council should not lose a moment in carrying the black levy plan into execution but I know that unless they are goaded upon the subject their deliberations and delays will lose the opportunity which now offers." On 21 January, the same day that Laurens took his seat in the House of Representatives, Greene wrote a second letter to Governor Rutledge in which he pulled out all the stops to further his plea. One might interpret the first, long sentence of his letter as a series of exaggerations to bolster his case, but I believe that he truly meant what he wrote.[18] "When I view the present crisis of the American war and consider the obstinacy of the british court, the critical situation of South Carolina and Georgia as the last object of the national grasp and take into consideration the precarious and uncertain support of the northern States owing to the situation of their finance and the prejudices respecting the climate I cannot help repeating my recommendation of raising some black regiments for the more effectual protection and security of this country."[19]

He was well aware, he continued, of the miseries, the calamities foisted upon "this unfortunate country . . . for these past two years." He had witnessed them, and "knowing the uncertainty of the events of war I cannot help wishing all the resources of the country may be employed to guard against further misfortunes." Yes, "the remedy may be disagreeable," but would the country have fallen so easily to British forces "had this great resource" been used before "the reduction of Charlestown[?]"

He floated before Rutledge the danger of a negotiated "peace upon a principle of Uti possidetis" and "how you will reproach yourselves that you did not improve the means in your power to prevent it? And will not the northern States justify themselves in giving you up when that will procure to them peace and security after you have refused to avail yourselves of those means[?]"

He raised the specter of the British "now arming" large numbers of slaves and aiming to enlist 3,000 to defend Charleston. He claimed that his information was good, but it was not. British use of blacks as soldiers was strictly limited. Greene would later admit in letters to Francis Marion and George Washington to 700 blacks raised, yet that number too was certainly an exaggeration. No evidence has been found of the British raising and training blacks as infantry, just a small number of dragoons. At the time Greene wrote, however, he argued that the larger number could not be doubted given that "Lord Sandwich declared in Parliament that the Ministry would avail themselves of every thing that God and Nature had put in their power to crush this rebellion." We know, however, as noted in chapter 12, that sentiment in London for further prosecuting the war against the Americans was rapidly weakening, and that a little over a month after Greene wrote his letter the House of Commons voted to abandon the war in America. Greene, of course, did not know what was going on in London and could only act on what he knew and believed to be true, and he was adamant in his belief that the Cause remained in jeopardy.[20]

It was a powerful letter. Greene had now done all he could to present his case to the governor and the legislature. Now it was up to John Laurens to carry the torch, to sell to his fellow Rice Kings the idea that it was in their interest to agree to the unpalatable. He was a busy legislator, serving on nine committees, one of which was germane to his desire to raise black regiments and of which he was the chairman: the committee to decide which Tory estates should be confiscated "and to what purpose the Profits arising from them may be best applied." Well aware that to threaten the property of Rebels would get him nowhere, Laurens submitted to the House what was meant as a clever proposition: 2,500 slaves to be taken from confiscated Tory plantations for black regiments commanded by white officers. The question came to the floor the next day. Anger permeated the debate. Governor Rutledge's brother Edward reported that "We have had another hard Battle on the Subject of arming the Blacks," and he feared that early on the majority were with Laurens, and "I assure you I was very much alarmed." Yet "upon a fair full Argument, people in general returned to their senses." He wrote that "about 12 or 15 were for it & about 100 against it." John Laurens was livid, writing to George Washington, "The single voice of reason was drowned by the howlings of a triple-headed monster in which prejudice Avarice & pusillamimity were united."[21]

One of the opponents, Aedanus Burke, in a letter to Arthur Middleton, a South Carolina delegate to Congress, stated his suspicion that emancipation was the purpose of the proposed legislation. "Genl Greene favored it—wished for its success—The northern people I have observed regard the condition in which we hold our slaves in a light different from us. I am much deceived indeed, if they do not secretly *wish* [italics Burke's] for a general Emancipation, if the present struggle was over." Given Greene's acceptance from South Carolina and Georgia after the war of confiscated Tory plantations and his efforts to obtain slaves to work them, Burke was wrong about Greene's attitude on general emancipation. But he was right about some northerners. When Congress in 1779 had recommended that South Carolina and Georgia raise black regiments, a New Hampshire delegate, William Whipple, pondered on their reaction and wrote to Josiah Bartlett that if those states accepted and carried out the plan, "it will produce the Emancipation of a number of those wretches and lay a foundation for the Abolition of Slavery in America." Greene later wrote to Washington that the rejection of the proposal was not about money "(for they give a most enormous bounty for white men, and pay in Slaves) but from an apprehension of the consequences." By "consequences," was Greene referring to a subject that Burke commented on in his letter to Middleton? "A very sensible m[a]n whom you well know in Philade[lphi]a once mentioned seriously to me, that our Country [i.e., South Carolina] wd be a fine one, if our whites & blacks inter-married—the breed wd be a hardy excellent race, he said, to bear our climate." Fear of miscegenation, dread of armed blacks, the need for slaves to work the great rice and indigo plantations, and the concept of those slaves as less than human, as property—all combined to doom the proposal by Nathanael Greene and John Laurens to harness the untapped military resource at hand. Yet one wonders if any among those who howled down the proposal had at least an inkling that their own revolution would help hasten the day in a modern world taking shape in which human bondage would become a moral and political anachronism?[22]

15

Departures

"Beg Not to Be Honour Again with Any of Your Commands"

The war was winding down. The stalwarts were leaving. Badly wounded at Eutaw Springs, it took Lieutenant Colonel John Eager Howard two months to recover enough to set out for Maryland in mid-November 1781. Captain Robert Kirkwood was furloughed on 1 January 1782 and three days later left for Delaware. Colonel Otho Holland Williams departed for Maryland in early February 1782. They made no fuss as they left the army. They had served honorably with steady consistency, and in Howard's case brilliantly at Cowpens. Drama on departure was left to others.[1]

Thomas Sumter had followed Greene's orders, as described in chapter 13, and had done good work at Orangeburg in welcoming repentant Tories back into the fold. Backsliding by many and the outbreak of civil war in the Orangeburg District were not his fault. That would have happened no matter who was in command. When Greene asked Sumter to send away the horses of his infantry, the Gamecock complied, although he noted, "It is Not easie to Reconcile the Troops to this Measure, and the undertaking more disaGreable by Reason of their being So much Neglected by the Publick." Greene acknowledged the difficulty of such a move and the neglect but pointed out that there was little the public could do, for "poverty and want stares us in the face on every side." He continued to stroke Sumter: "we shall triumph at last, and your Country if they have any justice and gratitude will not fail to bless and reward you for your exertions made in the darkest hours they ever felt. I shall always bear testimony

John Eager Howard, 1752–
1827; oil painting by Charles
Willson Peale. (Courtesy
Independence National Historical Park Collection)

to your services and dont fail to tell the people how much you did when
many others hid their heads." He then ordered Sumter to send any cavalry he could spare to "Georgia immediately; and give the Officer pointed
Orders not to plunder." By 22 December, Sumter had dispatched most
of the cavalry, Major Francis Moore commanding, to join General John
Twiggs in Georgia.[2]

In a second letter of 22 December, Sumter wrote that "Your Notice and
Generous acknowledgment of My having done any thing advantageous to
the public Confers the Greatest Obligations upon me." That penultimate
sentence, however, was preceded by a litany of complaints that took up most
of the letter. He challenged the "equity and policy" of "Reducing and Dismounting the battallions of State troops[,]" although "fully Complied with
. . . Not without Reluctance." The dismounting had caused a morale problem among the state troops. He pointed out that they had been "Raised as
light dragoons, of Course Mounted, and Shoud have been equipped as Such,
but has hitherto been Neglected by the public." The militia serving as infantry "also think themselves much injured by being obliged to perform a Two
months & ten days tour of duty on foot, Not even Suffered to Ride from
home & Send their horseback [i.e., horse back]." Then came what Sumter
and his dismounted militia certainly considered as insult heaped on injury.

His men "are told that Govr Rutledge Suffers other divisions of Militia to do duty as horse or Mounted Infantry & Remain but one Month in the field before relieved." It was obvious, he continued, "that the Brigades I Commd has been Ludicrously treated . . . in consequence of Which I have Wrote his excellancy Govr Rutledge Who I hope will take measures to prevent any farther Complain[t]s."[3]

Rutledge bristled at Sumter's accusations. "I do not understand the passage of your letter which Says, 'the State Brigade is too little the object of publick attention, and in various cases ludicrously treated.' I am not conscious of treating any man, or body of men, ludicrously, nor do I know what attention Government could, or should, have paid, which it has not, to that Brigade." All "Brigadiers of militia" had been treated the same. That, however, was not true, and Rutledge admitted it. All militia had been ordered to report to camp "on foot, instead of coming on horseback," with one exception: Francis Marion's Brigade, and that had been upon "General Greene's recommendation."[4]

If we accept the governor's explanation, and I do, Greene's disappoints. He wrote to Sumter two days after Rutledge. "I do not know of any partiality respecting the Militia, nor did I give any orders in the matter; but General Marion being near the enemies lines I suppose led to the indulgence if any was granted." Shame on you, Nathanael. Why did you not admit that you recommended to Governor Rutledge that Marion's Brigade remain mounted? The case for doing so was excellent. Being near the British lines and British regulars meant Marion's situation was more perilous than Sumter's back in Orangeburg. Sumter had admitted that "The enemy in this quarter are numerous in horse, but not formidable." Marion, however, needed mobility in case the British launched a surprise attack against him and to defend against raids for provisions. Sumter, of course, was not assuaged, and Greene's weak attempt to wriggle out of the situation probably increased his anger and frustration. The Gamecock, heretofore engaged in or planning sweeping offensives, was now reduced to command of a garrison engaged in the day-to-day, down-and-dirty work of what we call counter-insurgency. Most of his command was reduced to infantry bereft of their beloved horses. And to make matters worse from his point of view, he was no longer the free agent of the first phase of the Rising, no governor or Continental general to oversee him and issue hated orders. The situation grated on this proud, irascible man.[5]

Perhaps to change the subject by seeking Sumter's advice on what was a very important matter, and at the same time attempt to mollify the Gamecock, Greene asked "whether the Tories join you in duty or whether they deliver up their arms and go home." Greene doubted that they could be trusted in arms and that "their neutrality" instead of "their service" would be of more benefit. Did Greene really believe this? By then he must of have learned that for Back Country men, Rebel or Tory, arms ranked with their beloved horses. Whatever Greene thought, Sumter disagreed with what he wrote—and he was right. On 2 January 1782 Sumter replied that they must be allowed to "Retain their arms whether they do duty or no," for "arms are So Very essential to the Support of families, and the Tenaciousness of people for that article, and the degradation of parting with them" would be insulting. There were advantages to be gained "from their doing their Duty, provided they are Treated as people in our Service ought to be." The more than 100 Tories who had surrendered since Sumter's arrival in early November came in well equipped, and he had no fear of their "Joining the enemy" even if they marched "through their settlements." Why? Because Sumter had cleverly made them "Conspicuous and obnoxious to the enemy." He had commissioned some of the "best Characters" among them as officers and kept them "detached" in pursuit of die-hard Tories. And "What ever the enemy Suffers is Charged to them, thus their lives would be imperiled if captured." Sumter's policy worked. The Tories who had surrendered had killed or captured "Several" die-hards, among them some of "the Greatest offenders in the state." Sumter ended the letter requesting Greene's permission to "Quite this Place," as he had been elected to the Assembly.[6]

This is not to say that the Orangeburg District had become quiet and peaceful since Sumter's arrival. The civil war continued to rage. An officer of the Pennsylvania Line on his way to join Greene's army stopped at a settlement near Orangeburg and described it as "Totaly abandoned to the Torys, and the Roads Dayly infested by those Miscreants." Yet Sumter's efforts were positive and had succeeded to some extent. Relations between Greene and Sumter seemed to be better than they had ever been. Greene constantly praised Sumter. But in the final sentence of his final letter to Greene, Sumter allowed his true feelings full sway. After imparting information about troop movements and his reason for ordering them, he turned to his previous request to leave Orangeburg to attend the Assembly. "I hope to be Indulged, and Beg Not to be honour again With any of your Commands Untill a proper inquiry Can be Made Whether I am Worth[y] of them."[7]

Greene claimed not to understand what Sumter meant. Furthermore, "I have heard no person intimate anything of the kind nor do I believe an enquiry is either wished or desired respecting any part of your conduct." He gave Sumter "my full consent to attend the house of Assembly." That was the end, the last letter between them that has been found. Sumter attended the full session of the Jacksonborough Assembly, which began 17–18 January

1782. On 26 February the Assembly adjourned, whereupon Sumter immediately resigned his military commission. In a letter of the following day, the new governor of South Carolina, John Mathews, informed Greene of Sumter's action. The South Carolina historian and Sumter champion Edward McCrady believed that the Gamecock resigned because Greene and Light Horse Harry Lee had formed a "cabal" against him and forced him out. But McCrady offered no evidence for this. A reasonable speculation is that Sumter knew his day had passed. Grand schemes and bold movements had been succeeded by the grinding effort to root out Tory partisans. No longer his own master, forced to dismount most of his troops while Marion kept his horses, condemned to a secondary role he could not accept—he quit. It is quite clear that there was no love lost between Greene and Sumter. There is no evidence that Sumter revealed his feelings about Greene to others, although it certainly would have been human of him to confide in close friends. In any case, lodged within him was a bitterness against the Rhode Islander that came out nine years later when he was a U.S. congressman. In a debate over whether to indemnify Greene's widow Caty for debts incurred by Greene in his desperate efforts to obtain clothing for his army, Sumter rose and spoke against the measure. He claimed that there had been no need for Greene to incur the debt as the army had received enough supplies; and further, "it does not appear to me that the family is reduced to that disagreeable situation which has been represented." Those, however, were not the real reasons behind Sumter's opposition. "Mr. Sumpter," the *Annals of Congress* recorded, "closed the debate in sundry remarks on extracts of letters written by General Greene during the late war, inserted in Gordon's History of the American Revolution," containing "unfavorable reflections on the militia of South Carolina, and the patriotism of the inhabitants of that State. These reflections Mr. Sumpter said, were gross calumnies on, and misrepresentations of the character of that people . . . invalidated by facts . . . and by the general tenor of the conduct of South Carolina throughout the whole course of the war." But Greene's friends and old comrades eventually prevailed and Caty received her indemnity. It was unseemly behavior by a man who, in his heyday, during the first phase of the Rising, in the words of Lord Cornwallis, "certainly has been our greatest plague in this country."[8]

"Disquietude of Mind and Infirmity of Body"

Thomas Sumter was not the only officer who would bedevil Greene in these waning months of the war. In late January 1782 Light Horse Harry Lee sent Greene a remarkable letter.[9]

I must at length ask permission to absent myself from the army. Disquietude of mind and infirmity of body unite in giving birth to my request. The first arises from the indifference with which my efforts to advance the cause of my country is considered by my friends, the persecution of my foes, and my consciousness that it is not in my power to efface the disagreeable impression. The second owes its birth to the fidelity with which I have served, and is nourished by my continuance in the same line of conduct.

However disgusted I am with human nature, I wish, from motives of self to make my way easy and comfortable. This, if ever attainable, is to be got in an obscure retreat.

There is no salutation, and he ended the letter without the usual courtesies. "I have nothing more to say, and will but add, my prayers for the honours and prosperity of your arms."

Greene was aware of Lee's condition and in his reply revealed once again his gifts as a letter writer. "I have beheld with extreme anxiety for some time past a growing discontent in your mind and have not been without my apprehensions that your complaints originated more in distress than in the ruins of your constitution." He regretted his inability to "heal" the "source of your wounds." If Lee meant that it was he, Greene, who failed "to do justice to your exertions," and if anything "in my conduct" should "confirm it, it has been owing to error in judgment or accident." He pronounced a "partiality" for Lee from their first days together. Yes, there were a few from "ignorance and malice" who wished Lee ill, "but it is out of their power to injure you." He entreated Lee "not to think of leaving the Army. Every body knows that I have the highest opinion of you as an officer and you know I love you as a friend." Whatever Lee decided, "my affections will accompany you," and "I shall always take a pleasure in paying a just tribute to your merit."[10]

A contrite Lee replied, "I am very sorry that any loose expression in my lettr should have permitted a construction so widely different from my meaning." If that were the case, then Lee's first letter was one "loose expression" after another. "I candidly told you," he continued, "that I read some of your public reports with distress, because some officers & corps were held out to the world with a lustre superior to others, who to say the least deserved equally." Here Lee was referring to Greene's report to Thomas McKean on the Battle of Eutaw Springs. Yet in his report Greene wrote that "Lt. Colo Lee had with great address, gallantry, and good conduct, turned the enemy's left flank, and was charging them in the rear at the same time the Virginia and Maryland Troops were charging them in front." In this action Lee had led the Legion infantry, and Greene referred to that unit with words of high praise. "I think myself principally indebted for the victory we obtained to the free use of the Bayonet made by the Virginians and Marylanders, the Infantry of the Legion, and Captain Kirkwood's Light Infantry, and tho' few Armies ever exhibited equal bravery with ours in general, yet the conduct of the Corps were peculiarly conspicuous." Both were handsome tributes. But perhaps Lee felt that Greene had not gone far enough in his praise. Was he jealous of Greene's acknowledgment of "my obligations to Colo [Otho Holland] Williams for his great activity on this and many occasions in forming the Army, and for his uncommon intrepidity in leading the Maryland Troops to the charge, which exceeded anything I ever saw"? And despite Greene's praise of the Legion infantry it was included with other units, unlike the North Carolina Continentals, of whom Greene wrote, "These were all new levies, and had been under discipline but little more than a month, notwithstanding they fought with a degree of obstinacy that would do honor to the best of veterans; and I could hardly tell which to admire most the gallantry of their Officers or the bravery of the Troops." And there was the matter of the Legion cavalry. When Greene wrote of the "Legion baffled in an attempt upon the right," he was referring to the failure of the Legion cavalry's charge led by Captain Joseph Eggleston. Greene had wanted Lee to lead that charge but as we know he could not be found. The only mention of Lee being with his cavalry is after the battle: Greene's detachment of Marion and his horse with "Colo Lee with the Legion Horse between Eutaw and Charles Town, to prevent any reinforcements from coming to the relief of the Enemy, and also to retard their march should they attempt to retire, and give time for the Army to fall upon their Rear, and put a finishing stroke to our successes." But reinforcements did reach the British army, "General Marion and Lieut Colo Lee not having force sufficient to prevent it." Added to that was talk in the army that if Lee had been with his cavalry toward the end of the battle and had made the charge Greene wanted, the British army would have been routed and victory assured.[11]

Lee assured Greene that "My attachment to you will end only with my life." He was "candid to acknowledge my imbecillity of mind, and hope time and absence may alter my feelings." For the "present my fervent wish, is the most hidden obscurity." He claimed to have struggled against the demons afflicting him, "but the sores of my wounds are only irritated afresh by such efforts." Light Horse Harry was obviously a deeply troubled man. Given the difficulty in understanding what motivates our contemporaries, even family and friends, one should hesitate to analyze a person at a distance of over two centuries. But had some six years of war gotten to him? Despite the occasional cruelties he had inflicted upon the enemy, his nature, in the words of a friend, was of a "delicate sensibility." Combined with his overweening thirst for fame and public praise, it left him vulnerable to slights real and imagined. The failure at Johns Island must have affected him deeply, for he meant that operation to be his crowning martial glory. And there was the presence of John Laurens. Prior to his arrival Lee had been the *beau sabreur* of the Southern Army. But his rival was senior in time in rank and a favorite of Washington, and Lee suspected that to please the Great Virginian Greene favored Laurens over him. So the camp rumors went. In a letter of 10 February, Lee recommended to Greene as his successor to command the Legion "an officer of great oeconomy," for "If he is an experimenter, he will waste the troops very fast." In using the word "experimenter" Lee could only have meant the imprudent Laurens. Two days later, however, Greene informed Lee that "Col Lawrens will take command of the light troops, as soon as you are gone."[12]

Lee avoided a meeting to say goodbye. For "The ceremony of parting from you & my friends in the army is so affecting, that I wish to decline it personally & hope you will consider me, as you always have experienced me[,] your devoted friend. Whenever you think me necessary to you, I will come at the risk of every thing convenient." Greene had offered Lee a letter of introduction to Comte Rochambeau, who was still in Virginia with his French Expeditionary Force. Lee declined. He had "no inclination to mix with the great."[13]

Lee had expressed his complaints to two of Greene's aides, Captain William Pierce Jr. and Colonel Lewis Morris Jr., and they had reported them to Greene. John Laurens and Colonel Morris had gone to Lee's camp, thinking he had left, but he was still there as he had not been able to obtain a carriage for his return to Virginia. Lee expressed his discontent, if not to Laurens, definitely to Morris. On 18 February Greene made a final attempt to assuage Lee. "I am exceeding sorry," he wrote, "to find that notwithstanding all that has passed between us upon the subject of your discontent that your disgust increases and that you harbour sentiments respecting me no less groundless than unfriendly." Greene defended his actions and noted that he had "honorably mentioned" Lee in "eleven public reports." He also recalled that he himself had served honorably in several actions in the North, yet had not been mentioned in reports, "notwithstanding I was a General Officer." He expressed his "love and esteem . . . and wish you not to think meanly of me, as some of your insinuations seem to impart." He denied taking any action just to please George Washington, "As nothing is more remote from the truth . . . nothing more wounding to my feelings. I despise a mean act, and am above duplicity." Nor in his reports had he favored William Washington over Lee. It was, as usual, an excellent letter—with one exception: "Col Lawrens thinks you have no reason in the World to complain; and that you do injustice to your own importance to dwell upon single expressions." One can imagine Lee grinding his teeth over that sentence.[14]

In reply Lee was "much mortified at the trouble which my stupid conduct gives you." He denied that he ever "mentioned any insinuation of the sort you express, & I am much hurt that you can ever think it possible." At the least, a questionable assertion. Jealousy, he claimed, "does not make up the causes of my grief." Well, perhaps not all the causes. He was "distressed at your countenancing reports so contrary to truth, hostile to my proffessions, and derogatory to my honor." He ended "unalterably your friend most affy."[15]

Greene had had enough. "Your parting letter gives me no small pain." He defended Colonel Morris, and though he said Morris "must have mistaken" what Lee said, "be assured he wishes not to injure you either with me or with the World." We can safely say that Morris did not misinterpret what Lee said, that Greene knew it, and papered it over for Lee's sake. He noted that negative remarks on Lee's conduct at Eutaw Springs were circulating prior to Greene's report being made public, probably by a "Maryland officer who was on his way home." Furthermore, "The people of Virginia are very jealous of your merit and growing consequence." Greene's aide, Captain William Pierce Jr., had carried Greene's battle report north to Congress in Philadelphia and to Washington in Virginia. Upon his return Pierce told Greene that Mr. Custis—Washington's stepson, John Parke Custis, who served his stepfather as a civilian aide during the siege of Yorktown—had "taxed him roundly with my [Greene's] partiality [of Lee] to the prejudice of other Officers. Your family and name must be very obnoxious that the people should refuse you the glory due to your merit and exertions." That must have stung. Especially as it was true. Many Virginians resented the arrogance of the Lees and had been spreading vicious gossip about Light Horse Harry at least since the action at Paulus Hook in New Jersey in 1779. The ending of Greene's letter was courteous but not fulsome. "I will only add that you maybe assured of my friendship and attachment." They never met again.[16]

In June 1782, long after Lee's departure, another of Greene's aides, Major Ichabod Burnet, after an absence returned to South Carolina and was himself "a little mortified to find you" gone, and the "tenor of your letters to General Greene affected me terribly." Addressing Lee as "My Dear Friend," he argued that though he did "not expect you to hear the ill natured insinuations of the insignificant without feeling ... I am confident they are not such as ought to make you distressed. Look around with an impartial eye and judge whether any person has so great a right to be happy in this situation as yourself." Burnet stressed that "Your military reputation is unsullied and unequalled & your judgment command that respect which you must wish to receive and I cannot conceive why you wish to contend with the envious and ill natured part of society. The line of conduct you have adopted as a military character, certainly places you out of their power, and I am surprised your cool reflections do not dispel every idea of their being worthy of your notice." Burnet signed his letter as "Your Sincere Friend." It was a good letter, a rational letter. Light Horse Harry, however, had crossed into an irrational world of his own making.[17]

How should we judge Lee's military performance? He was not at his best in big, set-piece battles. He tended to wander and meddle. Accustomed to being turned loose with general orders to carry out partisan missions, given a great deal of slack, he was not cut out for the command and control demanded when armies clashed head on. Until his breakdown, however—if that is what it was—Light Horse Harry Lee was a brilliant partisan commander, the leading Continental officer in that mode of warfare. He was at his best when sent off on detachment with his beloved Legion to carry out missions on his own. Except for a few minor bumps along the way, his partnerships with Francis Marion in taking the river forts and the operation at Augusta with Andrew Pickens were first rate. (Of Sumter, it might be said that the two men engaged in a mutual loathing society.) Scouting, raiding, collecting intelligence, acting as a cavalry screen—they were second nature to this young warrior. And he performed well in the static warfare of besieging forts. His youth should be emphasized. He joined the army when he was twenty, left it at twenty-six. In that period he strove mightily, gallantly, and often brilliantly for the Cause. He was one of the major players in the success of Greene's Southern Campaign. Yet he left it under circumstances that sullied his reputation.

A reputation, sad to say, that sank lower in the thirty-six years left to him. After initial political success, his desperate efforts to become rich by speculating in land led to financial disaster after disaster to a point that he was publicly proclaimed "the Swindling Harry Lee." He was such a failure in handling money that his in-laws used legal means to keep him from using his second wife's inheritance. He was imprisoned for debt, and it was in jail that he wrote his *Memoirs*. He was beaten senseless in Baltimore by a pro–War of 1812 mob. They attempted to cut off his nose and gouge out an eye. He never regained full health from that terrible ordeal and bore the scars for the years left to him. In a vain attempt to recover his health, he spent five years in the West Indies, never again to see wife and children. Finally, in 1818 he sailed from the islands and asked the ship's captain to put him ashore on Cumberland Island, Georgia. It was a fitting place for the end, for it drew him near the memory of the man he had served so well until the ignominious end. Nathanael Greene, long dead, had built a home on the island, Dungeness Plantation, and Greene's daughter, Mrs. Louisa Catharine Shaw, took Lee into the plantation house and provided a servant to nurse him. Army officers from Amelia Island and naval officers from the squadron stationed offshore took turns sitting with Lee at night. He lived for about two weeks. In his final days Mrs. Shaw and her family could hear his screams over the sound of the surf.[18]

Lee was buried with full military honors on Cumberland Island in the Greene family plot. A large crowd assembled: men from the two services, an army band, a marine guard, men and women from the islands. The pallbearers were six of the officers who had sat with him and listened to him talk of the Revolution and its aftermath. As the procession wended its way to the grave-yard, the band played the dead march from Handel's oratorio *Saul,* and U.S.S. *John Adams* fired a gun every minute upon the minute. The gun did not cease firing until Light Horse Harry was lowered into the earth.[19]

Like other young warriors whose life reached a pinnacle in wartime but in peace went downhill until they shattered, Light Horse Harry should not have died a broken, crippled old man. He should have died gloriously, leading his Legion into battle.

"They Are Absolutely No Better than Children"

While Lee's personal tragedy played out, and despite Cornwallis's surrender at Yorktown, the war went on in the Carolinas and Georgia, with all the disasters to civilians that entailed. Leslie's army was in no condition to challenge Greene to a major battle. It was "not above 3500 men fit for duty and wants confidence," Leslie reported to Clinton. Greene's army, even smaller, was in no condition to mount a conventional siege of Charleston. Nevertheless, the garrison and populace of the city were in dire need of food. Fresh "meat and vegetables etc. . . . are almost unavailable," wrote General Hans von Knoblauch, "due to the proximity of the enemy, only 10–12 Eng. miles from us." Military operations therefore centered on British foraging expeditions into the Low Country and Rebel attempts to foil them. And at long last the British had a cavalry commander who proved himself more than equal to the task.[20]

Colonel Benjamin Thompson of Massachusetts and New Hampshire, a confidante of Lord Germain and formerly an under secretary of state, arrived by chance at Charleston in December 1781. He was a passenger in a fleet carrying provisions and supplies for New York that was held in Charleston because it was thought too dangerous for it to proceed northward during the winter. Thompson, of modest birth and education, was a social climber who had honed his talent of insinuating his way into the good graces of powerful people. With time on his hands, he offered his services to General Leslie, who accepted and put the new colonel in charge of his various cavalry units.

Thompson's job was to forge a force capable of dealing with Rebel cavalry on even terms.[21]

At 11:00 A.M. on 14 January 1782, Lieutenant John Kilty and a small detachment of 3rd Light Dragoons (William Washington's command before he was captured at Eutaw Springs) were leaving Dorchester when sixty British cavalry emerged from the woods at the edge of town, attacked, and captured Kilty and six of his men. A corporal escaped by swimming the Ashley River and carried the word to Major Richard Call, who reported the incident to Greene. This minor skirmish is of interest because of what Colonel Thompson had to say about Lieutenant Kilty and his men: "if the prisoners we took the other day (which by the bye belonged to Col. Washington's Regiment) are a fair specimen of their cavalry, I would venture to attack the whole with 150 of the dragoons that are under my command. They are absolutely no better than children, and their horses are as much too fat as ours are too lean. A long march would knock one-half of them up." A far different assessment from what we have previously learned of American cavalry.[22]

In late February intelligence received in Charleston placed Marion's Brigade, now at about half strength, near Wambaw Bridge northeast of Charleston. In Marion's absence at the legislature in Jacksonborough, Colonel Peter Horry commanded the Brigade. Horry became ill, turned the command over to Colonel Archibald McDonald, and went home to his plantation. On 23 February Thompson marched against Marion's Brigade with his cavalry, mounted militia, and infantry from the jaegers and Volunteers of Ireland. The following day Captain William Bennett, leading an American patrol, spotted Thompson's movement and galloped off to warn the brigade. Major William Benison, in temporary command of Horry's dragoons, in his camp on one side of Wambaw Creek, was too busy eating to take Bennett's warning seriously. Bennett then rode across Wambaw Bridge to warn Colonel McDonald. He was also eating and scoffed at Bennett's warning, although he did send Major John James to take temporary command of the brigade, which was some measure of help when Thompson struck. Thompson attacked Benison and his dragoons first. Surprised, they fled across Wambaw Bridge and attempted to make a stand on a knoll just beyond but were attacked and broken by Tory militia. Horry would blame Major Benison for "neglect of duty," but Benison would not be punished, as he paid for his mistake with his life in the melee at Wambaw Bridge. American militia stationed nearby, largely consisting of former Tories, also took to their heels. Major James rallied Marion's Brigade and stopped the British advance. Night drawing nigh, Thompson withdrew his cavalry and rejoined his infantry eight miles away. He claimed forty American dead, twenty-five horses captured, and one British dragoon slightly wounded.[23]

General Marion and Major Hezekiah Maham had left the legislature in Jacksonborough when they received news that the British were advancing toward Marion's Brigade. They joined Maham's command at their camp several miles up the Santee River from Wambaw. The separation from Horry's force had come about because of the intense rivalry between Maham and Horry over command. Their rivalry was a festering wound that bedeviled both Marion and Greene but need not detain us. As Maham's home was only twelve miles from the camp, he asked and received permission from Marion to visit there. While he was gone, Marion learned of his brigade's defeat by Thompson. Without waiting for Maham's return or sending for him, on 25 February Marion immediately marched for Wambaw with Maham's dragoons. He set a fast pace and after thirty miles stopped at Tidyman's Plantation on the South Santee River not far from Wambaw Bridge.[24]

Upon learning of Marion's presence nearby, Thompson deigned to withdraw and ordered his cavalry to march up the Santee. At Tidyman's the opposing forces came within sight of each other at "about Three Hundred yards distant, directly in front of us," Thompson wrote. The Santee River was to Marion's rear, cutting off a retreat. After Thompson's force marched quickly through a narrow lane, they emerged onto what he described as a "Field extended at least Two Hundred yards to our right and to our left." This open space was obviously a fine spot for cavalry, and Marion ordered Maham's dragoons to charge. Captain John Carraway Smith commanded the dragoons. According to Greene's biographer, instead of charging, Smith "dashed into the woods on the right and drew after him the whole regiment in irretrievable confusion." Thompson immediately ordered his own charge and Marion and his force were driven from the field. Some men fled to the Santee swamps in attempts to get to the river. Lieutenant Jacob Smizer of Horry's corps drowned "in Crossing the river," Marion reported, and others were probably shot by Thompson's men and sank into the swamp. Marion wrote that he rallied some of the dragoons in less than half a mile. Thompson, victorious and satisfied with the damage he had done, withdrew. He was not sure of Marion's losses, but he had captured forty horses and much baggage, including "General Marion's Tent and his Canteens full of Liquor, which afforded a timely supply for the troops."[25]

Now the blame game began. Colonel Horry in a letter to Greene claimed, "I think was the General [Marion] with the Brigade the Enemy would not have returned in Tryumph," and that he had "Repeatedly wrote him of the Necessity of his Presence & urged as much as possible his return." He did admit that Marion had tried to leave Jacksonborough earlier but the legislature refused to allow him to go due to the press of important business. Major Maham complained to Greene that Marion had ridden off without giving him notice and had "not Even Left one of my dragoons To go down with me." He also asserted that instead of ordering a charge Marion directed the troops to "file of[f] to the Rite which struck the officers & men, that they wast to Retret, which thay did in the Greatest Confution." With regard to this accusation, given Maham's character flaws we would do best to stick with Marion's version. Marion's biographer stated that the many redeemed Tories in Maham's command were not eager to fight their former comrades and also feared punishment, perhaps execution, if captured. Marion's report on the action to Greene has not been found, but in another letter he wrote, "We lost a Glorious opertunity the 25th of Cutting up the British Caveldry, if Our Troops Would have Charged; for I had no Idea of a retreat when they broke." He added more detail and put the onus on Captain Smith in a letter to Colonel Horry. "We lost a fine opportunity to cut the enemy's Horse to pieces, by Maham's Horse not charging as it was ordered, but I believe it was principally owing to Capt. Smith not telling his officers and men what they were going about. I rallied a part of the Horse less than half a mile, and sent them to cover the scattered men." Marion gave his losses as eight killed, seven wounded, and thirteen missing. William Dobein James, who rode with Marion, put the affair best: "The loss was but little . . . but the disgrace was great." Greene, however, was not unduly agitated and in a letter to Marion dealt with it in two sentences. "I am sorry they have succeeded so well as it will revive the drooping spirits of their troops and give a disponding temper to our Militia. But there is no guarding against so superior a force." He then offered Marion part of Sumter's Brigade.[26]

Colonel Benjamin Thompson was obviously an aggressive and skillful combat commander, and he deserves plaudits for his performance. But not too much should be made of these skirmishes in judging the overall record of Rebel and Tory partisans. Marion's command at the time was much depleted and the controversy over command between Horry and Maham weakened it further. And unlike Marion and other Rebel partisan leaders, who proved themselves over the long haul, Thompson's tenure was but a few months. The convoy for New York sailed in late March 1782 and Thompson left with it. Again, William Dobein James put it best: "he was a burning meteor but soon disappeared." Thompson's best years lay ahead of him. After the war he went to Europe and gained an international reputation as a scientist and social reformer, and by the elector of Bavaria was made Count Rumford of the Holy Roman Empire.[27]

"They Seem to Be Afflicted with a Kind of Hydrophobia"

Another successful British foray was made at Beaufort, about fifty miles south of Charleston as the crow flies. Getting there by land was impossible with Greene's army near Jacksonborough blocking the way. But the British still controlled the sea. Preparations for a raid probably began in late February, as a woman had come out of Charleston and told John Laurens that "gallies and flat bottomed boats" were being readied and there were rumors of "some southern expedition." On 3 March General John Barnwell, who commanded the militia assigned to protect the barrier islands from the Edisto River to the Georgia line at the Savannah River, "received intelligence that two British Gallies & a Sloop were in St. Helena Sound," on the northern side of Port Royal Island, on which Beaufort was located. Barnwell "immediately" requested assistance from the militia on the mainland, "but I must say without much expectation of their assistance having long known how very difficult it had ever been to prevail on them to Cross Salt Water: they seem to be afflicted with a kind of Hydrophobia which increases at the view of sea water. Nor have they disappointed me." Ten men appeared from the mainland. The problem lay in that old devil command jealousy: the commanders on the mainland, Colonel William Harden and Colonel William Davis, denied Barnwell's authority. The British vessels anchored off Beaufort on 4 March. Barnwell wisely made an agreement with the British commander, the South Carolina Tory Major Andrew De Veaux, that "should he treat the Women and Children with politeness & prevent his men from plundering, his men Shoud not be fired on in the Town." Sources differ on the purpose of the raid, from recapturing a British sloop to recovering Tory property and gathering provisions. De Veux's force stayed in Beaufort for three weeks.[28]

"Col Lawrens Is by No Means Popular with the Legion"

Greene had a more serious problem to deal with than De Veaux's raid at Beaufort. As stated in the previous chapter, on 12 February Greene informed Light Horse Harry Lee that "Col Lawrens will take command of the light troops, as soon as you are gone; which I mean to consist of the Legion[,] Washington's horse and the Dela[ware]." It was not a wise choice. Lee had engaged in daring operations but was thorough and prudent. Now he was to be succeeded by an officer lacking in both categories. Lee was careful of his men's lives, Laurens was careless of them, by his record criminally careless in his ceaseless quest for personal glory. No wonder, then, that "Col Lawrens is by no means popular with the Legion," as Greene wrote to Lee, who by then was in Virginia, newly married, never to return. Later Greene described the toxic situation of command in even stronger terms: the officers took a "great dislike to Lawrens . . . and they were determined to be removed from under his command if possible, and would listen to nothing that opposed it." Major John Rudulph of the Legion felt that he should have succeeded to command of the Legion, or as Greene put it, "Major Rudulph wanted to personate you but nature never formed him for it. He is a brave officer; but is too petulant and impatient at times." It may well be that Rudulph was not up to the top command, but surely his impatience could not have come close to equaling that of Laurens. The Legion was an elite unit, its officers a proud, arrogant lot, accustomed to special treatment. Dredging up his knowledge of Roman history, Greene wrote that "The pride of the Corps from long indulgence and from their great reputation made them not unlike the Pretorian guards difficult to govern and impatient of subordination." Despite his faults one must sympathize with Laurens, for he was placed in a very difficult situation. And to this was added a war that had wound down to British foraging raids and Rebel attempts to foil them. It was not the kind of war John Laurens fervently wished for: "the campaign is become perfectly insipid," he wrote to a friend.[29]

So matters stood through the late winter, spring, and early summer of 1782. Renowned for its discipline, the Legion began to unravel. Greene's aide Major Ichabod Burnet wrote to Major John Rudulph that the Southern Army's monthly returns of strength "have been repeatedly delayed by the neglect" of submitting the Legion's returns, and warned that General Greene "will not suffer that inattention to discipline." He reminded Rudulph that the Legion's "honor" and the "reputation of its Officers are nearly connected with the perfection of its discipline," and that his adjutant should be ordered "to observe in future the greatest punctuality and accuracy in making the Returns." Burnet wrote to Lee, "Your absence from the Corps has been too evident to escape even the unobserving."[30]

The blow-up came in June 1782. In his Orders of 13 June, Greene announced the reorganization of the Light Corps and in so doing separated the Legion cavalry from the Legion infantry. The Legion horse and the cavalry of the 3rd and 4th Regiments comprised one corps under Colonel George Baylor. The second corps included the Legion infantry, dismounted dragoons from the 3rd Regiment, the Delaware Line, and 100 men "fit for light infantry service . . . the whole of the Infantry to be commanded by Lt Colonel Laurens." General Mordecai Gist was given overall command of the two corps. Neither Colonel Baylor nor General Gist was a Legion officer, and Laurens was considered beyond the pale by Rudulph and his colleagues. The Legion's officers were incensed at the separation of the Legion cavalry and infantry and that both would be combined with other units. Major Rudulph and the five captains of the Legion wrote to Greene five days later that his "orders contain such injustice & are so repugnant" they could not "consistant with our established rights[,] serve you any longer," and they resigned en masse. Greene replied the same day rejecting their "accusation" as "no less indelicate than unjust," and noted that "You have not distinguished between what have been matters of indulgence and what are rights." He had no problem submitting the matter to "our superiors in Congress, the Board of War, the commander in Chief, or either of them." He ended his long letter advising them not "to suppose the public cannot do without you. I know your value and shall feel your loss and wish you to reconsider the matter before you take your final resolution." The officers replied the next day. They disagreed with Greene, believed their services were "no longer wanted," and could not "think of waiting the decision of Congress [while] labouring under the Grievance." Whereupon Greene on the same day sent them a one-sentence reply. "As I find you are determined not to listen to reason, I shall not hesitate to accept your resignations; and shall report the same to the board of war."[31]

It was apparently then that Captain Patrick Carnes, one of the Legion officers objecting to Greene's reorganization, began backing off and using his influence with his fellow officers to do the same. Greene wrote to Lee the following October, "where temper is wanting and claims run high reason is often rejected. This was too much the temper of your officers. Nor do I know where the matter might have ended had it not been for Captain Carnes's good sense and better way of thinking." The officers withdrew their resignations, agreed to refer the dispute to Congress, and Captain Carnes was sent north with the relevant documents. On 23 August Congress resolved to uphold Greene in all aspects of the matter.[32]

"Open a Door for the Disaffected"

While Greene dealt with prima donnas, Major General Anthony Wayne maintained his vigil close to Savannah. The short distance between British lines and Wayne's patrols gave opportunities for deserters to cross to the Rebels. One enticement for Tories to desert was provided by the new governor of Georgia, John Martin, who had been urged by Greene, in furtherance of his policy of reconciliation, "to open a door for the disaffected of your State to come in with particular exceptions. It is better to save than destroy especially when we are obliged to expose good men to destroy bad." On 20 February 1782 Martin issued a proclamation offering pardons to all who "wish to return to their allegiance and atone for their past conduct by assisting their

fellow Citizens to rescue their Country from British Tyranny & oppression."
James Wright, the royal governor of Georgia, was aware of Greene's policy
before Martin's proclamation and warned in a letter of 12 February that unless
the "Great Many Truly Loyal Inhabitants here" could be "Subsisted etc. at
a Vast Expence," they would "go off & make the best Terms they can." On
21 February, two important and respected Tories went over. Sir Patrick Hous-
ton and Major David Douglass left Savannah and "surrendered themselves to
me," Wayne reported, and added that "a considerable number of Hessian &
other Deserters have also lately come out."[33]

Although desertion of soldiers did not seriously weaken the garrison, Hessians fleeing the ranks worried Governor Wright. On 4 March he wrote that
"The Hessians Continue to Desert & it becomes a most Serious & Dangerous matter." Wayne reported that the British commander, Brigadier General
Alured Clarke, "filled the swamps round their works with Tories, Indians, &
armed Negroes, to prevent desertions, notwithstanding which a Number of
Hessians find the way out, and the defection in that Corps is so general, that
they are not trusted to mount guard but in the Center of the Town."[34]

"I Ordered the Vanguard to Charge"

Even with desertions from the garrison, Wayne remained outnumbered, which
forbade an assault on Savannah. But on 21 May General Clarke sent Colonel
Thomas Brown, whom we met during his 1775 travail outside Augusta and
again during the two sieges of that town, into the countryside with a 350-
man mixed force of regulars, provincials, militia, and some Choctaw braves
to meet and escort a band of Creek warriors into the city. Wayne was unaware
of Brown's mission but he craved action, and when "I received intelligence of
the enemy being out in force from *Savannah,*" dragoons and infantry "were
put in motion" to intercept Brown. Failing to find the Creeks, Brown had
turned back. He and Wayne met on the night of 21 May on a causeway cut
through a swamp on the road to Savannah. When Wayne became aware of
Brown's column, "I ordered the Vanguard to charge, which was obeyed with
such vivacity as to immediately terminate in total defeat, & Dispersion of all
the British Cavalry, & a large body of Infantry." This was Wayne tooting his
horn. The clash was a skirmish in which Brown lost five men killed and nineteen taken prisoner. Wayne lost two men. Brown was driven off the causeway
into the swamp, but he had militia who knew the ground, took an alternate
route, and in the morning was in Savannah. Emboldened by this minor affair,
Wayne refreshed his men and on the morning of the 23rd advanced within
sight of the British redoubts outside Savannah and detached "a few Infantry

& Dragoons to draw the Enemy out, but they declined the invitation." The reason for the British declining to engage is made clear when one recalls that London was winding down the war, and all commanders were under orders not to engage in offensive operations.[35]

"A Most Furious Attack"

If the short-lived clash on the causeway was but a skirmish, the following month Wayne was engaged in another encounter by night, this one a hot fight that began when he and his soldiers were totally surprised. The Creek party that failed to make contact with Brown was still intent on gaining Savannah. One hundred and fifty strong, it was led by Emistisiguo, one of the most important Creek leaders. He was described by an American, Alexander Parker, who was in the thick of the fight, as "the largest and bravest of the warriors—six feet, three inches high—weighing about two hundred and twenty pounds—of a manly and expressive countenance, and thirty years of age." At that time Wayne had moved from his camp at Ebenezer to Sharon, only five miles from Savannah and directly in the path of the Creeks. Unseen, unheard, the warriors scouted Wayne's position. Emistisiguo decided to attack Wayne's pickets and overrun them the next night. On the evening of 23 June, following his customary practice, Wayne moved his camp to where his pickets had been. Wayne's rear was unguarded.[36]

At 1:30 on the morning of 24 June, the night air erupted with the shrill cries of the warriors. Wayne reported that they launched "a most furious attack" upon a light infantry company guarding the army's two field pieces, "their onset ... so impetuous, and their numbers so superior, as to cause that little gallant Corps to fall back a few paces, which put the Enemy for a few moments in possession of that Artillery." Then the Creeks made a mistake. They temporarily halted their advance and attempted to use the field pieces against the Americans. Wayne, his officers and men, though initially "thrown into disorder" by the "fury and violence" of the attack, gathered themselves. Led by Colonel Thomas Posey and Captain Alexander Parker, the light infantry charged with the bayonet. It was the perfect weapon in the hand-to-hand fighting that followed. Wayne paid tribute to Emistisiguo and his warriors, who "met our charge with that ferocity for which they are famous at the first onset, not a little heightened by their temporary success." Wayne had his horse shot from under him. Emistisiguo died on the field, pierced with sword and bayonet. Many warriors died there, along with two white guides, and Wayne thought many wounded probably sought sanctuary in a nearby swamp.[37]

In the aftermath there occurred an incident that stained Wayne's honor. Colonel Posey was sent in pursuit of the retreating Creeks and captured twelve who thought Posey and his men were British troops because they approached from the direction of Savannah. He returned with his prisoners and met Wayne with the rest of the army. Colonel Posey related the end of the story. "The general appeared in good humor until he discovered the Indian prisoners, his countenance then changed, and he asked Posey in a very peremptory manner, how he could think of taking those savages prisoners. Posey related the circumstances in the manner in which they were decoyed, and observed that he thought it wrong to put them to death after they became prisoners; he [Wayne] said they should not live, and they were accordingly put to death."[38]

There would be no more major engagements in Georgia; thus we can return to the disgruntled officers of the Legion and events in South Carolina.

"Glorious Death, or the Triumph of the Cause"

Whatever the officers thought of Congress's decision to uphold Greene, one of their objections soon disappeared. On 21 August General Leslie wrote letters to Major John Doyle and Major William Brereton. Doyle was ordered to proceed to Beaufort, collect rice and cattle, then join forces with Major Brereton. Brereton's mission was to proceed up the Combahee River to "collect as much rice as possible" before joining Doyle. Two days later Captain William Pierce Jr. informed General Mordecai Gist of intelligence that the "Enemy mean to forage up Gumbahee [Combahee] River" and transmitted Greene's orders to "strike at" the foragers. On the 24th Captain William McKennan, commanding the Delaware Line, was so ill with malaria that he was "scarcely able to cross my Room." He had ordered out the local militia "but afraid their numbers will be small as they appear much discontented." McKennan could not fathom the raiders' intentions, "there being no Rice on the Cambahee, but imagine, they are in pursuit of Negroes, and Corn, as there are great Quantities of the latter planted on the River swamps." (McKennan was wrong about there being no rice on the Combahee.) Gist marched that day and on the 25th arrived on the north side of the river at Combahee Ferry. The redoubtable veteran Sergeant Major William Seymour of the Delaware Line recorded that "The enemy this time lay in the river with two row galleys, some top-sail schooners, and other small craft, the whole amounting to eighteen sail and three hundred regular troops and two hundred refugees."[39]

Greene had temporarily detached John Laurens from the Light Corps to gather intelligence. Laurens then became ill with malaria and was in bed when he learned of the British flotilla. Despite his illness, and without permission, he abandoned his intelligence assignment to rejoin his unit, for an opportunity for glory might arise.[40]

On 27 August General Gist reported the outcome to General Greene. Gist and his main force and the British foragers had arrived at Combahee Ferry on the 25th. Gist ordered Major Richard Call with 3rd Light Dragoons to cross to the south bank of the river, "Join the Infantry, and attack them at Day Break the next morning." That attack did not come off because Major Brereton learned that the "Americans were collecting in force, & throwing up works on the heights of Cambee," and he therefore ordered his troops to embark the night of the 25th. They took with them slaves and 300 barrels of rice.[41]

Downriver about twelve miles from Combahee Ferry Gist had ordered a "work to be thrown up" on Tar Bluff at Chehaw Neck "to annoy their shipping on their return." At that point John Laurens entered the story. Upon his arrival he solicited from General Gist "command at that post." Gist agreed and sent Laurens downriver with "50 infantry wth some matrosses [assistants to gunners] and a Howitz[er]." There are two versions of what happened at Chehaw Neck. One has it that the British landed troops on the north bank of the Combahee and occupied Tar Bluff before Laurens and his command arrived and that Laurens marched into a trap. The other account, by participants of both sides, claims that the British did not land troops until after Laurens fired upon the flotilla and "stopped them in the river," wrote Sergeant Major Seymour, and they then "tacked about and landed above where our men were." Seymour claimed that the British put 300 men ashore and that Laurens had only 40 men. Another account has British strength on shore at 150. Major Brereton reported that he put 60 men ashore. General Gist in the meantime had learned that the British had left Combahee Ferry in the night and stolen a march on him. Aware of the danger Laurens was in, he immediately began a forced march to Chehaw Neck. Lieutenant C. P. Bennett of the Delaware Line was with Laurens. Bennett wrote several decades later that Laurens appeared "anxious to attack the enemy previous to the main body coming up . . . and at the head of troops, although few in number, were as he supposed sufficient to enable him to gain a laurel for his brow previous to a cessation of arms, and . . . could not wait until the main body of the detachment would arrive, but wanted to do all himself, and have all the honor." Laurens ordered a charge, the British volleyed, several of the Delaware Line were "dangerously wounded"—and John Laurens fell dead.[42]

It was not unexpected. Greene wrote to Otho Williams, "Poor Lawrens has fallen in a paltry little skirmish. You knew his temper; and I predicted his fate." Laurens himself had written three and one-half years before his death: "You ask me, my Dear Father, what bounds I have set to my desire of serving my Country in the Military Line—I answer glorious Death, or the Triumph of the Cause in which I have engaged." Yet how glorious was death in a "paltry little skirmish" on the Combahee?[43]

However distressed he might be over Laurens's death, Nathanael Greene had more important things to concern him. First the Legion had unraveled, now the army threatened to do the same, and any hope that de Grasse would relent and appear off Charleston with the French fleet vanished under the waters of the Caribbean.

16

Greene Was the Maestro

"Injured Officers"

On 9–12 April 1782 a series of actions took place in the West Indies between de Grasse's fleet and a British fleet under Admiral George Rodney. Rodney bore a large share of responsibility for Cornwallis's disaster at Yorktown by dallying on the island of St. Eustatius in order to line his pockets with loot instead of intercepting de Grasse's fleet on its way to the capes of the Chesapeake. Now he redeemed himself. De Grasse's goal was the rich British colony of Jamaica. But on the 12th, in the passage between Dominica and Guadeloupe called Les Saintes, the final encounter between the two fleets became a crescendo of broadsides. De Grasse's 110-gun flagship, *Ville de Paris,* was pounded into nearly a wreck by a seventy-four-gun ship commanded by Captain William Cornwallis, Lord Cornwallis's younger brother, whose gallantry that day was described as "like Hector . . . as if emulous to revenge his brother's cause." De Grasse, his flagship, and four other ships containing the siege artillery for the invasion were taken by Rodney. The some 6,000 French dead included many of the troops who had served at Yorktown. The destruction of de Grasse's fleet spelled the end of any hope Greene had of a French naval operation off Charleston.[1]

Greene also faced a serious challenge by his officers and the threat of mutiny by the rank and file. He rebuked a logistics officer because "the troops have been three days without rice," which had brought the army to a "mutinous condition." To Governor Mathews he wrote, "The beef is really so bad and the discontent through the line so great that I begin to be very apprehensive of the consequences." That was on top of no pay for years, or clothing to replace the rags that in many cases barely covered the soldiers. Upon his arrival on 7 April 1782 at the main army's camp at Bacon's Bridge, Captain Walter Finney found the troops "remarkably healthy, but badly fed, and wretchedly Cloathed, at least one third of the men as Naked as they came to the world, thire Blankit & Hat excepted, which the belted round them to defend from the . . . weather, or well as to preserve . . . Deacency."[2]

The clothing crisis never went away and led Greene to enter into agreements the following year with a merchant, a shady character named John Banks, to procure clothing for the troops, and later provisions, for he could expect help from neither Congress nor South Carolina. During this affair Greene signed notes to guarantee payment to Banks's creditors. When John Banks & Company went bankrupt it left Greene personally responsible for £30,000 owed the creditors. The episode damaged his reputation and left him in debt for the rest of his life—and haunted his widow, as discussed in the previous chapter.[3]

To add to his distress, near the end of March 1782 Greene was plagued by the grumblings of officers of the Pennsylvania Line, and in their telling General Greene was the culprit for their hurt feelings. Greene ordered a detachment out to conduct a raid on an enemy position. By his order it was left up to the captain in charge to choose his junior officers. A Pennsylvania lieutenant "whose tower [tour] it was for command" reported for duty but was told the captain had chosen another. According to a fellow Pennsylvania officer, the lieutenant demanded to "see an order from the Gen'l for this irregular manner of proceeding; which was presented to him." He then left, "his feelings injured much." And to add insult to injury the captain who had been a party to the offense was a Maryland officer. Good Heavens! Obviously, this was not a matter to be taken lightly by men whose sense of honor was worn on their sleeves. A letter of protest signed by thirty-six ensigns, lieutenants, and captains was sent to Greene. Their rights had been "infringed on," and they required an "explanation." Had the general intended to form the detachment as he did, or was it a mistake? If the latter, they hoped the general's "sense of equity and honor will lead him to do justice to the feelings of a body of injured officers."[4]

Greene was exasperated. They were soldiers, not civilians. In his reply he reminded the "injured officers" that "You are to consider yourselves as Officers of the continental Army bound by its laws and governed by Military maxims. You are under military and not civil government." He lectured them on the general principles of forming detachments, and explained that "I have ever made it a rule . . . to detach such men and officers as I may think requisite for the service to be performed." He softened a bit toward the close of his letter but ended on a firm note. "You may be assur'd I have the strongest disposition to oblige and do justice to the merit and services of every Officer but I must confine myself to the maxims of Military government as are necessary to do justice to the public and to the Army at large."[5]

The officers' tender feelings were not assuaged. Lieutenant John Bell Tilden confided to his diary that "Our determination of sending in our resignations to him gains." Sanity, however, prevailed. In their reply of 3 April, the officers disagreed with Greene's reasoning but "are induced, from the peculiar situation of the army, and our zeal for the public good, to decline any further steps on the occasion."[6]

In the midst of despair over clothing and food and other supplies for the army, and officers behaving like spoiled brats, a ray of sunshine appeared. On 25 March Greene rode twelve miles from his headquarters at Bacon's Bridge to meet on the road his beloved Caty. She had finally succeeded in what she had wanted from her husband's first posting to the Southern Command: to be with him. In a century in which travel resembled an endurance contest, Major Ichabod Burnet, who had accompanied Catharine Littlefield Greene, praised the manner in which she had taken the journey. "She performed her part exceedingly well and retained a much greater Share of Health than could have been expected. A few weeks more rest I trust will restore that blooming countenance which she possessed in Phila." Caty had looks, wit, and according to tradition "her power of fascination was absolutely irresistible." A contemporary described her as a "small brunette with high color, a vivacious expression, and a snapping pair of dark eyes." Those eyes tantalized men, and she would become a victim of gossips. After the war a Georgia congressman who liked and admired Caty left us her own charming summary of her predicament and how she met it. "She confesses she has passions and propensities & that if she has any virtue 'tis in resisting and keeping them within due bounds." Greene was deeply in love with Caty, and certainly her presence brightened his days and nights.[7]

"The Prisoner to Be Shot to Death"

As happy as his domestic situation was, the opposite was true of the Southern Army. General Leslie in Charleston was well aware of the sufferings of the American troops, and in April 1782 there appeared a broadside called by Americans the "King's Proclamation." It listed the hardships and privations endured by Greene's army and announced that there was "*No scarcity of Rum, Salt, Clothing, Gold or Silver in Charlestown*" (italics in the original). To make matters worse, another element had been added with the newly arrived

Pennsylvania Line. Over a year before, on the night of 1 January 1781, wrote James Madison to Greene, "a mutinous spirit which had been some time working in the Pennsylvania Line . . . broke out with such violence that the utmost efforts of the Officers were insufficient to suppress it." One officer was killed, another mortally wounded. Madison noted that "many of the troops were foreigners & not a few deserters from the British Army." All or at least some of the sergeants who had led the mutiny had marched south with the Pennsylvania Line. They had come out victors in the northern mutiny, even winning pardons for the mutineers, and no doubt expected a similar result in the South.[8]

On 20 April 1782 Greene issued a general order attacking the "shameful practice of Desertion prevailing among the troops" and offered "ten guineas in hand, to any person who will discover them." His message did not alleviate the situation. Eight men of the Pennsylvania Line deserted between 3 and 5 May. One of its officers wrote, "A lamentable circumstance indeed that desertion is like to continue in our army; but what can we expect in their situation, without cloathes and pay for two years. Every person must allow there is still virtue in the army when we have any left." On the same day Greene issued his order, Sergeant George Gosnell of the Pennsylvania Line was arrested for attempting to incite mutiny. A woman named Becky, probably a camp follower, had turned him in. To counter any attempt to free the prisoner, Colonel Josiah Harmer recommended that Lee's Legion provide Gosnell's guards. Gosnell was a British deserter who had joined the Pennsylvania Line in the North and had been a ringleader in the January 1781 mutiny at the Northern Army's camp in Morristown, New Jersey. If he expected to get away with it in the South, he was mistaken. The day after his arrest Gosnell was court-martialed, found guilty, and sentenced to die. The next day Greene approved the sentence "and orders the prisoner to be shot to Death, on the Field in the rear, this afternoon at 3:00 oclock. 100 Men from each Brigade properly officered to attend the execution." The sentence was duly carried out.[9]

On the day Gosnell was executed, Greene wrote to Anthony Wayne of the army's "constant fever of discontent." The troublemakers lay "principally" in the Pennsylvania Line, but the mutineers "are trying to bring in the Maryland Line to join them." Greene was well aware, as he informed Otho Holland Williams, that "the troops have great reason to complain," but "this disposition in that line, has a deeper root than suffering." He also revealed that he was "almost certain the Enemy have been tampering with my Steward." Greene's steward was Richard Peters of the Maryland Line. Sergeant Major Seymour of the Delaware Regiment confided to his journal that Peters had corresponded with the British, "some of the letters being found about him." But General Gist, the presiding judge at Peters's trial, notified Greene that there was no evidence "to criminate him." There were in addition four Pennsylvania Line sergeants, also British deserters, under suspicion of fomenting mutiny: John Nicholson, Terrence Connell, John Speer, and Thomas Hustlar. They petitioned Greene and he decided not to court-martial them. But they and Richard Peters were dismissed from the service and "with their wives and families" taken into custody and marched to Salisbury, North Carolina, to work in the Continental manufactures. According to Light Horse Harry Lee, another of Greene's servants, Owens by name, was also suspected, and that "Twelve others deserted in the course of the night, and got safe to Charleston." That may well be, but Lee had already left the army and wrote that many years later.[10]

Greene reported to John Hanson, president of the Continental Congress, that the banishment of Peters and the sergeants "had a better effect upon the Army then even their execution." And he wrote to Otho Holland Williams in June that "The discipline of the Army is as rigid as ever. I hung a Sergeant and sent away five others among whom was Peters the Steward. This decisive step put a stop to it; and you cannot conceive what a change it made in the temper of the Army." Once again Greene is revealed as a hard man, which he needed to be, but also astute in the ways of managing an army. As he explained to Hanson, "I knew that mutiny must be checked in its first appearance, or else it would soon become too bold for resistance; for authority depends more on opinion than force." Those final words reveal a commander with a mind sensitive to nuance.[11]

The unrest in the army may have been due partly to the feeling that the war was almost over, therefore why must we continue to exist in such misery? Officers in Greene's army knew of reports in the North that the British were going to evacuate Savannah and Charleston, and surely their knowledge filtered down, first to sergeants, then to men in the ranks. An excerpt from one officer's letter on the subject was printed on 14 May in the *Pennsylvania Packet.* "Our little army lies at Bacon's Bridge, about 20 miles from Charles-town. Every preparation is making in the town for an evacuation: some circumstances have put the matter almost out of doubt." In late April Baron Ludwig von Closen, serving with Rochambeau's army in Virginia, entered in his journal that "We had intelligence from several places that Charleston would be abandoned" and that "Governor Harrison himself, who arrived in Williamsburg on the 27th ... confirmed this news, which he had been told verbally by Governor [John] Rutledge, who had come up from South Carolina."[12]

Greene disagreed—strongly. In his letter of 18 May to Hanson he wrote, "I fear the prevailing opinion to the northward of the enemy's intention of evacuating this country will delay our supply of stores. I can see nothing to warrant an opinion of this kind; on the contrary every appearance is against it." Although Greene did not use the sobriquet *perfidious Albion* (coined in the seventeenth century), it represented his attitude. He did not trust the British, was convinced that they meant to reinforce Leslie and take the offensive, and he stuck to his opinion throughout most of the summer. Events in Britain, however, had taken an entirely different course after Cornwallis's surrender at Yorktown in October 1781; thus we should go back and look at what happened among the British ruling class after news of the disaster reached London.[13]

"Oh, God! It Is All Over"

It took over a month for London to learn of Cornwallis's fate. On the early afternoon of 25 November 1781, Lord Germain hastened to Downing Street and informed George III's first minister, Lord North, of the calamity. Germain later reported that North received the news "as he would have taken a ball in the breast," and cried out, "Oh, God! It is all over." He was right. When Cornwallis lost his army, he lost America. Politically the war was over. Although men would continue to die in the Carolinas and Georgia in skirmishes over rice and slaves, the fighting was reduced to John Laurens's "insipid campaign." In the words of the British historian Piers Mackesy, "The surrender at Yorktown was to break the British will to continue the fight for the colonies." For John Brooke, George III's biographer, Yorktown "broke the morale of the governing class and paralyzed the national will to make war."[14]

The king and Lord Germain rejected the consensus. Both men fervently believed that the loss of America would be the end of Britain as a great nation, Germain declaring, "We should sink into perfect insignificance." Germain huffed and puffed about *uti possidetis:* retain Savannah, retain Charleston, retain New York, "to provide winter stations and staging posts" for troops fighting the French and Spanish in the West Indies. In his speech of 27 November opening Parliament, George III remained steadfast: the "late misfortune [Yorktown] in that quarter calls loudly for your firm concurrence and assistance, to frustrate the designs of our enemies, equally prejudicial to the real interests of America, and to those of Great Britain." Greene's reaction to the king's speech was pessimistic: "The enemy are determined to prosecute the war; and ... there can hardly be a doubt of the operations being principally to the southward." George Washington was privy to better intelligence. Writing on 18 March, he informed Greene that "By late advices from Europe and from the Declarations of the British Ministers themselves, it appears, that they have done with all thoughts of an excursive War, and that they mean to send small if any reinforcements to America. It may also be tolerably plainly seen that, they do mean to hold all their present posts, and that New York will be occupied in preference to any other. Hence, and from other indications, I am induced to believe that an evacuation of the southern States will take place." Washington's view was on the mark, although events would not move as rapidly as he apparently believed. According to the king's biographer, George III realized "that it was no longer possible to conduct offensive operations in America, and he accepted the cabinet's advice that no further reinforcements should be sent." This was confirmed on 12 December in a speech by Lord North to Parliament, in which he foreswore further offensive operations in America as well as replacements for the "Army lost in Virginia," for "it could not possibly be the intention of government to proceed with the war in America on the same scale as hitherto." But he also stressed that maintaining coastal ports and garrisons on the mainland was necessary to protect loyal subjects "within our lines" and to safeguard trade and British vessels "against the armed ships and privateers of America." And in the words of the historian of North's ministry, by the end of 1781 George III was still not "prepared to accept a separation from America."[15]

Yet the overall thrust of British policy crept steadily toward disengagement on the mainland while efforts moved inexorably to the salvation of other parts of the empire. Minorca fell to the Spanish in early February 1782. Britain was determined that Minorca's fate would not befall Canada, Jamaica, Gibraltar, India. On 9 February Germain resigned. In late February the House of Commons voted to abandon the war in America, and on 4 March it resolved that all who advocated or prosecuted offensive war in America were enemies of Britain. Two and one-half weeks later, 20 March, Lord North's ministry fell. On 27 March the opposition formed a new ministry whose policy was to conduct no offensive operations in America and to withdraw the army from the mainland.[16]

"Distrust Is the Mother of Security in War"

Greene was not convinced that the British meant what they said. On 19 May he replied to Washington's letter of 18 March that "I am not agreed with your Excellency in opinion that the enemy mean to evacuate this country; on the contrary I am fully convinced they do not." Such an opinion "has delayed our stores and will lessen the general exertion for the more effectual support of these states." On the day he wrote Greene learned of de Grasse's defeat at the Battle of Les Saintes, and he immediately wrote Washington another letter stating, "I have always been of opinion that farther attempts should be made for the subjugation of this Country should fortune favor them in the West Indies. I can see no other reason for having held footing in it so long."[17]

On 20 May General Leslie sent to the American lines by his aide, Captain Francis Skelly, a copy of Parliament's resolution of 27 February foreswearing further offensive operations in America. Captain Skelly, waiting with the American advance guard while notice of his arrival was sent to Greene, told the guard commander, Lieutenant William McDowell, that "He hop'd that matters were on a fare footing for peace; he hop'd that we would soon have the pleasure of drinking a glass of wine and taking each other by the hand in peaceable terms. He then asked me to take a drink of porter with him." Greene arrived about sunset and conversed with Skelly until 8:00 P.M. During that time, Skelly relayed to Greene General Leslie's verbal proposal of a cease-fire. Skelly also informed Greene that Sir Henry Clinton had been succeeded as commander in chief in America by General Sir Guy Carleton, who had arrived in New York on 5 May. What General Leslie would not know until some two weeks later, in early June, was that Carleton carried orders from the new secretary of state, the Earl of Shelburne, to withdraw from New York to Halifax; and "the same steps are to be taken with respect to the garrisons of Charleston and Savannah." Quite incredibly, the orders also read that if it was not in Carleton's "power to effect the evacuation without great hazard of physical loss, an early capitulation upon the terms which may secure the main object is thought preferable by His Majesty's confidential servants to an obstinate defense of the place without hope of answering any rational purpose by it."[18]

Greene sent the resolution and Leslie's verbal proposal to President Hanson, and awaited Congress's pleasure. Not surprisingly, he added his opinion on the proper course of action. He could not act on Leslie's proposal "without the order of Congress." "Nor can I conceive ourselves at liberty" to act upon the proposal without the "consent and approbation of our Ally" France. Since Britain seemed bent on continuing its war with France, American agreement to a cessation of hostilities would be regarded by France as a "violation of the alliance. And as the Marine of France has met with a misfortune in the West Indies our conduct will be regarded with a stricter Eye of jealousy." This raises an interesting speculation. Congress had instructed the American peace commissioners in Paris to negotiate with the British commissioners under French direction and not to sign a treaty without French consent. After heated debate among the American commissioners, they disobeyed their instructions, negotiated separately with the British commissioners, and signed the very favorable Treaty of Paris of 1783. If Greene had been a member of the American diplomatic team in Paris negotiating a peace treaty with the British, would he have resisted the decision by the other commissioners to sign off on the treaty without the advice and consent of "our Ally"?[19]

The letter also revealed Greene's deep distrust of British intentions, bordering on paranoia. His motto was simple: "Distrust is the mother of security in war." He believed one object of their approach was "to detach us from our alliance"; another, "to relax our exertions"; and if America refused to renounce its alliance with France, it "may serve to unite all parties in the justice and necessity of pushing the American War. They will urge that they have offered us peace and we will not accept it. They have offered us Independence if we will renounce our alliance with France, and we refuse it, therefore to push the War is both just and indispensable."[20]

Events, however, mirrored the new British policy. The garrison at Savannah evacuated the city at high noon on 11 July and proceeded twelve miles to Tybee Island to await embarkation. Their departure was peaceful, "leaving the Works and town perfect," Anthony Wayne wrote, "for which the Inhabitants are much Obligated to that Worthy humane officer Brigr Genl [Alured] Clarke." To prove his peaceful intention, General Clarke even allowed "Rebel officers to inspect our encampment at Tybee Island," wrote a Hessian officer. In recognition of his "severe and fatiguing service," Wayne designated Colonel James Jackson of Georgia to lead the American advance into Savannah. Further revealing the civilized nature of this transfer of power, a group of British officers handed over the keys to the city to Colonel Jackson.[21]

Greene believed the Savannah garrison would join General Leslie's in Charleston and therefore urged General Wayne to join the main army with his force as soon as Savannah fell, "for I am not without my apprehensions that as soon as the enemy combine their force they will fall upon us." He also alerted Francis Marion to be ready to join him with his militia. As it turned out, Greene's fear was for naught. General Sir Guy Carleton had ordered the Savannah garrison and its artillery field train to New York and the heavy artillery to Halifax, Nova Scotia.[22]

"Sickness Rages to an Amazing Degree"

All the while malaria swept through the army. Seeking a healthier location, on 7 July Greene moved the army from its encampment at Bacon's Bridge, where it had been since late March, seven miles down the south side of the Ashley River to Ashley Hill Plantation, eight or nine miles from the British position at Quarter House on Charleston Neck, fifteen miles from Charleston. He wrote Washington that "The ground is high and dry, the water is good and it has the appearance of the most healthy place this country affords." Colonel Lewis Morris Jr. agreed. "This is a fine commanding position that we are now in. They say it is healthy, and I shall believe it so." Their optimism was misplaced. Captain Walter Finney reported that "We had not ben three Days on this Ground, before two-thirds of our men and Officers were laid up with Intormitting & Flametory fevours. They have not proved mortal but in a few instances, one officer (Lt. McCullough) and two Soldiers ... ware removed to the Silant Grave." And in August he recorded that the "Intormitting Fevours so prevelant amongst our Troops, operate Diferently this month from it Did last, the great Mortalety produced in the first two Weeks, hais struck a Damp to all the survivers." In his journal entry of 8 September, Lieutenant McDowell recorded "Three hundred and seventy sick in General Hospital out of this small army, and better than half of the men sick in camp. We are scarcely able to relieve our guards." On the 21st he reported "Gen'l Greene exceedingly sick. Gen'l Wayne getting better." Colonel Josiah Harmer wrote on 29 September, "Sickness rages to an amazing degree; in the course of this month we have buried near one hundred men." By 2 November some two hundred soldiers had been lowered into silent graves. Greene wrote, "This has been one of the sickliest seasons known this thirty years. The only consolation and security we had had [is] the enemy have suffered no less than we." Indeed, General Leslie had been forced to evacuate Quarter House because of malaria, and a German officer reported that "The number of sick [in the Charleston garrison] increased highly during July, and many officers especially, were taken down by the malignant fever [malaria]." The only thing both armies could be thankful for was the absence of an even deadlier killer—yellow fever.[23]

The experience of one soldier reveals what the men were going through. On 29 September Lieutenant McDowell recorded, "This morning I took the fever." The next day "I took a vomit and was very sick." While he was sick he reported that "Lt Story of the 4th Regt died," then "sergt Welch of our company ... both buried this afternoon." Did McDowell wonder if he was next to be lowered into a silent grave? He recovered somewhat, but on 20 October "took very sick" while on guard and couldn't take the wine and soup sent to him by the mistress of Middleton Plantation. The next day "I took a vomit; after this I was something better." But on the following day "I had a violent fever and pain in my head and bones." On 12 November, as one of the officers retiring from the army, and after procuring a saddle for his horse, he began his journey home. It would take him one month and nine days to reach Pennsylvania and he was sick most of the way. On 1 December in Virginia "had to take a vomit which almost killed me." He could not travel the next day. He reached "Frederick Town" in Maryland on 19 December and "took very sick." But he pushed on twenty-six miles the next day to Hagerstown, Maryland, and on 21 December, traveling twenty-two miles that day, he arrived at his home. "The number of miles which I have traveled since the 26th of May 1781 is 2755 miles."[24]

The specter of the dead and the dying cast such a pall over the Continental camp that on 26 August Greene issued a poignant general order. "The general has observed, that the custom of beating the *dead march* at Soldiers funerals, has a tendency to depress the Spirits of the Sick in camp, & he is therefore pleased to order, that in the future this practice be discontinued."[25]

Passersby and people arriving at the camp were well aware of the presence of illness before they got there, and repelled by the stench even in an age of strong, offensive odors. Major General William Moultrie, taken prisoner in Charleston upon its surrender in 1780, returned to South Carolina in September 1782 after his exchange and visited the camp at Ashley Hill. "The next day we arrived at General Greene's camp; on our near approach, the air was so infected with the stench of the camp, that we could scarcely bear the smell; which shows the necessity of moving camp often in the summer, in these hot climates. General Greene expecting the evacuation to take place every week, from the month of August, was the reason he remained so long on the same ground."[26]

For August had brought a change to Greene's thinking on Britain's intention to evacuate. With regard to a peace treaty, however, he remained cautious, and continued to harbor his basic distrust of the British. "Peace seems to be probable and yet I would believe nothing until it was signed sealed and delivered. The Nation that is wicked enough to begin an unjust war will be base enough to practice every deception." On 5 August a Rebel spy brought word that "Every thing announces an approaching evacuation of Charlestown. Nothing but the want of transports expected from N. York is said to delay it." The report was true. General Leslie had received orders from Sir Guy Carleton on 1 August, stressing that the operation should proceed "with the utmost dispatch." It was "not a matter of choice," Carleton wrote, "but of deplorable necessity, in consequence of an unsuccessful war." Although not privy to the Carleton-Leslie correspondence, Greene was convinced. He wrote sundry persons, including Marion, of the "Great preparations . . . for the evacuation" and "I am persuaded it will take place soon"—"in a few weeks," he wrote to another, and to his friend Charles Petit, "the matter is now reduced to a certainty." Indeed it was. But it would not happen in a few weeks—far from it.[27]

The reason was lack of adequate shipping. Between 1775 and 1782, almost two thousand British merchant ships had been destroyed or captured. The new government issued the order for the evacuation of mainland America but left it at that: an order without planning how to carry out the order. The ministers in London paid no attention to how the evacuation was going to be done. And evacuation meant not only the garrison. The problem was magnified by the large numbers of civilians fleeing the country of their birth or adoption. Charleston was packed with Tory inhabitants and refugees, Americans all, who had no desire to stay in a land controlled by Rebels, for they rightly feared the well-known vengeance of the victors. Britain offered free transportation to secure realms of the British Empire, so best to go forth and, in the words of David Fanning, "begin the world anew." In even greater numbers were slaves accompanying their masters. Some free blacks would also leave. Savannah had already gone through it, and though the numbers there had been smaller they were not inconsiderable. The first convoy of thirteen vessels that sailed from Savannah to Port Royal, Jamaica, contained 50 whites and 1,900 blacks, mostly slaves who would be hired out or sold again into slavery in the West Indies even more brutal than on the mainland. When evacuation orders were posted in Charleston, 4,230 Tories signed up. Going with them: 7,163 blacks, most of them slaves. Charleston and Savannah combined would send more than 20,000 Tories, slaves, and troops to various parts of the British Empire. It would take four months of work by men on the spot, Generals Carleton and Leslie and Admiral Robert Digby, to gather the necessary shipping to evacuate troops and civilians from Charleston.[28]

"It Is One of the Most Pleasing Events of My Life"

As mid-December approached, the tempo quickened. The civilians had sailed. Now it was the garrison's turn. A fleet of some 130 sail awaited them in Charleston Harbor. Arrangements had been made for the peaceful transfer of power from General Leslie's garrison to Greene's army. Leslie proposed that upon the firing of the morning gun an American advance march to the outermost British redoubt. If it had been evacuated, they should continue their march until sighting the British rear guard, whereupon the Americans would maintain a distance of 200 yards. When the British rear guard turned to proceed to Gadsden's Wharf, the American advance "may immediately proceed into Town, & put into execution their directions towards the preservation of Peace & Good Order, during the whole of this it is to be understood that no hostility is to take place untill our troops have got on board their transports." Greene recorded that the Americans would "let them embark without molestation, they agreeing not to fire upon the Town after getting on board." The proposal was sent to Major General Anthony Wayne through a civilian intermediary. Wayne accepted the proposal and sent it to Greene for approval. Greene not only approved but informed Wayne that he and Governor Mathews intended to arrive in Charleston on evacuation day for a celebratory dinner, that he was forwarding "three or four quarters of beef and some poultry" for the occasion, and requested Wayne to contribute any beef and poultry that he might have on hand. He noted that Leslie's proposal gave "additional security to the Town which at this period of the war is a capital object."[29]

Governor Mathews and his council were especially concerned with the security of Charleston, thus they banned from the city as "dangerous spectactors" men who had played a key role in the Southern Campaign. They were the partisan militia: men who had put their lives and the well-being of their families on the line and saved the Revolution in the Carolinas and Georgia during the first phase of the Rising ... men who had changed the course of the war during those desperate months in 1780 following the surrender of Charleston and a Continental army to the British ... men who had fought on despite the devastating defeat of a second Continental Army ... men who had combined with Greene's Continentals since April 1781 in driving the British within their lines at Charleston ... men of Eutaw Springs who had advanced with élan against British regulars, marching "over dead men," hearing "without concern the groans of the wounded." Those men were not invited to share in the glory of that day. On the 14th of December 1782, the Back Country partisan militia was deliberately excluded by the civilian authorities from the capital of the Rice Kings. After all, they were just a "Pack of Beggars."[30]

Greene made sure that Marion knew he had played no role in the decision and added, "I should not have thought this necessary." He invited Marion "with three or four of your particular friends to enter the Town with the party that takes possession or as soon after as possible and remain there until the Governor arrives." Marion declined. He claimed that the militia "do not wish to go in to town, & my reason for not wanting to go in is that I never had the small pox & it may be in town & I would not wish to take it naturally." Thus ended this shameful episode.[31]

Over two days 4,127 British officers and men evacuated Charleston. The "inhabitants of the towns were forbidden, under penalty of strict punishment, either to show themselves in the streets, or to open their doors and shutters, but to keep them closed." The first units embarked in two waves on Friday, 13 December. At 7:00 A.M. on Saturday, the first embarkation of 14 December took place. Following that the British rear guard marched for Gadsden's Wharf: a detachment of artillery, jaegers, 63rd Foot, and a detachment from 3rd and 4th battalions of 60th Foot: 498 officers and men.[32]

Two hundred yards or so behind them marched the Continental advance, 400 strong, Major General Anthony Wayne commanding: 300 light infantry, 80 of Lee's cavalry, and 20 gunners and assistants with two 6-pounders. The Americans marched with "great order and regularity, except now and then the British called to General Wayne that he was too fast upon them, which occasioned him to halt a little." Apparently there were some desertions among British and German soldiers. A Hessian source recorded that of soldiers who returned to their quarters to fetch belongings they had forgotten, "many remained behind and forgot to come back. The subordinate officers were therefore obliged to bring in all that could be found, and then we went forward." General Alexander Leslie was the last man to board the last long-boat at Gadsden's Wharf.[33]

Wayne's advance "entered the Town in Triumph at 9 oClock A.M.," Captain Walter Finney of 1st Pennsylvania recorded in his diary entry of 14 December. They marched to the State House, arriving at 11:00 A.M., then returned to the "Berracks and Announced our Arrival by the Discharge of thirteen Cannon & thre Cheers." After that, for Finney and his comrades, all went downhill. His reaction to the populace of Charleston is worth quoting at some length. Leaving the enlisted men in their barracks, Finney and presumably some of his fellow officers "took a stroll thorow the Town, but Didn't meet with that Friendly Reception that might reasonably be expected on such an Event."

> Hear we experienced a most shameful Neglect, by the publick, Notwithstanding we ware but few in number, and doing hard Duty in the Matropelass of a State that Abounds with welth, we could not be furnished with either Fuel or provisions, the Soldiery was obliged to pull down the old Redoubts and carry the timber on thire Sholders near half a mile. How they contriv'd to get provisions, Am not able to account but certain I am that for Six Days they only Draw'd 1½ lb of Beef & 2 lb of Rice.
>
> In this Disagreeable Situation we remained without any Intercours, or conexion with the Inhabitants, to the 24th when we had the agreeable Orders to Rejoin our Respective Regts being relieved by the Virginia, & S. Carolina Troops.[34]

By the testimony of Major General William Moultrie, who also was there, the reception given the dignitaries that afternoon was entirely different. At three o'clock Major General Nathanael Greene, the victorious commander of a small, ragged, unpaid, malaria-ridden army, rode into Charleston behind an officer and thirty dragoons from the Legion. Greene escorted Governor Mathews. Behind them rode General Moultrie and General Mordecai Gist followed by the Governor's Council, "citizens and officers, making altogether about fifty." Behind them was a rear guard of 180 cavalry. The procession dismounted on Broad Street. The cavalry was discharged and sent to quarters. Then "every one went where they pleased; some in viewing the town, others in visiting their friends." Moultrie was elated. "I cannot forget that happy day when we marched into Charlestown with the American troops; it was a proud day to me, and I felt myself much elated, at seeing the balconies, the doors, and windows crowded with the patriotic fair, the aged citizens and others, congratulating us on our return home, saying, 'God bless you, gentlemen! you are welcome home, gentlemen!' Both citizens and soldiers shed mutual tears of joy."[35]

What of Nathanael Greene? Moultrie, the governor, his Council, the dignitaries—they were there because of him. He was the maestro. It was he who had directed the most brilliant campaign of the War of the Revolution. Had it not been for Greene the partisan militia resistance of the first phase of the Rising would have been for naught. So what was his reaction upon his entrance to the Citadel of the Rice Kings? His impression was mixed. "The town is neither so large or elegant as I expected, and yet it contains a great number of houses and many of them are spacious and noble buildings." After two bitter, bloody years, Greene had to have been exultant to have at last attained his goal. Yet his letters announcing the long-awaited day were restrained, his prose felicitous in its spareness. To Elias Boudinot, president of the Continental Congress, "I have the honor to communicate to your Excellency the agreable information of the evacuation of Charles Town, and beg leave to congratulate you upon the event." To friends he dropped the formal language. "It is one of the most pleasing events of my life," he wrote to Charles Petit. "It has long been in expectation; and the issue in doubtful suspence. My mind on this subject is now at ease." To Jeremiah Wadsworth he had cutting remarks for his critics. "Now let malice swell, and envy snarl, the work is compleat; and adds a finishing lustre to all our operations." To General George Weedon he quoted the gospel of Matthew 5:12—"now rejoice and be exceeding glad." Greene always had civic duty and the future in mind, and after commenting on the "happy deliverance of an oppressed people" he confided to Dr. John Witherspoon that "I wish private re[pose?] may not seduce Minds of the people from their public obligations. Pleasure is too apt to steal upon us after a long series of hardships and sufferings."[36]

He did not forget the army, the long-suffering Continentals who had, to paraphrase one of Nathanael Greene's most famous statements, fought, got beat, rose, fought again. He paid tribute to the army in his official letter to Elias Boudinot.[37] "I should be wanting in gratitude to the Army was I to omit expressing my warmest acknowledgements for the zeal and activity with which they attempted and persevered in every enterprise, and for the patience and dignity with which they bore their sufferings. Perhaps no army every exhibited greater proofs of patriotism and public virtue. It has been my constant care to alleviate their distresses as much as possible, but my endeavors have been far short of my wishes, or their merit."

Finally, he allowed himself a boast for his victory in the South that is a fitting end to our tale.

"I found it in confusion and distress and have restored it to freedom and tranquility."[38]

Epilogue

War and revolution bring to the fore men and women who otherwise, said Alexander Hamilton, "might have languished in obscurity or only shot forth a few scattered and wandering rays." Such a man was Nathanael Greene, called upon, Hamilton continued, "to act a part on a more splendid and ample theater." Plucked from a provincial neighborhood he rose to high fame in his time and rests now in the pantheon of heroes of the Revolution and a Founder of the new nation.[1]

There are two absolute requirements for a commander: physical and mental toughness. A commander may be brilliant, but if he lacks the physical constitution and mental balance to overcome, in the memorable words of Winston Churchill about his great ancestor John, Duke of Marlborough, "all the chances and baffling accidents of war," then all is lost. Nathanael Greene was blessed with those attributes. He carried burdens that would have crushed many commanders. His four predecessors in the South would have folded under the pressure. Of all Washington's lieutenants, Greene was the only one who possessed the skill, the judgment, and the character to undergo the extreme vicissitudes of the Southern Campaign and emerge triumphant.[2]

Had Nathanael Greene lived he would have been a mover and a shaker in the new Republic. We can certainly see him at the Constitutional Convention. Secretary of war? President? What a tragedy that this vital man, this brilliant intellect, who had so much to offer his country, was taken so early, three years after the war, age forty-six.

Greene and Caty had gone to Savannah, where he spent two days conferring with one of his creditors, E. John Collett, about the crushing debt brought on by the Banks affair. A miserly Congress had refused to relieve the hero of a debt incurred for the Cause. It would haunt his final days. They were returning to their plantation home, awarded to Greene by the grateful state of Georgia, and stopped at the plantation of a neighbor, William Gibbons. Greene and Gibbons inspected the plantation's rice fields under a hot Georgia sun. On the way home he complained of a headache. The pain continued the next day and on the day following was severe, especially over his eyes. His forehead swelled. He became depressed and spoke little. A doctor came and took blood. Another doctor arrived. The physicians conferred and took more blood. His head swelled greatly and he fell into a stupor from which he never emerged. Caty and Anthony Wayne were at Greene's bedside when he died at Mulberry Plantation, 6:00 A.M., 19 June 1786. That day Wayne wrote a letter to Colonel James Jackson about funeral arrangements and included an apology that serves as Nathanael Greene's epitaph.[3]

"Pardon this scrawl; my feelings are but too much affected because I have seen a great and good man die."[4]

Notes

Abbreviations

AC *Journal of . . . Archibald Campbell, Esquire, Lieut. Colo. of His Majesty's 71st Regimt. 1778,* ed. Colin Campbell (Darien, GA: Ashantilly Press, 1981)

AHR *American Historical Review*

Anderson, "Journal" "The Journal of Lieutenant Thomas Anderson of the Delaware Regiment, 1780–1782," *Historical Magazine* 1, no. 4 (April 1967)

AR Sir Henry Clinton, *The American Rebellion: Sir Henry Clinton's Narrative of His Campaigns, 1775–1782, with an Appendix of Original Documents,* ed. William B. Willcox (New Haven, CT: Yale University Press, 1954)

BHP British Headquarters Papers, Manuscript and Archives Division, New York Public Library, Astor, Lenox, and Tilden Foundations

Buchanan, *GCH* John Buchanan, *The Road to Guilford Courthouse: The American Revolution in the Carolinas* (New York: John Wiley & Sons, 1997)

CC *Correspondence of Charles, First Marquis Cornwallis,* 3 vols., ed. Charles Ross (London: John Murray, 1859)

Collins, *Autobiography* James Potter Collins, *Autobiography of a Revolutionary Soldier,* 1859; reprinted in Susan Francis Miller, *Sixty Years in the Nueces Valley: 1870–1930* (San Antonio, TX: Naylor Printing Company, 1930)

Commager and Morris *The Spirit of 'Seventy-Six: The Story of the American Revolution as Told by Participants,* 2 vols., ed. Henry Steele Commager and Richard B. Morris (Indianapolis: Bobbs-Merrill, 1958)

CP *The Cornwallis Papers: The Campaigns of 1780 and 1781 in the Southern Theatre of the American Revolutionary War,* 6 vols., ed. Ian Saberton (Uckfield: Naval and Military Press, 2010)

DAR *Documents of the American Revolution, 1770–1783* (Colonial Office Series), 21 vols., ed. K. G. Davies (Shannon: Irish University Press, 1972–1981)

Davie, *Sketches* *The Revolutionary War Sketches of William R. Davie,* ed. Blackwell P. Robinson (Raleigh: North Carolina Department of Cultural Resources, Division of Archives and History, 1976)

Davis, *Diary* "Diary of Capt. John Davis of the Pennsylvania Line," ed. John Davis and Jas. A Waddell, *Virginia Magazine of History and Biography* 1, no. 1 (July 1893), 1–16

Draper Mss Draper Manuscripts, Wisconsin Historical Society, Madison

EM Thomas Addis Emmet Collection, Manuscript and Archives Division, New York Public Library, Astor, Lenox, and Tilden Foundations

Feltman, *Journal* *The Journal of Lieut. William Feltman of the First Pennsylvania Regiment, 1781–82. Including the March into Virginia and the Siege of Yorktown* (1853; reprint, San Bernardino, CA: Nabu Press, 2013)

Finney, "Diaries" "The Revolutionary War Diaries of Captain Walter Finney," ed. Joseph Lee Boyle, *SCHM* 98, no. 2 (April 1997), 126–52

Garden, *Anecdotes* Alexander Garden, *Anecdotes of the Revolutionary War, with Sketches of Persons the Most Distinguished in the Southern States, for Civil and Military Service* (Charleston, SC: A. E. Miller, 1822)

GHQ *Georgia Historical Quarterly*

Gibbes, *Doc. Hist.* R. W. Gibbes, *Documentary History of the American Revolution, Consisting of Letters and Papers Relating to the Contest for Liberty, Chiefly in South Carolina*, 3 vols. (New York: D. Appleton & Co., 1855, 1857; Columbia, SC: Banner Steam-Power Press, 1853)

GLL Alexander Leslie's letterbooks, Thomas Addis Emmett Collection, Manuscript and Archives Division, New York Public Library, Astor, Lenox, and Tilden Foundations

"Gray's Observations" Robert Gray, "Colonel Robert Gray's Observations on the War in the Carolinas," *SCHGM* 11, no. 3 (July 1910), 139–59

Greene, *Greene* George Washington Greene, *The Life of General Nathanael Greene: Major-General in the Army of the Revolution*, 3 vols. (1867–1871; reprint, Freeport, NY: Books for Libraries Press, 1972)

"Itinerary PA Line" "Itinerary of the Pennsylvania Line from Pennsylvania to South Carolina, 1781–1782," *Pennsylvania Magazine of History and Biography* 36, no. 3 (1912), 273–92

JA *The Adams Papers Digital Edition*, ed. C. James Taylor (Charlottesville: University of Virginia Press, Rotunda, 2008–2017)

James, *Marion* William Dobein James, *A Sketch of the Life of Brig. General Francis Marion and a History of His Brigade* (1821; reprint, Marietta, GA: Continental Book Co., 1948)

JCC *Journals of the Continental Congress, 1774–1789*, 34 vols., ed. Worthington C. Ford et al. (Washington, DC.: U.S. Government Printing Office, 1904–1937)

Johnson, *Greene* William Johnson, *Sketches of the Life and Correspondence of Nathanael Greene, Major General of the Armies of the United States, in the War of the Revolution*, 2 vols. (1822; reprint, New York: Da Capo Press, 1973)

JSH *Journal of Southern History*

JW John Wilson, *Encounters on a March Through Georgia in 1779: The Maps and Memorandums of John Wilson, Engineer, 71st Highland Regiment*, ed. Robert Scott Davis (Sylvania, GA: Partridge Pond Press, 1986)

Kirkwood, *Journal* *The Journal and Order Book of Captain Robert Kirkwood of the Delaware Regiment of the Continental Line* (1910; reprint, San Bernardino, CA: N.p., 2013)

Lee, *Memoirs* Henry (Light Horse Harry) Lee, *The American Revolution in the South*, ed. Robert E. Lee (1869; reprint, New York: Arno Press, 1969)

Lee Jr., *Campaign of 1781* Henry Lee Jr., *The Campaign of 1781 in the Carolinas with Remarks Historical and Critical on Johnson's Life of Greene* (1824; reprint, Chicago: Quadrangle Books, 1962)

Massey, *Laurens* Gregory D. Massey, *John Laurens and the American Revolution* (Columbia: University of South Carolina Press, 2000)

McCrady Edward McCrady, *The History of South Carolina in the Revolution, 1780–1783* (New York: Macmillan, 1902)

McDowell, "Journal" "Journal of Lieut. William McDowell, of the First Penn'a Regiment, in the Southern Campaign, 1781–1782," *Pennsylvania Archives,* 2d ser., 15 (1890), 295–340

MHS H. Furlong Baldwin Library, Maryland Historical Society, Baltimore

Moultrie, *Memoirs* William Moultrie, *Memoirs of the American Revolution* (1802; reprint, Bedford, MA: Applewood Books, n.d.)

NCSR *Colonial and State Records of North Carolina,* 26 vols., ed. William L. Saunders and Walter Clark (Raleigh: State of North Carolina, 1886–1905), http://docsouth.unc.edu/csr/index.html/volumes

NYHS New-York Historical Society, New York City

NYPL New York Public Library, New York City

PAHDE *The Papers of Alexander Hamilton Digital Edition,* 27 vols., ed. Harold C. Syrett (Charlottesville: University of Virginia Press, Rotunda, 2011–2017)

PGW: Rev War *The Papers of George Washington: Revolutionary War Series,* ed. Philander D. Chase (Charlottesville: University Press of Virginia, 1985–)

PGW: Rev War DE *The Papers of George Washington: Revolutionary War Series Digital Edition,* ed. Theodore J. Crackel (Charlottesville: University of Virginia Press, Rotunda, 2008–2017)

PHL *The Papers of Henry Laurens,* 16 vols., ed. David R. Chesnutt et al. (Columbia: University of South Carolina Press, 1968–2002)

PNG *The Papers of General Nathanael Greene,* 13 vols., ed. Richard K. Showman, Dennis Conrad, and Roger N. Parks (Chapel Hill: University of North Carolina Press, 1976–2005)

Ramsay, *Rev. of S-C* David Ramsay, *A History of the Revolution of South Carolina, from a British Province to an Independent State,* 2 vols. (Trenton, NJ: Isaac Collins, 1785)

SCAR *Southern Campaigns of the American Revolution,* www.southerncampaign.org

SCHGM *South Carolina Historical and Genealogical Magazine*

SCHM *South Carolina Historical Magazine*

Seymour, "Journal" William Seymour, "A Journal of the Southern Expedition, 1780–1783," *Pennsylvania Magazine of History and Biography* 7, nos. 3, 4 (1883), 286–98, 377–94

Tilden, "Journal" "Extracts from the Journal of Lieutenant John Bell Tilden, Second Pennsylvania Line, 1781–1782," *Pennsylvania Magazine of History and Biography* 19, no. 2 (1895), 208–33

WGW *The Writings of George Washington from the Original Manuscript Sources, 1754–1799,* 39 vols., ed. John C. Fitzpatrick (Washington, DC: U.S. Government Printing Office, 1931–1944)

WHS   Wisconsin Historical Society

WLCL   William L. Clements Library, University of Michigan, Ann Arbor

Prologue

1   "The Siege of Charleston: The Journal of Captain Peter Russell, December 25, 1779, to May 2, 1780," *AHR* 4, no. 3 (1899), 484; Captain Johann Ewald, *Diary of the American War: A Hessian Journal,* trans. and ed. Joseph P. Tustin (New Haven, CT: Yale University Press, 1979), 196–97; Johann Hinrichs, "Diary," in *The Siege of Charleston,* trans. and ed. Bernhard A. Uhlendorf (1938; reprint, New York: Arno Press, 1968), 183; Peter Wood, *Black Majority: Negroes in South Carolina from 1670 through the Stone Rebellion* (1974; reprint, New York: Norton, 1975), 67 (for quotations on "Heat" and "charnel house"); J. R. McNeill, *Mosquito Empires: Ecology and War in the Greater Caribbean: 1620–1914* (Cambridge: Cambridge University Press, 2010), 198–234.

2   James Haw, *John and Edward Rutledge of South Carolina* (Athens: University of Georgia Press, 1997), 64; Henry Laurens to John Laurens, 8/14/1776, *PHL,* 11:228.

3   Richard Walsh, *Charleston's Sons of Liberty: A Study of the Artisans, 1763–1789* (Columbia: University of South Carolina Press, 1959), 53 (first Drayton quotation); William R. Ryan, *The World of Thomas Jeremiah: Charles Town on the Eve of the American Revolution* (New York: Oxford University Press, 2010), 36 (second Drayton quotation); for Drayton's mission to the Back Country, see Buchanan, *GCH,* 90–103, and Keith Krawczynski, *William Henry Drayton: South Carolina Revolutionary Patriot* (Baton Rouge: Louisiana State University Press, 2001), 127, 153–95, 206–9.

4   In two other ways the American Revolution also differed from the French and Russian upheavals. With the exception of offensives in 1776 and 1781 against the Cherokee in the southern Appalachians, and in 1779 in central and western New York against the Iroquois, Rebel terror was not state sanctioned, but instead more in the nature of vigilante actions. Nor was there a Thermidor in America: the original revolutionary leaders maintained control throughout and went on to lead the new nation. For my thinking on why the Rice Kings rebelled, and how they overcame Tory resistance, see Buchanan, *GCH,* ch. 8; Cornwallis to Clinton, 8/29/1780, *CC,* 1:58; for copious evidence of Rebel terror, see Jim Piecuch, *Three Peoples, One King: Loyalists, Indians, and Slaves in the Revolutionary South, 1775–1781* (Columbia: University of South Carolina Press, 2008), passim.

5   See the discussion of British plans by Piers Mackesy, *The War for America, 1775–1783* (1964; reprint, Lincoln: University of Nebraska Press, 1993), 43–44, 110, 157–58; for the war in the North, see John Buchanan, *The Road to Valley Forge: How Washington Built the Army That Won the Revolution* (Hoboken, NJ: John Wiley & Sons, 2004); Germain to Clinton, 12/3/1778, Clinton Papers, vol. 47:32, WLCL.

6   Andrew Jackson O'Shaughnessy, *The Men Who Lost America: British Leadership, the American Revolution, and the Fate of Empire* (New Haven, CT: Yale University Press, 2013), 53 (first quotation), 114–15; JW, 42; William John Hale to Admiral

Hale, 4/2/1778, in Harold Wilkin, *Some British Soldiers in America* (1914; reprint, Milton Keynes: General Books, 2010), 114; Troy Bickham, *Making Headlines: The American Revolution as Seen through the British Press* (DeKalb: Northern Illinois University Press, 2009), 197.

7   Mackesy, *War for America,* 159.

8   Clinton to Campbell, 11/8/1778, Clinton and Commissioners to Campbell, 11/3/1778, and Campbell's remarks, in *AC,* 4–7; Prevost to Lord Germain, 3/5/1779, *DAR,* 17:77.

9   The contemporary descriptions of Campbell are in Edward J. Cashin, *The King's Ranger: Thomas Brown and the American Revolution on the Southern Frontier* (Athens: University of Georgia Press, 1989), 83–84. For the capture of Savannah, *AC,* 22–30, and Charles E. Bennett and Donald R. Lennon, *A Quest for Glory: Major General Robert Howe and the American Revolution* (Chapel Hill: University of North Carolina Press, 1991), 94–99; for Howe's distress, Kenneth Coleman, *The American Revolution in Georgia, 1763–1789* (Athens: University of Georgia Press, 1958), 121.

10   *AC,* 45–46, for Campbell's statement on the number of troops who accompanied him upcountry, 47, for the dates of his march, 53, and for his description of Augusta and the surrounding countryside, 54–55; Campbell to Henry Clinton, 3/4/1779, *DAR,* 17:73 for slightly different troop strength, and 74 for description of the Savannah River; JW, 19, for the figure of 900 men; William Bartram, *The Travels of William Bartram: Naturalist's Edition,* ed. Francis Harper (1958; reprint, Athens: University of Georgia Press, 1998), 200. Unless otherwise indicated, the rest of the discussion in this paragraph and those following on the Georgia campaign of 1778–1779, including the Battles of Kettle and Briar Creeks, are drawn from Robert S. Davis, "The Battle of Kettle Creek," *SCAR* 3, no. 2.3 (February 2006), 30–35; Steven J. Rauch, "Kettle Creek Battlefield, Washington, GA," *SCAR* 3, no. 2.3 (February 2006), 38–43; Robert S. Davis, "Battle of Briar Creek," *SCAR* 3, no. 10.11 (October–November 2006), 26–27; and Joshua Howard, "The American Defeat at Briar Creek," *GHQ* 88, no. 4 (Winter 2004), 477–98. Quotations are cited.

11   Cornwallis to John Harris Cruger, 8/5/1780, *CP,* 1:256; *AC,* 60, 64; Campbell to Clinton, 3/4/1779, *DAR,* 17:74–75; JW, 42–43.

12   Dooly to Samuel Elbert, 2/16/1779, *SCAR* 3, no. 2.3 (February 2006), 39; Pickens to Henry Lee, 8/28/1811, Draper Mss, 1 VV 107, WHS.

13   Pickens to Lee, 8/28/1811; Dooly to Elbert, 2/16/1779.

14   Ibid.

15   *AC,* 64–65, and 87–91 for the Creek failure to rally to the British cause; JW, 43; Prevost to Campbell, 2/17/1779, Misc. Coll., WLCL.

16   *AC,* 57–58.

17   *Times Literary Supplement,* 11/13/2015, 29 (Moltke quotation); Ashe to Lincoln, 2/4/1779, Miscellaneous Manuscripts, EM.A (microfilm), NYPL.

18   *AC,* 68.

19   *AC,* 48.

20   John C. Dann, ed., *The Revolution Remembered: Eyewitness Accounts of the War of Independence* (Chicago: University Press of Chicago, 1980), 178–79.

21 Howard, "Briar Creek," 491; Harold L. Peterson, *The Book of the Continental Soldier* (Harrisburg, PA: Stackpole Books, 1968), for illustrations and an informed discussion of cartridge boxes.

22 *Orderly Book of Lieut. Gen. John Burgoyne,* ed. E. B. O'Callaghan (Albany, NY, 1860), 3; "political socialite" is the term used by Howard, "Briar Creek," 482.

23 Howard, "Briar Creek," 495; Dann, *Revolution Remembered,* 181.

24 *AC,* 77; Howard, "Briar Creek," 496.

25 Howard, "Briar Creek," 496.

26 Augustine Prevost to Germain, 3/5/1779; John Mark Prevost to Germain, 4/14/1779, *DAR,* 17:79, 101.

27 Lieutenant Heinrich Carl Phillip von Freilitzsch and Lieutenant Christian Friedrich Bartholomai, *Diaries of Two Ansbach Jaegers,* trans. and ed. Bruce E. Burgoyne (Bowie, MD: Heritage Books, 1997), 145; *John Peebles' American War: The Diary of a Scottish Grenadier, 1776–1782,* ed. Ira D. Gruber (Mechanicsburg, PA: Stackpole Books, 1998), 372.

28 Washington to John Mathews, 10/23/1780, *WGW,* 20:248–49.

29 Collins, *Autobiography,* 292.

30 *Men and Times of the Revolution; or, Memoirs of Elkanah Watson,* 2nd ed., ed. Winslow C. Watson (New York: Dana and Co., 1857), 290; The "Pack of Beggars" quote is in *The Carolina Backcountry on the Eve of the Revolution: The Journal and Other Writings of Charles Woodmason, Anglican Itinerant,* ed. Richard J. Hooker (Chapel Hill: University of North Carolina Press, 1953), 273.

31 For the training of Henry "Light Horse Harry" Lee's Legion as partisans and its use as such in the North, and the experience of partisans in the War of Austrian Succession, I am indebted to James R. McIntyre, who generously shared with me his unpublished paper, "Freemen or Freikorps? Light Horse Harry Lee and His Legion, American Partisans." On the matter of partisan warfare being waged from at least antiquity onward, cf. Michael C. Scoggins, *The Day It Rained Militia: Huck's Defeat and the Revolution in the South Carolina Backcountry, May–July 1780* (Charleston, SC: History Press, 2005), 159, especially the first sentence in the second paragraph.

32 For the number of actions, I have relied on the careful and conservative estimate in Terry W. Lipscomb, *Battles, Skirmishes, and Actions of the American Revolution in South Carolina* (Columbia: South Carolina Department of Archives & History, 1991).

33 Cornwallis to Rawdon, 8/4/1780, *CP,* 1:227; Mackesy, *War for America,* 342; Lyman C. Draper, *King's Mountain and Its Heroes* (Cincinnati: Peter G. Thompson, 1888), 230; Cornwallis to Germain, 8/20/1780, *CC,* 1:503; "Gray's Observations," 140, 148; Robert Stansbury Lambert, *South Carolina Loyalists in the American Revolution* (Columbia: University of South Carolina Press, 1987), 321. With regard to the strength of the British regular cavalry, in Buchanan, *GCH,* I placed it at 240. That was careless of me, since that number included Banastre Tarleton's Legion infantry, whereas his Legion cavalry numbered about 100 and the 17th Light Dragoons, also under Tarleton, about 40 to 50.

34 Brown to William Campbell, 10/18/1775, quoted in Cashin, *The King's Ranger,* 33; Balfour to Cornwallis, 6/7/1780, *CP,* 1:78; "Gray's Observations," 144.

35   I am grateful to Ben Rubin for the insight regarding the long Rebel rule in the Back Country. Prevost to Henry Clinton, 3/1/1779, *DAR*, 17:69; I am grateful to Jim Piecuch for allowing me to use his "The Loyalist Exodus from South Carolina in 1778," a paper presented to the Society for Military History Conference in Ogden, Utah, April 2008; Cornwallis to Alexander Leslie, 11/12/1780, *CC*, 1:69; Balfour to Cornwallis, 11/5/1780, *CP*, 3:65; Cruger to Cornwallis, 11/23/1780, quoted in Piecuch, *Three Peoples*, 233; Ferguson to Cornwallis, 7/20/1780, *CP*, 1:293.

36   "The attitude of the Loyalists in America and particularly in the South," [n.d., after 1781], attributed to Lord Rawdon, Alexander Wedderburn Papers, 1: 46, WLCL.

37   "Gray's Observations," 144; A. R. Newsome, "A British Orderly Book, 1780–1781," *NCHR* 9, no. 4 (October 1932), 381; Charles Stedman, *History of the Origin, Progress, and Termination of the American War*, 2 vols. (London, 1794), 2: 225–26 (for extended Cornwallis and Stedman quotations, see Buchanan, *GCH*, 243–44); Harold A. Larrabee, *Decision at the Chesapeake* (New York: Clarkson Potter, 1964), 32 (Germain quotation).

38   The first claim is in Rachel N. Klein, *Unification of a Slave State: The Rise of the Planter Class in the South Carolina Backcountry, 1760–1808* (Chapel Hill: University of North Carolina Press, 1990), 106–8; the second claim is in Sylvia R. Frey, *Water from the Rock: Black Resistance in a Revolutionary Age* (Princeton, NJ: Princeton University Press, 1991), 113, and passim; "Theirs was a revolution …" is in Simon Schama, *Rough Crossings: Britain, the Slaves, and the American Revolution* (London: BBC Books, 2005), 73; for "considerable overstatement," see Piecuch, *Three Peoples*, 10; for the other refutation of the racial motive, see the article by the late and much lamented dean of Revolutionary War studies, Don Higginbotham, "Some Reflections on the South in the American Revolution," *JSH* 73, no. 3 (August 2007), 661–63; Henry Laurens to Thomas Fletchall, 7/14/1775, *PHL*, 10:214.

39   "Memoir of Thomas Young, A Revolutionary Patriot of South Carolina," *The Orion, a Monthly Magazine of Literature and Art (1842–1844)* 3, no. 3 (November 1843), 101; Michael R. Nifong, "In the Provincial Service: The British Legion in the American Revolution, 1778–1783" (MA thesis, University of North Carolina, Chapel Hill, 1976), for the makeup of the Legion.

40   Cornwallis to Tarleton, 4/25/1780, *CP*, 1:25. For incidents of brutality prior to the Waxhaws engagement, see Buchanan, *GCH*, 62–63.

41   Tarleton to Cornwallis, 8/5/1780, *CP*, 1:365; *Reynolds*, ed. Nicholas Penny (New York: Abrams, 1986), 377–78.

42   C. Leon Harris, "What Can Pension Applications Contribute to Understanding the Battle of the Waxhaws and Other Events of the Revolutionary War?" *SCAR* 10, no. 2 (Summer 2014), 6. For more by Harris, see "American Soldiers at the Battle of Waxhaws, SC, 29 May 1780" (http://revwarapps.org/b221.pdf), and an unpublished paper, "Massacre at Waxhaws: The Evidence from Wounds" (2016), which deserves to be published. The revisionist arguments can be found in Thomas A. Rider, "Massacre or Myth: No Quarter at the Waxhaws" (MA thesis, University of North Carolina, Chapel Hill, 2002); Jim Piecuch, "Massacre or

Myth: Banastre Tarleton at the Waxhaws, May 29, 1780," *SCAR* 1, no. 2 (October 2004), 4–10; Jim Piecuch, *The Blood Be Upon Your Head: Tarleton and the Myth of Buford's Massacre: The Battle of the Waxhaws, May 29, 1780* (Lugoff, SC: Southern Campaigns of the American Revolution Press, 2010).

43 Banastre Tarleton, *A History of the Campaigns of 1780–1781 in the Southern Provinces of North America* (London, 1787), 30–31; Stedman, *History,* 2:193; Piecuch, *The Blood Be Upon Your Head,* 33.

44 Rider, "Massacre or Myth," 28 (1st quotation); Tarleton, *History,* 30; Pension Application of Obed Britt, S1499 (http://revwarapps.org); Piecuch, *The Blood Be Upon Your Head,* 91, for casualties.

45 Don Higginbotham, *The War of American Independence: Military Attitudes, Policies, and Practice, 1763–1789* (New York: Macmillan, 1971), 361.

46 For Hammond's Store and Pyle's Massacre, see Buchanan, *GCH,* 302, 363–64.

47 Buchanan, *GCH,* 106–10, for details. I am indebted to Ben Rubin for sharing with me his researches on the action at Ramseur's Mill.

48 George C. Rogers Jr., ed., "Letters of Charles O'Hara to the Duke of Grafton," *SCHM* 65, no. 3 (July 1964), 176; Cornwallis to Rawdon, 6/29/1780, *CP,* 1:185; William Richardson Davie, *The Revolutionary War Sketches of William R. Davie,* ed. Blackwell P. Robinson (Raleigh: North Carolina Division of Archives & History, 1976), 8.

49 Cornwallis to Clinton, 6/30/1780, *CP,* 1:161; Collins, *Autobiography,* 239; and for an excellent description of Huck's Defeat, see Scoggins, *The Day It Rained Militia*; Elizabeth Jane [Doss?] to Lyman C. Draper, 12/20/1873, Draper Mss, 14 VV 10–13 (microfilm), WHS. It should be noted that Draper's informant got her battles mixed up and placed the setting for Captain Huck's death at Kings Mountain.

50 Cornwallis to Nisbet Balfour, 7/17/1780, *CP,* 1:250; for a sketch of Thomas Sumter's background, see Buchanan, *GCH,* 115–21, and the best biography, Anne King Gregorie, *Thomas Sumter* (Columbia, SC: R. L. Bryan Co., 1931).

51 Draper Mss, 16 VV 37 (microfilm), WHS; Davie, *Sketches,* 13–16 and 15 for the quote.

52 "A Narrative of the Campaign of 1780, by Colonel Otho Holland Williams, Adjutant General," in Johnson, *Greene,* appendix B, 1:497; Finney, "Diaries," 133; Davis, *Diary,* 15; "Itinerary PA Line," 290; Tilden, "Journal," 216; Otho Holland Williams to Alexander Hamilton, 8/30/1780, Alexander Hamilton to James Duane, 9/6/1780, *PAHDE,* 2:386, 421. For the Battle of Camden, see Buchanan, *GCH,* ch. 12.

53 Draper Mss, 16 VV 27 and passim (microfilm), WHS, for "Sumter's Surprise," and 16 VV 28 for a description of how some Rebels escaped; Evan McLaurin to Balfour, 8/22/1780, EM, Miscellaneous Manuscripts (microfilm), NYPL. For a biographical sketch of McLaurin, see Bobby Gilmer Moss, *Journal of Capt. Alexander Chesney* (Scotia, SC: Hibernia Press, 2002), 124–25; Cornwallis to Clinton, 8/29/1780, *CC,* 1:58.

54 Greene to Hamilton, 1/10/1781, *PNG,* 7:88.

55 "Kings Mountain: Letters of Colonel Isaac Shelby," ed. J. G. deRoulhac Hamilton, *JSH* 4, no. 3 (August 1938), 372, for Shelby's quotations; Samuel Hammond's

undated account is in Joseph Johnston, *Traditions and Reminiscences Chiefly of the American Revolution in the South: Including Biographical Sketches, Incidents and Anecdotes* (Charleston, SC: Walker & James, 1851), 519–22; for an excellent up-to-date description of the battle and much ancillary information of interest, see Christine R. Swager, *Musgrove Mill Historic Site* (Conshohocken, PA: Infinity Publishing, 2013). The keen student is Brigadier General George Fields (ret.).

56 Evan McLaurin to Balfour, 8/22/1780, EM, Miscellaneous Manuscripts (microfilm), NYPL.

57 Hugh Rankin, *Francis Marion: The Swamp Fox* (New York, Thomas Y. Crowell, 1973), 26; Rawdon to Clinton, 3/23/1781, *AR*, 501.

58 For Cornwallis's thinking on securing South Carolina, see Mackesy, *War for America*, 404; *AR*, 186, for Clinton's orders to Cornwallis.

59 Cornwallis to Clinton, *AR*, 59; Clinton's Instructions to Major Ferguson, Inspector of Militia, 5/22/1780, *CP*, 1:103–5.

60 Draper, *King's Mountain and Its Heroes*, 169.

61 Ibid., 176.

62 *Virginia Gazette*, 11/11/1780.

63 *AR*, 226; for my opinion on why Ferguson chose to fight instead of withdrawing within Cornwallis's lines at Charlotte, see Buchanan, *GCH*, 223–24, 234–35.

64 Cruger's opinion is in Rawdon to Clinton, 10/29/1780, *CC*, 1:63.

65 Alexander Hamilton to James Duane, 9/6/1780, *AH*, 2:420.

66 For a sketch of Greene's life up to his assuming command of the Southern Department, see Buchanan, *GCH*, 260–75; Theodore Thayer, *Nathanael Greene: Strategist of the Revolution* (New York: Twayne Publishers, 1960), 67, for the first Washington quote; Greene to Knox, 11/17/1776, *PNG*, 1:352; Washington to Mathews, 10/23/1780, *WGW*, 20:249.

67 Greene to Robert Howe, 12/29/1780, *PNG*, 7:17; William Gordon, *History of the Rise, Progress, and Establishment of the Independence of the United States of America . . .*, 4 vols. (London, 1788), 4:28.

68 Greene to Morgan, 12/16/1780, Greene to Samuel Huntington, 12/28/1780, *PNG*, 6:589–90, 7:7; Anderson, "Journal," entry of 1/17/1781; Morgan to William Snickers, 1/26/1781, Horatio Gates Papers, Manuscript Collection 240 (microfilm, reel 13), NYHS. The superbly researched and definitive history of the battle is Lawrence E. Babits, *A Devil of a Whipping: The Battle of Cowpens* (Chapel Hill: University of North Carolina Press, 1998).

69 Cornwallis to Rawdon, 1/21/1781, Cornwallis to Germain, 3/17/1781, *CP*, 3:251; 4:12; for estimates of British prisoners, see Babits, *Devil of a Whipping*, 142.

70 Greene to Hamilton, 1/10/1781, Greene to Huger, 1/30/1781, *PNG*, 7:90, 220; David Halberstam, *The Coldest Winter: America and the Korean War* (New York: Hyperion Press, 2007), 299.

71 *The Twilight of British Rule in Revolutionary North America: The New York Letter Book of General James Robertson, 1780–1783*, ed. Milton M. Klein and Ronald W. Howard (Cooperstown, NY: New York State Historical Association, 1983), 170–71.

72 Lee, *Memoirs*, 237; Richard Pindell to My Dear Friends, 12/8/1816, in "A Militant Surgeon of the Revolution: Some Letters of Richard Pindell, M.D.," *MHS* 18, no. 4 (December 1923), 317.

73   The reader's attention is drawn to the excellent exhibit on the crossing of the Dan at the Prizery in South Boston, Virginia, the result of the unstinting efforts of the Halifax County Historical Society and local volunteers, a superb example of what dedicated local people can do to maintain the nation's precious historical heritage. It merits a detour off the interstate.

74   Greene to Joseph Reed, 3/18/1781, *PNG,* 7:450; Hugh F. Rankin, *The North Carolina Continentals* (Chapel Hill: University of North Carolina Press, 1971), 310; *Diaries of Two Ansbach Jaegers,* 161. For the definitive account of the battle, see Lawrence E. Babits and Joshua Howard, *Long, Obstinate, and Bloody: The Battle of Guilford Courthouse* (Chapel Hill: University of North Carolina Press, 2009), and for breakdowns of British and American numbers and casualties, see this work, 173 and appendices A and B.

1. "We March Tomorrow Directly for South Carolina"

1   "Glorious Cause" are George Washington's words in his Address to the Continental Congress accepting his appointment as general and commander in chief of the American forces, 6/16/1775, *PGW: Rev War,* 1:1.

2   William Smallwood to Greene, 5/4/1781, *PNG,* 8:204; Clinton quoted in Walter B. Willcox, *Portrait of a General: Sir Henry Clinton in the War of Independence* (New York: Knopf, 1964), 392.

3   Washington to John Cadwalader, 10/5/1780, *WGW,* 20:122.

4   Washington to Greene, 12/31/1780, *PNG,* 6:569.

5   Washington to Greene, 10/14/1780, 10/22/1780, *PNG,* 6:385, 424–25, and 426n6.

6   Greene to Ichabod Burnet, 4/5/1781, *PNG,* 8:54; Return of Troops remaining in South Carolina under Rawdon, 15 January 1781, *CP,* 3:255–64; Cornwallis to Clinton, 1/6/1781, *CP,* 3:33–34.

7   Greene to Lee, 4/4/1781, Lee to Greene, 4/4/1781, General Greene's Orders, 4/5/1781 and 4/6/1781, *PNG,* 8:46–47, 54, 58.

8   The quotations are in the introduction to *The Revolutionary War Memoirs of General Henry Lee,* ed. Robert E. Lee, new introduction by Charles Royster (1869; reprint, New York: Da Capo Press, 1998), iv. I am indebted to Christine Swager for bringing them to my attention.

9   The quotations on Lee's physical appearance are in Royster, *Lee,* 15, and Dann, *Revolution Remembered,* 20; Charles Lee, "Proposals for the Formation of a Body of Light Troops Ready to be Detach'd on Emergent Occasions," [1778], Lee Papers, *New-York Historical Society Collections,* 4–7 [New York, 1872–75], 6:287; Ewald, *Diary of the American War,* 121; Friedrich von Muenchhausen, *At General Howe's Side, 1776–1778: The Diary of General William Howe's Aide de Camp, Captain Friedrich von Muenchhausen,* trans. Ernst Kipping, annotated Samuel Smith (Monmouth Beach, NJ: Philip Freneau Press, 1974), 47; John Laurens to Henry Laurens, 1/23/1778, *PHL,* 12:330–31.

10   General Orders, 1/20/1781, Lee to Washington, 1/20/1781 (two letters), Washington to Lee, 1/20/1781, *PGW: Rev War,* 13:287, 292–94.

11   Washington to William Buchanan, 2/7/1778, Washington to Lee, 2/16/1778, Washington to Smallwood, 2/16/1778, *PGW: Rev War,* 13:465, 561–64. For an

excellent account of this little-known episode of Lee's career, see Ricardo A. Herrera, "'[T]he zealous activity of Capt. Lee': Light Horse Harry Lee and *Petite Guerre," Journal of Military History* 79, no. 1 (January 2015), 9–36.

12   Lee to Washington, 3/31/1778, Washington to Lee, 4/1/1778, *PGW: Rev War,* 14:368–69, 379–80.

13   Washington to Henry Laurens, 4/3/1778, Laurens to Washington, 4/8[–9]/1778, *PGW: Rev War,* 14:390–91, 425–26n2.

14   This paragraph is based on the account in Jim Piecuch and John H. Beakes Jr., *"Light Horse Harry" Lee in the War for Independence* (Charleston, SC: Nautical and Aviation Publishing Company, 2013), 35–40.

15   Ibid., 40–41; Capt. Levin Handy to George Handy, 8/22/1779, in Commager and Morris, 2:726–27; Washington to Gates, 8/24/1779, *PGW: Rev War DE,* 22:236, gives the number of prisoners as 158: 7 officers and 151 privates.

16   George Washington, General Orders, 8/22/1779, Washington to John Jay, 8/23/1779, Washington to John Parke Custis, 8/24/1779, *PGW: Rev War DE,* 22:207, 230, 233.

17   George Washington, General Orders, 9/11/779, *PGW: Rev War DE,* 22:396; Templin, *Lee,* 70; John Adams to Abigail Adams, 5/22/1777, *JA,* 2:245.

18   Piecuch and Beakes, *"Light Horse Harry,"* 55–56; George Washington, General Orders, 9/11/1779, Washington to John Parke Custis, 8/24/1779, Washington to Lee, 10/7/1779, *PGW: Rev War DE,* 22:396, 233, 660; *JCC,* 9/24/1779, 15:1099–1100; R. E. Lee, "The Life of General Henry Lee," in Lee, *Memoirs,* 22.

19   Thomas E. Templin, "Henry 'Light Horse Harry' Lee" (PhD diss., University of Kentucky, 1975), 72; Paul C. Nagel, *The Lees of Virginia: Seven Generations of an American Family* (New York: Oxford University Press, 1990), 162.

20   Washington to John Mathews, 10/23/1780, *WGW,* 20:249.

21   Greene to Lee, 4/4/1781, *PNG,* 8:46.

22   Greene to Washington, 3/18/1781, Greene to Lee, 3/19/1781 (two letters), 3/21/1781, *PNG,* 7:452, 454, 456, 461n3; Lee, *Memoirs,* 287; Tarleton, *History,* 279.

23   Seymour, "Journal," 379; the execution was also reported in Kirkwood, *Journal,* 15; Cornwallis to Cruger, 8/18/1780, *CP,* 2:19; Cornwallis to Clinton, 8/29/1780, *CC,* 1:58; L. P. Hartley, *The Go-Between* (London: Hamish Hamilton, 1953), 9.

24   Greene to Nash, 3/18, 29/1781, Greene to Reed, 3/18/1781, Greene to Washington, 3/18/1781, *PNG,* 7:448, 480, 450, 452.

25   Greene to Burnet, 4/5/1781, *PNG,* 8:54; Lee, *Memoirs,* 315–25; see *PNG,* 7:482n4, for a convincing analysis that Greene, not Lee, was the author of the plan.

26   Greene to Burnet, 4/5/1781, *PNG,* 8:54.

27   Greene to Samuel Huntington, 4/22/1781, *PNG,* 8:130; Troop Return, 5/1/1781, *CP,* 4:184.

28   Greene to James Emmett, 4/2/1781, *PNG,* 8:33.

29   Greene to Sumter, 1/8/1781, Greene to Lee, 4/4/1781, *PNG,* 7:75; 8:46; see also Dennis Conrad, "General Nathanael Greene: An Appraisal," in *General Nathanael Greene and the American Revolution in the South,* ed. Gregory D. Massey and Jim Piecuch (Columbia, SC: University of South Carolina Press, 2016), 14, and the entire article by the most knowledgeable and perceptive student of Greene.

30   Greene to Sumter, 3/30/1781, *PNG,* 8:12–13.

31 Greene to von Steuben, 3/22/1781, to Jefferson, 3/23/1781, to Mordecai Gist, 3/30/1781, to Thomas Sim Lee, 4/7/1781, to von Steuben, 4/6/1781, *PNG,* 7:463–64, 466, 8:5 and n3, 60, 62.

32 Greene to Washington, 3/29/1781, *PNG,* 7:481–82.

33 Seymour, "Journal," 380; Amos Kendall, *The Life of General Andrew Jackson* (New York, 1843–44), 45; Greene to Samuel Huntington, 12/28/1780, *PNG,* 7:9; "Memoirs of Tarlton Brown," *Magazine of History with Notes and Queries,* extra no. 101 (1924), 25, 29; for the Battle of Moore's Creek Bridge, see Buchanan, *GCH,* 4–5.

34 Elizabeth Lichtenstein Johnston, *Recollections of a Georgia Loyalist* (New York and London: M. F. Mansfield & Company, 1901), 32–33.

35 John F. Stegeman and Janet A. Stegeman, *Caty: A Biography of Catharine Littlefield Greene* (1977; reprint, Athens: University of Georgia Press, 1985), 10; Greene to Catharine, 3/18/1781, 6/23/1781, *PNG,* 7:446, 8:443–44.

36 *PNG,* 5: appendix II, 616–23.

37 Washington to Henry Laurens, 8/3[–4]/1778, *PGW Rev War,* 16:238–39; Greene to Joseph Reed, 3/9/1778, Greene to Washington, 4/24/1779, *PNG,* 2:307, 3:427; Clearchus quoted in Xenophon, *Anabasis,* 1:3, c. 360 B.C.; Washington to John Mathews, 10/23/1780, *WGW,* 20:249.

38 Watson, *Men and Times of the Revolution,* 297.

39 Greene to Clement Biddle, 2/14/1778, Greene to Washington, 2/15/1778, *PNG,* 2:283, 285.

40 Greene to the Board of War, 4/4/1781, John Hamilton to Greene, 8/31/1781, 9/10/1781, *PNG,* 8:45, 9:273, 312.

41 For logistics problems in the North, and for the American political culture and spirit of localism that led to difficulties throughout the country, see Buchanan, *The Road to Valley Forge,* 190–93; Greene to Long, 1/18/1781, Long to Greene, 3/2/1781, Wade to Greene, 4/4/1781, Greene to Board of War, 3/30/1781, 5/2/1781, *PNG,* 7:140–41, 457–58; 8:53, 3, 188; for further documentation of this problem, see Greene to Jethro Sumner, 1/19/1781, and William Pierce to John Mazaret, 3/13/1781, *PNG,* 7:148, 429.

42 Cornwallis to Charles O'Hara, 8/2/1781, *CP,* 6:43; Dann, *Revolution Remembered,* 244; Holly A. Mayer, "Wives, Concubines, and Community: Following the Army," in *War and Society in the American Revolution: Mobilization and Home Fronts,* ed. John Resch and Walter Sargent (De Kalb: Northern Illinois University Press, 2007), 238 and 246 (for the Washington quotation); for the full gamut of civilian support of the Continental Army, see the excellent work by Holly A. Mayer, *Belonging to the Army: Camp Followers and Community during the American Revolution* (Columbia: University of South Carolina Press, 1996).

43 Jefferson to Greene, 4/5/1781, *PNG,* 8:57. The controversy over horses can be traced in this paragraph and those following in *PNG,* as follows: Greene to Jefferson, 2/15/1781, Jefferson to Greene, 2/19/1781, Greene to William Washington, 2/16/1781, Greene to Henry Lee, 2/17/1781, Jefferson to Greene, 3/24/1781, 7:289, 317, 301–2, 467, and Jefferson to Greene, 4/1/1781, 4/5/1781, Greene to Jefferson, 4/6/1781, 4/28/1781, 8:20–21, 57–59, 165–67.

44 For the Rudder incident, see Buford to Jefferson, 3/20/1781, *The Papers of Thomas Jefferson*, ed. Julian Boyd et al. (Princeton, NJ: Princeton University Press, 1950–), 5:187.

45 Greene's comments on Congress are in a letter to an unknown recipient, 5/20/1777, *PNG*, 2:87. For citations to the following quotations in the narrative, see n44, above.

46 Ewald, *Diary of the American War*, 305.

47 Greene to Board of War, 5/2/1781, Washington to Greene, 2/27/1781, Greene to Lafayette, 5/1/1781, *PNG*, 7:363; 8:189, 183; Washington to Lafayette, 4/6/1781, *WGW*, 21:421.

48 Greene to Board of War, 5/2/1781, *PNG*, 8:189; for the Wellington and Napoleon quotes, see *The Greenhill Dictionary of Military Quotations*, ed. Peter G. Tsouras (London: Greenhill Books, 2000), 29.

49 William Tecumseh Sherman, *Memoirs of General W. T. Sherman* (1886; reprint, New York: Library of America, 1990), 880.

50 Greene to Pickering, 4/4/1781, *PNG*, 8:48, and 49n2; Davie quoted in *PNG*, 6:517n2; Pickering's obnoxious personality and bumbling career are skewered in Stanley M. Elkins and Eric L. McKitrick, *The Age of Federalism: The Early American Republic* (New York: Oxford University Press, 1993), 623–26.

51 The exchange can be followed in Greene to Davie, 12/11/1780, *PNG*, 6:561–62; and Davie, *Sketches*, 39.

52 "Proclamation, 1781," *CP*, 4:55; Buchanan, *GCH*, 363–64, for Pyle's Massacre; Otho Holland Williams to Greene, 3/4/1781, *PNG*, 7:393–94 and n3, for attack on Tories by the British Legion; Rankin, *North Carolina Continentals*, 292, for the drover incident.

53 Cornwallis to Clinton, 4/10/1781, *CP*, 4:110; Stedman, *American War*, 2:348.

54 Johnston, *Recollections of a Georgia Loyalist*, 44–45.

55 *Diary of Frederick Mackenzie, Giving a Daily Narrative of His Military Service as an Officer of the Regiment of Royal Welch Fusiliers during the Years 1775–1781 in Massachusetts, Rhode Island, and New York* (Cambridge, MA: Harvard University Press, 1930), 581–82.

56 Cornwallis to Clinton, 4/10/1781, *CP*, 4:110; Graves quoted in Mackesy, *War for America*, 252.

57 Balfour to Craig, 1/15/1781, Balfour to Clinton, 1/25/1781, *GLL*, EM.15488, EM.15493, NYPL; Craig to Cornwallis, 4/12/1781, *CP*, 4:133; Gregory de Van Massey, "The British Expedition to Wilmington, January–November 1781," *North Carolina Historical Review* 66, no. 4 (October 1989), 390, provides an excellent description of the war in southeastern North Carolina. Another valuable, well-researched study is Robert M. Dunkerly, *Redcoats on the Cape Fear: The Revolutionary War in Southeastern North Carolina*, rev. ed. (Jefferson, NC: McFarland and Company, 2012): chs. 7 and 8 cover Craig's expedition and Cornwallis's arrival in Wilmington.

58 "Charles O'Hara to the Duke of Grafton, 4/10/1781, "Letters of Charles O'Hara," 178 (1st quotation); Cornwallis to Craig, 2/21/1781, Craig to Cornwallis, 3/22/1781, *CP*, 4:25, 27–28; Cornwallis to Clinton, 4/10/1781, *AR*, 508–9.

59 Roger Lamb, *An Original and Authentic Journal of Occurrences during the Late American War, from Its Commencement to the Year 1783* (Dublin, 1809), 360; Greene to Isaac Huger, 1/30/1781, *PNG,* 7:220.

60 Cornwallis to Clinton, 4/10/1781, *AR,* 509; Clinton to Cornwallis, 4/13/1781, *CP,* 5:94. With regard to the Royal Navy favoring a port in Chesapeake Bay, I have benefited from the thoughts of Dennis Conrad.

61 Cornwallis to Balfour, 4/5/1781, 4/24/1781, Cornwallis to Phillips, 4/24/1781, *CP,* 4:42, 122, 116.

62 Cornwallis to Phillips, 4/10/1781, 4/24/1781, Cornwallis to Germain, 4/23/1781, Cornwallis to Clinton, 4/23/1781, *CP,* 4:114–16, 108, 113.

63 For a defense of Cornwallis, Franklin and Mary Wickwire, *Cornwallis: The American Adventure* (Boston: Houghton Mifflin, 1970), 311–21; for a harsh view, William B. Willcox, *Portrait of a General: Sir Henry Clinton in the War of Independence* (New York: Knopf, 1964), 381–91, with the quote on 386.

2. "We Must Endeavor to Keep Up a Partizan War"

1 Greene to Marion, 12/4/1780, Greene to Jacob Greene, 9/28/1776, Greene to von Steuben, 2/3/1781, *PNG,* 6:519; 1:303; 7:243.

2 Greene to Huntington, 4/22/1781, *PNG,* 8:131–32.

3 Greene to Nelson, 8/10/1781, *PNG,* 9:160.

4 Reed to Greene, 6/16/1781, *PNG,* 8:396–97. As noted on 402n9 of this citation, Reed paraphrased two lines from "An English Padlock," a poem by Matthew Prior (1664–1721): "Be to her virtues very kind / Be to her faults a little blind."

5 Greene to Reed, 8/6/1781, Greene to McKean, 9/2/1781, Greene to Huntington, 4/22/1781, *PNG,* 9:135, 278; 8:131.

6 Greene to Marion, 12/4/1780, *PNG,* 6:520.

7 Washington to William Heath, 2/3/1777, *PGW: Rev. War,* 8:230.

8 Lipscomb, *Battles, Skirmishes, and Actions,* 12–14.

9 Sumter to Greene, 3/9/1781, 1/13/1781, *PNG,* 7:417, 118n2; Sumter to Marion, 2/20/1781, Gibbes, *Doc. Hist.,* 3:23.

10 For a defense of Sumter, see Thomas L. Powers, "In Defense of General Thomas Sumter," *SCAR* 5, no. 2 (2008), 31–34.

11 Greene to Marion, 2/11/1781, *PNG,* 7:281; Rankin, *The Swamp Fox,* 163.

12 Unless otherwise indicated, the subsequent maneuverings and actions until Sumter's withdrawal from the field can be followed in Rawdon to Cornwallis, 3/7/1781, *CP,* 4:47–49.

13 The Watson quotation is in Russell E. Weigley, *The Partisan War: The South Carolina Campaign of 1780–1782,* Tricentennial Booklet no. 2 (Columbia: University of South Carolina Press, 1970), 48.

14 John Watson Tadwell Watson, undated letter to an unnamed recipient, Clinton Papers, vol. 232/21:8, WLCL.

15 Ibid., 8–9.

16 Robert D. Bass, *Gamecock: The Life and Campaigns of General Thomas Sumter* (New York: Holt, Rinehart and Winston, 1961), 134–35; "Gray's Observations," 152.

17   Balfour to Clinton, 2/24/1781, GLL, EM.15503, NYPL; Rawdon to Cornwallis 3/7/1781, *CP,* 4:49.

18   Robert S. Davis, "Elijah Clarke: Georgia's Partisan Titan," *SCAR* 4, no. 3 (January–March, 2007), 38–40; Isaac Shelby, "King's Mountain Letters of Colonel Isaac Shelby," ed. J. G. de Roulhac Hamilton, *JSH* 4, no. 3 (August 1938), 372.

19   For the circumstances that led Greene to order Pickens back to South Carolina, see Buchanan, *GCH,* 366–68; Pickens to Henry Lee Jr., 11/25/1811, Draper Mss, 1 VV 108 (microfilm), WHS; Pickens to Greene, 4/8/1781, *PNG,* 8:70–71.

20   Pickens to Greene, 4/8/1781, *PNG,* 8:71.

21   With regard to the series of actions in this and the following paragraphs, see *PNG,* 8:121–22n1, for a succinct description of the British plan and its outcome; Rankin, *The Swamp Fox,* 165–79; James, *Marion,* 98–104; William Gilmore Simms, *The Life of Francis Marion: The True Story of South Carolina's Swamp Fox,* with a new introduction by Sean Busick (1844; reprint, Charleston, SC: History Press, 2007), 140–42, with Watson's reputed quotation on 142; John Oller, *The Swamp Fox: How Francis Marion Saved the American Revolution* (Boston: Da Capo Press, 2016), 141.

22   *PNG,* 8:32n2; James, *Marion,* 104; Washington to Orange County Committee of Public Safety, 7/14/1776, *PGW: Rev War,* 5:314.

23   Rutledge to Marion, 3/6/1781, Sumter to Marion, 2/10/1781, 2/28/1781, 3/4/1781, Gibbes, *Doc. Hist.,* 3:32–33, 23–24, 27–28, 44–47, 49.

24   Rankin, *Swamp Fox,* 182–83; James, *Marion,* 106; for the Black Dog, see the *Oxford English Dictionary.*

25   James, *Marion,* 107–8; Marion to Greene, 4/23/1781, *PNG,* 8:139.

26   Greene to Sumter, 3/30/1781, Sumter to Greene, 4/7/1781, Greene to Lee, 4/12/1781, Marion to Greene, 4/23/1781, *PNG,* 8:12–13, 66–67, 85–86, 139.

27   Lee, *Memoirs,* 325; Greene to Huntington, 4/22/1781, *PNG,* 8:131; Howard quoted in Piecuch and Beakes, *"Light Horse Harry,"* 153; Lee to Greene, 4/2/1781, *PNG,* 8:28

28   Balfour to Clinton, 1/31/1781, GLL, NYPL; James, *Marion,* 108.

29   I am indebted to that font of knowledge on South Carolina, Charles Baxley, for distances. Marion to Greene, 4/23/1781, *PNG,* 8:139; Lee, *Memoirs,* 331–32. For the probable height of the Indian mound in 1781 (and its height now) I have benefited from conversations and correspondence with Dr. Steven D. Smith, director of the South Carolina Institute of Archaeology and Anthropology, University of South Carolina, who also brought to my attention the very helpful article by Leland G. Ferguson, "Archeology at Scott's Lake: Exploratory Research 1972, 1973" (1975), Research Manuscript Series, Book 14 (http://scholarcommons.Sc.edu/arcanth_books/141).

30   Marion to Greene, 4/23/1781, Lee to Greene, 4/18/1781, Greene to Lee, 4/19/1781, *PNG,* 8:139, 113, 117–18; Lieutenant McKay quoted in Piecuch and Beakes, *"Light Horse Harry,"* 157.

31   Lee to Greene, 4/23/1781, Greene to Lee, 4/22/1781, *PNG,* 8:138, 133.

32   Lee, *Memoirs,* 332; Marion to Greene, 4/23/1781, *PNG,* 8:139–41; Piecuch and Beakes, *"Light Horse Harry,"* 158; for siege towers in the ancient world, see Duncan B. Campbell, *Besieged: Siege Warfare in the Ancient World* (Oxford: Osprey Publishing, 2006), 46–47 and passim.

33　McKay quoted in Piecuch and Beakes, *"Light Horse Harry,"* 158; *PNG,* 141nn4 and 5; Marion to Lee, 4/23/1781, *PNG,* 141–42.

34　Lee to Greene, 4/23/1781, *PNG,* 8:139.

35　Greene to Marion, 4/24/1781, *PNG,* 8:144.

3. "We Fight Get Beat Rise and Fight Again"

1　Greene to Sumter, 4/5/1781, Greene to Marion, 4/17/1781, 4/24/1781, Marion to Greene, 4/30/1781, Greene to Marion, 5/1/1781, *PNG,* 8:100, 106, 145, 179, 184.

2　Greene to Sumter, 3/30/1781, Sumter to Greene, 4/7/1781, *PNG,* 8:12–13, 66.

3　Sumter to Greene, *PNG,* 8:66; Richard Hampton to John Hampton, 4/1/1781, Gibbes, *Doc. Hist.,* 3:47–48.

4　Gregorie, *Sumter,* 146–48; Klein, *Unification of a Slave State,* 103; Higginbotham, *War of American Independence,* 164–65, for British and German transgressions; Lord Rawdon to the Earl of Huntington, 8/5/1776, in Commager and Morris, 1:424.

5　Greene to Sumter, 4/15/1781, *PNG,* 8:100–101; Haw, *John and Edward Rutledge,* 158–59.

6　Klein, *Unification of a Slave State,* 106–8; McCrady, 147–48; Haw, *John and Edward Rutledge,* 158; Sara Lipton to the Editor, *New York Review of Books* (August 13, 2015), 85, for the observation on chronology.

7　For the Fort Washington fiasco, see Buchanan, *The Road to Valley Forge,* 112–19.

8　Greene to Sumter, 4/14/1781, *PNG,* 8:94.

9　Greene to John Butler, 4/19/1781 (in letters to others Greene put the distance as either two or four miles), Greene to Samuel Huntington, 4/22/1781, *PNG,* 8:117, 131–32; Seymour, "Journal," 380.

10　For Cornwallis specifically giving Rawdon command on the frontier, see Enclosure in Cornwallis to Clinton, 1/6/1781, entitled "Disposition of the Troops in the Southern District," stating, "Lord Rawdon to command on the frontier of South Carolina," listing locations and units, including the "garrison of Charlestown," and "Return of Troops Remaining in South Carolina under Rawdon," 1/15/1781, both in *CP,* 3:34–35, 255–64; see also Paul David Nelson, *Francis Rawdon-Hastings, Marquess of Hastings: Soldier, Peer of the Realm, Governor General of India* (Madison, NJ: Farleigh Dickinson University Press, 2005), 27–29, 49 (for the quotation), 87–88, and the entire work for the life of one of the more interesting builders of the Second British Empire; Rawdon to Lee, 6/24/1813, in Lee, *Memoirs,* 615–16, denying that he commanded.

11　Rawdon to Cornwallis, 4/26/1781, *CP,* 4:180; Christopher Ward, *The War of the Revolution,* 2 vols. (New York: Macmillan, 1952), 2:802; Kirkwood, *Journal,* 16; Greene to Thomas Polk, 4/21/1781, Greene to Samuel Huntington, 4/22/1781, Greene to Lee, 4/22/1781, Lee to Greene, 4/23/1781, General Greene's Orders, 4/24/1781, Greene to Huntington, 4/27/1781, *PNG,* 8:127, 131, 133, 138, 142, 155.

12　Dann, *Revolution Remembered,* 219.

13　Ibid., 218. There is no mention of this incident in the Greene Papers.

14　Rawdon to Cornwallis, 4/26/1781, *CP,* 4:180; Nelson, *Francis Rawdon-Hastings,* 93.

15 Greene to Samuel Huntington, 4/27/1781, General Greene's Orders, 4/25/1781, *PNG,* 8:155, 146; John Eager Howard to John Gunby, 3/22/1782, Bayard Family Papers, Box 1, Fldr. 14, MHS; Christopher L. Ward, *The Delaware Continentals, 1776–1783* (Wilmington, DE: Historical Society of Delaware, 1941), 430.

16 Rawdon to Cornwallis, 4/26/1781, with enclosed Return of killed, wounded, and missing, *CP,* 4:181–82; Jim Piecuch and John H. Beakes Jr., *"Cool Deliberate Courage": John Eager Howard in the American Revolution* (Charleston, SC: Nautical and Aviation Publishing Company, 2009), 102.

17 For the width of the road, see "Samuel Mathis' Account of the Battle of Hobkirk's Hill," transcribed by Sam Fore, annotated by Charles B. Baxley, *SCAR* 5, no. 2 (April–December 2008), 39; Greene to Samuel Huntington, 4/27/1781, *PNG,* 8:155–57; Lee, "Sketch of the Battle of Hobkirk's Hill Near Camden," *Memoirs,* facing 336.

18 Howard to Gunby, 3/22/1782, Bayard Papers, Box 1, Fldr. 14, MHS; Davie, *Sketches,* 43.

19 Rawdon to Cornwallis, 4/25/1781, *CP,* 4:181.

20 Greene, *Greene,* 3:245; Johnson, *Greene,* 2:77; Seymour, "Journal," 381; Rawdon to Cornwallis, 4/25/1781, *CP,* 4:181.

21 Greene to Samuel Huntington, 4/27/1781, *PNG,* 8:155; Lee, *Memoirs,* 336; Davie, *Sketches,* 43; Howard to Gunby, 3/22/1782, Bayard Papers, Box 1, Fldr. 14, MHS; Moultrie, *Memoirs,* 2:276; Seymour, "Journal," 381.

22 George Hanger, *To All Sportsmen and Particularly Farmers and Gamekeepers* (London, 1814), 205; for more detail on the eighteenth-century musket and tactics, see Buchanan, *GCH,* 158–61, and sources cited there. It has been suggested that Hanger's statement is misleading, that an experienced shooter could hit a man-sized target at 100 yards nine out of ten shots, and not miss at 50 yards, and this may be true for modern shooters using these muskets on a firing range. But it does not hold for the average soldier in the heat of battle.

23 Mark M. Boatner III, *Encyclopedia of the American Revolution,* 3rd ed. (Mechanicsburg, PA: Stackpole Books, 1994), 506, 508; John S. Pancake, *This Destructive War: The British Campaign in the Carolinas, 1780–1782* (Tuscaloosa: University of Alabama Press, 1992), 198; Lee, *Memoirs,* 340.

24 Greene to Huntington, 4/27/1781, *PNG,* 8:156; Rawdon to Cornwallis, 4/26/1781, *CP,* 4:181; Seymour, "Journal," 381.

25 Lee, *Memoirs,* 340–41; Davie, *Sketches,* 44.

26 Piecuch and Beakes, *"Cool Deliberate Courage,"* 104; General Greene's Orders, 5/2/1781, *PNG,* 8:187, for the distance Gunby withdrew; Howard to Gunby, 3/22/1782, Bayard Papers, Box 1, Fldr. 14, MHS.

27 For an excellent, detailed description of the rearward movement and face about at Cowpens, see Babits, *Devil of a Whipping,* 109–19.

28 Dann, *Revolution Remembered,* 220; Davie in Johnson, *Greene,* 2:94–95; Greene to Samuel Huntington, 4/27/1781, *PNG,* 8:157, 159n3; Rawdon to Cornwallis, 4/26/1781, *CP,* 4:181.

29 The claim that Washington's mission was to "cut off the British retreat" is in Lee F. McGee, who quotes the letter to von Steuben in "The Object Was Worthy of the Cast: The Patriot Cavalry Reexamined at Hobkirk's Hill," *SCAR* 3, no. 4 (April 2006), 13. Another defender of Washington is Daniel Murphy, *William*

Washington, American Light Dragoon: A Continental Cavalry Leader in the War of Independence (Yardley, PA: Westholme, 2014), 129–30, 134–35; Greene to von Steuben, 4/27/1781, Steuben Papers (microfilm, Reel 3), NYHS.

30 Greene to Huntington, 4/27/1781, *PNG,* 8:155; Howard to Henry Lee [Jr.], 1/19/1819, in Lee Jr., *Campaign of 1781,* 281 (for the date of Howard's letter see *PNG,* 8:158n1).

31 Rawdon to Cornwallis, 4/26/1781, *CP,* 4:181; Howard to Lee [Jr.], 1/19/1819; Davie in Johnson, *Greene,* 2:83; Greene to Huntington, 4/27/1781, Rawdon to Greene, 4/26/1781, Greene to Rawdon, 4/26/1781, *PNG,* 8:157, 152, 154.

32 Among Washington's modern critics are Ward, *The War of the Revolution,* 2:807; Pancake, *This Destructive War,* 198–99.

33 Rawdon to Cornwallis, 4/26/1781, *CP,* 4:181; Greene to Samuel Huntington, 4/27/1781, *PNG,* 8:156.

34 Pancake, *This Destructive War,* 198.

35 *PNG,* 8:160n7; Rawdon, "RETURN of the Killed, Wounded and Missing . . . April the 25th 1781," *CP,* 4:182.

36 Greene to Joseph Reed, 8/6/1781; Greene to Samuel Huntington, 4/26/1781, *PNG,* 9:135; 8:156–57.

37 Greene to Joseph Reed, 8/6/1781, General Greene's Orders, 4/28/1781, *PNG,* 9:135; 8:164–65.

38 General Greene's Orders, 5/2/1781, *PNG,* 8:187; Howard to Gunby, 3/22/1782, Bayard Family Papers, Box 1, Fldr. 14, MHS.

39 Greene to von Steuben, 4/27/1781, Greene to Lee, 4/29/1781, Greene to Abner Nash, 5/2/1781, Greene to Reed, 5/4/1781, Greene to Sumter, 5/5/1781, Greene to Reed, 8/6/1781, Greene to Gates, 10/4/1781, *PNG,* 8, 162, 172, 190, 201, 208; 9:135, 425–26; Greg Brooking, "'I am an independent spirit, and confide in my own resources': Nathanael Greene and His Continental Subordinates, 1780–1781," in *Greene,* ed. Massey and Piecuch, 97–100, is very critical of Greene regarding his performance and especially his treatment of Gunby.

40 Greene to Lee, 4/29/1781, Lee to Greene, 4/30/1781, Greene to Sumter, 4/14/1781, 4/30/1781, *PNG,* 8:173, 178, 94, 176–77; Davie, *Sketches,* 44.

41 Greene to Chevalier Anne-Cesar de la Luzerne, 4/28/1781, *PNG,* 8:168.

4. "The Revolt Was Universal"

1 Dann, *Revolution Remembered,* 220.

2 Greene to Samuel Huntington, 5/5/1781, General Greene's Orders, 4/30/1781, *PNG,* 8:175–76, 206; Dann, *Revolution Remembered,* 221; Kirkwood, *Journal,* 17; Seymour, "Journal," 382.

3 Greene to Samuel Huntington, 5/5/1781, Greene to Sumter, 5/4/1781, Emmet to Greene, 4/28/1781, Greene to Lee, 5/4/1781, Lee to Greene, 5/6/1781, *PNG,* 8:206, 202, 170, 198, 214.

4 Kirkwood, *Journal,* 17.

5 Cornwallis to Rawdon, 12/13/1781, *CP,* 3:209; Watson to unnamed correspondent, n.d., vol. 232:21:13, WLCL; Marion to Greene, 5/6/1781, *PNG,* 8, 215 and n3; Rawdon to Cornwallis, 5/24/1781, *CP,* 5:288–89.

6   Watson to unnamed correspondent, n.d., Clinton Papers, vol. 232:21:14, WLCL; Rawdon to Cornwallis, 5/24/1781, *CP,* 5:289.

7   Dann, *Revolution Remembered,* 222–24; Rawdon to Cornwallis, 5/24/1781, *CP,* 5:288–89. The topography around Sawney's Creek and Colonel's Creek remains rugged, and I am indebted to Charles Baxley for driving me through it.

8   Rawdon to Cornwallis, 5/24/1781, *CP,* 5:288.

9   Davie, *Sketches,* 44–45; Greene to Lee, Greene to Marion, Greene to Pickens, all 5/9/1781, *PNG,* 8:227–28, 230–32.

10 Davie, *Sketches,* 46.

11 Rawdon to Cornwallis, 5/24/1781, *CP,* 5:288–89; Moultrie, *Memoirs,* 2:279.

12 Notes taken from Alexis Helsley, "Rebecca Brewton Motte: Revolutionary Heroine" (Paper presented at the 11th Annual Francis Marion Symposium, Central Carolina Technical College, Sumter, SC, 10/18/2013). I am beholden to my friend Luther Wannamaker for giving me access to the site of Fort Motte, and to Dr. Steven D. Smith, director, South Carolina Institute of Archaeology and Anthropology, who has conducted several important excavations on the site.

13 Steven D. Smith et al., *"Obstinate and Strong": The History and Archaeology of the Siege of Fort Motte* (Columbia: South Carolina Institute of Archaeology and Anthropology, 2007), 17–18, 21–22. An engineering drawing of Fort Motte done shortly after the siege is in *PNG,* 8:252.

14 Nisbet Balfour to Cornwallis, 5/21/1781, *CP,* 5:276; Smith, *"Obstinate and Strong,"* 22 and n51.

15 Helsley, "Rebecca Brewton Motte: Revolutionary Heroine"; Lee, *Memoirs,* 345–47.

16 Lee, *Memoirs,* 345–46; conversation with Steven D. Smith, 11/30/2015; Robert D. Bass, *Swamp Fox: The Life and Campaigns of General Francis Marion* (1959; reprint, Orangeburg, SC: Sandlapper Publishing Company, 1974), 193; on the controversy, Steven D. Smith to John Buchanan, 11/30/15, and Charles Baxley to John Buchanan, 11/30/15 and 12/1/15.

17 With regard to the information on archaeological excavations at Fort Motte, as of November 2015, I am indebted to Steven D. Smith; Marion to Greene, 5/12/1781, *PNG,* 8:246; Lee, *Memoirs,* 346–47.

18 James, *Marion,* 120–21; Smith, *"Obstinate and Strong,"* 24–26; Rawdon to Cornwallis, 5/24/1781, *CP,* 5:289.

19 Lee, *Memoirs,* 347–48.

20 Ibid., 348–49.

21 Ibid., 348.

22 Catherine S. Crary, *The Price of Loyalty: Tory Writings from the Revolutionary Era* (New York: McGraw-Hill, 1973), 288–90.

23 Lee to Greene, 5/8/1781; Hyrne to Greene, 5/8/1781, Greene to Maham, 6/21/1781, *PNG,* 8:222–23, 433.

24 Lee, *Memoirs,* 349.

25 Greene to Marion, 1/4/1781, Marion to Greene, 1/9/1781, Greene to Marion, 1/16/1781, Greene to Marion, 4/26/1781, 4/27/1781, *PNG,* 7:47, 86, 131; 8:151–52, 160–61.

26 Sumter to Greene, 5/2/1781, Lee to Greene, 5/2/1781, Greene to Marion, 5/4/1781, *PNG,* 8:192–94, 214–15.

27　Greene to Sumter, 1/8/1781, *PNG*, 7:74–75.

28　Marion to Greene, 5/6/1781, *PNG*, 8:214–15.

29　Greene to Marion, 5/9/1781, *PNG*, 8:230–31.

30　Greene to Rutledge, 5/14/1781, *PNG*, 8:256.

31　Greene to Lee, 5/13/1781, *PNG*, 8:249; Lee, *Memoirs*, 349; Rawdon to Cornwallis, 5/24/1781, *CP*, 5:289–90.

32　Sumter to Greene, 5/11/1781, 5/12/1781, *PNG*, 8:244, 248; Thomas Young quoted in Alexander S. Salley, *The History of Orangeburg, South Carolina, from Its First Settlement to the Close of the Revolutionary War* (Orangeburg, SC, 1898), 516n.

33　Lee's brief operation at Fort Granby and the negotiations for its surrender can be followed in this and succeeding paragraphs in Lee to Greene, 5/15/1781, *PNG*, 8:262–64; and Lee, *Memoirs*, 349–52.

34　William Gordon, *History of the Rise, Progress, and Establishment of the Independence of the United States of America*, 4 vols. (1788; reprint, Freeport, NY: Books for Libraries Press, 1969), 4:90; *PNG*, 8:264–66n6, for editorial comment on the relationship between Gordon and Otho Williams.

35　Greene to Lee, 5/21/1781, *PNG*, 8:290 and n4.

36　Sumter to Greene, 5/14/1781, *PNG*, 8:258–59.

37　Sumter to Greene, 5/16/1781, Greene to Sumter, 5/17/1781 (2), *PNG*, 8:274, 277–78.

38　Rawdon to Cornwallis, 5/24/1781, *CP*, 5:290.

39　Proclamation, 6/2/1781, Gibbes, *Doc. Hist.*, 3:88–89.

40　Greene to Lee, 5/29/1781, *PNG*, 8:326.

41　Pickens to Greene, 5/3/1781, 5/8/1781, 5/[12?]/1781, *PNG*, 8:197–98, 223–24, 246–47; Edward J. Cashin Jr. and Heard Robertson, *Augusta and the American Revolution: Events in the Georgia Back Country, 1773–1783*, Richmond County Historical Society, Augusta, GA (Darien, GA: Ashantilly Press, 1975), 55.

42　Greene to Lee, 5/16/1781, Greene to Pickens, 5/16/1781, 5/20/1781, *PNG*, 8:272, 286.

5. A "Judicious and Gallant Defense"

1　Lee to Greene, 5/16/1781, *PNG*, 8:273; Johnson, *Greene*, 2:126; Piecuch and Beakes, *"Light Horse Harry,"* 168; Lawrence E. Babits and Joshua B. Howard, *"Fortitude and Forbearance": The North Carolina Continental Line in the Revolutionary War, 1775–1783* (Raleigh: Office of Archives and History, North Carolina Department of Cultural Resources, 2004), 154.

2　Lee, *Memoirs*, 353; Lee to Greene, 5/22/1781, Greene to Lee, 5/22/1781, Pickens to Greene, 5/25/1781, *PNG*, 8:293, 291, 310.

3　My description of the Fort Galphin operation in this and succeeding paragraphs in this section is based on several sources and the following correspondence in *PNG*, vol. 8: Lee to Greene, 5/22/1781, 5/24/1781, 6/1/1781, 6/4/1781, 293, 309–10, 334, 346; Greene to Lee, 5/22/1781, 5/29/1781, 6/3/1781, 291–92, 326, 340; Pickens to Greene, 5/25/1781, 6/1/1781, 6/2/1781, 6/4/1781, 310–11, 334–45, 339, 347; Pickens and Lee to Greene, 6/5/1781, 351–52; Greene to Pickens, 5/29/1781, 6/1/1781, 6/3/1781, 328, 332, 341. See also William Bartram, *The Travels of William*

Bartram: Naturalist's Edition, ed. Francis Harper (1958; reprint, Athens: University of Georgia Press, 1998), 199; Lee, *Memoirs,* 354–55; Steven J. Rauch, "Prelude to Augusta: The Capture of Fort Galphin, 21 May 1781," and "A Judicious and Gallant Defense: The Second Siege at Augusta, Georgia, 22 May–5 June 1781," *SCAR* 3, no. 5 (May 2006), 22–23, and 3, nos. 6–8 (June–August 2006), 32–56; Cashin, *The King's Ranger,* 131; Piecuch and Beakes, *"Light Horse Harry,"* 169–71; for the question of whether Lee was actually present at the taking of Fort Galphin, see the comments by Rauch, "Prelude to Augusta," 22n29; for a description of the boats used on the Savannah River for the Indian trade, see Robert Paulett, *An Empire of Small Places: Mapping the Southeastern Anglo-Indian Trade, 1732–1795* (Athens: University of Georgia Press, 2012), 64–65.

4   Rauch, "A Judicious and Gallant Defense," 35.

5   Cashin, *The King's Ranger,* 27–29.

6   Ibid., 12–13.

7   Ibid, 13; the quotations are in Cashin, *The King's Ranger,* 118.

8   Rauch, "The First Siege of Augusta"; Hugh McCall, *The History of Georgia* (1784; reprint, Atlanta, GA: A. B. Caldwell, 1909), 486–87.

9   Lee, *Memoirs,* 356; Paulett, *Empire of Small Places,* 1, 77–78; Rauch, "A Judicious and Gallant Defense," 33, 50.

10 Lee, *Memoirs,* 356.

11 Ibid.; Lee to Greene, 5/24/1781, Pickens to Greene, 4/25/1781, *PNG,* 8:309, 311.

12 Lee, *Memoirs,* 356–57; Rauch, "A Judicious and Gallant Defense," 35–37; Cashin, *The King's Ranger,* 132, states that "Every second man was equipped with an axe" but does not give a source.

13 Beckaem is quoted in Rauch, "A Judicious and Gallant Defense," 37; Lee, *Memoirs,* 356–57; Pickens to Greene, 5/25/1781, *PNG,* 8:311.

14 Greene to Pickens, 5/29/1781, *PNG,* 8:328.

15 Lee, *Memoirs,* 361.

16 Ibid., 357, 361.

17 Ibid., 361–62

18 Ibid., 362.

19 Ibid, 362–63.

20 Ibid., 363.

21 Ibid., 367.

22 Ibid., 363–64.

23 Ibid., 364–65.

24 Greene to Lee, 5/22/1781, General Greene's Orders, 5/26/1781, Greene to Lewis Morris Jr., 5/27/1781, Greene to Samuel Huntington, 5/29/1781, Greene to Pickens, 5/29/1781, 6/1/1781, Lee to Greene, 6/1/1781, Pickens to Greene, 6/1/1781, Greene to Pickens, 6/3/1781, *PNG,* 8:291–92, 312, 315–16, 325, 328, 332, 334, 334–35, 341.

25 Lee to Greene, 6/4/1781, *PNG,* 8:346.

26 Lee, *Memoirs,* 365–66.

27 Ibid., 366.

28 Pickens to Greene, 6/4/1781, *PNG,* 8:347; Lee, *Memoirs,* 367–69.

29 Lee, *Memoirs,* 369–70.

30 Ibid., 370–71; "Memoirs of Tarlton Brown," 25; Cashin, *The King's Ranger*, 136, for Armstrong's reminiscences.

31 Pickens to Greene, 6/7/1781, *PNG*, 8:359.

32 Ibid.; Thomas Brown to David Ramsey, 12/25/1786, cited in Rauch, "A Judicious and Gallant Defense," 51–52; Brooks and Taylor quoted with citations in Cashin, *The King's Ranger*, 137.

33 A Proclamation, *PNG*, 8:370.

6. Surrender Is "Inadmissible"

1 Lee to Greene, 6/1/1781, 6/4/1781, *PNG*, 8:334, 346.

2 Greene to Clarke, 5/29/1781, Greene to Clay, 6/9/1781, *PNG*, 8:324–25, 361–62; *PNG*, 7:39n4; Edward J. Cashin Jr., "Nathanael Greene's Campaign in Georgia in 1781," *GHQ* 61, no. 1 (Spring 1977), 44.

3 To the Inhabitants Upon the Saluda, 6/5/1781, Greene to Pickens, 6/5/1781, *PNG*, 8:349–50; Robert Stansbury Lambert, *South Carolina Loyalists in the American Revolution* (Columbia: University of South Carolina Press, 1987), 110.

4 William Sharpe to Greene, 6/21/1781, *PNG*, 8:436.

5 Jamison to Greene, 7/2/1781, *PNG*, 8:338–39 and n2.

6 Greene to Clarke, 6/7/1781, *PNG*, 8:356.

7 Greene to John Wilkinson, 6/13/1781, *PNG*, 8:386–87.

8 The date is from Jerome B. Greene, *Historic Resource Study and Historic Structure Report, Ninety Six, a Historical Narrative* (Denver: National Park Service, 1978), 5–6.

9 "Diary of Lieutenant Anthony Allaire, of Ferguson's Corps," entry of 6/22/1780, in Lyman C. Draper, *King's Mountain and Its Heroes* (Cincinnati: Peter G. Thompson, 1881), 498–99; *Captured at Kings Mountain: The Diary of Uzal Johnson, a Loyalist Surgeon*, ed. Wade S. Kolb III and Robert M. Weir (Columbia: University of South Carolina Press, 2011), 19.

10 "Diary of Edward Hooker, 1805–1808," in *Report of the American Historical Association for the Year 1896*, 2 vols. (Washington, DC: Government Printing Office, 1897), 1:891.

11 Greene, *Historic Resource Study*, 99–100, with Allen's quote on 100.

12 Ibid., 100–101.

13 Ibid., 101–7; Greene to Huntington, 6/20/1781, *PNG*, 8:421.

14 Greene, *Historic Resource Study*, 112.

15 Ibid., 111; Robert M. Dunkerly and Eric K. Williams, *Old Ninety Six: A History and Guide* (Charleston, SC: History Press, 2006), 48. I am indebted to Ranger Sarah Cunningham of Ninety Six National Historic Site for the distances between the Town Stockade and the jail and from the jail to the Spring Branch.

16 Greene to Huntington, 6/20/1781, *PNG*, 8:419; Greene, *Historic Resource Study*, 108–11.

17 Cruger's order of battle is in Dunkerly and Williams, *Old Ninety Six*, 66, which is based on the extensive research of the late Bobby G. Moss; Greene, *Historic Resource Study*, 113–14, 123; Roderick Mackenzie, *Strictures on Lt. Col. Tarleton's*

History of the Campaigns of 1780 and 1781, in the Southern Provinces of North America (London, 1787), 144–47.

18 Dunkerly and Williams, *Old Ninety Six,* 65.

19 Greene to Lee, 5/22/1781, *PNG,* 8:291, for Greene's arrival at Ninety Six, and 230n10 and 248n3, for Rawdon's orders to Cruger.

20 For a sketch of Vauban and his method, see Buchanan, *GCH,* 53–55, and the valuable citations.

21 Miecislaus Haiman, *Kosciuszko in the American Revolution* (New York: Polish Institute of Arts and Sciences in America, 1943), 3, 6, 9, 11–13 16–21, 43–45; John F. Luzadar, *Saratoga: A Military History of the Decisive Campaign of the American Revolution* (New York: Savas Beatie, 2008), 48, 206, 279, 372, 376–77.

22 Haiman, *Kosciuszko,* 103–4; Greene to Kosciuszko, 12/3/1780, *PNG,* 6:515.

23 Greene to Kosciuszko, 12/8/1780, 1/1/1781, Colonel Lewis Morris Jr. to Kosciuszko, 2/1/1781, *PNG,* 6:554; 7:35, 232.

24 Johnson, *Greene,* 2:143; Haiman, *Kosciuszko,* 112; Mackenzie, *Strictures,* 147–48.

25 Haiman, *Kosciuszko,* 112. Haiman cites other sources giving the distance at 350 to 400 yards, 112n8.

26 Lee, *Memoirs,* 377–78n.

27 Haiman, *Kosciuszko,* 112–13; Otho Williams to Cruger, 6/3/1781, Cruger to Williams, 6/3/1781, *PNG,* 8:339–40; Greene, *Historic Resource Study,* 138.

28 Lee, *Memoirs,* 371. Kosciuszko as well as Lee state that Lee arrived at Ninety Six on 8 June, but Greene to Pickens, 6/7/1781, *PNG,* 8:357, states in a postscript that "Lt Colonel Lee has just arrived in camp."

29 Lee, *Memoirs,* 371–72.

30 Haiman, *Kosciuszko,* 150; Commager and Morris, 2:1184.

31 Greene to Pickens, 6/1/1781, Pickens to Greene, 6/2/1781, *PNG,* 8:332, 339; Commager and Morris, 2:1183.

32 Lee, *Memoirs,* 373–74; Haiman, *Kosciuszko,* 147–48.

33 Rawdon to Cornwallis, 6/5/1781, 6/7/1781, *CP,* 5:290–93; "62 sail" in Baron von Bose to Baron von Knyphausen, 6/7/1781, quoted in *PNG,* 8:369n5; Isaac Huger to Greene, 6/6/1781, *PNG,* 8:355n2; Captain William Feilding to the Earl of Denbigh, 6/30/1781, in *The Lost War: Letters from British Officers during the American Revolution* (New York: Horizon Press, 1975), 209. Feilding was a marine officer with the fleet that brought the reinforcements and dated their landing as 5 June.

34 Rawdon to Cornwallis, 6/5/1781, 6/7/1781, *CP,* 5:291–93.

35 Greene to Sumter, 6/10/1781 (2 letters), Greene to Marion, 6/10/1781, Greene to Elijah Clarke, 6/12/1781, Greene to Sumter, 6/12/1781, *PNG,* 8:374–75, 379, 382.

36 Gregorie, *Sumter,* 122–23; Sumter to Greene, 6/11/1781, Greene to Sumter, 6/13/1781, *PNG,* 8:378, 385.

37 Greene to Sumter, 6/12/1781, *PNG,* 8:382; Rawdon to Cornwallis, 6/5/1781, 6/7/1781, *CP,* 5:291–93.

38 Huntington to Greene, 10/31/1780, Greene to Galvez, 6/12/1781, *PNG,* 6:451; 8:379–80; David J. Weber, *The Spanish Frontier in North America* (New Haven, CT: Yale University Press, 1992), 267–68.

39   Greene to Gamble, 6/12/1781, Greene to Nash, 6/12/1781, *PNG,* 8:379–81.

40   Sumter to Marion, 6/13/1781, 6/14/1781, 6/15/1781, Gibbes, *Doc. Hist.,* 96–97; Sumter to Greene, 6/13/1781 (two letters), Greene to Pickens, 6/14/1781, Burnet to Rudulph, 6/14/1781, Greene to Washington, 6/14/1781, Sumter to Greene, 6/14/1781, *PNG,* 8:388–90 and n1, 390–91; Johnson, *Greene,* 2:153.

41   Marion to Greene, 6/16/1781, *PNG,* 8:394. I am indebted to Charles Baxley for the location of Rock's Plantation.

42   Greene to Sumter, 6/17/1781, Rudulph to Greene, 1/18/1781, *PNG,* 8:404–5, 412.

43   Sumter to Greene, 6/19/1781 (2 letters), and editorial notes; Rawdon to Cornwallis, 8/2/1781, *CP,* 6:63.

44   Commager and Morris, 2:1183; Haiman, *Kosciuszko,* 114.

45   Lee, *Memoirs,* 374.

46   Greene to Huntington, 6/20/1781, *PNG,* 8:419; Lee, *Memoirs,* 375; Haiman, *Kosciuszko,* 114.

47   Haiman, *Kosciuszko,* 114; Greene to Huntington, 6/20/1781, *PNG,* 8:421; Commager and Morris, 2:1184–85.

48   Mackenzie, *Strictures,* 159–60; Alexander Garden, *Anecdotes of the Revolutionary War in America* (Charleston, SC: A. E. Miller, 1822), 408; Greene to Huntington, 6/20/1781, *PNG,* 8:421 and n6.

49   General Greene's Orders, 6/18/1781, Greene to Huntington, 6/20/1781, *PNG,* 8:408–9, 421; Kirkwood, *Journal,* 19.

50   Lee, *Memoirs,* 377–78n.

51   Garden, *Anecdotes of the Revolutionary War,* 408.

7. A Bravura Performance

1   Lee, *Memoirs,* 371.

2   Haiman, *Kosciuszko,* 115–16; Johnson, *Sketches,* 2:142–43; Dunkerly and Williams, *Old Ninety Six,* 23; "Memoir of Major Thomas Young," 103–4.

3   General Greene's Orders, 6/20/1781, Greene to Huntington, 6/20/1781, *PNG,* 8:419; McCrady, 296; Rankin, *Marion,* 217; Pickens to Henry Lee Jr., 11/25/1811, Draper Mss, 1 VV 108, WHS.

4   Greene to Marion, 6/25/1781, *PNG,* 8:457–58.

5   Greene to Jefferson, 3/23/1781, Jefferson to Greene, 3/30/1781, Lafayette to Greene, 5/18/1781, Greene to Jefferson, 6/27/1781, *PNG,* 7:466; 8:13, 280, 463–65; Jefferson to Robert Lawson, 5/8/1781, *The Papers of Thomas Jefferson,* 5:613.

6   Rawdon to Cornwallis, 8/2/1781, *CP,* 6:64; Greene to McKean, 7/17/1781, *PNG,* 9:28.

7   Rawdon to Cornwallis, 8/2/1781, *CP,* 6:64.

8   Ibid., 65.

9   Draper, *King's Mountain and Its Heroes,* 113; Greene to Shelby, 6/22/1781, Shelby to Greene, 7/2/1781, 8/3/1781, Sevier to Greene, 8/6/1781, Marion to Greene, 11/2/1781, *PNG,* 8:439, 482; 9:129, 143, 522; Davie, *Sketches,* 13.

10   Greene to Locke, 6/21/1781, 7/1/1781, Pierce to Greene, 6/26/1781, Malmedy to Greene, 6/29/1781, 7/10/1781, *PNG,* 8:432, 479, 463, 476, 517; JW, 43.

11 Greene to Locke, 7/30/1781, Locke to Greene, 8/10/1781, Pickens to Greene, 2/20/1781, *PNG*, 9:108, 162–63; 7:325.

12 Greene to Lee, 6/24/1781, Greene to Pickens, 6/23/1781, *PNG*, 452, 448; Clyde R. Ferguson, "General Andrew Pickens" (PhD diss., Duke University, 1960), 232; Ramsay, *Rev. of S-C,* 2:246.

13 Greene to George Washington, 6/22/1781, Greene to von Steuben, 5/1/1781, Greene to Nash, 5/2/1781, 4/13/1781, Greene to Maham, 6/21/1781, Horry to Greene, 6/28/1781, Ichabod Burnet to Horry, 7/2/1781, *PNG*, 8:441, 184, 191, 89–90, 433, 471–72, 481; Cornwallis to Rawdon, 8/4/1780, *CP,* 1:227; Carrington to Long, 7/15/1781, *NCSR,* 15:534.

14 Lee, *Memoirs,* 379 and n.

15 Greene to Lee, 6/25/1781, Lee to Greene, 6/30/1781, Greene to Marion, 7/1/1781, General Greene's Orders, 7/1/1781, William Pierce Jr. to Edward Carrington, 7/1/1781, *PNG*, 8:455, 478, 479–80, 479.

16 Rawdon to Cornwallis, 8/2/1781, *CP,* 6:65; Sir John Fortescue, *The War of Independence: The British Army in North America, 1775–1783* (1911; reprint, with new introduction by John Shy, London: Greenhill Books; Mechanicsburg, PA: Stackpole Books, 2001), 240; William Washington to Greene, 7/2/1781, Lee to Greene, 7/3/1781, *PNG*, 8:483, 486; Lee, *Memoirs,* 381.

17 Rawdon to Cornwallis, 8/2/1781, *CP,* 6:65; Greene to William Washington, 7/3/1781, *PNG*, 8:486; John C. Parker Jr., *Parker's Guide to the Revolutionary War in South Carolina: Battles, Skirmishes, and Murders,* 2nd ed. (West Conshohocken, PA: Infinity Publishing, 2013), 313, for the sites of the actions and Congaree Creek in relation to the Congaree River.

18 Lee, *Memoirs,* 383–84.

19 Marion to Greene, 7/7/1781, *PNG*, 8:505.

20 Rankin, *Swamp Fox,* 222–23; Marion to Greene, 7/8/1781 (2 letters), *PNG*, 8:508–9.

21 Marion to Greene, 7/10/1781, Pickens to Greene, 7/10/1781, 7/19/1781, *PNG*, 8:518–19; 9:48–50 and n2.

22 Greene to Lee, 7/4/1781, Pierce to Greene, 7/8/1781, Williams to Greene, 7/8/1781, *PNG*, 8:489, 509, 511–12.

23 Rawdon to Cornwallis, 8/2/1781, *CP,* 6:65; Williams to Major Nathaniel Pendleton, 7/16/1781, Gibbes, *Doc. Hist.,* 3:105; General Greene's Orders, 7/12/1781, *PNG*, 9:3.

24 Lee, *Memoirs,* 384–85; Williams to Pendleton, Gibbes, *Doc. Hist.,* 3:106; Greene to McKean, 7/17/1781, *PNG*, 9:29; Rawdon to Cornwallis, *CP,* 6:65.

25 Lee, *Memoirs,* 385; Greene to McKean, *PNG*, 9:29; Williams to Pendleton, Gibbes, *Doc. Hist.,* 3:106; Rawdon to Cornwallis, *CP,* 6:65–66.

26 McCrady, 343; Pancake, *This Destructive War,* 215; Greene to McKean, 7/17/1781, *PNG*, 9:29; Kirkwood, *Journal,* 19–20; Lee, *Memoirs,* 386.

27 Rawdon to Cornwallis, 8/2/1781, *CP,* 6:66; Lambert, *South Carolina Loyalists in the American Revolution,* 173–74, for the number of Loyalists with Cruger.

28 Fortescue, *The War of Independence,* 240; Rawdon to Cornwallis, *CP,* 6:66.

8. Dog Days

1 Rawdon to Cornwallis, 6/5/1781, *CP,* 5:291.

2 Greene to McKean, 7/17/1781, Greene to Marion, 6/25/1781, Greene to Sumter, 6/15/1781, Greene to Lee, 6/25/1781, Greene to Sumter, 7/14/1781, *PNG,* 9:29; 8:458, 455; 9:8.

3 Gregorie, *Sumter,* 172; Sumter to Greene, 7/15/1781, 7/22/1781, *PNG,* 9:17–18, 63; and in *PNG,* 9:13–17, see "Headnote on the Dog Days Expedition" by the editors of the Greene Papers, which is a valuable summary of the raid and explains how it got the name Dog Days.

4 Sumter to Greene, 7/15/1781, 7/22/1781, *PNG,* 9:17–18, 62–63.

5 Lee to Greene, 7/15/1781, *PNG,* 9:12; Lee, *Memoirs,* 387.

6 Sumter to Greene, 7/15/1781, *PNG,* 9:18.

7 Sumter to Greene, 7/17–19/1781, *PNG,* 9:51 and n6, 53; Captain David John Bell to Charles [Masterson?], 8/11/1781, *Papers of the Continental Congress* (Washington, DC: National Archives, 1957–59), vol. 1, Item 51: 659 (microfilm) (I am indebted to Charles Baxley for providing me with a transcript of this letter and the correct name of the writer); "Diary of Samuel Mathis," entry of 7/16/1781, in *Historic Camden, Part One: Colonial and Revolutionary,* by Thomas J. Kirkland and Robert M. Kennedy (1905; reprint, Camden, SC: Kershaw County Historical Society, 1963), 403.

8 Sumter to Greene, 7/17–19/1781, *PNG,* 9:51.

9 Greene to Lafayette, 7/24/1781, *PNG,* 9:72; Johnson, *Greene,* 2:170; David John Bell to Charles [Masterson?], 8/11/1781.

10 David John Bell to Charles [Masterson?], 8/11/1781; Sumter to Greene, 7/17–19/1781, Marion to Greene, 7/19/1781, *PNG,* 9:50–51, 47; Lee, *Memoir,* 388.

11 Lee, *Memoir,* 389–90; David John Bell to Charles [Masterson?], 8/11/1781.

12 Lee, *Memoir,* 390; David John Bell to Charles [Masterson?], 8/11/1781.

13 Sumter to Greene, 7/22/1781, Greene to Thomas McKean, 7/26/1781, *PNG,* 9:63, 84; David John Bell to Charles [Masterson?], 8/11/1781.

14 Sumter to Greene, 7/17–19/1781, Marion to Greene, 7/19/1781, *PNG,* 9:52, 47; David John Bell to Charles [Masterson?], 8/11/1781.

15 Marion to Greene, 7/19/1781, Sumter to Greene, 7/25/1781, *PNG,* 9:47–48, 81.

16 Ibid.

17 Marion to Greene, 7/19/1781, Sumter to Greene, 7/17–19/1781, *PNG,* 9:47–48, 52.

18 David John Bell to Charles [Masterson?], 8/11/1781; Sumter to Greene, 7/17–19/1781, 7/25/1781, Marion to Greene, 7/19/1781, *PNG,* 9:48, 52, 81.

19 Lee, *Memoirs,* 393, editor's note; Sumter to Greene, 7/25/1781, *PNG,* 9:81; Draper Mss, 16 VV 35 (microfilm), WHS, for the confrontation, and 16 VV 38 for the description of Colonel Taylor. The veracity of what Colonel Taylor's son told Lyman Draper is supported by descendants, who have passed the story down through the generations: author's conversation with Francis Chandler Furman, a direct descendant of Colonel Thomas Taylor.

20 Greene to Sumter, 7/21/1781, Greene to Pickens, 7/22/1781, Greene to Lafayette, 7/24/1781, Greene to Morgan, 8/26/1781, Greene to Sumter, 6/23/1781, *PNG,* 9:55, 60, 72, 256; 8:449; McCrady, 2:325.

21 Balfour to Clinton, 7/20/1781, *CP,* 6:249.

22 Greene to Samuel Huntington, 1/14/1781, Georgia Delegates to Greene, 4/26/1781, *PNG,* 7:119–20; 8:154–55.

23 Greene to Georgia Delegates, 7/18/1781, Greene to Colonels Elijah Clarke, John Twiggs, and William Few, 7/24/1781, Greene to Joseph Clay, 7/24/1781, *PNG,* 9:34, 69–70.

24 Nathan Brownson to Greene, 8/29/1781, *PNG,* 9:270. For the anemic attempts to establish Rebel civil government in Georgia prior to Greene's involvement, see Kenneth Coleman, *The American Revolution in Georgia, 1763–1789* (Athens: University of Georgia Press, 1958), 155–61.

25 Greene to Joseph Clay, 7/24/1781, *PNG,* 9:70.

26 This and several following paragraphs covering the European scene and its players follows closely the narrative in Richard B. Morris, *The Peacemakers: The Great Powers and American Independence* (New York: Harper & Row, 1965), 152–90, with quotations from that narrative cited separately, followed by page numbers; Morris's quote on Maria Theresa, 153; Joseph II quote, 154; Morris's quote on Kaunitz, 154.

27 "Several icy interviews," and William Lee quote, Morris, *Peacemakers,* 152.

28 "Played no significant role," and "to have a finger in every pie," ibid., 158, 160.

29 "Unless any of our mediators," and "*Aut nunc aut nunquam,*" ibid., 157, 113.

30 "Declared a free republic," ibid., 179; "Clumsy gestures," *The New Yorker,* 4/28/2014, 53.

31 William Sharpe to Greene, 5/28/1781, Samuel Huntington to Greene, 6/3/1781, John Mathews to Greene, 7/4/1781, *PNG,* 8:323, 341–42, 347; the quotations "prepared to yield" and "even ... the American-held portion of South Carolina," Morris, *Peacemakers,* 180.

32 Huntington to Greene, 6/3/1781, *PNG,* 8:341–42; Huntington to the States, 6/1/1781, 6/2/1781, *Letters of Delegates to Congress, 1774–1789,* ed. Paul H. Smith et al. (Washington, DC: Library of Congress, 1976–), 17:283–86; the previous source also contains letters of delegates that mention the danger of *uti possidetis* in 17:274, 279, 297, 309; on mediation, see also William Sharpe to Greene, 5/28/1781, John Mathews to Greene, 7/4/1781, *PNG,* 8:322–23, 347; McDowell to Campbell, 7/25/1781, Gibbes, *Doc. Hist.,* 3:107–8.

33 Greene to Mathews, 7/18/1781, *PNG,* 9:38–39.

9. The "Confidence and Good Opinion of Those in Power"

1 General Greene's orders, 7/16/1781, Greene to Thomas Burke, 7/16/1781, *PNG,* 9:18, 20; James, *Marion,* 138; Lee, *Memoirs,* 393.

2 Greene to Burke, 7/16/1781, *PNG,* 9:20.

3 Lee, *Memoirs,* 393; Lee to Greene, 7/29/1781, Greene to Lafayette, 7/22/1781, Greene to Lee, 7/29/1781, *PNG,* 9:101, 58–59, 102–3.

4 Lee to Greene, 7/29/1781, Greene to Lee, 7/29/1781, *PNG,* 9:101, 103.

5 Ibid., 101, 104.

6 Lee to Greene, 7/30/1781, Marion to Greene, 11/30/1781, Greene to Lee, 7/29/1781, *PNG,* 9:114, 642, 104.

7 Lee, *Memoir,* 446; Greene to Burke, 8/12/1781, *PNG,* 9:166.

8 Piecuch and Beakes, *"Light Horse Harry,"* 195; Lee to Greene, 8/8/1781, Greene to Lee, 8/9/1781, *PNG,* 9:150–51, 153.

9 Lee to Greene, 8/10/1781, Greene to Lee, 8/12/1781, *PNG,* 9:162, 170.

10 Sumter to Davis, quoted in McCrady, 429; Lee to Greene, 7/29/1781, Greene to Lee, 7/29/1781, *PNG,* 9:102–3; Marion to Sumter, 7/26/1781, quoted in Gregorie, *Sumter,* 181, and 183 for the final quotation in the paragraph.

11 Gregorie, *Sumter,* 182–83; Henderson to Greene, 8/14/1781 (2 letters), *PNG,* 9:182–83.

12 Greene to Henderson, 8/16/1781, *PNG,* 9:188; Gregorie, *Sumter,* 184.

13 Greene to Marion, 8/10/1781, Greene to Henderson, 8/12/1781, Greene to Lee, 8/12/1781, Marion to Greene, 8/13/1781, Marion to Greene, 8/20/1781, Marion to Greene, 9/3/1781, *PNG,* 9:158–59, 169–70 and n3, 170, 179–80, 216–17, 288; James, *Marion,* 126–27.

14 Marion to Greene, 9/3/1781, Marion to Greene, 9/27/1781, *PNG,* 9:288–90, 403n1.

15 Marion to Greene, 9/3/1781, *PNG,* 9:289–90.

16 Stephen Jarvis, "An American's Experience in the British Army," *Journal of American History* 1, no. 4 (1907), 728.

17 Marion to Greene, 9/3/1781, Rutledge to Greene, 9/6/1781, 11/1/1781, *PNG,* 9:290, 304 and n2, 516–17; Rutledge to Marion, 9/14/1781, Gibbes, *Doc. Hist.,* 3:159–60.

18 Greene to Malmedy, 7/17/1781, Greene to Gist, 7/19/1781, Gist to Greene, 5/29/1781, Greene to Henderson, 7/22/1781, Greene to Pickens, 7/22/1781, *PNG,* 9:21, 44–45, 57, 61; 8:321.

19 Greene to Sumner, 7/19/1781, Davidson to Greene, 7/18/1781, Greene to Davidson, 7/26/1781, Greene to Hamilton, 7/27/1781, Pendleton to Mazaret, 7/26/1781, *PNG,* 9:46, 43, 83, 89, 86.

20 Jonathan Bryan to Greene, 8/27/1781, *PNG,* 260–61 and n1.

21 David K. Bowden, *The Execution of Isaac Hayne* (Orangeburg, SC: Sandlapper Publishing, 1977), 15–16, 18, 29–34; *Royal Gazette,* Charlestown, August 8, 1781; *PNG,* 251–52n2; for an excellent discussion of the Hayne affair, see Benjamin Rubin, "The Rhetoric of Revenge: Atrocity and Identity in the Revolutionary Carolinas" (MA thesis, Western Carolina University, 2010).

22 Greene to Henderson, 8/12/1781, Greene to Lee, 8/12/1781, *PNG,* 9:169, 171.

23 From the Officers of the Southern Army to Greene, 8/20/1781, Greene to Balfour, 8/26/1781, Balfour to Greene, 9/3/1781, Greene to Washington, 11/21/1781, Washington to Greene, 12/15/1781, *PNG,* 9:217, 250, 284, 605; 10:61–62; for the congressional motion, see *PNG,* 9:252n2.

24 Pickens to Greene, 7/19/1781, Greene to Pickens, 7/30/1781, Colonel Robert Anderson to John McCarter, 8/31/1781, *PNG,* 9:48–49, and 50n3 for Anderson letter on the policy of expelling Tories.

25 Pickens to Greene, *PNG,* 9:48–49; Lambert, *South Carolina Loyalists,* 206–7.

26 Pickens to Greene, 7/25/1781, *PNG,* 9:77.

27 Hampton to Greene, 7/29/1781, Greene to Hampton, 7/30/1781, *PNG,* 9:105–7.

28 For the full text of Rutledge's proclamation, see Moultrie, *Memoirs,* 2:407–9; *PNG,* 9:100n3.

29 Catharine Greene to Samuel Ward Jr. and Celia Greene, 12/23/1782, quoted in *PNG,* 12:328n3.

30 Greene to Lee, 8/19/1781, Lee to Greene, 8/23/1781, *PNG,* 9:205–6, 226–27.

31 The information for this brief sketch of Rutledge's early life is based on Haw, *John and Edward Rutledge,* 1–15, with the quotations on 11, 15; Ramsay, *Rev. of S-C,* 2:269.

32 Haw, *John and Edward Rutledge,* 17, 19, 22, 35, 79–80, with quotations on 35 and 80; for the 1775 Rebel campaign against the Tories in the Back Country, see Buchanan, *GCH,* ch. 8.

33 Haw, *John and Edward Rutledge,* 81, 86–87; Garden, *Anecdotes of the Revolutionary War,* 8n; for the Battle of Sullivan's Island, see Buchanan, *GCH,* ch. 1.

34 Rutledge to South Carolina Delegates to Congress, 8/6/1781, "The Letters of John Rutledge," ed. Joseph W. Barnwell, *SCHGM* 18, no. 3 (July 1917), 136–37.

35 Rutledge to Marion, 9/2/1781, 9/3/1781, Gibbes, *Doc. Hist.,* 3:131, 134.

36 In this paragraph I have followed Haw, *John and Edward Rutledge,* 142; for the allegiance document, see Moultrie, *Memoirs,* 2:386–88.

37 Rutledge to Marion, 9/2/1781 (2 letters), Gibbes, *Doc. Hist.,* 3:132–33.

38 General Greene's Orders, 8/5/1781, 8/6/1781, Death Warrant for Sergeant John Hadley, 8/6/1781, *PNG,* 9:131, 133–34.

39 General Greene's Orders, 8/5/1781, 8/6/1781, Warrant for the Execution of Private Joden Roziers, 8/10/1781, Warrant for the Execution of Private John Barrott, 8/10/1781, Warrant for the Execution of Private James Pallet, 8/10/1781, *PNG,* 9:131, 134, 158. Private Barrott's name is also spelled Barrett in the records.

40 General Greene's Orders, 7/25/1781, 8/5/1781, *PNG,* 9:76, 131.

41 General Greene's Orders, 8/6/1781, *PNG,* 9:133–34.

42 Greene to Luzerne, 8/7/1781, Washington to Greene, 7/1/1781, Lafayette to Greene, *PNG,* 9:145–46, 8:336–37, 9:279–80 and nn1, 3; Don Higginbotham, *War of American Independence,* 380, 388n50.

43 Greene to Washington, 8/6/1781, 8/7/1781, *PNG,* 9:138–41, 146–47.

44 Rochambeau to de Grasse, 5/28/1781, quoted in Charles Lee Lewis, *Admiral De Grasse and American Independence* (Annapolis, MD: United States Naval Institute Press, 1945), 120–21, 136; Greene to Washington, 8/7/1781, *PNG,* 9:146; for Washington's initial reaction to and then acceptance of de Grasse's decision to sail to the Chesapeake instead of New York, see Buchanan, *The Road to Valley Forge,* 317–18, 320.

10. "We Obtained a Complete Victory" (Greene)/ "I Totally Defeated Him" (Stewart)

1 General Greene's orders, 8/22/1781, *PNG,* 9:222.

2 Greene to Lee, 8/21/1781, *PNG,* 9:218; Stewart to Cornwallis, 8/15/1781, Balfour to Clinton, 10/2/1781, *CP,* 6:75, 252–53; James Weymss, "Sketches of the characters of the General Staff officers and Heads of Departments of the British Army that served in America during the Revolutionary War, (the Northern Army

excepted) with some remarks connected therewith," Draper Mss, 17 VV 192–215 (microfilm), WHS.

3   Greene to McKean, 8/25/1781, *PNG*, 9:242.

4   Lee to Greene, 8/20/1781, Greene to Lee, 8/22/1781, *PNG*, 9:214–15, 223.

5   General Greene's Orders, 8/24/1781, Hyrne to Gamble, 8/24/1781, Greene to Henderson, 8/24/1781, Colonel Charles Harrison to Greene, 8/28/1781 (re the negative prospects of obtaining arms from Salisbury), Greene to Lee, 8/25/1781, Greene to Sevier, 9/1/1781, Greene to Shelby, 9/1/1781, *PNG*, 9:233–35, 265, 239–40, 276–77.

6   Greene to Lee, 8/25/1781, *PNG*, 9:239.

7   General Greene's Orders, 8/27/1781, 8/30/1781, 9/1/1781, Lee to Greene, 9/1/1781, Lafayette to Greene, 9/2/1781, *PNG*, 9:259, 271, 274, 278, 279–80 and n2. On de Grasse's arrival at the Chesapeake, see Lewis, *Admiral De Grasse and American Independence,* 141, 354n9.

8   Greene to Thomas McKean, 9/5/1781, Greene to Marion, 9/5/1781, Nathan Pendleton to Pickens, 9/5/1781, Pickens to Greene, 9/5/1781, *PNG*, 9:298–300.

9   Stewart to Cornwallis, 9/9/1781, *DAR*, 20:227.

10   Greene to McKean, 9/11/1781, *PNG*, 9:328; Stewart to Cornwallis, 9/26/1781, *CP*, 6:169. The exceptions are Jim Piecuch, "The Evolving Tactician: Nathanael Greene at the Battle of Eutaw Springs," in *Greene,* ed. Massey and Piecuch, 226; and Robert M. Dunkerly and Irene B. Boland, *Eutaw Springs: The Final Battle of the American Revolution's Southern Campaign* (Columbia: University of South Carolina Press, 2017), 109–18.

11   In estimating Stewart's strength, I have used the "Returns" in *DAR*, 19:229, and figures in Piecuch, "The Evolving Tactician," 226, although I disagree with Piecuch on how many troops Stewart fought.

12   Stewart's Return of Rooting Party, 9/8/1781, *DAR*, 19:229; Lee, *Memoirs,* 466; Williams in "Battle of Eutaw," Gibbes, *Doc. Hist.,* 3:145; Anderson, "Journal," 9/8/1781; Kirkwood, *Journal,* 23; Stewart to Cornwallis, 9/19/1781, *CP*, 6:167.

13   John Rutledge to South Carolina Delegates, 9/9/1781, *SCHGM* 18, no. 3 (July 1917), 139.

14   Piecuch, "The Evolving Tactician," 226–27; "Field Return of the No. Carolina Militia Commanded by Colonel Malmady, August 25th, 1781," Greene Papers, WLCL; Henderson to Greene, 8/25/1781, *PNG*, 9:245; John Rutledge to South Carolina Delegates, 9/9/1781, 139; General Greene's Orders, 9/4/1781, *PNG*, 9:291; Johnson, *Greene,* 2:219.

15   General Greene's Orders, 9/6/1781, Greene to McKean, 9/11/1781, *PNG*, 9:302, 305, 328, 333–34n4; James, *Marion,* 132; Johnson, *Greene,* 2:219. Note: A jill, or gill, is equal to four U.S. fluid ounces or five Imperial fluid ounces.

16   For George Washington's reaction to the Morgan/Greene method of deploying regulars and militia for set-piece battles, see Buchanan, *The Road to Valley Forge,* 314–16.

17   Greene to McKean, 9/11/1781, *PNG*, 9:302, 305, 328, 333–34n4.

18   Ibid., 328–29.

19   Ibid., 329; "Battle of Eutaw," Gibbes, *Doc. Hist.,* 3:144.

20   Stewart to Cornwallis, 9/9/1781, *DAR*, 20:226–29; Greene to McKean, 9/11/1781, *PNG*, 9:329; Jim Piecuch, "The Battle of Eutaw Springs, September

8, 1781," *SCAR* 3, no. 9 (September 2006), 28; "Battle of Eutaw," Gibbes, *Doc. Hist.,* 3:145.

21 Greene to McKean, 9/11/1781, *PNG,* 9:302, 305, 328, 333–34n4; "Battle of Eutaw," Gibbes, *Doc. Hist.,* 3:146; Williams to Edward Giles, 9/23/1781, quoted in *PNG,* 9:334n5.

22 Stewart to Cornwallis, 9/9/1781, *DAR,* 20:226–29.

23 Greene to McKean, 9/11/1781, *PNG,* 9:329; "Battle of Eutaw," Gibbes, *Doc. Hist.,* 3:146.

24 Greene to McKean, 9/11/1781, *PNG,* 9:329; Stewart to Cornwallis, 9/9/1781, *DAR,* 20:226–29.

25 Stewart to Cornwallis, 9/9/1781, *DAR,* 20:226–29.

26 "Battle of Eutaw," Gibbes, *Doc. Hist.,* 3:147; Stewart to Cornwallis, 9/9/1781, *DAR,* 20:226–29.

27 William Henry Gaines to Henry Lee Jr., 4/1/1810, *Southern Literary Messenger* 29, no. 4 (October 1859), 291.

28 Ibid., 291–92; "Battle of Eutaw," Gibbes, *Doc. Hist.,* 3:148.

29 Greene to McKean, 9/11/1781, *PNG,* 9:329; "Battle of Eutaw," Gibbes, *Doc. Hist.,* 3:148; Greene to Jacob Greene, 9/28/1776, *PNG,* 1:303; Collins, *Autobiography,* 253; Federal Pension Application of Jim Capers R1669, transcribed and annotated by C. Leon Harris, posted on Southern Campaigns Revolutionary War Pension Statements & Rosters (revwarapps.org); Federal Pension Application of William Griffis R4322, transcribed and annotated by Will Graves, posted on Southern Campaigns Revolutionary War Pension Statements and Rosters (revwarapps.org).

30 "Battle of Eutaw," Gibbes, *Doc. Hist.,* 3:148–49; Greene to von Steuben, 9/17/1781, Greene to McKean, 9/11/1781, *PNG,* 9:360, 329; Stewart to Cornwallis, 9/9/1781, *DAR,* 20:228.

31 "Battle of Eutaw," Gibbes, *Doc. Hist.,* 3:149–51; Greene to McKean, 9/11/1781, *PNG,* 9:331.

32 "Battle of Eutaw," Gibbes, *Doc. Hist.,* 3:151.

33 Ibid., 3:152–53; Greene to McKean, 9/11/1781, *PNG,* 9:331; John Eager Howard to Henry Lee [Jr.], 1/19/1819, in Lee Jr., *Campaign of 1781,* 281 (for the date of Howard's letter, see *PNG,* 8:158n1); John Chaney, Pension Application, in Dann, *Revolution Remembered,* 232; Piecuch, "Nathanael Greene and the Battle of Eutaw Springs," 237n54. Washington is defended in Lee F. McGee, "Most Astonishing Efforts: William Washington's Cavalry at the Battle of Eutaw Springs," *SCAR* 3, no. 3 (March 2006), 15–33, and Daniel Murphy, *William Washington, American Light Dragoon: A Continental Cavalry Leader in the War of Independence* (Yardley, PA: Westholme, 2014), 159–65.

34 Greene to McKean, 9/11/1781, *PNG,* 9:331; Lee, *Memoirs,* 470.

35 "Battle of Eutaw," Gibbes, *Doc. Hist.,* 3:153–54.

36 Ibid.; "Personal Reminiscences of Dr. William Read, Arranged from His Notes and Papers," Gibbes, *Doc. Hist.,* 2:282; "A Militant Surgeon of the Revolution: Some Letters of Richard Pindell, M.D.," *Maryland Historical Magazine* 18, no. 4 (December 1923), 319.

37 Cf. Piecuch, "Nathanael Greene at the Battle of Eutaw Springs," 231, with whom I respectfully disagree. For the layout of British field camps, see Lewis Lochee,

An Essay on Castrametation (London, 1778), 17, 20; pension application of James Magee S1555, transcribed by Will Graves (revwarapps.org).

38 "Battle of Eutaw," Gibbes, *Doc. Hist.,* 3:154–55.

39 Draper Mss, 1 DD 234 (microfilm), WHS; Lee, *Memoirs,* 471n473.

40 "Battle of Eutaw," Gibbes, *Doc. Hist.,* 3:155–56; Gaines to Lee, 4/1/1810, *Southern Literary Messenger,* 292; Stewart to Cornwallis, 11/29/1781, *CP,* 6:171; Stewart to Cornwallis, 9/9/1781, *DAR,* 20:228–29; Andrew Roberts, *Napoleon and Wellington: The Battle of Waterloo—and the Great Commanders Who Fought It* (New York: Simon & Schuster, 2001), 237.

41 Seymour, "Journal," 386; William Howard to Robert Walsh Jr., 12/10/1830, Howard Papers, Box 23, Fldr. 21, MHS; Greene to Rutledge, 9/9/1781, Greene to McKean, 9/11/1781, *PNG,* 9:308, 332; James, *Marion,* 136n1; "Battle of Eutaw," Gibbes, *Doc. Hist.,* 3:156–58; Stewart to Cornwallis, 9/29/1781, *CP,* 6:171. The casualties among American officers and sergeants is from Kirkwood, *Journal,* 24, whose numbers total fifty-five officers and forty sergeants, and "Battle of Eutaw," Gibbes, *Doc. Hist.,* 3:157–58, which includes only officers and numbers fifty-six.

42 Greene to Burke, 9/17/1781, *PNG,* 9:355; Stewart to Cornwallis, 9/9/1781, *DAR,* 20:227; Stewart's "Return" of casualties, 9/8/1781, *DAR,* 19:229; for American casualties, *PNG,* 9:338n24, and Kirkwood, *Journal,* 24; "Battle of Eutaw," Gibbes, *Doc. Hist.,* 3:157.

11. High Drama on Cape Fear

1 Stewart to Cornwallis, 11/29/1781, *CP,* 6:171; "Battle of Eutaw," Gibbes, *Doc. Hist.,* 3:157; Marion to Greene, 9/9/1781, *PNG,* 9:309.

2 Marion to Greene, 9/11/1781, *PNG,* 9:341.

3 Lee, *Memoirs,* 476–77.

4 Draper Mss, 1 DD 234 (microfilm), WHS; the quotation "smarter than people" are the words of Daniel Murphy, an authority on horses.

5 Marion to Greene, 9/13/1781, General Greene's Orders, 9/12/1781, 9/13/1781, *PNG,* 9:342–43; Gould to Clinton, 9/30/1781, quoted in *PNG,* 9:357n1.

6 Greene to Isaac Shelby and John Sevier, 9/16/1781, *PNG,* 9:351, for his location.

7 Dann, *Revolution Remembered,* 184; Browne to Greene, 9/2/1781, Pierce to Greene, 9/13/1781, Greene to Governor Thomas Nelson, 9/16/1781, for his location, Williams to Greene, 9/16/1781, *PNG,* 9:279, 344, 350, 353–54.

8 Williams to Greene, 9/16/1781, *PNG,* 9:354. For more contemporary comments on the horrors undergone by the wounded at military hospitals, see Caroline Cox, *A Proper Sense of Honor: Service and Sacrifice in George Washington's Army* (Chapel Hill: University of North Carolina Press, 2004), 147–48.

9 For the Battle of Moore's Creek Bridge, see Buchanan, *GCH,* 4–5, and for a fuller description Robert M. Dunkerly, *Redcoats on Cape Fear: The Revolutionary War in North Carolina,* rev. ed. (Jefferson, NC: McFarland and Company, 2012), 54–74; Craig quoted in Babits and Howard, *Long, Obstinate, and Bloody,* 5.

10 For the contemporary description of Craig, see Dunkerly, *Redcoats on Cape Fear,* 95; *Dictionary of National Biography,* for Craig's American and postwar career

and 2nd quotation. Lower Canada (1791–1841) included the southern part of the modern province of Quebec plus Labrador.

11   The quotations are in Massey, "British Expedition to Wilmington," 393–94, 399.

12   This paragraph is based on the essay in *American National Biography,* where the quotations are also located; and John Sayle Watterson, *Thomas Burke: Restless Revolutionary* (Washington, DC: University Press of America, 1980), 83–88, for the Sullivan affair.

13   Burke to Greene, 7/30/1781, Greene to Burke, 8/12/1781, *PNG,* 9:112, 166–67.

14   Massey, "British Expedition to Wilmington," 396–97.

15   Quoted in ibid., 397.

16   Ibid., 398; Craig to Cornwallis, 12/3/1781, *CP,* 6:181.

17   Craig to Balfour, 7/30/1781, *CP,* 6:70; Massey, "British Expedition to Wilmington," 401.

18   Quotations in *The Narrative of Col. David Fanning,* ed. Lindley S. Butler (Davidson, NC: Briarpatch Press, 1981), 2–3, 6, with the exception of the quotations and remarks about Fanning's alleged scalp disease and alleged mistreatment by his guardian, which may be found in the essay on Fanning in *American National Biography.*

19   Fanning, *Narrative,* 3–4, 19–22, 25.

20   Ibid., 25–30.

21   Ibid., 29–33 and n37.

22   Ibid., 33–39.

23   Massey, "British Expedition to Wilmington," 403; Burke to Greene, 8/9/1781, *PNG,* 9:154 and n11.

24   Massey, "British Expedition to Wilmington," 404–6, with quotations on 404; Fanning, *Narrative,* 49–53. Craig to Balfour, 10/24/1781, *CP,* 6:178; Dunkerly, *Redcoats on Cape Fear,* 39, discusses the importance of salt to the life and economy of early America.

25   Lafayette to Greene, 7/23/1781, 8/25/1781, Burke to Greene, 8/31/1781, *PNG,* 9:67 and n8, 246–47 and n12, 271.

26   Lee, *Memoirs,* 446–48; Greene to Martin, 9/27/1781, Greene to Wayne, 9/29/1781, Greene to Washington, 10/7/1781, *PNG,* 9:409, 413, 430.

27   Lee, *Memoirs,* 447–48.

28   Massey, "British Expedition to Wilmington," 405–6, and quotations; Algie I. Newlin, *The Battle of Lindley's Mill* (Burlington, NC: Alamance Historical Association, 1975), 3–4.

29   Fanning, *Narrative,* 54–55. For the probable strength of Fanning's force that marched to Hillsborough, see Massey, "British Expedition to Wilmington," 407n68; and Newlin, *Lindley's Mill,* 3–4.

30   Newlin, *Lindley's Mill,* 7–8; Fanning, *Narrative,* 55.

31   Fanning, *Narrative,* 54–57; Newlin, *Lindley's Mill,* 7–17; Dunkerly, *Redcoats on the Cape Fear,* 149.

32   Newlin, *Lindley's Mill,* 20.

33   Massey, "British Expedition to Wilmington," 408; Dunkerly, *Redcoats on Cape Fear,* 155–57, has an excellent description of the fight at Raft Swamp.

34   Greene to Rutherford, 10/18/1781, 10/20/1781, *PNG,* 9:452–53, 456–57; Massey, "British Expedition to Wilmington," 408, on Rutherford's reputation for "cruelty."

35 Dunkerly, *Redcoats on Cape Fear,* 158–59.

36 Quotations in Massey, "British Expedition to Wilmington," 409.

37 Fanning, *Narrative,* 9–12, 76; Rankin, *Marion,* 284; Greene to Marion, 7/9/1782, *PNG,* 11:422.

38 Watterson, *Burke,* 187–92; Burke to Greene, 1/19/782, Otho Holland Williams to Greene, 2/23/1782, *PNG,* 10:219–21 and n11, 404 and nn13, 14; William Richardson Davie to Burke, 2/23/1782, Burke to Otho Holland Williams (incorrectly given as William Williams), 3/28/1782, *NCSR,* 16:202, 251–55.

39 This paragraph is based on *American National Biography* (including 1st quotation), and Watterson, *Burke,* 213ff (including 2nd quotation).

40 Greene to Burke, 8/25/1781, *PNG,* 9:237.

12. "Like Goths and Vandals of Old"

1 The victory at Yorktown had not yet taken place, but Greene presented the most positive outcome in order to bolster his argument to send de Grasse's fleet south. Washington to Greene, 9/4/1781, Greene to Washington, 9/7/1781, Greene to Lafayette, 9/8/1781, *PNG,* 9:295, 430, 436.

2 Greene to Lafayette, 9/8/1781.

3 Greene to Shelby and Sevier, 10/11/1781, Sevier to Greene, 10/13/1781, *PNG,* 9:442, 445.

4 Williams to Greene, 10/10/1781, Greene to McKean, 10/25/1781, *PNG,* 9:440–41, 482–83.

5 Rutledge to Marion, 10/16/1781, Gibbes, *Doc. Hist.,* 3:192; Greene to Davie, 10/18/1781, Davie to Greene, 10/27/1781, Martin to Greene, 11/5/1781, Greene to Davie, 11/26/1781, *PNG,* 9:451, 464, 531, 629.

6 Ramsay, *Rev. of S-C,* 4:172–74 (given the date of Griffin's Death Warrant, the date for the night the troops left camp was probably 20 October); Death Warrant for Private Timothy Griffin, 10/21/1781, *PNG,* 9:459.

7 Balfour to Germain, 10/12/1781, GLL, EM.15531, NYPL.

8 Rutledge to Greene, 10/15/1781, Greene to Rutledge, 10/15/1781, *PNG,* 9:446–47.

9 Washington to William Crawford, 9/21/1767, in *Washington-Crawford Letters: Being the Correspondence between George Washington and William Crawford, from 1767 to 1781, Concerning Western Lands,* ed. Consul W. Butterfield (Cincinnati: Robert Clarke, 1877), 3–4; Byrd to Mr. Collenson, 7/18/1736, *Virginia Magazine of History and Biography* 34, no. 4 (October 1928), 354; for the "West in their eyes," I am indebted to Professor John D. W. Guice for permitting me to use the phrase, which was coined in Thomas D. Clark and John D. W. Guice, *The Old Southwest, 1795–1830: Frontiers in Conflict* (1989; reprint, Norman: University of Oklahoma Press, 1996); Bernard W. Sheehan, *Seeds of Extinction: Jeffersonian Philanthropy and the American Indian* (1973; reprint, New York: Norton, 1974), 266; Alexander McGillvray to Vizente Manuel de Zepadas, 5/22/1785, in John Walton Caughey, *McGillvray of the Creeks* (Norman: University of Oklahoma Press, 1938), 87; Captain Basil Hall, *Travels in North America in the Years, 1827–28,* 3 vols. (Edinburgh, 1829), 3:131–33. For readers interested, I have discussed the subject of conquest at some length in *Jackson's Way: Andrew Jackson*

and the People of the Western Waters (New York: John Wiley & Sons, 2001), 34–38, and passim.

10 Reverend James Creswell to William Henry Drayton, 7/27/1776, Gibbes, *Doc. Hist.,* 2:31; William Sharpe to Cornelius Harnett, 7/27/1776, quoted in Piecuch, *Three Peoples,* 69. For the Cherokee offensive west of the mountains, see Buchanan, *Jackson's Way,* 28–31.

11 Christian to Patrick Henry, 10/27/1776, and Stuart to Germain, 8/23/1776, quoted in James H. O'Donnell III, *Southern Indians in the American Revolution* (Knoxville: University of Tennessee Press, 1973), 48–50.

12 O'Donnell, *Southern Indians,* 106–7, 118–19.

13 Ibid., 119; Ferguson, "Pickens," 253; McCrady, 477–78.

14 Ferguson, "Pickens," 253.

15 McCrady, 467–70; Lambert, *South Carolina Loyalists,* 206–7; Pickens to Greene, 7/19/1781, *PNG,* 9:49 and n4.

16 Lambert, *South Carolina Loyalists,* 207; Greene to Sumter, 11/2/1781, Sumter to Greene, 11/14/1781, *PNG,* 9:517–18 and n1, 575–76 and n2; *Parker's Guide,* 367, for the location of the Moore-Cunningham fight.

17 Sumter to Greene, 11/17/1781, 11/23/1781, *PNG,* 9:586, 615 and n1.

18 *Parker's Guide,* 341, 482; Hammond to Greene, 12/2/1781, *PNG,* 9:651 and n2.

19 Hammond to Greene, 12/2/1781, *PNG,* 9:651 and n4. For readers interested in the locations of the various actions, see *Parker's Guide,* passim.

20 Hammond to Greene, 12/2/1781, Brownson to Greene, 12/1/1781, *PNG,* 9:651, 645; Ferguson, "Pickens," 256–57.

21 *PNG,* 9:653n5; Sumter to Greene, 12/9/1781, *PNG,* 10:24–25 and n2.

22 Buchanan, *GCH,* 215–16, 240.

23 For readers who wish to delve in detail on the Yorktown campaign, two books are recommended: Harold A. Larrabee, *Decision on the Chesapeake* (New York: Clarkson Potter, 1964), especially for the crucial naval aspect; and Jerome A. Greene, *The Guns of Independence: The Siege of Yorktown, 1781* (New York: Savas Beatie, 2005).

24 Lee, *Memoirs,* 513.

25 Greene to Thomas Nelson Jr., 8/10/1781, Washington to Greene, 10/24/1781, 10/31/1781, St. Clair to Greene, 11/14/1781, Carrington to Greene, 1/2/1782, *PNG,* 9:160, 480–81, 504–5, 573–74; 10:184. For de Grasse's orders and the French goal of taking Jamaica, see Andrew Jackson O'Shaughnessy, *An Empire Divided: The American Revolution and the British Caribbean* (Philadelphia: University of Pennsylvania Press, 2000), 232–33, and Lewis, *Admiral De Grasse,* 190–91.

26 Davies to Greene, 11/10/1781, Carrington to Greene, 1/12/1782, Arthur St. Clair to Greene, 12/5/1781, Christian Febiger to Greene, 1/29/1782, *PNG,* 9:555; 10:184; 8:280–81; Febiger to William Davies, 2/23/1782. *Calendar of Virginia State Papers and Other Manuscripts from January 1, 1782, to December 31, 1784,* ed. Wm. P. Palmer (1883; reprint, New York: Kraus Reprint Corp., 1968), 3:72.

27 Charles B. Baxley, "'An Enterprise on John's Island': Nathanael Greene's Winter Campaign and the Jacksonborough Assembly," *Army History* (Winter 2016), 30–52, for details and excellent maps; Greene to John Farr, 10/24/1781,

Marion to Greene, 11/2/1781, Greene to Marion, 11/15/1781, General Greene's Orders, 11/18/1781, *PNG,* 9:389n7, 469–70 and n3, 521–22, 588; Johnson, *Greene,* 2:259.

28 *PNG,* 9:655n4; Johnson, *Greene,* 2:264; Baxley, "'An Enterprise on John's Island,'" 36–38; Greene to McKean, 12/9/1781, *PNG,* 10:17–18.

29 The action and aftermath are described in Greene to Sumter, 12/2/1781, Greene to Williams, 12/2/1781, Greene to McKean, 12/9/1781, *PNG,* 9:648–50; 10:17–18.

30 Jarvis, "An American's Experience in the British Army," 728–29.

31 Leslie to Germain, 1/3/1782, BHP, Doc. 4035, Box 19, NYPL; Leslie to Germain, 12/31/1781, *DAR,* 19:237.

32 Leslie to Clinton, 12/4/1781, BHP, Doc. 3926, Box 18, NYPL; Lewis Morris Jr. to General Lewis Morris, 12/19/1781, "Letters to General Morris," New-York Historical Society, *Collections for the Year 1875* (New York, 1876), 495–96.

33 Jarvis, "An American's Experience in the British Army," 729.

34 Leslie to Germain, 1/3/1782, BHP, Doc. 4035, Box 19, NYPL.

13. "They Would Make Good Soldiers"

1 Greene to Sumter, 12/2/1781, Greene to Williams, 12/2/1781, *PNG,* 9:648–49.

2 Greene to Sumter, 10/3/1781, Sumter to Greene, 9/19/1781, 11/14/1781, 11/27/1781, Pickens to Greene, 3/5/1781, *PNG,* 9:423 and n1, 378, 575–76, 633; 7:399; Cornwallis to Germain, 8/20/1780, *CC,* 1:503.

3 Greene to Sumter, 12/2/1781, 11/28/1781, Sumter to Greene, 11/27/1781, *PNG,* 9:633, 648.

4 Greene to Sumter, 11/2/1781, *PNG,* 9:517–18; "Gray's Observations," 503.

5 Rutledge to Francis Marion, 9/2/1781, Rutledge Proclamation, 9/27/1781, Gibbes, *Doc. Hist.,* 3:131, 175–78; Gregorie, *Sumter,* 190.

6 Sumter to Greene, 11/23/1781, 11/24/1781, 12/9/1781, 12/19/1781, 12/22/1781, Greene to Sumter, 12/12/1781, *PNG,* 9:615, 623–24, 633; 10:24, 40, 81, 90.

7 Sumter to Greene, 12/19/1781, *PNG,* 10:81.

8 Greene to Sumter, 11/25/1781, 11/28/1781, *PNG,* 9:627, 633–34.

9 Ramsay, *Rev. of S-C,* 2:275; Moultrie, *Memoirs,* 2:303.

10 Collins, *Autobiography,* 271.

11 Ibid., 271–72.

12 Greene to Rutledge, 12/9/1781, *PNG,* 10:20–22.

13 Ibid., 22–23.

14 Walter Edgar, *South Carolina: A History* (Columbia: University of South Carolina Press, 1998), 78, for statistics; Jack P. Greene, *Understanding the American Revolution: Issues and Actors* (Charlottesville: University Press of Virginia, 1995), 143, for 1st quotation; Buchanan, *GCH,* 22, for "internal enemies"; Rutledge to Greene, 12/24/1781, *PNG,* 10:101.

15 John Laurens to Henry Laurens, 2/18/1774, *PHL,* 9:293.

16 Massey, *Laurens,* 14–16, 19, 62–63, 93; John Laurens to Francis Kinloch, 4/12/1776, Miscellaneous Papers (John Laurens), EM.L, NYPL.

17 John Laurens to Henry Laurens, 2/18/1775, *PHL,* 10:75–76.

18   Chamberlain quoted in Max Hastings, *Warriors: Portraits from the Battlefield* (New York: Knopf, 2005), 48.

19   Massey, *Laurens,* 73–77, 79, 110, 119–21 (Lafayette quotation, 75); James McHenry to Elias Boudinot, 7/2/1778, EM.9294, NYPL; Greene to George Washington, 8/28–31/1778, *PNG,* 2:502.

20   Massey, *Laurens,* 123–24 (quotes on 124).

21   Ibid., 93–97, 132; Krawczynski, *Drayton,* 308–10.

22   Hastings, *Warriors,* xv, for Frederick the Great's quote; Massey, *Laurens,* 135–36; Moultrie, *Memoirs,* 1:403–4.

23   Gadsden quote in Massey, *Laurens,* 140, and see 140–43 for an excellent discussion; David Ramsay to William Henry Drayton, 9/1/1779, Gibbes, *Doc. Hist.,* 2:121.

24   Massey, *Laurens,* 147–48, 158–59 (quotes). The assessment of Laurens's being unfit for troop command is mine.

25   Massey, *Laurens,* 170, 172, 187, 194 (Vergennes quote, 187; Massey's judgment, 194), and all of ch. 9 for a judicious description of a fish out of water.

26   Ibid., 196–99.

27   Ibid., 199–200.

28   Lewis Morris Jr. to Greene, 12/2/1781, Rutledge to Greene, 12/18/1781, *PNG,* 9:653; 10:74; Massey, *Laurens,* 206.

29   On malaria, see McNeill, *Mosquito Empires,* an excellent work, which has a chapter on the Southern Campaign. Although it is undeniable that both armies suffered from malaria, especially when campaigning in the Low Country during the hot, sickly season from June to about mid-October, McNeill's claims that it was malaria that drove Cornwallis north out of South Carolina (219) and that it was malaria "in part" that led to Yorktown because British "forces were much more susceptible to malaria than were the Americans" (199) are far-fetched. Morris to Greene, 12/2/1781, Greene to Williams, 12/2/1781, Lee to Greene, 12/4/1781, Greene to Lee, 12/7/1781, *PNG,* 9:643–54, 649–50; 10:6, 12–13; Lee, *Memoirs,* 524–25.

30   For factionalism in Georgia during the Revolution, see Harry H. Jackson, "The Rise of the Western Members: Revolutionary Politics and the Georgia Backcountry," in *An Uncivil War: The Southern Backcountry during the American Revolution,* ed. Ronald Hoffman, Thad W. Tate, and Peter J. Albert (Charlottesville: University Press of Virginia, 1985), 276–320.

31   Brownson to Greene, 10/30/1781, Greene to Brownson, 11/6/1781, Greene to Twiggs, 11/6/1781, *PNG,* 9:498, 535–38.

32   Greene to Twiggs, 12/7/1781, Brownson to Greene, 12/15/1781, *PNG,* 10:13–14, 58–59.

33   Brownson to Greene, 12/17/1781, *PNG,* 10:70–71.

34   Twiggs to Greene, 12/16/1781, *PNG,* 10:65–67.

35   Greene to Brownson, 12/24/1781, *PNG,* 10:95–98.

36   Greene to Twiggs, 12/25/1781, *PNG,* 10:102–3.

37   General Greene's Orders, 1/4/1782, *PNG,* 10:157 and nn2, 3.

38   Feltman, *Journal,* 26; Paul David Nelson, *Anthony Wayne: Soldier of the Early Republic* (Bloomington: Indiana University Press, 1985), 16–17 and passim for the

Wayne–St. Clair feud, 145 for Wayne's delay in marching, 164 for Wayne's arrival at Round O; Greene to John Hanson, 1/23/1782, *PNG*, 10:243.

39   Greene to Wayne, 1/9/1782, Greene to Twiggs, 1/10/782, *PNG*, 10:175–76 and n1, 177; Nelson, *Wayne*, 164.

40   Wayne to Greene, 1/17/1782, 1/23/1782, 1/26/1782, Greene to Wayne, 1/9/1782, 2/4/1782, *PNG*, 10:175–76 and n1, 215 and n4, 246–47 and n4, 267, 310–11.

41   Posey to Greene, 2/22/1782, 3/11/1782, 4/10/1782, Greene to Wayne, 3/12/1782, Greene to Posey, 3/24/1782, *PNG*, 10:396–97, 484–85 and n3, 490, 535; 11:30.

42   Greene to Rutledge, 12/14/1781, Rutledge to Greene, 12/24/1781, Greene to Rutledge, 12/27/1781, Rutledge to Greene, 12/31/1781, *PNG*, 10:51, 101, 116–17, 143.

14. Missions Impossible

1   Lee to Greene, 12/11/1781, *PNG*, 10:34.

2   Lee to Greene, 12/12/1781, *PNG*, 10:44.

3   Lee to Greene, 12/14/1781, 12/15/1781, 12/20/1781, Laurens to Greene, 12/20/1781, *PNG*, 10:54, 59, 83–84; Laurens to Lee, 12/27/1781, quoted in Massey, *Laurens*, 203–4.

4   Greene to Lee, 12/21/1781, *PNG*, 10:85.

5   Lee, *Memoirs*, 535; Lee to Greene, 12/28/1781, Greene to Lee, 12/28/1781, Greene to John Hanson, 1/23/1782, *PNG*, 10:126–27, 243.

6   Charles Baxley, "General Nathanael Greene's Moves to Force the British into the Charlestown Area, to Capture Dorchester John's Island, and to Protect the Jacksonborough Assembly," *SCAR* 12, no. 1.1 (January 23, 2015), 16–17; and Baxley, "'An Enterprise on John's Island,'" 44–46, for the Johns Island operation.

7   Lee, *Memoirs*, 528; Baxley, "'An Enterprise on John's Island,'" 44 and n89 for the probable location of the ford and description of pluff mud.

8   Lee, *Memoirs*, 528–29 and 528n.

9   Ibid., 529.

10   Lee to Greene, 12/29/1781, 12/31/1781, Greene to Lee, 1/1/1782, *PNG*, 10:135, 142, 144; Leslie to Clinton, 12/27/1781, *DAR*, 20:287.

11   Lee to Greene, 12/11/1781, 12/20/1781, *PNG*, 10:34–35 and n2, 84 and n3; Baxley, "Greene's Moves," 16; Leslie to Clinton, 12/4/1781, Leslie to Germain, 1/3/1782, BHP, Doc. 3926, Box 18, Doc. 4035, Box 19.

12   Seymour, "Journal," 387; General Greene's Orders, 1/11/1782, 1/12/1782, John Laurens to Greene, 1/11/1782, Greene to John Hanson, 1/23/1782, *PNG*, 10:180, 183, 243; Tilden, "Journal," 219; Lee, *Memoirs*, 532–35; Feltman, *Journal*, 37; Baxley, "Greene's Moves," 22 and n104 for air and water temperatures.

13   Lee, *Memoirs*, 533–34.

14   Ibid., 534; Greene to John Hanson, 1/23/1782, *PNG*, 10:243; Tilden, "Journal," 219.

15   Lee, *Memoirs*, 534–36; Greene to Rutledge, 1/16/1782, *PNG*, 10:206.

16   Lee, *Memoirs*, 529–31; Leslie to Clinton, 1/29/1782, quoted in *PNG*, 10:209n5.

17   Feltman, *Journal*, 35–36; General Greene's Orders, 1/16/1782, 1/23/1782, *PNG*, 10:201 and n1, 241.

18   Laurens to Greene, 12/28/1781, *PNG*, 10:130–31.

19 Greene to Rutledge, 1/21/1782, *PNG*, 10:228–29 and n4. Unless otherwise indicated, the discussion in the following paragraphs, including quotations, is taken from this source.

20 Greene to Marion, 4/15/1782, Greene to Washington, 4/15/1782, *PNG*, 11:64–66 and n5; Frey, *Water from the Rock*, 137–39, for Britain's limited use of slaves as soldiers.

21 Massey, *Laurens*, 206–8; Edward Rutledge to Arthur Middleton, 2/8/1782, "Correspondence of Hon. Arthur Middleton, Signer of the Declaration of Independence," *SCHGM* 27 (January 1926), 4; Laurens to George Washington, 5/19/1782, quoted in Massey, *Laurens*, 208.

22 Aedanus Burke to Arthur Middleton, 1/25–2/5/1782, "Correspondence of Arthur Middleton," *SCHGM* 26 (October 1925), 194; Whipple to Bartlett, 4/27/1779, in Smith, ed., *Letters of Delegates*, 12:398; Greene to George Washington, 3/9/1782, *PNG*, 10:472.

15. Departures

1 Greene to an unidentified person, 11/14/1781, Greene to Williams, 2/9/1782, *PNG*, 9:571; 10:341; Kirkwood, *Journal*, 27.

2 Greene to Sumter, 12/22/1781, *PNG*, 9:648; Sumter to Greene, 12/13/1781, Greene to Sumter, 12/15/1781, Sumter to Greene, 12/22/1781 (1st letter of that date), *PNG*, 10:49, 57–58, 89–90.

3 Sumter to Greene, 12/22/1781 (2nd letter of that date), *PNG*, 10:92.

4 Rutledge to Sumter, 12/25/1781, quoted in *PNG*, 10:93n4.

5 Greene to Sumter, 12/27/1781, *PNG*, 10:120; Sumter to Marion, 11/23/1781, Gibbes, *Doc. Hist.*, 3:214; Gregorie, *Sumter*, 191.

6 Greene to Sumter, 12/27/1781, Sumter to Greene, 1/2/1782, *PNG*, 10:120, 252–53.

7 Finney, "Diaries," 134; Sumter to Greene, 1/4/1782, *PNG*, 10:159.

8 Greene to Sumter, 1/8/1782, Mathews to Greene, 2/27/1782, *PNG*, 10:168, 416; McCrady, 534; Gregorie, *Sumter*, 198–99, 233; for the debate, see "Petition of Catherine Greene," *Annals of Congress*, House of Representatives, 2nd Congress, 1st Session, January 1792, 316–27, with the quotations on 322, 326–27; Cornwallis to Tarleton, 11/23/1780, *CP*, 3:342.

9 Lee to Greene, 1/26/1782, *PNG*, 10:264–65.

10 Greene to Lee, 1/27/1782, *PNG*, 10:268–69.

11 Lee to Greene, 1/29/1782, Greene to McKean, 9/11/1781, *PNG*, 10:282–83; 9:329, 331–33.

12 Lee to Greene, 1/29/1782, 2/10/1782, Greene to Lee, 2/12/1782, *PNG*, 10:282–83, 350, 358; Ichabod Burnet to Henry Lee, 6/20/1782, Misc. Ichabod Burnet, Misc. microfilm, Reel 71, NYHS; Massey, *Laurens*, 212–13.

13 Lee to Greene, 2/13/1782, Greene to Lee, 2/12/1782, Lee to Greene, 2/17/1782, *PNG*, 10:361, 358, 375.

14 Lee to Greene, 1/29/1782 (re his communication to Pierce), Greene to Lee, 2/18/1782, 3/12/1781 (2nd letter re Morris as his informant), *PNG*, 10:283, 378–79, 486.

15 Lee to Greene, 2/19/1782, *PNG*, 10:389–91.

16 Greene to Lee, 3/12/1782, *PNG,* 10:486–87.

17 Burnet to Lee, 6/20/1782, Misc. Ichabod Burnet, Misc. microfilm, Reel 71, NYHS.

18 Royster, *Lee,* 3–7, 164, 171, 251–52.

19 This paragraph is a brief summary of the brilliant epilogue by Royster, ibid., 251–52.

20 Leslie to Clinton, 12/1/1781, *DAR,* 19:229; von Knoblauch to Baron von Jungkenn, 3/9/1782, quoted in *PNG,* 10:419n3.

21 Donald M. Londahl-Smidt, "After Eutaw Springs: The Last Campaign in South Carolina" (MA thesis, University of Delaware, 1972), 43; Leslie to Germain, 12/31/1781, *DAR,* 19:237.

22 Major Richard Call to Greene, 1/14/1782 (2 letters), *PNG,* 10:192 and n2 of the first letter for the Thompson quotation.

23 Londahl-Smidt, "After Eutaw Springs," 43; James, *Marion,* 161–62; Horry to Greene, 2/28/1782, *PNG,* 10, 419–20 and n5.

24 Maham to Greene, 3/1/1782, *PNG,* 10:429–30.

25 My description is largely based on the editorial notes of both actions, bringing together various sources, in *PNG,* 10:420–21nn5–7; Maham to Greene, 3/1/1782, *PNG,* 10:421–22; Marion to Horry, 3/2/1782, Gibbes, *Doc. Hist.,* 3:260–61; Rankin, *Marion,* 274–75.

26 Horry to Greene, 2/28/1782, Maham to Greene, 3/1/1782, Marion to Greene, 3/1/1782, Greene to Marion, 3/1/1782, *PNG,* 10:419, 430–31, 427; Rankin, *Marion,* 275; Marion to Horry, 3/2/1782, Gibbes, *Doc. Hist.,* 3:260–61; James, *Marion,* 163.

27 James, *Marion,* 165.

28 Laurens to Greene, 2/28/1782, Barnwell to Greene, 3/6/1782, *PNG,* 10:422 and n2, 457 and nn2, 3.

29 Greene to Lee, 2/12/1782, 6/6/1782, 10/7/1782, *PNG,* 10:358; 11:295, 670; 12:38–39; Laurens to Thomas Bee, 4/14/1782, quoted in Massey, *Laurens,* 216.

30 Burnet to Rudulph, 5/5/1782, *PNG,* 11:157; Burnet to Lee, 6/20/1782, Misc. Ichabod Burnet, Misc. microfilm, Reel 71, NYHS.

31 General Greene's Orders of 6/13/1782, and the correspondence of 6/18–19/1782 between Greene and Major John Rudulph and the captains of Lee's Legion, are in *PNG,* 11:323–24, 346–48, 350.

32 Greene to Hanson, 7/11/1782, Greene to Lee, 10/7/1782, *PNG,* 11:432–34; 12:36; *JCC,* 23:529–30.

33 Greene to Martin, 1/9/1782, Martin to Greene, 2/9/1782, Wayne to Greene, 2/22/1782, *PNG,* 10:173, 342–45 and n5, 398, and 174n7 for Wright quotation.

34 Wayne to Greene, 2/22/1782 (for Wright quotation), Wayne to Greene, 3/11/1782, *PNG,* 10:398n5, 485–86.

35 Wayne to Greene, 5/24/1782, *PNG,* 11:241 and nn1, 2; Nelson, *Wayne,* 171–72.

36 Lee, *Memoirs,* 560n; Thomas Brown to Lord Shelburne, 9/23/1782, *DAR,* 21:122.

37 Wayne to Greene, 6/24/1782, *PNG,* 11:365–66 and notes; Lee, *Memoirs,* 557–59, including Thomas Posey's statement.

38 Colonel Posey's statement, in Lee, *Memoirs,* 559.

39 Leslie to Doyle, 8/21/1782, EM.15637, Leslie to Brereton, 8/21/1782, EM.15636, NYPL; Pierce to Gist, 8/23/1782, McKennan to Greene, 8/24/1782, *PNG,* 11:570, 573–74; Seymour, "Journal," 392.

40 Johnson, *Greene,* 2:339.

41 Gist to Greene, 8/27/1782, 579–82 and nn1–11, *PNG,* 11:579–82; Brereton to Leslie, 8/27/1782, quoted in *PNG,* 11:581n3.

42 Gist to Greene, 8/27/1782, *PNG,* 11:579–82 and nn1–11; Massey, *Laurens,* 225–27; Seymour, "Journal," 392; C. P. Bennett, "The Delaware Line in the Revolution: Narrative of the Services of the Delaware Regiment with Captain McKennan during the Revolutionary War," *Pennsylvania Magazine of History and Biography* 9, no. 4 (January 1886), 461.

43 Greene to Williams, 9/17/1782, *PNG,* 11:670; John Laurens to Henry Laurens, 1/23/1778, *PHL,* 12:330.

16. Greene Was the Maestro

1 O'Shaughnessy, *An Empire Divided,* 232–37, and his *The Men Who Lost America,* 314–15 (quotation), and 309–10 and passim for Rodney's dalliance on St. Eustatius; Mackesy, *War for America,* 456–59.

2 Greene to John Kean, 3/30/1782, Greene to Mathews, 3/30/1782, *PNG,* 10:562; Finney, "Diaries," 136.

3 For a discussion of the Banks affair, see Thayer, *Nathanael Greene: Strategist of the Revolution,* 413–20.

4 Johnson, *Greene,* 2:324; McDowell, "Journal," 316–17; Tilden, "Journal," 224; Officers of the Pennsylvania Continental Line to Greene, 3/28/1782, *PNG,* 10:555.

5 Greene to Officers of the Pennsylvania Line, 3/29/1781, *PNG,* 10:559–60.

6 Tilden, "Journal," 224; Officers of the Pennsylvania Continental Line to Greene, 4/3/1782, *PNG,* 10:580–81.

7 Burnet to Charles Petit, 4/12/1782, *PNG,* 11:38; John F. Stegeman and Janet A. Stegeman, *Caty: A Biography of Catharine Littlefield Greene* (1977; reprint, Athens: University of Georgia Press, 1985), 10, 121.

8 The broadside is printed in *SCHGM* 17, no. 1 (January 1916), 7; Madison to Greene, 1/13/1781, *PNG,* 7:116–17; Ward, *War of the Revolution,* 2:625.

9 General Greene's Orders, 4/20/1782, Harmer to Greene, 4/20/1782, General Greene's Orders, 4/21/1782, Harmer to Mordecai Gist, 4/21/1782, Gist to Greene, 4/21/1782, General Greene's Orders, 4/22/1782, *PNG,* 11:80 and n1, 81 and n1, 82, 85, 87 and n1; McDowell, "Journal," 321; Finney, "Diaries," 137; Seymour, "Journal," 389.

10 Greene to Wayne, 4/21/1782, Gist to Greene, 4/21/1782, Greene to Otho Williams, 4/22/1782, Four Sergeants to Greene, 4/27/1782, Ichabod Burnet to William Alexander, 4/29/1782, *PNG,* 11:83, 85, 100–101, 129–30, 142; Seymour, "Journal," 389; Lee, *Memoirs,* 547–48.

11 Greene to John Hanson, 5/18/1782, Greene to Otho Holland Williams, 6/6/1782, *PNG,* 11:199, 300.

12 The quotation from the *Pennsylvania Packet* is in *PNG,* 11:200n2; *The Revolutionary Journal of Baron Ludwig von Closen, 1780–1783,* trans. and ed. Evelyn A. Acomb (Chapel Hill: University of North Carolina Press, 1958), 195.

13 Greene to Hanson, 5/18/1782, *PNG,* 11:199–200.

14 Mackesy, *War for America,* 424 (for Mackesy quote), 434–35 (for North's reaction); John Brooke, *King George III* (New York: McGraw-Hill, 1972), 219; see

also Ian R. Christie, *The End of North's Ministry, 1780–1782* (London: Macmillan, 1958), xii.

15 Mackesy, *War for America,* 461; Christie, *The End of North's Ministry,* 277 (for Germain quotation), and 274 for the king's stance; Greene to Washington, 3/9/1782, Washington to Greene, 3/18/1782, *PNG,* 10:471, 525; for late advices, see *JCC,* 22:150–51; for the Parliamentary debate and North's speech, see *The Parliamentary History of England, from the Earliest Period to the Year 1803,* 36 vols. (London, 1806–1820), 22:802–31 (microform).

16 Mackesy, *War for America,* 466, 468, 470, 473–75, and for an extended and authoritative discussion of this tangled tale and an appreciation of Britain's worldwide commitments, 433–500; also important is Christie, *The End of North's Ministry,* chs. 3 and 4.

17 Washington to Greene, 3/18/1782, Greene to Washington, 5/19/1782 (2 letters), *PNG,* 10:525; 11:213, 215.

18 Greene to Francis Skelly, 5/21/1782, *PNG,* 11:229 and n1; McDowell, "Journal," 322; Shelburne to Carleton, 4/4/1782, *DAR,* 21:53; for Carleton to Leslie, 5/23/1782, with orders to prepare for evacuating Savannah and Charleston, see n3 of Morris to Greene, 5/10/782, *PNG,* 11:179; Carleton to Leslie, 5/23/1782, GLL, EM.15587, NYPL.

19 Greene to Hanson, *PNG,* 11:227–28. See Morris, *Peacemakers,* 309–10 and passim, for details of the actions of the diplomats in Paris.

20 Greene to David Howell, 9/1/1782 (for the first quotation), Greene to Hanson, 5/21/1782, *PNG,* 11:617, 228.

21 Wayne to Greene, 7/12/1782, 7/17/1782, *PNG,* 11:439, 441nn1, 2, 448.

22 Greene to Wayne, 6/21/1782, Greene to Marion, 7/9/1782, *PNG,* 11:353 and n5, 422; Carleton to Leslie, 5/23/1782, GLL, EM.15587, NYPL.

23 General Greene's Orders, 7/6/1782, Greene to Washington, 7/11/1782, *PNG,* 11:397, 435–36; "Letters from Col. Lewis Morris [Jr.] to Miss Ann Elliott," ed. D. E. Huger Smith, *SCHGM* 40 (1939), 122; Finney, "Diaries," 143; McDowell, "Journal," 328–29; Harmer to Arthur St. Clair, 9/29/1782, quoted in Londahl Smidt, "After Eutaw Springs," 77; Seymour, "Journal," 392; Laurens to Greene, 7/5/1782, *PNG,* 11:396 and n6, on sickness among the British and the quotation from the British officer; on the absence of yellow fever, McNeill, *Mosquito Empires,* 234.

24 McDowell, "Journal," 331–34.

25 General Greene's Orders, 8/26/1782, *PNG,* 11:576.

26 Moultrie, *Memoirs,* 2:356.

27 John Laurens to Greene, 8/5/1782 (includes the Carleton quotation in n3), Greene to Robert Forsyth, 8/9/1782, Greene to Marion, 8/9/1782, Greene to Pettit, 8/14/1782, Greene to Otho Williams, 9/17/1782 (for the quotation on his distrust of the British), *PNG,* 11:489 and nn3, 4, 508, 510, 540, 669.

28 Laurens to Greene, 8/5/1782. I have gratefully mined two excellent works for this paragraph: Eldon Jones, "The British Withdrawal from the South, 1781–1785," in *The Revolutionary War in the South: Power, Conflict, and Leadership,* ed. W. Robert Higgins (Durham, NC: Duke University Press, 1979), 265–66; and Maya Jasanoff, *Liberty's Exiles: American Loyalists in the Revolutionary World* (New York: Knopf, 2011), 68–77, which also contains the Fanning quote on 69. It should be noted that

Jasanoff is especially rewarding. See also Joseph W. Barnwell, "The Evacuation of Charleston by the British in 1782," *SCHGM* 11, no. 1 (January 1910), 26.

29 Wayne to Greene, 12/13/1782, Greene to Wayne, 12/13/1782, Greene to Elias Boudinot, 12/19/1782, *PNG,* 12:290–91 and n2 of Greene's letter. Note 2 of Greene's letter to Boudinot, citing a Hessian source, gives 130 ships in the harbor, whereas Moultrie, *Memoirs,* 2:360, says "upwards of 300 sail."

30 Greene to Marion, 11/15/1782, Mathews to Greene, 11/17/1782, *PNG,* 12:187–88, 198. The term "dangerous spectators" was used by James, *Marion,* 176; the other quotation is Greene's in a letter written early in the war in which he described some of his requirements for soldiers: Greene to Jacob Greene, 9/28/1776, *PNG,* 1:303.

31 Greene to Marion, 11/22/1782, Marion to Greene, 11/24/1782, *PNG,* 12:210–11, 217.

32 "Evacuation of Charleston, SC, 1782," *Magazine of American History* 8 (1882), 828–29; "Journal of the Regiment von Huyn/von Bening," in *PNG,* 12:282n2 of Greene's letter to Wayne of 12/12/1782.

33 Moultrie, *Memoirs,* 2:358–59; "Evacuation of Charleston," 830.

34 Finney, "Diaries," 147–48.

35 Moultrie, *Memoirs,* 2:358–60.

36 Greene to Boudinot, 12/19/1782, Greene to Petit, 12/21/1782, Greene to Wadsworth, 12/21/1782, Greene to Weedon, 12/21/1782, Greene to Witherspoon, 12/21/1782, *PNG,* 12:301, 324, 326, 329–30.

37 Greene to Boudinot, 12/19/1782, *PNG,* 12:303.

38 Greene to Wadsworth, 12/21/1782, *PNG,* 12:326.

Epilogue

1 "Eulogy on Nathanael Greene," 7/4/1789, *PAHDE,* 5:348.

2 Winston S. Churchill, *Marlborough, His Life and Times,* 6 vols. (New York: Scribner's, 1933–1938), 1:3.

3 Johnson, *Greene,* 2:419–20; for a discussion of Greene's death by the editors of the Greene Papers, see the Epilogue, *PNG,* 13:697–705.

4 Wayne's letter is in Greene, *Greene,* 3:534.

Index

Italicized page numbers refer to illustrations, and entries on individual battles are listed under "Battle of."

96–100; Battle of Ninety Six and, 152, 154, 155

Watson, Elkanah, 53

Watson, John Watson Tadwell, 72, 73–74, 77–78, 81, 82, 105–6; Battle of Hobkirk's Hill and, 91–92

Waugh, David, 177

Wayne, Anthony, 42–43, 58, 244, 282–83, 320, 325, 326–27; Charleston evacuation and, 328–29; Greene's death and, 334; Savannah campaign of, 311–14

Webster, James, 63

Weedon, George, 331

Wellington, Arthur Wellesley, Duke of, 59, 89, 232

West, Rebecca, 190

West Indies, 3, 153, 213, 214, 262, 272, 322, 323, 328; de Grasse's defeat in, 316, 317, 323; Lee in, 304

Weymss, James, 30, 215

Whipple, William, 294

Willcox, William, 65

Williams, Daniel, 260

Williams, Henry, 136–37

Williams, Hezekiah, 259–60

Williams, James, 27

Williams, Otho Holland, 26, 91, 94, 117, 148, 159, 172–73, *222*, 235, 250, 252, 264, 267, 295; Battle of Eutaw Springs and, 219, 221–34, 301; Greene's letters to, 315, 320, 321; on the wounded, 238

Wilson, John, 5, 8, 9, 165

Witherspoon, George, 331

wounded, treatment of the, 237–38, 252

Wright, James, 283, 312

Wright, John, 177

Yorke, Joseph, 189

Young, Thomas, 20–21, 115, 160